# Self-Management and
# the Crisis of Socialism

# Studies in Social, Political, and Legal Philosophy
### Series Editor: James P. Sterba, University of Notre Dame

This series analyzes and evaluates critically the major political, social, and legal ideals, institutions, and practices of our time. The analysis may be historical or problem-centered; the evaluation may focus on theoretical underpinnings or practical implications. Among the recent titles in the series are:

# Self-Management and the Crisis of Socialism

*The Rose in the Fist of the Present*

Michael W. Howard

ROWMAN & LITTLEFIELD PUBLISHERS, INC.
*Lanham • Boulder • New York • Oxford*

ROWMAN & LITTLEFIELD PUBLISHERS, INC.

Published in the United States of America
by Rowman & Littlefield Publishers, Inc.
4720 Boston Way, Lanham, Maryland 20706
http://www.rowmanlittlefield.com
12 Hid's Copse Road
Cumnor Hill, Oxford OX2 9JJ, England

British Library Cataloguing in Publication Information Available

**Library of Congress Cataloging-in-Publication Data**

Howard, Michael Wayne, 1952–
  Self-management and the crisis of socialism : the rose in the fist of the present /
Michael W. Howard.
    p.  cm.  — (Studies in social, political, and legal philosophy)
    Includes bibliographical references (p.   ) and index.
    ISBN 0-8476-8904-2 (cloth : alk. paper) — ISBN 0-8476-8905-0 (pbk. : alk. paper)
    1. Management—Employee participation.  2. Employee ownership.  3. Socialism.
I. Title.  II. Series.

  HD5650.H68   2000
  331'01'12—dc21                                              99-045034
                                                                  CIP

Printed in the United States of America

♾™ The paper used in this publication meets the minimum requirements of
American National Standard for Information Sciences—Permanence of
Paper for Printed Library Materials, ANSI/NISO Z39.48–1992.

# Contents

# Acknowledgments

My thinking about self-managed market socialism extends back over twenty years to the late 1970s when I wrote a dissertation on the topic (only traces of which are in this book), and I am indebted to the faculty in philosophy at Boston University, and particularly Elizabeth Rapaport and the late Marx Wartofsky for their invaluable mentoring and inspiration. I also received useful criticism and encouragement from Fred Gordon, Charles Heckscher, and Chris Mackin, fellow members of the Group for Work Democracy, during my years in Boston and subsequently. Over the last decade, the International Institute for Self-Management (IIS) has provided a forum for earlier versions of several chapters, invaluable exchanges of ideas, and moral support, as has the Radical Philosophy Association. The IIS, in addition, has facilitated visits to self-managed, cooperative, and worker-owned enterprises and support organizations in the former Yugoslavia, Hungary, the Basque country, the Czech Republic, Germany, and Italy. This book would be inconceivable without the support of these comradely networks, their memberships too numerous to mention. My colleagues in the philosophy department at the University of Maine have been thoroughly supportive, even of some parts of my research that some in the profession would consider "not really philosophy." I thank the University of Maine for a Summer Faculty Research Grant in 1998. The European University Institute in Fiesole and Stanford University provided hospitality during earlier stages of my work, and I thank the philosophy department at the University of Connecticut, for inviting me to present an earlier version of what has become chapters 2 and 9, and the Social Science Research Centre at Northumbria University, for hosting an earlier version of chapter 7. I am grateful to Mauro Romoli for arranging a tour of the Lega delle Cooperative and cooperatives in Reggio-Emilia in 1991.

Several people have read most or all of the manuscript at some stage of its development and offered helpful criticism, notably Doug Allen, Valerie Carter, Frank Cunningham, Milton Fisk, Len Krimerman, David Schweickart, Thomas Simon, James Sterba, and Philippe Van Parijs.

Many more have given me helpful suggestions on one or more chapters, including Paul Adler, Karen-edis Barzman, Betsy Bowman, Stephen Clifford, David Ellerman, Ann Ferguson, Maurice Glasman, Koldo Gorostiaga, Paul Grosswiler, John Hanson, Gabriele Herbert, Sharryn Kasmir, Roger King, Frank Lindenfeld, Steven Lukes, Mark Lutz, Greg MacLeod, Tomaš Mastnak, Kevin McCarron, Mike McCauley, Andrew McCulloch, Véronique Munoz-Dardé, Bill Murphy, Mario Nuti, Henning Oleson, Rodney Peffer, Laura Pennacchi, Bob Prasch, the late George Potts, Kenton Robinson, Loren Rodgers, Michele Salvati, Jana Sawicki, Karsten Struhl, Bob Stone, Salvatore Veca, Paul Warren, Jeff White, the students in my political philosophy seminars, and no doubt others whom I regretfully may have forgotten to mention. The final result I am sure falls short of their best expectations. But it is a far better book than it would have been without their input. I am grateful to Eva McLaughlin, Brenda Collamore, and Marilyn Costanzo for their excellent word processing, and for additional valuable help from Tiffany Beaulieu, José Guzman, Toby Jandreau, Lewis McEachern, and Maria Saravia. Maureen MacGrogan and Collette Stockton of Rowman & Littlefield were very cooperative in the process of preparing the final draft, and Katherine Kimball's copyediting much improved the manuscript. I thank my wife, Valerie Carter, and my daughter, Emma, for tolerating my workaholism and providing support of the deepest kind, and I dedicate this book to them.

Parts of chapter 4 of the present work appeared in a longer version in "From Commodity Fetishism to Market Socialism: Critical Notes on Stanley Moore," *Philosophy and Social Criticism* 7, no. 2 (Summer 1980): 187–214, reprinted with permission of Sage Publications.

Parts of chapter 7 appeared in earlier versions in: "Does Generalizing the Mondragon Model Require Revising It?" in *Social Economy and Social Participation: The Ways of the Basques* (Madrid and Donostia-San Sebastian: Marcial Pons and GEZKI, 1996), 175–84, reprinted with permission of GEZKI; "Worker Self-Management, the Market and Democracy," in *Rights, Justice, and Community*, ed. Creighton Peden and John K. Roth (Lewiston, N.Y.: Edwin Mellen Press, 1992), 187–99, reprinted with permission of The Edwin Mellen Press; "Where Do We Go From Here? Another View," *Grassroots Economic Organizing Newsletter*, no. 25 (Jan.–Feb. 1997): 1–2; and "Mondragon at 40," in *Grassroots Economic Organizing Newsletter*, no. 20 (Jan.–Feb. 1996): 3–4, reprinted with permission of Grassroots Economic Organizing Newsletter.

Parts of chapter 8 appeared in shorter versions in "Market Socialism and the International Mobility of Capital," *Radical Philosophy Review of Books*, nos. 11–12 (1995): 1–5; and "Review of *A Future for Socialism*, by John Roemer," in

*Radical Philosophy Review of Books*, no. 10 (1994): 44–48, reprinted with permission of the Radical Philosophy Association.

Parts of chapter 11 appeared in shorter versions in: "Media Democratization: Access or Autonomy," *Socialist Forum*, no. 20 (Spring 1993): 53–57, reprinted with permission of the Socialist Forum; and "Self-Management, Ownership, and the Media," *Journal of Mass Media Ethics* 8, no. 4 (1994): 197–206, reprinted with permission of Lawrence Erlbaum Associates, Inc.

# Preface

## What's Left?

We do not know what to call ourselves, we who came of age in the latter half of the twentieth century and developed political commitments and attitudes in struggles for civil rights, peace, social justice, a better relationship to the environment, women's emancipation, gay and lesbian rights, and so on (the list is not complete). Many of us who were once comfortable with *radical, progressive, socialist, Marxist, egalitarian, radical democratic* have seen these terms fall into disfavor among many of our still left-wing friends, for a variety of reasons, not all of them consistent with one another. "Progress" has been interrogated by feminists and postmodernists, as has "equality" of various kinds. Talk of rights is out of fashion in some circles. Socialism was always questioned by the anarchists among us, but now even some Marxist and former Marxist economists wonder whether it has any fundamental justification. Quite a few are now "post-Marxist," and analytical Marxists pick and choose what suits them from the corpus. *Radical* is a sort of weasel word, because one can be radical in any direction, and it leaves open the question of what one stands for when one has grasped things by the root. Even the term *liberal,* often used in derision during the 1960s, and by many Marxists throughout the twentieth century, is being embraced by quite a few leftists who want to exploit its more egalitarian implications, ironically, as the Right has managed to substitute the "*L*-word" as the favored term of derision in place of *socialist* and *communist.*

This plethora of—and nervousness about—self-descriptions of the Left is more than a symptom of an identity crisis of "tenured radicals." What the Left is has become problematic. At one time one could fairly easily place the Left on one side of each of a series of oppositions:

- with labor, against capital;
- for change, against the status quo;

- for the least advantaged, the dominated, and the oppressed, against the privileged;
- for the state, against the market;
- for more democracy, against limits on democracy;
- for internationalism, against nationalism;
- for scientific, technical and spiritual progress, against superstition, ignorance, and tradition.[1]

These oppositions no longer line up. Some leftists, even "communists," offer qualified defenses of capitalism. I have in mind here not the selling out of the old nomenclatura but rather principled defenses of private ownership under specific conditions. Philippe Van Parijs is one outstanding example. In addition, one can not always be uncritically pro-labor, when labor lines up against the environment or the welfare state (for example, unions supporting Ronald Reagan).

In recent years, the course of change has been reactionary in most of the capitalist world, with the right wing rolling back decades of egalitarian reforms, and with left-wing parties and movements struggling to preserve the status quo. The state is, after Communism and for many from the New Left on, understood as a potential source of domination on a par with private property. Markets, as I argue, may be a central part of a defensible alternative to capitalism as we know it.

Democracy can take reactionary forms. Moreover, for reasons to be explored, it may be less fundamental and in some ways at odds with deeper Leftist values of freedom and equality; and values of freedom, equality, and democracy may conceal multiple exclusions. National liberation movements align the Left with nationalism, not only in the postcolonial struggles in the former colonies of Europe and the United States, but also in contemporary movements for autonomy in the Basque country, Quebec, and elsewhere.

Karl Marx inherited the mantle of technical and scientific progress from the Enlightenment. The challenges to the Enlightenment faith in science and technology from communitarians, postmodernists, critical theorists, and ecologists, however, unsettle this alignment, with implications for the Left's relationship to labor, the market, democracy, and processes of change.

The only nonproblematic alignment is solidarity with the least advantaged. What is noteworthy here is how this has become decoupled from other dichotomies. The unemployed, particularly the chronically unemployed, loom large and often are distinct from, if not in opposition to, the more stable working class. Oppressions rooted in gender, race, and ethnicity cut across economic categories and contend for priority. As well, the status of the nonhuman world—animals, species, ecosystems—has become a serious topic of discussion and a focus of struggle. Advancing the cause of the least advantaged puts one in different positions vis-à-vis the oppositions between market and state, capital and labor and others, depending on one's focus, and in terms of how "least advantaged" is articulated. Following Michel Foucault, many are wary of ways in which resisting one kind of domination can involve one in perpetrating other sorts.

The status of the term *socialist* brings some of these issues into focus. Raymond Williams has observed that from the very beginning of the use of the term, *socialist* has denoted two distinct though often overlapping tendencies. The first was a continuation and fuller realization of liberal values, "political freedom, the ending of privileges and formal inequalities, social justice." The second counterposed to individualist values and individual ownership a more communal and cooperative way of life, conceived of as superior to liberalism but also as a precondition of its full realization.[2]

Similarly today, those on the Left who still consider themselves socialist understand different things by the term or defend their position in different ways with practical implications. There are still many who aspire to a more cooperative, participatory society and oppose individualism. Given the failure of state socialism in the Soviet Union and Eastern Europe, however, many who are socialists in this sense are not necessarily in favor of greater state ownership of the means of production or planning of the economy. Nonetheless, socialists, as distinct from other sorts of communitarians, generally see their ends as requiring some fundamental changes in the ownership and control of the means of production.

Some consider socialism to be primarily a means. Defining it as some form of social ownership of the means of production, some favor it as a means to the democratization of decision making. The root problem in this view is individual ownership, which leads to oligarchy. Others see it as a means to more equal opportunity to make choices, to make the best of one's capacity. The root problem here is exploitation and inequality of opportunity or welfare. Both groups see socialism as a means to equality, which in turn is important for the sake of freedom (whether the participatory "freedom to the ancients" or the individual "freedom of the moderns").[3]

The genius of Marx was to weave all these strands into a coherent whole; but contemporary socialists as often as not pick up on some strands in deliberate opposition to others. Inevitably, some, still recognizably on the Left, will call the term *socialist* into question, not just because of its tainted history but also because some of these strands can conceivably be advanced within the framework of a kind of capitalism. Thus, deploying an egalitarian left criticism of merely formal freedom, Van Parijs favors a capitalism that could deliver the highest sustainable basic income for all; and David Ellerman favors a market economy of worker-owned firms, on the basis of a left-Kantian critique of wage slavery.[4]

My own position on this map is still socialist. However, I respond at some length, in what follows, to those of us who have deserted the cause, because I find their arguments deserving of our respect. I incline toward the radical liberal camp that sees the socialist project as making good on the broken promises of the Enlightenment (although this project must take full note of the exclusions identified by feminists and postmodernists, and revise accordingly). Also, while

I personally find some communitarian ideas, particularly those of Marx, appealing, I argue that the strongest defense of social ownership and radical democracy is that they are necessary to secure each individual's freedom. As I see it, the idea that genuine equal opportunity and substantial freedom for all can be secured by an elitist system of political parties, judicial review, and minimal regulation of the market economy is pretty close to sheer fantasy. Positive rights exist because people have fought for them. They can be extended and protected only by a vigorous, informed, and motivated public in which each of us has roughly equal standing. Not everyone will agree that a society of social equals is a noble aspiration, but most can come to see it as necessary for the freedom each values and deserves.

## NOTES

Apologies to Steven Lukes for appropriating his intended book title for this preface.

1. The first five of these were suggested by Philippe Van Parijs, in conversation, along with some of the relevant points that follow.

2. Raymond Williams, *Keywords* (New York: Oxford University Press, 1983), 286–87.

3. Benjamin Constant, "Liberty of the Ancients Compared with That of the Moderns," (1819), in *Political Writings*, trans. and ed. Biancamaria Fontana (Cambridge: Cambridge University Press, 1988).

4. David Ellerman, *Property and Contract in Economics: The Case for Economic Democracy* (Oxford: Blackwell, 1992); Philippe Van Parijs, *Real Freedom for All: What (If Anything) Can Justify Capitalism?* (Oxford: Clarendon Press, 1995).

# Introduction

## The Rose in the Fist of the Present

> To recognize reason as the rose in the cross of the present, this is the rational insight which reconciles us to the actual.
>
> —G.W.F. Hegel, *Philosophy of Right*

> Nothing in the universe can be the same if somewhere, we do not know where, a sheep that we never saw has—yes or no?—eaten a rose. . . .
> Look up at the sky. Ask yourselves: Is it yes or no? Has the sheep eaten the flower? And you will see how everything changes.
>
> —Antoine de Saint-Exupery, *The Little Prince*

While some conclude from the revolutions of 1989 that the sheep has eaten the rose—that is, that socialism is dead—interest in socialism will inevitably continue because of the persistent injustices and devastation of contemporary capitalism.[1] Consider first the truly catastrophic environmental destruction wrought by the capitalist growth imperative and by industrialization more generally. Global warming, ozone depletion, the steady depletion of finite fossil fuels and other resources, pollution of air, water, and soil, and the large-scale loss of both species and habitat, all well documented in the environmental literature, are proceeding apace. Despite warnings from the scientific community, the world's leaders—particularly those in the United States—in the thrall of corporate interests, do little to address the problem. A growing world population compounds the environmental crisis immensely, and this, too, is connected to the logic of global capitalism, which perpetuates and deepens inequality.

> Over the past three decades, only 15 countries have enjoyed high growth whilst 89 countries are worse off economically than they were ten or more years ago. In 70

xv

developing countries, today's income levels are less than in the 1960s and 1970s. . . . "Economic gains have benefitted greatly a few countries, at the expense of many," says the [United Nations Human Development Report]. . . . To illustrate, it estimates that the assets of the world's 358 billionaires exceed the combined annual incomes of countries accounting for nearly half (45%) of the world's people.[2]

This inequality translates into hunger, mass migrations, militarism, and civil war. Twelve million children die every year as a result of hunger.[3] Fifty million people are refugees or displaced persons.[4] According to Oscar Arias, Jordana Friedman, and Caleb Rossiter,

> The world's governments spend $868 billion a year to support military forces of more than 27 million soldiers. This phenomenal expense of 12 percent of all governments' spending is itself a threat to security. Developed countries account for 82 percent of this total, with the United States alone spending $270 billion on its defense budget. They are also responsible for 90 percent of arms transfers to developing nations, which have contributed to inciting and prolonging many of the world's 44 regional and internal conflicts. The $221 billion that developing nations spend on armed forces exacts a particularly heavy toll on the social sector. New weapons procurements and larger armies usually mean less funds to invest in health, education, and economic development, even in resource-rich countries like Saudi Arabia and Nigeria. In developing nations, more than 900 million people are unable to read or write, yet military spending exceeds spending on education; one billion people never see a health professional and two million children die a year of preventable infectious diseases, yet military spending is more than twice as high as spending on health.[5]

Much of this spending is made to enable dictatorships to remain in power or to protect the property rights of transnational corporations—in other words, to defend the existing patterns of inequality. Inequality on such a scale and to such a degree is unjust in its own right. It also compounds the environmental crisis. Affluent citizens in wealthy countries consume excessively.[6] At the same time, poverty is the principal spur to population growth in poor countries, where the growing numbers then aspire to the consumption patterns of the rich. The earth cannot sustain a growing population on such a consumption trajectory.[7]

Even by narrow economic standards, the global capitalist system is not doing well. Many European nations suffer persisting double-digit unemployment, a colossal waste of human potential. The economies of Russia, Brazil, Indonesia, and other Asian nations, after years of following the prescriptions of the International Monetary Fund [IMF], have been experiencing major financial and economic crises. Stephen Cohen and Katrina vanden Heuvel describe Russia's recent transition to capitalism:

> Russia is in the throes of an economic disaster. Seven years of depression have halved its GDP [gross domestic product], decimated its banking system and cur-

rency, eroded essential infrastructures of modern life and left the state bankrupt and saddled with more than $150 billion of foreign debt. Some 70 to 80 percent of Russians now live precariously below or barely above the subsistence level, their wages unpaid, bank savings frozen, money in hand greatly devalued and welfare provisions evaporating. . . . Free-market, rigidly monetarist policies that Washington and its primary lending agency, the IMF, have made a condition of aid for nearly six years. . . . have greatly contributed to Russia's deepening crisis.[8]

Nor is the majority in the United States even benefiting. Despite small upturns in the late 1990s, real wages for most Americans have been falling since the 1970s, and income inequality has been growing.[9] The North American Free Trade Agreement (NAFTA) has not delivered on the promises of its promoters; instead, during the first five years of its existence it has resulted in the loss of hundreds of thousands of manufacturing jobs for U.S. workers, a 29 percent decline in Mexican wages and decimation of the Mexican middle class, and an environmental disaster in the *maquiladoras*.[10] Those Americans who have jobs find that their jobs pay less and are less secure. Poverty remains at 13.7 percent (in 1996), with more than one-quarter of African Americans and one-fifth of all children in poverty.[11] Poverty breeds crime, and rather than address the causes of crime, we attack the symptoms by building prisons. "The United States now imprisons more people than any other country in the world—perhaps half a million more than Communist China. . . . [The state of California] holds more inmates in its jails and prisons than do France, Great Britain, Germany, Japan, Singapore, and the Netherlands combined."[12]

Wealth inequality has also increased in the 1990s. In 1995 in the United States, the "richest ½% had a larger share of total nonresidential net worth than the bottom 90%. . . . Wealth is now the most concentrated it's been since the 1920s."[13] With inequalities of income and wealth come inequalities of power and status. In human terms, all this means increasing hunger, homelessness, and despair of ever having a flourishing life. This is but a thumbnail sketch of the ills of contemporary global capitalism, but it is enough to demonstrate why we cannot rest content with things as they are.

Yet, despite the crisis of capitalism, socialism seems to be faring even worse. Not only the practice but the very idea of socialism is in crisis. First, the collapse of communism in the Soviet Union and Eastern Europe has brought to a head the institutional crisis: if socialism is to survive, there must be found a noncapitalist alternative to the centrally planned economies and one-party states of these failed experiments. Second, socialists in the East and West are experiencing a crisis of identity concerning what it means to be a socialist and what the constituency for socialism is. For democratic socialists this has less to do with the collapse of communism than with changes in capitalism: the shift from industrial mass production to "flexible production" and services, the decline of unions, and the rise of new social movements (among them, feminism and environmentalism). Some question whether socialism can still be a movement that is simultaneously majoritarian, working class, and anticapitalist. Finally, there is a crisis of ideology, of what remains of the democratic socialist idea, and how it—or indeed any political philosophy—can be defended. Socialism, and particularly Marxism, as nineteenth-century offspring of the Enlightenment, share in the crisis of the Enlightenment heralded by postmodernists and antimodernist communitarians. Commitments to universalism, rationality, and progress long taken for granted are now being called into question.

This book addresses all three aspects of the crisis of socialism, in each case advancing an idea that is as old as the socialist movement itself, although not always central to particular socialist parties, projects, or economies: the idea of worker self-management. Participatory democratic councils of citizens and workers sprang up spontaneously in the Paris Commune in the 1870s, in the Russian Revolution, and in other uprisings toward the end of the second decade of the twentieth century from Turin, Italy, to Seattle, Washington. The idea of self-management emerged prominently in Yugoslavia after Marshal Tito's break with Stalin and was a central feature of the system from its remarkable growth in the 1960s and 1970s to its collapse in 1991. The idea was central to the Solidarity movement in Poland before the coup and was popular in the May 1968 French uprising and in Czechoslovakia before the Soviet invasion. Workers' councils were prominent in the socialist government of Salvador Allende in Chile before the coup. The idea has become increasingly popular, in muted form, in the United States in the form of worker ownership and worker participation. More American workers now work in at least partially worker-owned companies than belong to unions. Self-management has emerged at times of capitalist crisis but also of socialist renewal. For example, the emergence of worker control movements in the early twentieth century coincided with the rigidification of craft unions and was an important precursor to industrial unions. Solidarity was a challenge to the Polish Communist government's claim to be the representative of the workers.

A revival of the idea of self-management is critical to the revival of socialism today. Such a revival, however, must be no mere return to the past but a reworking of the concept for contemporary conditions, taking account of the changing nature of capitalism and the peculiar crises that socialism as a movement itself faces. This book is one attempt to reinsert the idea of self-management into the discourse of the Left by exploring its justification in political theory, its practicality in models of socialist alternatives, and its relevance in particular contexts of struggle. Among the more important changes in contemporary capitalism is the declining political centrality of full-time, permanent work, which, along with other considerations, leads me to advocate, as a necessary complement to self-management, an unconditional guaranteed income for everyone at the highest sustainable level (or "basic income"). Other more clearly socialist institutions, such as public property and public planning of investment, find their place in the argument as necessary supports for self-management, basic income, and the conception of social justice that supports and links them.

If I may for a moment shift from a tone of confidence, this book raises more questions than it answers and offers challenges to self-managed market socialism, not all of them resolved, as much as it makes a case for its importance. The Slovenian philosopher Tomaš Mastnak once remarked that he would rather read a book of questions than a book of answers. I hope this one is worthy of his and your attention.

The essays assembled in this book cluster around three areas of inquiry—principles, institutions, and practice—with significant overlap. In political theory, the core question is whether there is in our time a shared conception of justice, cutting across gender, class, race, and other differences. By *shared conception* I do not mean one around which there is an actually existing consensus—were that the case, the answer to the question would obviously be negative. Most of the more difficult social conflicts, from reproductive rights to labor law, reveal fundamental antagonisms not only of interests but also of judgments of what is fair. Rather, I have in mind a philosophical notion of a possible consensus about justice, one based on some plausibly widely shared commitments of a less controversial sort. The debates in political philosophy are over the candidates for such commitments, how to articulate them and how to connect them to a variety of competing conceptions of justice. At the center of these debates for the last quarter century has been John Rawls' liberal theory of justice. In addition to criticism from right and left, Rawls' theory has been assailed in another way from communitarians, on the one hand, who think he does not assume enough in the way of shared values—conceptions of the good. On the other hand, some Marxist, postmodernist, and feminist writers have challenged the very project of a theory of justice that articulates a shared conception of justice.

Chapter 1 defends self-management on the basis of a left liberal theory of justice. My aim in this chapter, in part, is to answer liberal critics who maintain that self-management is sectarian. Chapter 2 makes the left liberal case for basic income and begins a defense (completed in chapter 9) for its compatibility with self-management. Chapter 3 defends the liberal approach against postmodernist and relativist Marxist criticisms.

Some readers may find a defense of socialism in terms of liberal political theory—particularly a worker-managed *market* socialism—to be a betrayal of the more far-reaching goals of the Marxist tradition. Chapter 4 makes the case that such a "revisionist" socialism is fully consistent with Marx's critique of capitalism, even if it is not the model Marx himself favored. Chapter 5 is a defense of market socialism against critics who claim that it will degenerate into capitalism or be more exploitative than capitalism. Chapter 6 is a critique of a nonmarket alternative to both centrally planned socialism and capitalism. By the end of part 1, I hope to have defended from within both liberal and Marxist traditions the core idea of self-managed market socialism.

Part 2 takes up the institutional crisis of socialism. Focusing on cooperatives and other forms of worker ownership in the Basque country, Italy, and the United

States, I examine, in chapter 7, whether a system of cooperatives could provide an alternative to capitalism and centrally planned socialism that would be generalizable, replicable, and desirable. The limitations of privately owned cooperatives lead us to look for aspects of socialism additional to self-management. Chapter 8 examines two models of socialism: "Economic democracy" favors social ownership of the means of production, worker self-management, and democratic planning of investment. Managerial or "coupon" socialism distributes ownership widely to citizen shareholders, does not mandate self-management, leaves investment decisions to agents in the market, and, in general, incorporates more elements shared with capitalism. Both models have strengths and weaknesses, and although I favor the self-management model, I think the jury is still out in the debate on market socialism, and attempts to combine elements of each should be explored. Chapter 9 shows how a guaranteed basic income and economic democracy are mutually supporting.

By the end of parts 1 and 2 , I would hope to have convinced the reader that from the standpoint of political theory the idea of socialism is still very much alive, because it is unclear how the egalitarian aims still voiced in various ways by liberals, communitarians, Marxists, and others could be reached within the framework of capitalism. From the standpoint of economic models, there are still some models of socialism on the drawing board that cannot be ruled out on the basis of the evidence of socialist experiments that have failed. Still, some of the most vexing problems confronting socialists today have to do with the relevance of socialist ideals and models to the changing landscape of capitalism, both its inner social structure and its global reach. The traditional industrial working class is shrinking, and the Left itself has come to seem less a working-class movement and more a diverse coalition of oppositional groups, many finding the basis of their identity in noneconomic dimensions of social life. Socialism, defined as an alternative form of economy, hence declines in saliency. At the same time, the increasing mobility of capital and labor across national boundaries makes the engine of capitalism seem an even more prominent determinant of other aspects of social life than it earlier was. The globalizing effects of capitalism threaten to render obsolete not only socialist but also liberal ideals that are premised on national economies and national sovereignty.

In part 3, I examine three challenges to the socialist project arising from (1) the changing nature of productive firms in contemporary capitalism, (2) the shift to an information economy, and (3) the rise of identity politics and new social movements. In chapter 10, I argue that "communitarian" enterprises, modeled on Japanese firms, are likely to increase proportionately over "competitive" firms but that it is possible to distinguish democratic from authoritarian forms of communitarian enterprise. The democratic firm has a chance of prevailing only if it receives support within a broad political coalition supporting an economic bill of rights. Although favoring the communitarian firm, such an economic bill of rights is better articulated within a liberal theory of justice than in a communitarian political theory.

The challenge raised for models of socialism by the economic bill of rights is that it is premised on the increasing mobility of both labor and capital. For example, a demand for portable pension plans presupposes an increasingly mobile working class; prior notification of plant closings presupposes a context of capital flight. Economic democracy, as envisioned by David Schweickart, requires halting or reversing these trends. Managerial socialism, on the other hand, geared as it is toward being at least as efficient as capitalism by mimicking capitalist managerial incentives, may be favored comparatively by such trends; but even it may become difficult to imagine as ownership of enterprises becomes spread out across the globe.

A different kind of challenge to socialism arises from the shift from an industrial to a service and information economy. Chapter 11, on self-management and the media, addresses the complexity of the media, vis-à-vis factory production, and the problems this raises for democratizing the media. I argue for self-management of the media by media workers, thus augmenting the case for economic democracy. I also highlight the potential conflict between the autonomy to be realized through self-management and citizen access to media. The former is important for the sake of promoting independent journalism and an informed citizenry, the latter for opening up space for marginalized voices and challenging the cult of expertise. This is a special case of conflict between a Left envisioned as a workers' movement and a Left envisioned as radical democracy involving diverse social movements. I argue that a democratized media should include a large measure of worker self-management, not because of the centrality of the labor movement but because of special features of the media.

The third challenge for socialism is that posed by the fading of the working class as a revolutionary subject and the rise of new social movements. Is there any longer an agent analogous to Marx's revolutionary proletariat with the capability and will to bring about socialism? This challenge is taken up in chapter 12, which addresses the relevance of market socialism to the concerns of new social movements, particularly feminism and environmentalism.

This book has arisen out of conversations over the years with people researching or promoting cooperatives, self-management, and market socialism and so speaks particularly to them. The "rose in the fist" in the title, while playing on a Hegelian theme, is also an allusion to a longstanding symbol of democratic socialism. However, as the previous paragraph makes clear, another part of the intended audience consists of activists in egalitarian and potentially anticapitalist social movements and less-active concerned citizens who might not initially be sympathetic to socialism but are open-minded enough to consider it. Some parts of the book contribute to ongoing debates among philosophers and social scientists, but I have tried to contextualize the occasional more technical passages for the less specialized reader. In writing for a wide audience, it is my hope that the book will contribute not only to academic but also to civic discussion of alternatives to contemporary capitalism.

## NOTES

1. In 1989, the Berlin Wall fell and with it the Communist government of East Germany; Solidarity won the first post-Communist multiparty election in Poland; the dissident playwright Vaclav Havel was elected president of Czechoslovakia; multiple parties were also introduced in Hungary and Bulgaria; and Romania's dictator Nicolae Ceaucescu was executed after a popular uprising. Within two or three years there followed the breakup of the Soviet Union and a process of political democratization and economic liberalization throughout Eastern Europe.

2. Martin Khor, "Growing Consensus on Ills of Globalization," <http://www.twnside.org.sg/souths/twn/title/ills-cn.htm> (cited 12 March 1999).

3. Frances Moore Lappé, Joseph Collins, and Peter Rosset, with Luis Esparza, "Twelve Myths about Hunger," *Food First Backgrounder* 5, no. 3 (Summer 1998), 1-4, based on *World Hunger: Twelfth Myths*, 2d edition, by Frances Moore Lappé, Joseph Collins, and Peter Rosset, with Luis Esparza (New York: Grove/Atlantic and Food First Books, 1998).

4. United Nations High Commission for Refugees, "UNHCR by Numbers," <http://www.unhcr.ch/un&ref/numbers/table1.htm> (12 March 1999).

5. Oscar Arias, Jordana Friedman, and Caleb Rossiter, "Less Spending, More Security: A Practical Plan to Reduce World Military Spending," <http://www.fas.org/pub/gen/mswg/year2000/oped.htm> (12 March 1999).

6. According to a joint statement of the Councils of the Royal Society of London and the United States National Academy of Sciences,

Since 1950, the richest 20% of the world's population has increased its per capita consumption of meat and timber two-fold, its car ownership four-fold and its use of plastics five-fold. The poorest 20% has increased its consumption hardly at all . . . Because carbon dioxide emissions per person in Britain are 50 times higher than in Bangladesh, the [annual additional] 100,000 people in Britain cause more than double the carbon dioxide emissions of the [annual additional] 2.4 million people in Bangladesh.

Quoted by the Center for a New American Dream, "Towards Sustainable Consumption," <http://www.newdream.org/discuss/nas.html> (12 March 1999).

7. Mark Hertzgaard, "Our Real China Problems," *Atlantic Monthly*, November 1997, 97–114.

8. Stephen F. Cohen and Katrina vanden Heuvel, "Help Russia," *Nation* 11–18 January 1999, 8–9.

9. Lawrence Mischel, Jared Bernstein, and John Schmitt, *The State of Working America 1998–99* (Ithaca: Cornell University Press, 1999).

10. Lori Wallach and Michelle Sforza, "NAFTA at 5," *Nation,* 25 January 1999, 7.

11. Mischel, Bernstein, and Schmitt, *The State of Working America.*

12. Eric Schlosser, "The Prison-Industrial Complex," *Atlantic Monthly,* December 1998, 51-77, 52.

13. Doug Henwood, *Wall Street* (New York: Verso, 1998), 66.

# Part 1

## Principles of Self-Managed Market Socialism

# Introduction to Part 1

The first chapter of *Self-Management and the Crisis of Socialism* explores philosophical arguments for and against self-management and sometimes economic democracy more widely, the latter including democratic planning of investment as well as worker self-management of workplaces. Economists have examined the relative efficiency of worker-owned or worker-controlled, capitalist, and state-managed enterprises; and the evidence on that score clearly supports workplace democracy.[1] The focus in this book is on whether workplace democracy can also be defended as a matter of justice. If it can, then to the extent that considerations of justice trump considerations of efficiency, we have a strong case for workplace democracy, even if it should prove to be somewhat less efficient than capitalist organization of labor. As capitalist firms should be replaced by self-managed firms, so, I argue in chapter 2, significant parts of the welfare state should be replaced with a scheme of unconditional basic income, for various practical reasons but also as a matter of justice.

There is, unfortunately, no widespread agreement on principles of justice. Disagreements arise, sometimes rather technical disagreements, about whether justice should be grounded in a commonly shared conception of the good life or should instead abstract from differing views about the good (the liberal–communitarian debate); whether there are any universal principles of justice or whether justice is relative to the interests of particular groups (the modernist–postmodernist debate); whether there are any natural rights or whether all rights are constructed; whether justice is ultimately determined by the consequences of actions, principles, and policies or whether there are certain rights that hold regardless of consequences (the consequentialist–deontologist debate); and, on a more concrete level, whether such principles are entitlement conceptions or equal-

3

concern conceptions, whether they are purely distributive (for example, the principle of equality), purely aggregative (for example, the principle of utility), or something in between (for example, Rawls' difference principle) and whether they aim to equalize (or, alternatively, maximize the minimum) outcomes or opportunities.[2] I engage in these debates only insofar as they relate to the justification of workplace or economic democracy.

In chapter 1, I defend workplace democracy as an extension of the principle of political self-determination into the workplace against the criticism that such an extension violates liberal neutrality. The heart of my argument is that workplace democracy is an important means of enhancing the fair value of political liberty. I also consider more direct arguments based on the inherent value of democracy. In chapter 2, I defend on grounds of justice an unconditional basic income for everyone. In chapter 3, I defend the liberal approach against relativist criticisms from some Marxists and postmodernists.

Many socialists and Marxists will object to a socialism with markets because of the tendency of markets to generate inequality, encourage egoism, and generate unintended large-scale disasters such as economic crises and environmental devastation. In chapter 4, I defend the market part of market socialism against such criticism and argue that market socialism need not involve abandonment of the noblest aspirations of Marxism. In chapter 5, I take up criticism from the Right, particularly that of N. Scott Arnold, who tries to show that alienation and exploitation are inevitable, and hence, provide no basis for a radical socialist alternative to capitalism. His analysis of alienation shares with Marx the assumption that I criticize in chapter 4, that commodity production entails commodity fetishism. I also criticize his concept of exploitation, showing that it does not warrant the apparent charge of injustice against socialism. Finally, I argue that market socialism, although not as radical an alternative as Marx (according to Arnold) hoped for, still deserves to be considered as a legitimate third way between capitalism and central planning. Chapter 6 takes up Michael Albert and Robin Hahnel's criticism from the Left and their support for a planned economy, albeit decentralized and participatory. I argue that there is no desirable third way between market socialism and a centrally planned economy, but I take note of some ways that the market itself can be "socialized," thus mitigating some of its alienating tendencies. Chapter 6, being a discussion of one model of nonmarket socialism, forms a bridge to the next part, discussion of cooperatives and models of market socialism.

Some readers may be completely unfamiliar with the market socialism debate or the theories of justice I refer to in justifying the variant of the market socialism that I, following David Schweickart, call economic democracy. In the remainder of this introduction I provide some orientation on these topics. Greater detail is provided as the argument unfolds in subsequent chapters.

## THE THEORY OF JUSTICE

The theory of justice I use to justify a kind of market socialism is a left-wing variant of a theory put forward by John Rawls in *A Theory of Justice*. His theory is without doubt the most important contribution to political theory in the English-speaking world in the last quarter century, judging by the volume of books, articles, and debates it has generated. Rawls has been attacked from almost every part of the political spectrum; his retorts have won the respect of many early antagonists; and his theory now has many adherents.

Feminists and Marxists include in their ranks Rawlsians as well as critics of Rawls. Even those who are in no way Rawlsian find it necessary, if they write on the topic of justice, to frame their work in relation to that of Rawls. European philosophers writing on justice routinely refer to Rawls, and his book has now been translated into Chinese.

The theory is a descendant of the social contract theory of Thomas Hobbes, John Locke, Jean-Jacques Rousseau, and particularly Immanuel Kant. The basic idea is that the correct principles of social justice—principles that are to guide the construction and revision of the basic liberties and the distribution of wealth, income, power, and authority in society—are those that would be chosen in an ideal contractual situation in which each person is free, rational, equal, properly informed about the alternatives, and impartial about the effects on himself or herself. This last condition is modeled by assuming each person stands behind a "veil of ignorance," unaware of his or her gender, class position, or personal preferences. Rawls argues that from his "original position" the parties would choose the following principles:

*First Principle*
Each person is to have an equal right to the most extensive total system of equal basic liberties compatible with a similar system of liberty for all.

*Second Principle*
Social and economic inequalities are to be arranged so that they are both:

  a) [the difference principle] to the greatest benefit of the least advantaged, consistent with the just savings principle [concerning future generations], and
  b) attached to offices and positions open to all under conditions of fair equality of opportunity.[3]

Two priority rules stipulate the priority of liberty over the second principle and the priority of justice over efficiency and welfare.

Numerous and sometimes complicated arguments for and against the claim that these principles would be chosen in the original position make up the bulk of *A Theory of Justice*. At this introductory level it is sufficient to grasp the following three points:

1. The priority of liberty: Rawls assumes that at a certain level of affluence rational people, particularly behind the veil of ignorance, will be unwilling to sacrifice basic liberties such as freedom of speech or religious freedom for higher income and wealth. This is not to say that there are no people in the United States, say, willing to make such a trade-off but, rather, that if one were in the dark about one's tastes, one would want to secure the basic liberties to do as one wished. Without these, any number of ways of life, including possibly one's own, would be imperiled. At first glance, this may resemble classical liberalism's privilege of freedom over equality, when freedom is understood to include free trade, wealth accumulation, and other market exchanges. However, Rawls explicitly excludes the freedom to accumulate capital from the list of basic liberties, and his second principle, which governs wealth, income, and power, is strongly egalitarian.[4]

2. The difference principle: Granting the basic liberties, each party in the original position will seek to maximize the minimum distribution to him or her of wealth, income, power, and authority, once the veil of ignorance is lifted. This "maximin" principle will lead the parties to choose the difference principle as the principle maximizing the advantage of the least advantaged. Because anyone could end up in the least-advantaged group, and no one knows where he or she will end up, each will favor the best outcome for the worst position. This principle is strongly egalitarian: any departure from equality in the distribution of wealth, income, power, and authority must be shown to improve the prospects of those who would be in the lower positions as a result. "Trickle-down" economics was a cynical appeal to this moral intuition. Actually satisfying the principle would require a more exacting demonstration of the benefits to the worst-off of any social inequalities and the impossibility of achieving those benefits with more egalitarian arrangements.

3. The priority of persons over utility: At the time Rawls' book was written, the dominant approach to questions of social justice in Anglo-American discourse was utilitarian. For the utilitarian, justice is that which maximizes utility overall, or on the average. Classically, utility was understood as happiness or pleasure. More recently it has been defined by economists as preference satisfaction. But the key point is that, on whatever formulation, utilitarianism favors the general good over the dignity and rights of individuals. Rawls succeeded in developing a theory that was reasonably clear in its implications, which at the same time secured a priority of basic liberties over utility maximization and further constrained the pursuit of utility maximization by the requirement that the distribution of social goods be such that each person could consent to it in the original position. It is in this sense that Rawls' theory is "deontological," or "rights based," rather than "consequentialist," or looking only to the aggregate outcome.

By providing a theoretical elaboration of the fundamental objection against utilitarianism—that it does not do justice to the intrinsic worth of persons—Rawls revived contractualism and made clear that justice can and should take precedence over economic efficiency. The criticisms of utilitarianism were not new. What was new was a fleshed-out alternative approach to theorizing, with resulting principles of justice.

Rawls' theory came on the scene in the wake of the civil rights and antiwar movements in the United States, which more concretely advanced the importance of individual dignity and justice and challenged the prerogatives of governments and corporations bent on maximizing profits and economic growth at the expense of other values. Many of Rawls' students were shaped not only by his teaching but also by the social movements of those years and interpreted his writing in more explicitly egalitarian ways than even Rawls himself.

Rawls considered his theory to be neutral between capitalism and socialism. He entertains the idea that a kind of socialism, one that combines a market economy with worker-managed enterprises, could create a just society. He himself favors a constitutional democracy that is capitalist but with widely dispersed ownership of property (achieved through such means as a steep inheritance tax). What sorts of economic institutions—forms of property, allocation mechanisms such as markets or planning agencies—are to be preferred depend upon which will yield the results required by the principles of justice. This, in turn, may vary significantly with the circumstances and history of particular nations. Thus, it could be the case, Rawls would say, that in one country capitalism, though requiring inequalities of wealth and income, is so dynamic in creating new wealth that the least advantaged are better off than they would be in any feasible noncapitalist alternative. In a different country, it could turn out that a socialist system would improve the prospects of the least advantaged. Rawls himself has largely steered clear of the more concrete debate between capitalists and socialists.

Some Rawlsians agree with Rawls that the theory of justice is neutral between capitalism and socialism but then try to make a case for a particular kind of capitalism or socialism as the most likely to achieve justice.[5] Others argue that the principles themselves, properly interpreted, point toward a degree of egalitarianism more consonant with socialism than with capitalism. Norman Daniels has criticized Rawls' distinction between liberty, guaranteed equally for all by the first principle, and the conditions making liberty worthwhile, the distribution of which is left to the second principle and may be unequal. Daniels argues that if equality of the basic liberties is as important as Rawls thinks, valuable enough to be set up as a priority constraining the distribution of wealth and income, then we should also favor a rough equality in the conditions making liberty worthwhile. In the absence of the requisite conditions for its exercise, liberty loses much of its value. Furthermore, and this is Daniels' key insight, often it is not the absolute amounts of a good, such as wealth or income, but the relative difference in people's holdings that determine the effectiveness of their liberties.[6] For example, one's voting rights do not require any particular absolute level of wealth or income to be effective beyond the minimum necessary for transportation to the polls, acquisition of basic literacy, and leisure time to vote. However, another person's exorbitant resources for influencing political campaigns through contributions and lobbying may render one's vote nearly worthless.

Hence, Daniels recommends that inequalities sanctioned by the difference principle should not be allowed to exceed the level at which they would undermine liberty itself by threatening its worth. The first principle of justice may thus require a more far-reaching egalitarianism than the difference principle, which otherwise lends itself to "trickle-down" interpretations according to which the least advantaged are considered better off as long as their incomes are rising, even if their power is shrinking. Will such a liberty-restricted difference principle lead to socialism rather than capitalism? Some further argument is needed to answer that question affirmatively, but at least the starting point is more egalitarian than it first appeared.

Rodney Peffer proposes changing or modifying Rawls' principles in three ways.[7] First, he makes explicit the sort of liberty-oriented restriction on inequality Daniels has defended, and which Rawls himself seems to have intended in *A Theory of Justice* and later writings. Second, he presents as a prior principle, trumping even the system of equal basic liberties, the following: "Everyone's security rights and subsistence rights shall be respected." Rawls himself has acknowledged such a principle to be implicit in his conception of justice, so Peffer's modification really amounts to a clarification.[8] The idea is that in the original position—or out of it—a reasonable person wants above all to be able to survive physically and meet basic needs. If these basic conditions are lacking, then freedom of speech and other basic liberties lose their value; and if the only way to provide security and basic subsistence for everyone in some particular circumstances is to curtail some liberties, justice requires that that be done.

Third, Peffer recommends adding to the equal opportunity principle "an equal right to participate in all social decision-making processes within institutions of which one is a part." He uses this principle to defend democratization of workplaces, a measure that moves decisively beyond capitalism. I favor that outcome, but later I argue that Peffer's principle is flawed. One can get to his self-management results without it, by appeal to the principle of the fair value of political liberty. This point is argued at greater length in chapter 1.

My own position is thus close to that of Peffer and builds on the insights of Daniels and other "left" Rawlsians. I add one further qualification to this much over-simplified account of Rawls' theory of justice. Rawls recognizes, almost as an afterthought in *A Theory of Justice*, that the most important of the "primary goods" whose distribution is the concern of the theory is the good of self-respect.

Without self-respect, that is, a sense of one's own worth and the confidence that one can succeed, none of the other goods matter. Thus from the standpoint of the original position the parties would have to condemn any scheme that systematically undermines the self-respect of whole classes of people. Unequal liberties threaten this by marking out some people as second-class citizens; thus, one argument for equal liberties is that they provide conditions for maintenance of self-respect. Inequalities of wealth, income, power, authority, and status also could undermine self-respect. Rawls acknowledges this and holds that an "excusable envy"—envy springing from the undermining of self-respect—could warrant the elimination of an inequality otherwise justified as advantaging the least advantaged. Peffer includes the requirement that inequalities not be so great as to seriously undermine self-respect explicitly alongside the equal worth of liberty restriction on the difference principle. This I take to be a more perspicuous rendering of Rawls' theory, not a modification. I have argued elsewhere that this condition favors work democratization in at least some cases and hence a transformation of at least some capitalist enterprises into worker-managed firms.[9]

## CONTRACTARIANISM, COMMUNITARIANISM, AND POSTMODERNISM

I should make clear at the outset that I am not entirely comfortable with this alliance of contractarian liberalism and socialism. I have been impressed, and intermittently persuaded, by "communitarian" and other critics of liberalism who question the usefulness of the contract method and the model of utility-maximizing rationality it employs. Utility maximization cedes too much to the idea of the good life as mere preference satisfaction: social theory should have room for critique of actually existing preferences. Perhaps more importantly, the world is inhabited not by the ghostly creatures of the original position, shorn of class, race, gender, or ethnicity, but, rather, by particular individuals "encumbered" by particular traditions and commitments. Any meaningful political argument must start from these. Rawls also heard this criticism and reframed his theory as grounded in an "overlapping consensus." That seems to me a correct move philosophically and politically, but it does not force one to abandon the contract method. Rather, it underscores the fact that in a society consisting of diverse and often conflicting communities and traditions, the search for a common ground leads to some such abstracting approach. But the justification to each person lies not in the argument from the original position alone but also in the harmonization of the resulting principles with more particular traditions and allegiances. In this book I have not attempted this latter more diversified line of argument, though, in the long run, it might prove the most necessary and efficient. For example, I leave it to those more engaged in the Catholic tradition to work out the affinities between

economic democracy and Catholic social doctrine—of which there are many.[10]
Here I undertake the more limited task of showing that the principles and institutions I advocate are not so exclusively tied to one or two communities as to be
branded "sectarian." Beyond that, I think there are some promising attempts to
bridge the communitarian emphasis on particular traditions and substantial ethical foundations and a liberal project to articulate a conception of justice shared
by the entire community.[11]

Marxist and postmodern feminist criticisms of the very idea of a shared tradition, or a shared conception of justice, have raised suspicion about the liberal
project. Maybe there are unbridgeable divides between bourgeois and working-
class conceptions of justice, for example. Nonetheless, I argue in chapter 3 that
a shared conception of justice should be the goal and vision inspiring even the
most partisan of oppositional movements. One need not wait or plead for the endorsement of capitalists, male chauvinists, and racists to put forward an idea of
a just society that all its inhabitants could reasonably be expected to endorse, once
they got accustomed to living without special privileges. If that is liberalism then
I plead guilty.


## MARKET SOCIALISM

Before getting any deeper into the argument the reader will want to know more
about what is meant by *market socialism, economic democracy,* and *worker self-
management* and how these are related to one another and to justice. In the minds
of most people, at least most Americans, the term *socialism* conjures up an image of state ownership of the means of production, centralized planning, and a
cradle-to-grave welfare system. The concentration of economic power in the hands
of the state is apt to arouse fears of one-party dictatorship, as well. The former
Soviet Union and the countries under its hegemony in Eastern Europe more or
less conformed to this image. With the collapse of Communism in those states,
it should not be surprising if most people now think that "socialism" so understood is definitively dead. It never extricated itself from dictatorship, it failed to
innovate enough to keep pace with capitalist economies, inefficiencies mounted,
and many citizens were kept from emigrating only by force.

However, there have always been alternative ideas of socialism, among dissidents in the "actually existing socialist" states and among Marxists and other
socialists outside of Eastern Europe. The varieties and nuances are too many to
canvas here. I mention only those that concern me in this book, mainly varieties
of market socialism. They are socialist in that they replace private property with
some form of state or social ownership, and sometimes replace the employer–
employee relationship with some form of worker self-management. Either measure alone, and certainly both in conjunction, are such significant departures from

capitalist private property and the prerogative of capitalists to hire wage workers in the labor market that they deserve a name that marks a departure from capitalism to a more egalitarian "socialist" system. However, one will have to look far and wide to find any contemporary socialist who would defend one-party states or bureaucratic centralized planning. Chapter 6 is devoted to Albert and Hahnel's defense of a nonbureaucratic planning process that they hope would dispense with markets in consumer goods. However, I side with those socialists who now concede that markets in consumer goods are indispensable in order to provide a level of goods and services to consumers that can compete with capitalism and that consequently can compete when measured by principles of justice. The least advantaged will be better off in a market system than in a centrally planned economy.

That is the true verdict of history in the recent abandonment of socialism in Eastern Europe and the former Soviet Union. It by no means follows that capitalism has triumphed. We must bear in mind that capitalism has its own ongoing crises and problems: systematically generated and growing inequalities, pursuit of profit at the expense of the environment and community, and many more particular problems connected with these (such as the unfair burden that dislocated workers bear of the costs of adjusting to global competition).

The question that faces us today is whether an equitable distribution of income, wealth, and power and genuinely democratic self-determination of our common destiny (the chief goals of the socialist movement) are attainable *without* centralized state planning. In other words, how might we combine markets with social ownership of property, the democratic governance of economic enterprises, and democratic investment planning (as distinct from production and exchange coordinated in the market)? The market socialist debate is about different proposals for doing this, their feasibility, and how by standards of justice they compare with capitalism as it is or might be.

Some, like N. Scott Arnold, think that the market under market socialism will ultimately lead back to capitalism. I address his argument in chapter 5. Defenders of market socialism disagree in their models over a number of questions.

1. Ownership: Who should own the capital wealth of a society? Traditional socialists, the defenders of the worker-managed market economy in the former Yugoslavia, and David Schweickart all would keep the ownership of capital in the hands of the state, although in the case of Schweickart's economic democracy, as well as in the Yugoslav case, workers, not state appointed managers, are responsible for the management of the firms. The workers constitute the firm as an association, but they pay a tax for the use of the land, raw materials, and other resources and are responsible for maintaining them. They receive grants for new investments, which are then added to the stock of capital assets on which they pay a tax. In accounting terms, the arrangement is akin to paying rent and interest for leased capital assets

and borrowed investment funds. John Roemer thinks socialists have for too long made a fetish of private property. He proposes to issue shares of stock in enterprises to every citizen. Social property (in a transition from a formerly socialist society) would thus be privatized. However, it would not devolve into capitalism because these shares could not be traded for cash. They could only be traded for coupons tradable for other shares, and at a person's death his or her shares would be reappropriated by the state and reallocated to the next generation. In the meantime citizens would earn dividends on their shares and the performance of firms, indicated by their ability to pay dividends, would be shaped in much the same way that the stock market currently disciplines firms. Efficiency would be preserved. But, from a socialist point of view, so would a rough equality of ownership. Roemer's market socialism thus has markets in capital and labor, as well as producer and consumer goods. It is socialist mainly in the egalitarian constraints on the transfer of capital and in restrictions on convertibility of capital into other kinds of income and wealth.

2. Planning: Although all market socialists favor markets in consumer goods, some, such as Schweickart, wish to maintain the planning of investment, at least a democratic setting of the broad parameters for disbursement of investment funds that are collected centrally—in Schweickart's model through the tax on capital assets. The claim is that the real advantage of markets vis-à-vis central planning is at the level of production and consumption. It is here that producers must satisfy consumers or risk losing their main source of income. But privatizing investment funds and leaving investment entirely to the discretion of enterprises is not warranted with a view to levels of efficiency and satisfaction of consumer needs that can compete with capitalism. On the contrary, the advantages that investment planning can afford in terms of avoidance of environmental destruction and the achievement of full employment, to mention only the two most important "externalities" in capitalist market economies that can be tackled directly in the investment process (rather than indirectly through regulation), justify the maintenance of this plank of the socialist platform. This, as I argue, is the most controversial aspect of Schweickart's proposal.

3. Worker self-management: Since the beginnings of the socialist movement in the nineteenth century, critics of capitalism have condemned "wage labor," the system in which propertyless individuals are forced to sell their labor in order to gain access to the means of labor and the means of subsistence. Although wage earners may live in a politically democratic state, they enter into a tyranny of the owner once they pass through the doors of the enterprise.

Thus, for many socialists a core idea of socialism has been to extend the formal democracy of the state into the economic enterprise, and make it a substantial reality of everyday life, by requiring those who manage enterprises to be accountable to—elected by—those whom they manage. Lest this "self-management" itself become a mere formality, advocates of self-management usually couple demands for democratic accountability with efforts to support substantial worker participation, often entailing significant redesign and humanization of jobs and the division of labor in the workplace.

Self-management, though compromised by the intervention by the League of Communists, was a reality in the former Yugoslavia. It exists in microcosm in the Basque cooperatives of Mondragon and in many other cooperative and worker-owned enterprises throughout the world. Worker ownership, when combined with participation, is remarkably efficient in comparison with traditional capitalist enterprise. Some, such as David Ellerman, advocate only self-management, coupled with private property, and a market economy that includes a market for capital. Such a system would be sufficiently different from capitalism to deserve a new name, but the scope for inequalities of wealth, income, and power it affords make it unfit to be called socialist, and Ellerman rightly spurns the label. I refer to this model as worker ownership.[12]

Schweickart addresses some of the deeper egalitarian concerns that lead him to advocate investment planning and social ownership. The whole package he calls "economic democracy" because it democratizes the economy in two ways: it democratizes enterprises through self-management and it opens up the investment process to all citizens, not just to an elite of owners. The socialist qualifications that distinguish economic democracy from worker ownership may erode some of the efficiency advantages observed in worker-owned enterprises. The question is whether this happens to such a degree as to undermine the case for the superiority of self-managing socialism over capitalism or mere worker ownership. Some socialists, such as John Roemer, are also suspicious of worker self-management, fearing that workers' interests might conflict with efficiency at the enterprise level and generate social inequality.

## ECONOMIC DEMOCRACY

In this book I defend Schweickart's economic democracy against the more limited idea of worker ownership and against Roemer's stock-market socialism. So that the reader can clearly keep this model in view, I summarize here its main features and give some hints concerning its relevance and attractiveness.[13]

1. Unlike command economies such as the former Soviet Union, economic democracy involves a *market* in goods and services. At various points

throughout the book I defend this reliance on the market against the objections of some Marxists (in chapter 4), against a model of decentralized planning (in chapter 6), and in relation to environmental concerns (in chapter 12). But Schweickart's main reasons for supporting the market mirror problems that arise for central planning, concerning information, incentives, power, and entrepreneurship. (*a*) "A modern industrial economy is simply too complicated to plan in detail." It can be done, but not without considerable failure to meet the needs of consumers. (*b*) Under central planning, "enterprises have little incentive . . . to provide what consumers really want . . . [and] will be inclined to understate their capabilities and overstate their needs." Workers have little incentive to work, and planners have little incentive to close inefficient firms. (*c*) The concentration of power risks authoritarianism and corruption. (*d*) Because enterprises do not compete, there is little incentive for innovation or risk, possibly the Achilles' heel of centrally planned systems. In sum, to be competitive with capitalism, even on the grounds of justice, a socialist system needs a market in goods and services. Economic democracy is a system of independent enterprises, competing in such a market.

2. Worker self-management is "at the heart of the system." One reason for this is the demonstrated efficiency of worker cooperatives noted earlier, which meshes with some of the arguments for markets just listed. More important is the ethical argument for self-management. "An enterprise is not a *thing* that is *owned* by its workers, rather it is an *association* that is *governed* by them." For reasons elaborated in chapter 1, such an association should be structured by the democratic principle of one member, one vote. In a capitalist democracy, by contrast, citizens have equal voting rights and civil liberties, but equality stops at the door of the enterprise plutocracy. This contradiction is overcome, and political democracy is widened into economic democracy, as the domain of work is brought under democratic control. I have been inspired by the economic and ethical example of the highly successful network of cooperatives in the Basque town of Mondragon. In chapter 7, I consider whether worker ownership on the Mondragon model is a viable alternative to capitalism.

3. Although worker controlled, the enterprises in economic democracy are not worker owned. This distinguishes economic democracy from mere worker ownership and also from the Mondragon cooperatives. Rather, enterprise assets are publicly owned, and enterprises pay a tax (or rent) for the use of the assets. This recognizably socialist feature ensures that the system does not give rise to class division between owners and nonowners based on wealth deriving merely from property ownership, "a major source of capitalist inequality."

4. Economic democracy does away with a market in capital stimulated through interest on private savings and instead generates public funds for investment through a tax on capital assets of enterprises. The resulting investment funds "are returned to communities on a per capita basis (as a prima facie entitlement). Thus capital flows to where the people are. People are not forced to follow the flow of capital. Once in communities, the investment funds are then 'loaned' to the enterprises in the community . . . via a network of public banks." This scheme, together with public ownership, democratizes the economy in a second way (the first being self-management): the decisions concerning what, where, and when to invest, currently made by an elite of investors and bankers accountable mostly to a small minority of wealthy property owners, is opened to democratic deliberation, and because the funds are returned to communities, on a scale that permits meaningful participation and accountability, community priorities can be established directly in the investment process rather than indirectly through the regulation and subsidization of a purely profit-driven process. Employment creation (and, I might add, regard for the environment) could be additional criteria for the disbursement of loans. This is socialist planning of a sort, but with enterprises disciplined on the other side by the market. The devolution of decisions to communities not only allows for meaningful democracy, it also permits a variety of experiments yet none of the national-scale catastrophes, such as forced collectivization emanating from the brainstorms of an authoritarian bureaucratic center.

Economic democracy solves the four problems associated with central planning. The information and incentive problems are addressed through the market economy and the cooperative structure of firms. The innovation problem is addressed through entrepreneurial development out of the banks, as successfully pioneered by the Basque cooperatives, and through the incentives for workers in the form of "either monetary gains, shorter working hours, or better working conditions." Decentralized economic power of enterprises counterbalances the political power of the state.

In comparison with capitalism, economic democracy is at least as efficient, much more egalitarian, "since it eliminates property income," more democratic, "since it extends democracy downward into the workplace, and upward into the determination of macro-economic developmental policies," and more rational, in that it "confronts squarely what may be the single most destructive feature of contemporary capitalism: the hypermobility of capital," an element that results in "job insecurities, destruction of communities, and mass migrations" and a race to the bottom among communities competing with one another to retain capital ("by offering lower wages, or fewer environmental restrictions," or lower taxes and state expenditures).

In *Against Capitalism*, Schweickart argues for economic democracy both economically and ethically, in comparison with several variants of capitalism and
alternative models of socialism. This book complements Schweickart's work by
developing some further arguments from the theory of justice that support workplace democracy or self-management (I use the terms interchangeably). I also
elaborate the theory of justice to argue for the more general principle of egalitarian distribution of wealth, income, and power, which might lend support, in
comparison with capitalism, to any of a variety of socialist models and which
also supports an unconditional basic income.

These egalitarian underpinnings strengthen the case against more-limited departures from capitalism, such as the mere promotion of worker-owned cooperatives,[14] and Van Parijs's proposal for a basic-income capitalism. A strong commitment to egalitarianism not only strenthens the case for the clearly socialist
aspects of economic democracy, it also forces us to adumbrate the model with a
basic-income scheme to address some tendencies toward inequality that can be
expected from a worker-managed market economy.

Whereas general egalitarian arguments do not favor any one model of socialism (and may even open up the possibility of an egalitarian capitalism), the argument for economic democracy turns on secondary concerns such as relative
efficiency, alienation, environmental sustainability, and political feasibility. By
*political feasibility* I mean, first, the possibility that a model of socialism might
actually be embraced by social movements and made the goal of a political practice that has at least a remote chance of success. (Later, I argue that economic
democracy is politically feasible in relation to the concerns of the labor, environmental, unemployed, and women's movements, but only if complemented by
a substantial basic income for everyone.) Economic democracy together with
basic income is also well fitted as a response to trends in contemporary capitalism: globalization, two-tiered labor markets, communitarian and stakeholder
firms, long-term high levels of unemployment, capital flight, the growth of employee ownership, and the information economy. This fit with "material conditions" is the second aspect of political feasibility. In sum, the ideal is not just
desirable in the abstract, it fits with real-life circumstances and real human
yearnings.

## NOTES

1. David Levine and Laura D'Andrea Tyson, "Participation, Productivity, and the
Firm's Environment," in *Paying for Productivity: A Look at the Evidence,* ed. Alan Blinder
(Washington, D.C.: Brookings, 1990), 203–14. For other evidence and arguments, see
David Schweickart, *Against Capitalism* (Cambridge: Cambridge University Press, 1994),
chapter 3. For references to recent studies, see National Center for Employee Ownership,
"1998 an Eventful Year for Employee Ownership Research," *Employee Ownership Re-*

*port* 19, no. 2 (March–April 1999): 3; and "Employee Ownership and Corporate Performance," updated 1999, <http://www.nceo.org/library/corpperf.html> (10 March 1999). The last of these concludes, "Researchers now agree that 'the case is closed' on employee ownership and corporate performance. . . . We can say with certainty that when ownership and participative management are combined, substantial gains result."

2. Philippe Van Parijs, "Justice as the Fair Distribution of Freedom: Fetishism or Stoicism?" Unpublished manuscript.

3. John Rawls, *A Theory of Justice* (Cambridge: Harvard University Press, 1971), 302.

4. "The basic liberties of citizens are, roughly speaking, political liberty (the right to vote and be eligible for public office) together with freedom of speech and assembly; liberty of conscience and freedom of thought; freedom of the person along with the right to hold (*personal*) property; and freedom from arbitrary arrest and seizure as defined by the concept of the rule of law." Rawls, *A Theory of Justice*, 61; my emphasis.

5. See Van Parijs's defense of basic-income capitalism in *Real Freedom for All: What (If Anything) Can Justify Capitalism?* (Oxford: Clarendon Press, 1995).

6. Norman Daniels, "Equal Liberty and Unequal Worth of Liberty," in *Reading Rawls: Critical Studies on Rawls' "A Theory of Justice,"* ed. Norman Daniels (New York: Basic Books, 1975), 253. 81.

7. Rodney Peffer, *Marxism, Morality, and Social Justice* (Princeton: Princeton University Press, 1990), 418.

8. John Rawls, *Political Liberalism* (New York: Columbia University Press, 1993), 7, n7.

9. Michael W. Howard, "Worker Control, Self-Respect, and Self-Esteem," *Philosophy Research Archives* 10 (1984): 455–72.

10. Cooperatives and worker self-management are relatively strong in predominantly Catholic countries such as Italy and Spain, and the most impressive network of worker cooperatives in the Basque country was shepherded into existence by a Catholic priest. On the latter, see Greg MacLeod, *From Mondragon to America* (Sydney, Nova Scotia: University College of Cape Breton Press, 1997).

11. See, for example, Martha Nussbaum, "Aristotelian Social Democracy," in *Liberalism and the Good*, ed. R. Bruce Douglass, Gerald M. Mara, and Henry S. Richardson (New York: Routledge, 1990), 203–52.

12. David Ellerman, *Property and Contract in Economics: The Case for Economic Democracy* (Oxford: Basil Blackwell, 1992). For a critique, see Michael W. Howard, "Worker Ownership and Wage Slavery," unpublished manuscript, 1999.

13. Schweickart provides a useful summary of his position, and that of Roemer, in his contribution to *Market Socialism: The Debate among Socialists,* ed. Bertell Ollman (New York: Routledge, 1998), 7–22. My remarks here draw heavily on this summary, and all quotations are from this text. For his more extended defense, see *Against Capitalism*.

14. I devote chapter 7 to consideration of the theory and practice of worker ownership.

# 1

# Justifying Workplace Democracy

Power should need no sanction of violence but be exercised solely by virtue of rank and legality, while wealth should never be so great that a man can buy his neighbor, nor so lacking that a man is compelled to sell himself.
—Jean-Jacques Rousseau, *Social Contract*

When communist artisans associate with one another, theory, propaganda, etc. is their first end. But at the same time, as a result of this association, they acquire a new need—the need for society—and what appears as a means becomes an end. In this practical process the most splendid results are to be observed whenever French socialist workers are seen together. Such things as smoking, drinking, eating, etc., are no longer means of contact or means that bring together. Company, association, and conversation, which again has society as its end, are enough for them; the brotherhood of man is no mere phrase with them, but a fact of life, and the nobility of man shines upon us from their work-hardened bodies.
—Karl Marx, *Economic and Philosophic Manuscripts*

The proposal of mandated workplace democracy appears sectarian and hence unjustifiable.
—Richard Arneson, "Democratic Rights at National and Workplace Levels"

The image of a society of equals—in which each citizen has respect for every other, all are able to, and for the most part do, take turns in a process of shared self-governance, and suspicion and egoism give way to bonds of trust and friendship—has exerted a powerful pull on the human imagination over a wide stretch of history. It finds its roots in Christianity and in Aristotle's idealization of the polis, and it reemerges variously in Renaissance civic humanism, in Rousseau's

19

vision of the Roman Republic and the city of Geneva, in French Revolutionary ideology celebrating "fraternity" as well as liberty and equality, and, of course, in Marx's vision of socialism, articulated early on as a bringing down to earth of what humanity has been dreaming of all along.

Long before the fall of communism in the Soviet Union and Eastern Europe, Marxists and others elaborated variations on this communitarian ideal designed to avoid the centralization, bureaucracy, political domination, and inefficiency of the Soviet model. The worker-managed market socialism I am defending in this book is one such alternative. Along with other forms of communitarianism, some defenses of self-management are open to criticisms. I do not address here the issue of exclusion: the partisans of "fraternity" unselfconsciously excluded women, the polis rested on the backs of slaves, and self-management can reinforce gender inequalities in the division of labor. What concerns me in this chapter is the claim that, even if the ideal were modified so as to include all those unjustly excluded, it would still be objectionable because it could not be justified to significant numbers of people who would reasonably reject it as their image of a good society. It would, as current terminology puts it, violate liberal neutrality. Why should this matter? Defenders of liberal neutrality, an ambiguous notion admitting of several interpretations, all start from the fact of pluralism, the existence of many reasonable but incommensurable conceptions of the good life. They also regard these conceptions as deserving of toleration, because otherwise the persons holding them would not be treated with respect.

I find myself caught between, on the one hand, the pull of a communitarian–egalitarian ideal, one manifestation of which is workplace and economic democracy, and, on the other, the force of the liberal neutrality argument. One strategy when one finds oneself so positioned is to explore whether there might not be a way to arrive at the communitarian goal via liberal premises or to show that some version of the communitarian ideal is after all not so illiberal. In this chapter, after some preliminary remarks on justification, I defend against liberal objections the claim that democracy should be extended from the state to economic enterprises and decision making. Along the way it will be necessary to clarify more precisely what neutrality means and what a liberal theory of justice requires, particularly what is required for the "fair value" of liberty.

In Chapter 3, I address some misgivings about liberalism from postmodern and Marxist perspectives. In the final analysis, I argue, the best justification of workplace and economic democracy must be a liberal justification, even for those of us who may aspire to more than the rather austere and limited conception of the good life affirmed by liberalism. But first, I should be more explicit about what "justification" is all about.

I share with John Rawls and many other contemporary philosophers a conception of justification as "wide reflective equilibrium." What this means is that to justify a conception of justice, or a view of an ideal society, one must seek coherence of one's general principles with one's "considered judgments" about what is right and wrong. Abstract theories can help to organize the totality of one's beliefs, identifying core principles, tracing out their implications, and connecting them with one another and with one's concrete beliefs. This reflective equilibrium is "wide" in so far as it encompasses not just one's own beliefs but also those of reasonable people with whom one comes into contact, whom one must consider and deal with. Wide reflective equilibrium is thus something that each of us may strive toward but may never perfectly attain.

There is also the question of *to whom* the justification is addressed. One unavoidably writes from a perspective and, at least implicitly, to an audience, or multiple audiences, of friends, colleagues, co-workers, activists, fellow citizens. One can assume more in the way of shared values and assumptions the narrower the circle of one's audience is drawn. The wider the circle, the more one needs to resort to a lowest common denominator, or an abstract principle, to convince everyone, or else one needs to offer multiple, overlapping arguments.

Liberal theories of justice, particularly that of Rawls, aim to justify principles of justice to the widest audience, on the basis of the thinnest available raft of shared assumptions. The idea is that appeal to "thicker" conceptions of what is good in life will appeal only to some, not to others, and hence be parochial or "sectarian."

One can carry this line of thinking to an extreme, where one accepts as plausible only arguments that appeal to the rationality of self-interested individuals, in the tradition of Hobbes. The idea here need not be that no one ever rises above egoism. Rather, it is that in a society as diverse as ours, one can not take for granted shared principles of any kind, but one can at least assume that individuals will act in pursuit of their own interests, however they define these (their interests could be altruistic). A kind of "justice" is still possible as an agreement among such rational agents. I do not devote attention to this line of thinking, concurring with the judgment (and arguments) of others that from such a thin starting point, no robust and stable conception of justice can be reached. One need only look at the manifestly unjust, violent, and unstable modus vivendi that exists between nation-states to see how little such an approach can be expected to yield.

On the other hand, if we begin from too rich a conception of the good life, which might make a clear place for principles of justice of a particular sort as constitutive of such a life, we find that our argument will persuade only the community of those who share this conception. Then we fail to persuade the wider society, which we both need in order to put our ideal into practice and whom we want to draw into an association based on reasonable argument, not coercion. This cul-de-sac ends in violence, or despair.[1]

As an alternative, we need to begin from assumptions that are strong enough to yield determinate principles of justice yet weak enough to have wide appeal. There may be no such assumptions. But the project of the liberal theory of justice is to try to identify such a starting point, if it can be found.

Given the fact of value pluralism—the existence today in the United States and other liberal democratic states of diverse and conflicting conceptions of the good—one strategy is to strive for neutrality with respect to any particular conception. There are different versions of this neutral strategy. I focus in this chapter on the most famous, that of John Rawls, and on a couple of other variations, with a view to what can and can not be said in support of economic democracy from the standpoint of a neutral liberal theory of justice. My main concern is to defend workplace democracy against the charge that it violates neutrality.[2]

## THE DEMOCRATIC ANALOGY

Robert Dahl and Michael Walzer, among others, have argued that if democracy is warranted for a nation-state, then it should be warranted for the workplace.[3] I am calling this claim the "democratic analogy." Because democracy is a core value in contemporary liberalism, arguments for the democratic analogy carry us some distance toward a satisfactory justification, but certain objections force us to go deeper into political theory and examine the foundations of democracy itself, in order to establish to what extent they support workplace democracy.

Walzer develops his argument around the case of Pullman, Illinois, the town built by George Pullman for the workers of his railway-car factory and entirely owned and ruled by him until 1898, when the Illinois Supreme Court "ordered the Pullman Company . . . to divest itself of all property not used for manufacturing purposes. . . . Ownership of a town . . . [is] incompatible with the theory and spirit of our institutions."[4] Walzer argues that the reasons for prohibiting ownership of a town and for requiring democratic institutions extend, by analogy, to workplaces. The owner of a firm, like the owner of a town, has "sustained control over men and women."[5] The firm owner gives commands and applies sanctions to enforce them. Power is exercised in both cases and warrants democratic accountability of rulers to the ruled. The characteristics often cited as distinguishing workplaces are seen, particularly in the case of Pullman, to apply also to towns, so that arguments against workplace democracy would seem to entail arguments against municipal self-government, as well. The town of Pullman, like many factories, would not have come into being without entrepreneurial vision, energy, inventiveness, and the investment of private capital (municipal bonds). Residents of towns, like workers, are free to go, although the cost of doing so may be quite high and the alternatives not much more attractive. In fact, in times of high unemployment, it may be easier to change one's town of residence than to find another job. Towns, like factories, might be more efficiently run, with resources left over for other purposes, if they were governed autocratically, but arguments for efficiency are trumped by more basic requirements of respect for human dignity and rights to self-determination.[6]

Clearly, a society with workplace democracy would be more democratic than a capitalist society. But would it be more just? Would it even be compatible with justice? Robert Nozick argues that any scheme of mandatory worker control would violate liberty. However, his argument rests on dubious libertarian conceptions of what is "voluntary" and "coercive" (because others have adequately criticized this argument, I will not comment further).[7] More-difficult challenges to the democratic analogy come from within the framework of egalitarian theories of justice that take for granted the subordinate and instrumental character of any particular scheme of property rights and are at least compatible with some form of socialism.

## IS WORKPLACE DEMOCRACY SECTARIAN?

Richard Arneson considers political rights, and democracy, in particular, to be valuable only instrumentally, as a means to securing fundamental rights, and he rejects the parallel between political and economic democracy drawn by Walzer and Dahl. Arneson argues that, relatively speaking, one enters workplaces more voluntarily than political states. Through the right to exit one has some control over the conditions of work. A firm's policies at least do not have "intolerable consequences" for one's fundamental rights.[8]

Arneson admits that as one moves from standard cases toward the margins, the putative analogy may become stronger. A country permitting easy exit may not need to be a democracy; and "coal miners in an isolated region, culturally very different from the rest of the nation," may have a stronger claim for workplace democracy.[9] On the other hand, and apropos of Walzer's Pullman case, Arneson does not consider the case for democracy in municipalities to be as strong as that for democracies in nation-states, because, presumably, the threat to more fundamental rights is greater from a nondemocratic state than from a nondemocratic municipality.[10]

Even if labor market conditions are such that all the firms offer intolerable conditions, Arneson thinks the argument would not warrant universal workplace democracy. "At most, the argument would show that among the work and career options available to the individual, some fraction of these options must include the opportunity to carry out one's work in a labor-managed firm." By contrast, mandated universal workplace democracy would favor some workers, those who prefer worker control, over others, those who are indifferent or hostile to it. Assuming the state should maintain neutrality with respect to such varying preferences (or conceptions of the good life), "the proposal of mandated workplace democracy appears sectarian and hence unjustifiable."[11]

However, in a typical capitalist economy, it is not the case that workers enter workplaces voluntarily, even if it is the case that they enter workplaces more voluntarily than they change citizenship. A worker does not always have another job as an option upon leaving a firm, and the personal cost of unemployment can be very high—higher, in some cases, than moving to another town or even another country. Economic necessity forces workers into firms under conditions dictated by the prevailing labor market, and workers are thereby plunged into subjection to owners. It is true that typically owners (and also municipalities) do not have the power to execute people or imprison them for long periods. But the threat of firing, which often has a blackballing effect with respect to future job prospects, is a forceful sanction that gives the owner power over the worker.[12]

Even the possibility of becoming an owner is not real for most workers. G. A. Cohen compares workers as a class to a group of people imprisoned in a cell, from which a few occasionally slip past the door. Although it is true that each individual is free to leave, it is false that all or most are able to leave.[13] For entry and exit from firms to be voluntary, workers must be really free (not just legally free) to exit: the terms of the contract must be such that refusal does not entail catastrophe. A guaranteed minimum income is one measure that would free workers to refuse wage-labor contracts that are undignified. Alternatively, workers could be entitled to a voice in the management of the firm. (I take up the idea of guaranteed income in connection with Philippe Van Parijs's objections, to workplace democracy.) The alternative of a voice—of mandated workplace democracy—is, Arneson argues, at most an option that must be available in the labor market but not in all firms. However, is this kind of opportunity any different from the "opportunity" that exists in all capitalist economies, for a worker to open a small business? If not, then it is subject to Cohen's objection: the fact that some co-ops exist does not mean that workers are free. On the other hand, if Arneson's idea is that cooperatives should exist in sufficient numbers that all workers have a real option of choosing a worker-managed firm over a capitalist firm, then he is not too far away from mandated worker control. Indeed, most advocates of worker control recognize some exceptions for the sake of efficiency, on the margins of a predominantly worker-controlled economy, and the main difference between them and Arneson would appear to be over how large the co-op sector needs to be to afford a genuine choice for everyone.[14]

Assuming that it would have to be quite large, it is hard to see how anything less than either mandated worker control or tax breaks—and other conditions that so tipped the economic balance in favor of cooperatives over capitalist firms that the latter were substantially outnumbered—would fail to be arbitrary. On what grounds could one require some firms to be worker controlled, so that a significant option existed in the market, but other firms would be exempt from the requirement? Even a sizable worker-controlled sector would be subject, as much as full-blown mandated workplace democracy, to what I take to be Arneson's deepest objection, that mandated workplace democracy would violate liberal neutrality.

The thesis of liberal neutrality is that principles of justice should be neutral with respect to competing conceptions of the good life, not in their effects (which is impossible) but in the kinds of reasons considered relevant or the deliberate aim of a policy. Thus, to illustrate, laws that favored Catholic schools, supported them with tax dollars, and made the Catholic Church the official church—even if other churches and religions were tolerated—on grounds that the Catholic religion is superior would not be neutral. Laws that allowed each person to pursue whatever religion he or she preferred—or no religion—would be neutral (with the proviso that practices not violate justice in other ways), even if they unintentionally strengthened Catholicism.

Adhering to liberal neutrality, Arneson considers certain rights as fundamental: "freedom of speech, privacy, and individual liberty . . . [and] egalitarian rights to material resources such as are implied by John Rawls's difference principle regulating the shares of social primary goods or by Ronald Dworkin's principle of equality of resources or by some other principle in this family."[15] These rights are fundamental in that they give each person the freedom as well as the means to do what he or she wants but leave open to each how he or she will use that freedom and those resources. A similar idea informs Van Parijs's proposal for an unconditional basic income as a way of realizing "real freedom for all," the adjective "real" contrasting with formal freedom guaranteed by basic liberties without the means to exercise them.

Arneson and Van Parijs are "left" liberals insofar as they go beyond the constraints of classical liberals and libertarians, who favor equal liberties but support inequality of resources. But they draw the line at favoring any positive vision of what freedom should be used for. A neutral liberal will resist the suggestion that one is not "truly" free unless one is participating in civic life, or exercising essential human capacities, or objectifying one's imagination through work, or realizing one's social essence, or, in general, realizing some conception of the good life.

When Arneson claims that mandated workplace democracy would be "sectarian" he is charging that it would impose a particular vision of the good life on everyone: only work that is self-managed is acceptable; other forms, such as wage labor, conflict with a vision of liberated and self-actualizing work. Even if not everyone is compelled to participate in workplace democracy, all are required to support it insofar as its universalization involves some cost, some diminution of resources that might have gone elsewhere.

## COOPERATIVES FOR EFFICIENCY

Philippe Van Parijs is more sympathetic to cooperatives but shares Arneson's commitment to liberal neutrality. Hence, an examination of his views is a good case study to see how far one can go in defending workplace democracy on the basis of liberal neutrality.

In *Real Freedom for All*, Van Parijs provides a "real libertarian" defense of an unconditional basic income (BI) for everyone and argues that the capacity to deliver that at the highest sustainable level, subject to some qualifications mentioned momentarily, is the yardstick by which we should measure the relative merits of capitalism and socialism. (In order not to digress too far from the focus of this chapter, I defer most of the arguments for BI to the next chapter.) Ultimately, Van Parijs argues that the best feasible capitalism probably has the edge in efficiently producing what needs distributing, but socialism may have the edge in actually being able to carry out the fair distribution.

The qualifications are that basic security and self-ownership be respected and that "undominated diversity" be achieved. Respect for self-ownership is the libertarian element in real libertarianism: it involves not violating the integrity of the person. It does not entail absolute libertarian rights to private property as the fruit of one's labor, in Nozickian fashion, but only that there be neither slavery nor collectivism, neither private nor social ownership of persons.[16]

Undominated diversity is Van Parijs's answer to the problem, raised by A. K. Sen and others, of how to take account of differential individual capabilities for utilizing resources. They argue that in a Rawlsian distribution of primary goods, or an equal distribution of resources, people with disabilities are not able to use the resources as effectively as abled people; and hence, equal distribution is unjust.[17] Van Parijs, while arguing for the highest equal distribution of a basic income and thus for a version of equality of resources, does so on the assumption of an undominated diversity, which, for our purposes, means that disabilities have been adequately compensated for so that everyone is above a baseline.[18]

Having an unconditional basic income is what turns formal freedom—self-ownership—into real freedom, as much as a society is able to provide. It is not necessarily an equal distribution of wealth and income, because the highest sustainable basic income may require differential incentives to achieve the most efficient production and the highest minimum. But it is considerably more egalitarian than free-market capitalism, or free-market capitalism qualified by some minimum floor, qualified by means testing, and pitched below the maximum sustainable. With the priority given to formal freedom and undominated diversity and with the maximizing of minimum income, Van Parijs's position bears a strong resemblance to Rawls' theory of justice, particularly the "difference principle," which allows only such inequalities as contribute to the advantage of the least advantaged.

However, the focus on income in Van Parijs's formulation might seem narrower and more "consumerist" than Rawls' formulation, which includes as "primary goods" not only income and wealth but also power, authority, and the bases of self-respect. But Van Parijs's intention is exactly Rawlsian, for the point of an unconditional basic income is not merely to increase purchasing power for the least advantaged. It will also enhance their bargaining power vis-à-vis employers, ensure the worth of their liberty, enable them to have as wide a range of work and leisure options as is feasible, and augment their status as equal citizens by making a basic income an unconditional right of citizenship, thus contributing to the bases of self-respect.

Such a society would be favorable to the development of workplace democracy, even if it were not mandated as a direct requirement of justice. A basic income would reduce the personal risk involved in entrepreneurship, facilitating innovation and also start-ups of cooperatives, along with many other nonstandard forms of enterprise. The key advantage for self-management of a BI is the way it would strengthen the bargaining power of workers. There is also much to be said in favor of cooperatives from the standpoint of efficiency, and thus with a view to maximizing basic income. A cooperative economy promises at least a partial solution to unemployment from certain conditions. It could also increase savings to the extent that the rate is depressed by workers' lack of trust of capitalists. Inefficiencies arising from conflict at the point of production requiring capitalist supervision and control could be reduced by self-managing workers.[19]

Thus, Van Parijs thinks that a basic-income scheme and cooperatives can be mutually reinforcing (a thesis I elaborate below in chapters 2 and 9). However, he favors cooperatives only to the extent that they contribute to efficiency in such ways as I have mentioned. He rejects any mandate for workplace democracy on alleged grounds of justice, if that would involve inefficiencies in production.

Economists have demonstrated that an identical equilibrium can be reached in an economy whether capital hires labor, as in a capitalist economy, or labor hires capital, as in a cooperative economy: both are equally efficient in allocating factors of production.[20] However, the demonstration assumes that new firms can be created at will and that unlimited entrepreneurial talent is available. Because cooperative firms will tend to be less expansionary (see chapter 8 below) and full employment will depend more heavily on new start-ups, these assumptions are critical. They are also suspect. At the very least, they point to the necessity for effective educational institutions that generate entrepreneurship if a cooperative economy is to be as efficient as a capitalist economy in the allocation of resources.[21] Furthermore, most unbiased observers will wonder whether cooperatives can be as efficient as capitalist firms in all branches of business, given the relatively small inroad that worker ownership has made into capitalist economies anywhere. There are some explanations for this paucity of cooperatives (discussed below in chapter 7), but the burden of proof lies with the cooperative advocates, and most people will want to see some more-extensive concrete successes before universally mandating the cooperative form.

Given the possibility of some sacrifice of efficiency if workplace democracy were mandated universally, such a mandate would violate real freedom for all. First, the right to participate in decision making at work is a right that only workers can exercise, and we are workers only in different degrees. Some of us are unpaid household workers, others work in paid employment only part-time or intermittently. Second, because motivations and talents are distributed unequally, people will use this right effectively to varying degrees. Other rights, such as the right to vote, are not dependent for their meaningfulness on a differential ability to use them. Third, each person's power is enhanced to the extent that he or she can refuse to accept a job, and this power is higher the higher the level of BI. Inefficiencies resulting from mandated workplace democracy would lower the level of BI, reducing everyone's power. In this case, mandated workplace democracy would be unjustified, particularly from the perspective of those without jobs or those least in a position to benefit from the exercise of democratic rights.[22]

If one were to maintain, nevertheless, that self-managed work is intrinsically superior or more meaningful than wage labor or that exercising power collectively and socially is less alienating and, therefore, superior to having one's individual bargaining power enhanced (even if some are left out of the collective), then one would be introducing perfectionist premises in violation of liberal neutrality. Under real freedom for all, the bargaining power of each worker is enhanced to the maximum, putting workers, individually or as union members, in the strongest position to demand democratic rights, if they so choose. Mandated workplace democracy preempts this choice in favor of one ideal of work, an ideal that privileges work and workers over leisure and nonworkers.

This is a powerful criticism of the ideal of a worker-managed society. It rests on an assumption, shared with Arneson, that democracy at any level is instrumental to the protection of more basic rights and freedoms but is not constitutive of one's freedom. Van Parijs offers a conceptual argument to challenge the idea that a maximally free society is "a maximally democratic society, a society that subjects everything to collective decision-making and gives each of its members an equal power in the decision it takes." He asks us to contrast two situations:

> In Situation A, each of us can decide for herself whether to scratch her nose. In situation B, we decide together, in perfectly democratic fashion, whether nose-scratching is permissible. [In] both situations the weight of each person in decision-making is identical. But surely the freedom to scratch (or not to scratch) one's nose is not. Each of us enjoys this freedom in situation A. But there is no such freedom in Situation B, where scratching is subjected to collective approval.[23]

This argument leads Van Parijs to insist that self-ownership takes priority over maximizing people's equal power. In his own left-wing Rawlsian case for a guaranteed unconditional basic income, Van Parijs goes on to support measures that maximize (or, more precisely, leximin)[24] each person's individual freedom, and he discusses democracy at national and workplace levels, as does Arneson, only instrumentally, insofar as it is necessary for securing justice or for increasing efficiency.

But his argument fails to defeat the claim that a freedom-respecting economic democracy deserves to be described as an extension of one's autonomy. In the nose-scratching example, each individual is free in situation A but constrained by the collectivity in situation B. The example is not typical of the kinds of cases where participatory autonomy is at issue. Consider situation C, in which workers in an enterprise have no participation rights; their only choice is to submit to the authority of the owners and managers or to leave the firm. The necessity to labor for a decent level of subsistence and the lack of alternative kinds of enterprises make this a less than voluntary choice.[25] Contrast situation D, in which each worker has a vote in the selection of the manager and effective equal influence in the democratic process. How do situations C and D contrast vis-à-vis freedom?

In situation C, the workers have no freedom within the workplace and a limited freedom to exit. In situation D, the freedom to exit is unchanged, and the workers each have a voice, if not a choice. The freedom to exit is unchanged as long as any comparative inefficiencies resulting from mandated workplace democracy are small enough that the level of BI is not reduced significantly. In situation C, all workers have the right to their own firms and to run them as they choose, whereas in situation D, each is constrained by the collectivity, as in the nose-scratching example. In Van Parijs's conceptualization, is there less freedom in situation D? This would seem to commit him to a libertarian prioritization of freedom over the means that make freedom valuable, but this is not his position. He offers the example of an island in which one person owns everything and "can impose on the other inhabitants any condition she fancies. . . . On a libertarian account . . . such a society would not cease to be free. On any intuitively defensible interpretation of the ideal of a free society . . . this is plain nonsense. . . . A libertarian's maximally free society is a society in which the aggregate of individual freedom is maximized, not one in which all are as free as possible." Real freedom for Van Parijs, exists in a society if, in addition to being guaranteed basic security and the right to self-ownership, "each person has the greatest possible opportunity to do whatever she might want to do (leximin opportunity)."[26]

Presumably, Van Parijs wants to restrict the application of this principle to individuals, and so any empowerment of collectivities (for example, the members of cooperatives) is an extension of each individual's rights only in the fairly trivial sense that the individual is now free to mark a ballot. What the collective is free to do is not identical with what each individual in it might want to do.

Van Parijs's objection is not countered by saying that at least a majority of individuals have more freedom through democratization of some decision-making process because those individuals are each able to accomplish what they want through the democratic process (for example, if the majority votes to allow nose scratching, each is free to do so). The problem is that often majorities go against what each person wants—even those in the majority. Consider a parliamentary majority that can form only by coalition members each compromising their principles. Or consider voting paradoxes such as the following hypothetical situation:

Rosa prefers A to B and B to C
Vladi prefers B to C and C to A
Miguel prefers C to A and A to B

Two-thirds prefer A to B; two-thirds prefer B to C. This argues for Rosa's prioritization, but this will not satisfy Vladi or Miguel. On the other hand, two-thirds prefer C to A, and two-thirds prefer A to B. This argues for Miguel's preferences. An analogous argument can be made for Vladi's preferences. Whatever order is chosen, with majority support, will fail to express the will of two-thirds of the voters. Such paradoxes are inherent possibilities in democratic procedures requiring voting above the simplest "yes or no" level of complexity.[27]

Still, it is hard not to see the extension of one's democratic rights as an extension of one's autonomy, particularly in cases in which, unlike the nose-scratching example and more like workplace democracy, one is not giving up meaningful individual freedoms to the collective but, rather, is restricting the freedom of elites (owners, managers, stockholders) in ways that empower workers as a group and, as a result, protect each worker from oligarchical power. Although each worker may not have significantly greater individual choices, to the extent that his or her identity is bound up with the group, freeing the group is freeing the individual member. There are, of course, dangers inherent in such a collectivist notion of freedom. But to rule the idea out of court is to inject an individualist bias into one's allegedly neutral theory. It is to ignore ways in which individuals within a group are freer by virtue of the group's being free. For example, if my union secures the right to halt production on account of unsafe working conditions, I am freed from being forced to endure such conditions, and I am free to halt production in concert with others and often individually. Can this intuition of democracy, both at national and at workplace levels, as intrinsically worthwhile or as an expression of one's freedom be defended in a way that is consistent with liberal neutrality?

## THE FAIR VALUE OF POLITICAL LIBERTY

John Rawls' *Theory of Justice* provides a version of liberal neutrality that, both in Rawls' formulation and in some left-wing interpretations, seems to offer what we are looking for, in its requirement for roughly equal worth (or "fair value") of liberty. Liberal neutrality is a doctrine according to which in a society characterized by a plurality of religious, ethical, and metaphysical beliefs, the state should be neutral with respect to various conceptions of the good. That is, no one should receive any particular advantage—be it a right or a material benefit—simply because of the conception of the good he or she holds. Nor should the principles determining the allocation of rights, benefits, and burdens be shaped by any particular conception of the good.[28]

This would seem to imply that the theory of justice guiding a neutral state can make no reference to any idea of the good. But closer inspection of virtually any theory of justice reveals that some appeal to at least a "thin" theory of the good is necessary if any determinate principles of justice are to be derived at all. One might go a small step further and interpret the thin theory as allowing only instrumental goods. On one (mistaken) reading, Rawls' primary goods—goods that one wants, whatever else one may want—are of this sort. No matter what one's ideals, religion, or metaphysics, one wants more rather than less of the basic liberties, wealth, income, power, authority, and the bases of self-respect.[29] But even Rawls' neutralist liberalism goes further than this. Justice as fairness is grounded in a view of moral personality involving a sense of justice and the capacity to develop a conception of the good. This conception of the person defines the "thin theory" of the good, and the primary goods are needed for these moral powers to unfold.[30] Rawls thus, implicitly at least, relies on a partial conception of the good that, if William Galston is right, along with other liberal theories, asserts the worth of human existence, fulfillment of human purposes, and a commitment to rationality as the chief guide to life.[31]

So in what sense is Rawls' theory neutral? It avoids commitment to any "comprehensive" conception of the good, such as Kant's autonomy or Mill's individuality,[32] seeking "common ground" among the adherents of these various views. The theory is "political" in the sense that it is implicit in the public political culture and institutions of a democratic society. But it is "free standing," not derived from any particular conception of the good. It is Rawls' conjecture that this freestanding conception of justice can be grounded in different comprehensive conceptions of the good, themselves incompatible but overlapping in their endorsement of this conception of justice.[33]

In *A Theory of Justice,* Rawls spells out the implications of equal liberty when applied to the political process, arguing for a "principle of (equal) participation."[34] The "political" liberties here—"the liberty of the ancients," including the principles of democratic government and "one person, one vote," universal suffrage, free and fair elections, formally equal access to public office—are distinguished from such "liberties of the moderns" as the right to choose one's occupation, the right to privacy, and the right to hold personal property. There are some liberties that overlap with others, such as freedom of speech, but the justification of these differs depending upon whether one is relating them to the freedom of the person or the integrity of the democratic process.

What is relevant to my purpose is Rawls' discussion of the *worth* of political liberty—those conditions or means that make its exercise valuable. Each person should have a fair opportunity to take part in and influence the democratic process. "Those similarly endowed and motivated should have roughly the same chances of attaining positions of political authority irrespective of their economic and social class."[35] This principle obviously is far from being realized in the contemporary United States. Realizing it would involve giving each the means to be informed and a fair chance to add to the political agenda. Rawls suggests several measures that might accomplish this, such as government financing of political campaigns, of political education, and of political parties and also, most significantly for our purposes, a wide distribution of property and wealth.

As we shall see, the last of these measures could be fleshed out in a variety of ways, not all of which would include self-management. Moreover, this justification is compatible with an instrumental view of democratic rights. However, Rawls also acknowledges (contrary to Arneson) an intrinsic value to democracy. "The grounds for self-government are not solely instrumental. Equal political liberty when assured its fair value is bound to have a profound effect on the moral quality of civic life."[36] And the development of one's political opinions with a view to political participation "is an enjoyable activity in itself that leads to a larger conception of society and to the development of his intellectual and moral faculties."[37]

Can we extend this argument from political rights at the national level to economic rights for democracy in the workplace? The inequalities of power characteristic of capitalistic firms effectively vitiate the value of equal political liberties for workers and the unemployed in the following ways:

- Owners have undue political influence.
- Owners shape key decisions that are privatized and thus off the political agenda.
- Owners exercise political power within firms over their employees continuously, and in far-reaching ways.
- Those subject to such autocratic power are apt to become despairing, dependent, and cynical and so lose interest not only in controlling their working life but also in participating in the wider political process.

Such considerations would seem to support Rodney Peffer's proposed modification of Rawls' principles to the following, in order of lexical priority:

1. Everyone's security rights and subsistence rights shall be respected.
2. There is to be a maximum system of equal basic liberties, including freedom of speech and assembly; liberty of conscience and freedom of thought; freedom of the person along with the right to hold (personal) property; and freedom from arbitrary arrest and seizure as defined by the concept of the rule of law.
3. There is to be (a) a right to an equal opportunity to attain social positions and offices  and (b) an equal right to participate in all social decision-making processes within institutions of which one is a part.

4. Social and economic inequalities are justified if, and only if, they benefit the least advantaged, consistent with the just savings principle, but *are not to exceed* levels that will seriously undermine equal worth of liberty or the good of self-respect.[38]

The first of these is not explicit in *Theory*, but Rawls has acknowledged that it is implicit in his conception, and Peffer argues persuasively that parties in the original position would favor such a principle.[39] Peffer removes the political liberties from the second principle, grouping them with participatory rights in his third principle. This makes clearer what he takes to be Rawls' prioritization of "negative" over "positive" liberty, when these conflict, but otherwise does not alter Rawls' basic liberties principle.[40] The fourth principle renders more explicit in the difference principle itself what Rawls says in *Theory* and in subsequent writing about the worth of liberty and about self-respect. The precise implications of this are further explored below.[41]

It is only in the second part of principle 3 that Peffer departs from Rawls substantively, arguing not just for the familiar political liberties, defended by Rawls and most liberals, but also for equal rights to participate in "all social decision-making processes within institutions of which one is a part." (Unlike Arneson, Rawls does not rule this out as a possibility; he only questions whether it should be part of the principles of justice themselves.) This would include, importantly, democratization of workplaces.

Peffer rests his case on the value of "participatory autonomy," both intrinsic and instrumental. By *participatory autonomy* he means "the freedom to participate in social decision-making processes that affect one's life"—one aspect of one's "freedom to determine one's own life."[42] The intrinsic value of participatory autonomy comes from the "conception of persons as autonomous choosers of ends" that is central to Rawls' characterization of parties to the original position. Political liberties are important not just as means to protect one's civil liberties. As well, "These freedoms strengthen men's sense of their own worth, enlarge their intellectual and moral sensibilities, and lay the basis for a sense of duty and obligation upon which the stability of just institutions depends."[43] Peffer sees the extension of democratic rights from the political to the economic and social spheres as, at least prima facie, warranted by this fundamental commitment to freedom.[44]

Van Parijs's opposing view, which refuses to consider democratization as an expression of freedom, privileges an individualistic conception of freedom. Rawls actually remains more neutral by allowing for the intrinsic worth as well as instrumental value of political liberties. One can agree with the stipulation that self-ownership not be violated or that "negative liberties" ought not to be sacrificed to promote democracy. But this leaves a lot of space in which democracy can either flourish or languish.

Acknowledging the intrinsic worth of democracy is still compatible with Rawls' endorsement of classical republicanism, but his rejection of "civic humanism." *Classical republicanism* "is the view that if citizens of a democratic society are to preserve their basic rights and liberties, including the civil liberties which secure the freedoms of private life, they must also have to a sufficient degree the political virtues . . . and be willing to take part in public life." Rawls' theory is consistent with this, in that such virtues are endorsed as means to the stability of justice. Rawls is opposed to civic humanism, "the view that man is a social, even a political, animal whose essential nature is most fully realized in a democratic society in which there is widespread and vigorous participation in political life. Participation is not encouraged as necessary for the protection of the basic liberties . . . and is in itself one form of good among others. . . . Rather, taking part in democratic politics is seen as the privileged locus of the good life."[45]

Democracy can be understood as an extension of one's freedom. Political rights have intrinsic value, even in Rawls' political liberalism, insofar as they affirm the equal worth of each person and provide a partial basis for self-respect. But civic humanism exceeds the warrant of political liberalism. Justifications for democratization in the framework of political liberalism will need to proceed on the basis of the "fair value" of political liberty. In the next section I lay the groundwork for such a justification with a discussion of power.[46]

## FROM EQUALITY OF POWER TO EQUALITY OF STATUS

Equality of power is an important idea in some social contract theories of justice at a theoretical level, and when we reflect on why, we can better understand the temptation to make equality of power a goal of justice itself, even though in the end this idea must be rejected as incoherent. In Rawls' original position, the parties striving to reach agreement on principles of justice are free and equal. No one has power over any other. This is so that each can act rationally in his or her own interest—and also under the moral constraints of the original position itself—without being coerced or pressured to favor anyone in particular. The point of equality in such constructions is captured clearly by Rousseau, writing more directly about society, in his argument for a rough social equality: "life in a social community can thrive only when all its citizens have something, and none have too much." Lacking this social equality, under a bad government, legal equality "is but apparent and illusory. It serves only to keep the poor man confined within the limits of his poverty, and to maintain the rich in their usurpation."[47]

When clarifying what he means by equality, Rousseau states, "I do not mean that power and wealth must be absolutely the same for all, but only that power should need no sanction of violence but be exercised solely by virtue of rank and legality, while wealth should never be so great that a man can buy his neighbor, nor so lacking that a man is compelled to sell himself."[48]

A citizenry so constituted might be expected when assembled to express its collective will as a "general will," not partial to any individual or group. In saying this, however, it is important to add another important qualification, that the citizens not communicate with one another, or form "intriguing groups and partial associations."[49] Setting aside the dubious idea that the common interest can be arrived at by each separately, without the benefit of conversation, Rousseau's insight here is that, even if each person were endowed with equal wealth and resources, great inequalities, leading to injustices, could still prevail through the formation of factions and parties.[50]

If there must be "subsidiary groups," let them be numerous and roughly equal in power, as in the Roman Republic.[51] The laws issuing forth from such a citizen body could not be oppressive in Rousseau's view, because it would be irrational for each to impose on himself a burden greater than that required to maintain the sovereignty of the general will, and no one is in a position to advance any measure that can not gain general assent.[52] There is, thus, a link for Rousseau between the negative liberty of the moderns and the positive liberty of the ancients, which he makes primary: In a well-ordered society, the (negative) freedom of each will be secured by the rationality and restraint of the general will.

In the history of political thought from Kant to Rawls and Jürgen Habermas, it is now commonplace to observe, Rousseau's prescriptions have been idealized, made hypothetical, for the purpose of deriving theoretically some principles of justice binding on the reason of each.[53] But unless actual social conditions for the articulation of justice are kept in mind, a paradox can arise: If we imagine our free and equal parties choosing principles of justice that permit inequalities of wealth and power above a certain magnitude, then the society required by justice will be a society in which justice is corrupted by power.

It is presumably for this reason that Rawls argues that considerations of "stability" might force the parties in the original position to reconsider principles they might favor when not looking to the consequences for the maintenance of just institutions and modify them in the direction of greater equality. It is also a major reason that political liberties must not be merely formal but must have a "fair value . . . in the sense that everyone has a fair opportunity to hold public office and to influence the outcome of political decisions. . . . Unless the fair value of these liberties is approximately preserved, just background institutions are unlikely to be either established or maintained."[54]

Hence, although merely with a view to maximizing their own individual freedom consistent with others doing likewise and maximizing their minimum prospects in life, parties to the original position might construe the difference principle as allowing rather substantial inequalities,[55] when they consider the social and economic conditions necessary for justice to be possible—that is, for their political liberties to have a fair value—they will aim for a rough equality of wealth and power (of wealth to the extent that it impinges on power). Here we come full circle to Rousseau, as Rawls moves to institute in the constitution of a just society itself some of the key features of the original position.[56]

Having established the way in which the fair value of political liberty can "trump" inequalities otherwise allowed by the difference principle, we must now turn to some problems that this idea raises.The first is an empirical question: How much inequality is enough to undermine the fair value of political liberties? I will return to this later.

The second concerns equality of power. It is one thing to imagine a hypothetical situation in which parties are equal in power and all are focused on a particular choice. It is quite another to even conceptualize equality of power in an actual society. Consider, for example, the inequality of power that surfaces in unrequited love. It is hard to conceive of how it could be rectified socially or compensated for, even if it were thought to be desirable to do so. Nor can such an example be dismissed as merely personal, unrelated to the sorts of inequality and dependency that threaten political equality. One need think only of the role of love, and its various distortions and simulacra, in the family to see how important a factor it is in entrenching the subordination of women.

Consider again the way in which the power of individuals waxes and wanes by virtue of the circumstances they are in and the shifting preferences of others. The power of a teacher over a student may vanish when the importance of the grade to the student diminishes, as when a student athlete plans an athletic career for which academic performance is not weighed by his or her potential employers.[57] The power of a judge in the Supreme Court may go from decisive to irrelevant as retirement and replacement shift the balance from 4-4-1 to 5-3-1 on a range of issues.[58]

The goal of equalizing power, then, is a kind of mirage that we will forever chase but never reach. Even if we could clearly conceptualize it, it would not be a desirable goal, because it would require the neutralization of decisions springing from people's impartial judgment. For example, a person whose power is great because she has succeeded in winning the confidence of her supporters should not be subject to measures seeking to counterbalance her power, just because of the fact that she is powerful.[59]

It might nonetheless be thought that certain forms of power, or power deriving from certain sources, ought to be reduced: illegitimate power, arbitrary power, excessive power, power based on irrelevant distinctions. But then it seems the problem is not so much power as some connected injustice, which gives rise to it: resources unequally distributed according to birth or race or gender, for example, or authority going to those who are more articulate, when it ought to be rotated more widely.

The problem, it would seem, is one of identifying the bases of power and ensuring that they are distributed justly, such that the resulting inequalities of power reflect only the free association of free and equal citizens and the differential esteem accorded individuals in proportion to their perceived wisdom and talents. The difficulty with this is that we are apt to be aiming at a shifting target. If inequality of birth results in unequal power between nobles and commoners, let us get rid of titles. But then, money becomes dominant, and those with more end up with disproportionate political power. So then let us equalize the wealth and income. But then, skills or political acumen or connections take over.[60]

It is this insight that leads Walzer to shun "simple equality"—the equalization of a good that has become dominant across many spheres of social life—in favor of what he calls "complex equality." Complex equality is said to obtain if boundaries between distinct spheres (education, politics, commodity exchange, the family) are protected and no one monopolizes all the goods across all the spheres. In such a society, some may be preeminent in some spheres but not in others; and none will dominate in all areas. As David Miller has noted, "complex equality" is really a kind of simple equality, a kind of equality of status.[61]

Walzer's argument has been challenged on several points: that protecting the boundaries of the spheres would not result in equality of status; that such protection is not feasible side by side with rather large inequalities of some goods the mobility and convertibility of which is hard to contain (most notably, money); that his particular conceptualization of the proper boundaries of the spheres is not supportable merely through interpretation of shared beliefs of the culture; and, perhaps most fundamentally, that equality of status is not the only sort of equality we need to worry about.[62] But what is interesting in Walzer's arguments is his attempt to cash out something like Rousseau's idea of social equality for a society irreversibly differentiated into distinct spheres of activity with diverse and incommensurable standards of good practice. Something like his equality of status is a necessary precondition of the worth of political liberties and the stability of a just order.[63] How is equality of status to be achieved, such that the fair value of political liberties is secured?

## FAIR VALUE OF POLITICAL LIBERTIES AND WORKPLACE DEMOCRACY

As we have seen, Rawls thinks that the fair value of political liberty would be secure if lifetime limits were placed on campaign contributions, if the government funded political campaigns, political education, and political parties, and if wealth and property were widely distributed. Such a scheme is still compatible with capitalism. Walzer has a similar vision of politics, one that allows inequality in the "sphere of money and commodities" but limits the power of money in politics and restores a local participatory politics of caucuses versus a money-dominated politics carried on in the mass media. Although I agree with Rawls' proposed electoral reforms, they do not go far enough to ensure the fair value of political liberty.

First, even with a wider distribution of income and wealth through stiffer inheritance taxes and redistributive taxation, for example, capitalists still would be making major decisions about whether, where, in what, and how much to invest. The threat of a capital strike or capital flight is a tremendous source of power, independent of direct control of the electoral process, which can only be effectively curbed by democratizing those decisions. Moreover, many investment decisions have consequences for employment, the environment, and other matters of public concern yet are depoliticized, made privately by a corporate elite in a capitalist economy. Both of these points provide support for workplace democracy as one way of broadening the base of accountability of corporate decision making. If the base of workers in the firm is not broad enough, corporate boards could include other constituencies. In some German codetermined enterprises the board consists half of stockholder representatives and half of representatives of the workers, with an extra seat for the mayor, representing the public at large.[64]

I acknowledge, however, that there are other schemes for democratizing capitalist wealth and power. Roemer's proposal (discussed in chapter 8) to socialize all stock and distribute shares equally to all citizens is another way of rendering managers accountable to a wider public and is perhaps closer to Rawls' idea of "property owning democracy." But the lack of worker management on the enterprise level renders Roemer's scheme vulnerable to alienation of the managers from the stockholders, with the latter holding a formal right lacking fair value in comparison with the power of managers. Workers, although not necessarily as knowledgeable as managers about markets and investment, are closer to the firm, have more of a stake in its successful operation, form more of a real deliberating community, and so are apt to elicit more real accountability from managers than are citizen stockholders.

Rawls' electoral reforms would do little to address inequality of political skills. Walzer's return to caucuses promises to open a wider arena to party activists but does nothing for the general population. Worker control (which Walzer, incidentally, favors) would provide more opportunities in the daily lives of working people for democratic participation and deliberation and cultivation of the political virtues, which would carry over to political democracy. Edward S. Greenberg has found some evidence to support this in his study of the plywood cooperatives in the U.S. Northwest (though his conclusions are expressed pessimistically).[65]

Worker owners do tend to be more politically engaged, even if not at the optimal level envisaged by some advocates of workplace democracy.[66] George Potts's careful study of Yugoslav self-management also supports the idea that institutions that open up space for popular participation do tend to evoke higher levels of participation and accountability than less participatory political systems, though as with Greenberg's study, the evidence serves to temper excessive enthusiasm about what is possible.[67]

Workplace democracy would probably yield lower income differentials than capitalist enterprises, thus promoting greater equality of income, wealth, and status. The ratio of the incomes of the highest-paid manager to the lowest-paid worker in the Mondragon cooperatives is typically about 7:1, and even though there are signs of its creeping upward as Spain enters the European Community, it still remains far below the 419:1 of American firms or the 20:1 of Japanese and German firms. Assuming cooperatives can operate at least as efficiently as capitalist firms, they would receive direct support from the difference principle as well, as an institutional way of maximizing the minimum.[68]

Two important qualifications need to be made, however. First, not everyone is a worker, and care must be taken that lowering differentials within firms does not come at the cost of increasing differentials between the permanently employed and those not fortunate enough to have a job. (This topic is further explored in chapter 9.) Second, Roemer's scheme, mentioned earlier, promises a cleaner egalitarian distribution of income and wealth, in that it gives stock and associated dividends equally to all, whereas the profits of enterprises would go rather unevenly to different groups of workers under economic democracy. Roemer might argue that the labor market for managers would result in more or less the same differentials in his scheme as under worker control, but this is an empirical question for which there is little evidence one way or the other. Moreover, Roemer can claim plausibly that his proposal will eliminate a rentier class enhancing the fair value of political liberty, thus going beyond Rawls, without instituting workplace democracy.

In conclusion, we have found support for workplace democracy in liberal theories of justice, on the basis of the fair value of political liberty. This provides an answer to skeptics like Arneson. At the same time, we have to acknowledge that some other socialist models, such as that of Roemer, provide other routes to securing the fair value of political liberty. In part 2, I compare models of socialism, bringing in a wider range of criteria, to settle some of the indeterminacy we are left with on grounds of justice alone. What is clear at this point is that the theory of justice supports workplace democracy in combination with some kind of socialism.

One final remark on the fair value of political liberty: Walzer is on the right track when he identifies the marketing of politicians through the mass media as a major source of the degradation of political participation and political equality. But much more needs to be said about media institutions themselves and how they might be democratized. Workplace democracy has a role to play here, but it is not the whole story.

## NOTES

1. Alasdair MacIntyre writes, "Marxism is exhausted as a *political* tradition . . . [and] this exhaustion is shared by every other political tradition within our culture. . . . What matters at this stage is the construction of local forms of community within which civility and the intellectual and moral life can be sustained through the new dark ages which are already upon us"; *After Virtue*, 2d ed. (Notre Dame: University of Notre Dame Press, 1984), 262–63.

2. Not all liberalisms are neutral. Some liberals think it a mistake—or perhaps impossible—to abstract entirely from conceptions of the good, arguing instead for specifically liberal conceptions of the good. Martha C. Nussbaum and A. K. Sen, eds., *The Quality of Life* (Oxford: Clarendon Press, 1992); William Galston, *Liberal Purposes* (Cambridge: Cambridge University Press, 1991); Michael Walzer, *Spheres of Justice* (New York: Basic Books, 1983); Martha Nussbaum, "Aristotelian Social Democracy," in *Liberalism and the Good*, ed. R. Bruce Douglass, Gerald M. Mara, and Henry S. Richardson (New York: Routledge, 1990), 203–52; Richard Kraut, "Politics, Neutrality, and the Good," *Social Philosophy and Policy* 16, no. 1 (Winter 1999): 315–32.

3. "If democracy is justified in governing the state, then it must also be justified in governing economic enterprises; and to say that it is not justified in governing economic enterprises is to imply that it is not justified in governing the state"; Robert A. Dahl, *A Preface to Economic Democracy* (Berkeley: University of California Press, 1985), 111.

4. Walzer, *Spheres*, 55, 297–98.

5. Walzer, *Spheres*, 298.

6. Robert Dahl defends the democratic analogy against four objections: (1) that there is a "superior right to property"; (2) that decisions in economic enterprises are "not binding in the same sense as decisions made and enforced by the government of a state"; (3) that the presumptions of equality in the case of citizens does not apply in the case of employees; and (4) that tendencies toward oligarchy will win out, making democracy a sham. Dahl, *A Preface to Economic Democracy*, 111-12. Rather than summarize arguments here, I invoke them as needed in response to criticisms by Nozick, Arneson, and Arnold.

7. See Philippe Van Parijs, *Real Freedom for All: What (If Anything) Can Justify Capitalism?* (Oxford: Clarendon Press, 1995); G. A. Cohen, *Self-Ownership, Freedom, and Equality* (Cambridge: Cambridge University Press, 1995); also essays by Bernard Williams, Peter Singer, Robert Paul Wolff, Thomas Scanlon, Thomas Nagel, Onora O'Neill, and Cheyney Ryan in *Reading Nozick*, ed. Jeffrey Paul (Totowa, N.J.: Rowman & Littlefield, 1981); and Kai Nielsen, *Equality and Liberty: A Defense of Radical Egalitarianism* (Totowa, N.J.: Rowman and Allanheld, 1985). For what I would call a "left-libertarian" defense of self-management in terms of a natural right to the fruit of one's labor, see David Ellerman, *Property and Contract in Economics: The Case for Economic Democracy* (Oxford: Blackwell, 1992). See my critique in "Worker Ownership and Wage Slavery," unpublished manuscript, 1999.

8. Richard Arneson, "Democratic Rights at National and Workplace Levels," in *The Idea of Democracy*, ed. David Copp, Jean Hampton, and John E. Roemer (Cambridge: Cambridge University Press, 1993), 140.

9. Arneson, "Democratic Rights," 140.

10. "A related but different point: If a national democratic assembly institutes a program of centralized top-down municipal government, with local mayors appointed by the

national government, such a scheme might be objectionable on various grounds but not on the ground that it is undemocratic"; Arneson, "Democratic Rights," 148 (Would Arneson say the same about a dictatorship endorsed by plebiscite?)

11. Arneson, "Democratic Rights," 141, 143.

12. For an elaboration of the employer-employee relationship as a power relationship, see Samuel Bowles and Herbert Gintis, "A Political and Economic Case for the Democratic Enterprise," in Copp, Hampton, and Roemer, *The Idea of Democracy,* 375–99.

13. G. A. Cohen, "Capitalism, Freedom, and the Proletariat," in *The Idea of Freedom,* ed. Alan Ryan (Oxford: Oxford University Press, 1979), 9–25.

14. David Schweickart, *Against Capitalism* (Cambridge: Cambridge University Press, 1994); Alec Nove, *The Economics of Feasible Socialism Revisited* (London: HarperCollins, 1991).

15. Arneson, "Democratic Rights," 118.

16. Van Parijs, *Real Freedom for All,* 25, 58-84; G. A. Cohen has succeeded nicely in blunting the libertarian attempt to ground capitalist property rights on self-ownership, in *Self-Ownership.* See also Dahl's criticism of property rights arguments against self-management in *A Preface to Economic Democracy.*

17. A. K. Sen, *Inequality Reexamined* (Cambridge: Harvard University Press, 1992); Ronald Dworkin, "What Is Equality? Part One: Equality of Welfare," and "What Is Equality? Part Two: Equality of Resources," *Philosophy and Public Affairs* 10, nos. 3–4 (Summer–Fall 1981); John Rawls, *Political Liberalism* (New York: Columbia University Press, 1993).

18. There may be disagreements about his particular proposal for how to evaluate this baseline of comparison, but this need not concern us here.

19. Van Parijs, *Real Freedom for All,* 42, 223, 188, 213, 293, 216, 219.

20. Jacques Dréze, *Labour Management, Contracts, and Capital Markets: A General Equilibrium Approach* (Oxford: Blackwell, 1989); Jaroslav Vanek, *The General Theory of Labor-Managed Market Economies* (Ithaca: Cornell University Press, 1970).

21. David Schweickart discusses other forms of efficiency, ignored in the general-equilibrium analysis of Dréze and Vanek, in which cooperatives have the advantage over capitalist firms. See chapter 7 below for discussion of entrepreneurship in cooperatives.

22. This argument is reconstructed from a conversation with Philippe Van Parijs.

23. Van Parijs, *Real Freedom for All,* 8.

24. A good is distributed according to a lexicographical maximin (*leximin*) principle if certain conditions obtain: no inequality is allowed that would diminish the advantage of the least advantaged; between two systems that equally favor the least advantaged, that one is preferred that better contributes to the advantage of the next-least advantaged; and so on.

25. The unconditional basic income advocated by Van Parijs would, at a sufficiently high level, remove the necessity to labor.

26. Van Parijs, *Real Freedom for All,* 14, 25.

27. The paradox is that the "majority" seems to prefer each of these incompatible orderings. A univocal outcome could be achieved through adoption of some rules governing the order of voting, but no such rules could be neutral with respect to the outcome.

28. Rawls, *Political Liberalism,* 190–95, Ronald Dworkin, "Liberalism," in *Public and Private Morality,* ed. Stuart Hampshire (Cambridge: Cambridge University Press, 1978), 113–43.

29. Rawls, *Political Liberalism*, 191; William Galston, *Liberal Purposes: Goods, Virtues, and Diversity in the Liberal State* (Cambridge: Cambridge University Press, 1991).

30. Galston, *Liberal Purposes*, chapter six.

31. In addition (and in a way that Galston argues unnecessarily biases justice as fairness against some conceptions of the good), Rawls has a strong commitment against coercion, or for the freedom to choose one's own conception of the good, and to the overriding importance of justice following from the value of the two moral powers. My point here is not to endorse Galston's critique and his move toward a nonneutral liberalism. Rather, it is simply to underscore how nonneutral one of the central advocates of neutrality actually is. Charles Larmore's political liberalism is quite close to that of Rawls, and Larmore is quite explicit that political neutrality is a relative matter, extending only to those conceptions of the good life that are actually disputed; Larmore, *Patterns of Moral Complexity* (Cambridge: Cambridge University Press, 1987), 67.

32. Rawls does, however, seem to come close to the former.

33. If "common ground" is the aim, it may be the case that a theory that incorporates more in the way of a conception of the good could go further (cf. Galston on this), and it may be that Rawls' Kantian theory of the person, in the way that it privileges freedom and justice, provides a poor foundation for such common ground.

34. Rawls, *Theory*, 221–34.

35. Rawls, *Theory*, 225.

36. Rawls, *Theory*, 233.

37. Rawls, *Theory*, 234.

38. Rodney G. Peffer, *Marxism, Morality, and Social Justice* (Princeton: Princeton University Press, 1990), 418.

39. Rawls, *Political Liberalism*, 7–8, n7; Peffer, *Marxism, Morality*, 385.

40. In so doing, Peffer inadvertently weakens the case for participatory democracy, because Rawls himself does not assert a strong prioritization of individual over political liberties; John Rawls, "Reply to Habermas," *Journal of Philosophy* 92, no. 3 (March 1995): 132–80.

41. Also see my article, "Worker Control, Self-Respect, and Self-Esteem," *Philosophy Research Archives* 10 (1984): 455–72. I would now modify my argument in that article in the following ways:

1. I argued in that piece that meaningful work was essential for self-respect and self-esteem. I would now broaden the thesis to read that one's self-respect rests on one's making some meaningful contribution to society and on that contribution's typically being recognized. This weakens the case for workplace democracy, in that there are other contexts in which people can make meaningful contributions. But the workplace remains one of the major sources of personal identity and avenues for contribution.

2. My case against capitalism rested too heavily on Harry Braverman's thesis that capitalism tends toward the degradation of work. The evidence on balance shows conflicting tendencies for and against de-skilling within contemporary capitalism in different industries. In banking, for example, there is evidence that computer technology has enhanced the skills and power of lower-tier workers. See Paul S. Adler, "New Technologies, New Skills," *California Man-*

*agement Review* 29 (1986): 9–28; Paul S. Adler, ed., *Technology and the Future of Work* (Oxford: Oxford University Press, 1992); and Stephan Wood, ed. *The Degradation of Work?* (London: Heinemann, 1982). To the extent that Braverman's thesis is true in certain contexts, there might still be a case for transformation of work in those contexts.

3. I gave insufficient attention to the potential for new and creative initiatives in the "third sector"—neither market nor state—that might overlap with some traditional workplaces but is more often distinct and is arguably the burgeoning sector for work in the future. Van Parijs's basic-income scheme might be a more relevant institutional support for the standing of citizens in this sector than any attempt to impose a model of self-management. (For further discussion, see chapters 2 and 9 below.)

42. Peffer, *Marxism, Morality*, 397.

43. Peffer, *Marxism, Morality*, 398; Rawls, *A Theory of Justice*, 234. Peffer recognizes that Rawls' concern with moral autonomy in his Kantian conception of the person does not entail (though it is not inconsistent with) participatory autonomy, because the morally autonomous person may or may not value democratic participation.

44. Peffer's principle of participatory autonomy needs to be given a sharper formulation, as is done by Joshua Cohen, whose "deliberative democracy" I discuss below. As it stands, Peffer's principle would seem to illiberally sanction the democratization of the Catholic Church. I would like to see that happen, but not by legal imposition. Peffer acknowledges the problem but does not address it; Peffer, *Marxism, Morality*, 403.

45. Rawls, *Political Liberalism*, 206. It goes without saying that Rawls must also be opposed to Marxist variations on this civic humanist theme.

46. This section was motivated by a conversation with Van Parijs, in which he argued for a distinction between equal opportunity (which he favors) and equal power (which he sees as only one of a number of possible outcomes of equal opportunity, and not required by justice).

47. Jean-Jacques Rousseau, "The Social Contract," in *Social Contract Essays by Locke, Hume, and Rousseau*, ed. Ernest Barker (London: Oxford University Press, 1947), 189. There is a similar presumption of freedom and equality in Habermas's ideal speech situation, where the goal is to reach consensus on moral norms. For a good brief summary, see Thomas McCarthy, introduction to *Legitimation Crisis*, by Jürgen Habermas (Boston: Beacon Press, 1975), vii–xxiv.

48. Rousseau, "Social Contract," 217.

49. Rousseau, "Social Contract," 194.

50. See Joshua Cohen, "Reflections on Rousseau: Autonomy and Democracy," *Philosophy and Public Affairs* 15, no. 3 (Summer 1986): 275–97.

51. Rousseau, "Social Contract," 194–95.

52. Rousseau, "Social Contract," 198; 195–96; see Joshua Cohen, "Reflections on Rousseau," 293.

53. See Rawls, "Reply to Habermas," 150.

54. Rawls, *Political Liberalism*, 327–28.

55. "We cannot be sure that the inequalities permitted by the difference principle will be sufficiently small to prevent those with more combining against and excluding those with less"; Rawls, *Political Liberalism*, 328.

56. Rawls, *Theory*, 221–22; John Rawls, "The Basic Liberties and Their Priority," *Tanner Lectures on Human Values*, vol. 3 (Salt Lake City: University of Utah Press, 1982), quoted in Joshua Cohen's "Deliberation and Democratic Legitimacy," in *The Good Polity: Normative Analysis of the State*, ed. Alan Hamlin and Philip Pettit (Oxford: Basil Blackwell, 1989), 19; Rawls, *Political Liberalism*, 330.

57. Thomas Wartenberg, *The Forms of Power* (Philadelphia: Temple University Press, 1990).

58. See chapter eleven, "The Uses of 'Power,'" in Brian Barry, *Democracy, Power, and Justice: Essays in Political Theory* (Oxford: Clarendon Press, 1989), 307–21.

59. Recall that Rousseau accepts power "exercised solely by virtue of rank and legality"; "Social Contract," 217.

60. Walzer, *Spheres*. Michel Foucault also deserves mention for calling attention to the many forms that power takes. See, for example, "Disciplinary Power and Subjection," in *Power*, ed. Steven Lukes (Oxford: Basil Blackwell, 1986), 229–42. Despite the difficulties involved in pinning down his theoretical statements about power, Foucault's studies of prisons, hospitals, and other institutions of the modern world have deepened our understanding of the ways in which power operates through each of us, is internalized, and has an anonymous and often invisible character, resulting simultaneously in our domination and our empowerment through disciplines.

Foucaultian analyses applied to allegedly egalitarian institutions can expose deeper levels of inequality and domination than the modes of analysis I have been employing thus far. The classical liberal will identify and object to formal inequalities of legal status. The Marxist will identify inequalities in wealth and income and control over property. The Foucaultian identifies inequalities in knowledge, or, even where there is equal knowledge, the structuring of disciplines to the advantage of one over the other. How can we guard against egalitarian theories providing ideological rationalization for such subtler forms of inequality?

To illustrate the problem, consider one version of liberalism that defines freedom as the situation in which each person is able to do what he or she wants to do, subject to not violating anyone else's rights (leave aside the question of what these rights are). Foucault would focus on the formation of the wants themselves, the constitution of the self, and point out that a person who got what he or she wanted but whose tastes had been shaped by schools, prisons, media, and the like, would not be free but would have only an illusion of freedom. There is a rejoinder to this "adaptive tastes" objection, that what should matter is not having the ability to do what one wants but, rather, having the ability to do what one might want to do. (Van Parijs adopts such a formulation.) The reference point now is not one's actual preferences, which may be too adaptive, but rather the plurality of reasonable possibilities available in society.

Here, Foucault might respond with a deeper, but also more problematic, objection: that in a carceral society, the range of possibilities is itself adapted to prevailing power structures. Abjuring any transcendental standpoint from which to identify nonadaptive goods and preferences, there is no way out. This conclusion would be inconsistent, however, with Foucault's emphasis on discontinuities and points of resistance. Power is not monolithic, and alternatives always persist side by side with dominant views and indeed must be counted among the reasonable options, even if they are not featured on mainstream television.

61. David Miller, "Complex Equality," in *Pluralism, Justice, and Equality*, ed. David Miller and Michael Walzer (Oxford: Oxford University Press, 1995), 197–225.

62. See various essays in Miller and Walzer, *Pluralism, Justice, and Equality*.

63. Brian Barry, "Spherical Justice and Global Injustice," in Miller and Walzer, *Pluralism, Justice, and Equality*, 67–80.

64. Maurice Glasman, in conversation.

65. Edward S. Greenberg, *Workplace Democracy: The Political Effects of Participation* (Ithaca: Cornell University Press, 1986); also Philip Green, *Retrieving Democracy: In Search of Civic Equality* (Totowa, N.J.: Rowman and Allanheld, 1985), on democratic division of labor; and Iris Young, *Justice and the Politics of Difference* (Princeton: Princeton University Press, 1990).

66. Carole Pateman, *Participation and Democratic Theory* (Cambridge: Cambridge University Press, 1970), 22–44.

67. George A. Potts, *The Development of the System of Representation in Yugoslavia with Special Reference to the Period since 1974* (New York: University Press of America, 1996).

68. For data on executive compensation in American firms, including comparisons with European and Japanese firms, see AFL-CIO, "How Much Would You Be Making If Your Pay Had Grown As CEO Pay Has?" <http://www.aflcio.org/paywatch/ceou_compare.htm> (12 May 1999).

# 2

# Justifying Basic Income

In chapter 1, I argued for worker self-management on grounds of justice. Along the way I introduced the beginnings of a case for an unconditional basic income (BI), which appeared to be in tension with self-management. Self-management links work and income and fits neatly with the traditional socialist emphasis on the centrality of work and workers in alternatives to capitalist exploitation. Basic income decouples income from work and does not privilege the working class, at least not directly. I argue later that BI and economic democracy (which includes self-management) complement one another and can be combined in a strategy that is politically feasible. But for now my aim is to clarify the BI proposal, justify it pragmatically and on grounds of justice, and show why it requires something like socialism for its successful implementation at a high level.

What is proposed under a basic-income strategy is to guarantee to every resident an unconditional guaranteed income at the highest sustainable level. In contrast with current "make-up" guaranteed-income schemes, which supplement low wages and involve means testing, the BI is unconditional. Everyone would be entitled to it, regardless of wealth, household circumstances, employment status, or willingness to work.[1] Such a grant might replace, or correspondingly reduce, many existing social service transfer payments, such as those for unemployment, pensions, or aid to needy families. (Some additional transfers would still be needed for individuals with costly special needs or disabilities.)

Some of the pragmatic advantages of a basic income are as follows:[2]

- Compared with a means-tested guaranteed income, no degrading stigma would attach to recipients.
- By giving everyone an unconditional grant, one might have a higher rate of "target efficiency"—targeting needy groups, many of whom fall through the

cracks of means-tested programs as social change moves ahead of bureaucratic response.[3]

- Compared with means-tested programs, there would be no unemployment trap. Earned income would be on top of the basic income, and there would be no penalty involved in taking a job of any kind.
- Work sharing would become more feasible, because a full-time job would not be as necessary to make ends meet; this would tend to reduce unemployment.
- The coercive nature of the employment contract would be undermined: no one would be forced to work for wages out of economic necessity.
- A possible further consequence is a rise in income for unattractive, dangerous, or dirty work, because the economically desperate who now take such jobs at minimum wage would be free to refuse such work.
- Work conditions generally might be made more attractive, and work itself more intrinsically rewarding, as a way of attracting workers.
- A floor of income for everyone would make possible a deregulation of the labor market and greater flexibility and innovativeness in the economy.[4]
- BI is one way of internalizing externalities associated with environmental impacts and control over intellectual property.[5]

Following Van Parijs and Robert van der Veen, let us say that a society has achieved "weak abundance" when it is sufficiently affluent to be able sustainably to provide everyone with a basic income at a culturally defined decent minimum.[6] Then, it might be objected, for any society falling short of weak abundance, there must be a trade-off between giving everyone maximum basic income, which will be an amount below the poverty line, and giving larger *conditional* grants to the truly needy and those involuntarily unemployed. This group, excluding the voluntarily unemployed, arguably are the true least-advantaged group, and any worsening of their position to provide a basic income for everyone would be ruled out by the difference principle. Thus, below weak abundance, a society would have to balance basic income with means-tested transfers.

Even in weak abundance, why should the level of benefit to the involuntarily unemployed be lowered so that the voluntarily unemployed can enjoy a modest leisure? This objection seems sound so long as we take the difference principle to be covering only the distribution of income. However, it includes also the distribution of wealth, power, and the bases of self-respect. Remembering this, one can make a Rawlsian case for BI, as Van Parijs has done.

First, the BI is an "all-purpose means" to various ends, a primary good. Second, by removing the stigma attaching to recipients of means-tested welfare, self-respect is less likely to be undermined. Third, by making a basic income a right of citizenship, one makes equal citizenship more substantial as a basis for self-respect. One of the problems with Rawls' original formulation of justice as fairness is that he maintained that guaranteeing equality of the basic liberties is sufficient to support self-respect while also allowing substantial inequalities of wealth and power. But as Norman Daniels and others have argued, it is not consistent to favor equal liberty yet not favor at least a rough equality in the conditions making liberty valuable. A basic income would go some distance toward rendering the basic liberties valuable: for example, one would have the "real freedom" to engage in political work and expression of opinion, if the grant were at a sufficiently high level.[7]

Fourth, by granting to everyone the freedom to refuse wage labor contracts, the power of each person is enhanced, particularly that of workers in relation to capitalists but also, for example, non-wage-working wives in relation to husbands.[8] Fifth, basic income, unlike conditional transfers, does not discriminate between competing conceptions of the good, favoring those who embrace a work ethic over those who prefer not to work.

On the other hand, sixth, as Van Parijs notes, a basic income "enables those who attach importance to (paid) work *per se* to accept a low wage—lower than they could afford in the absence of a basic income—in exchange for actual access to waged, cooperative or self-employment. Whereas a rising means-tested benefit makes it increasingly difficult for unskilled people to find a job, a rising basic income makes it increasingly feasible."[9] Thus with a view to enabling each person to pursue his or her plan of life, a basic-income scheme has a lot to recommend it over alternative conditional transfers. It is not just about maximizing minimum income and consumption.

Still, other questions remain: Would it not be too costly? Would not too many people stop working? Would it not be unfair exploitation of workers by the lazy? Would there not be a flight of capital out of the country, or a capital strike? Who would support it?

## COST

Viewed statically, without regard to its consequences in practice over time, the introduction of a basic income might cost nothing at all. Existing welfare benefits would change form but not amount, and wages could be reduced by the amount of the grant. The net transfer in incomes could leave everything as it is. Adam Przeworski estimates that a basic income for everyone at half the average income would require a tax increase of at least 20 percent of gross domestic product (GDP). But such a tax burden would not be objectionable if one's net income after taxes were unchanged.[10]

A more difficult question is whether a basic income could be sustained over time, at a level adequate for basic needs, without reducing the aggregate income so much that even a basic income level would become impossible. The economist A. B. Atkinson has proposed a more modest BI scheme, one that would not replace but would be complemented by other forms of social insurance and provide a basic income to every child and to every adult willing to participate in some form of socially valuable activity (not just paid work but care for the elderly, child care, et cetera). Atkinson calculates that, with some tweaking of the tax system, in England every child could receive £12.50 a week, and every adult between £17.75 and £18.25 a week, without increasing taxes overall. "With such a citizen's income, the number dependent on means-tested benefits would be reduced by half a million. A third of families would be worse off in cash terms; ten percent would be virtually unaffected; and fifty-seven per cent would gain. Among the latter would be many women." An increase of about 10 percent in the tax rates would more than double the basic income to nearly £40 a week and more than quadruple the number freed from dependence on means-tested benefits.[11] Crudely extrapolating these figures to the United States, we might be able to introduce a revenue-neutral BI scheme, giving everyone twenty-five to thirty dollars a week—hardly enough to pay the rent but significant in conjunction with additional social insurance, a part-time job, a relatively low-wage full-time job, or higher-paying but intermittent work. If we were able to raise taxes on that richest 4 percent making as much as the bottom 51 percent, not to mention the richest 20 percent, this amount could be at least doubled.

## WORK INCENTIVES

Of course, the degree to which people will have incentives to work for wages will vary with the level of the grant. Note, however, that there is no lack of incentive to work today, even though, for practical purposes, at least in most Western European countries, everyone can find minimal subsistence without working. This incentive might decline if the grant were unconditional, with no stigma attached to being a recipient, and if the level were, say, half of the average income. On the other hand, those now facing "prohibitive marginal rates of benefit withdrawal"—especially in Europe, where the level of social services is higher—would have much greater incentives to take work once the unemployment trap was eliminated. Whether the latter effect would counterbalance an exodus from work of some of those currently employed is hard to judge.

Moreover, the income would valorize or make possible new forms of work. It would greatly facilitate child care, giving to mothers (or fathers), whether married or single, a measure of economic independence and the freedom to stay at home with children. It would also enable people to devote much time to community service, political work, and careers, the remuneration for which might otherwise be prohibitively low. It thus might encourage risk taking, innovation, and more small business initiatives, increasingly important in rapidly changing markets.

What is unlikely is that most people would do nothing at all. But a significant number would probably drop out of the paid labor market, bringing that market into equilibrium or even resulting in labor shortages. Keep in mind that the context for this discussion, especially in Europe, under the status quo is not full employment, with the prospect of millions of wage workers ceasing employment, but rather chronic high unemployment, with no clear solution for the problem of what to do with all the excess labor supply. A basic-income arrangement would help the unemployed price themselves into a job. In the United States, where unemployment is lower but so also are wages, benefits, and job security, the point of BI might be better framed as enabling people to price themselves into a *good* job. (See chapter 9 for further discussion of BI and unemployment.)

## EXPLOITATION

Would the proposed arrangement be fair to those who continued to work and pay taxes, particularly if their taxes went up to finance a basic income for significant numbers of people choosing not to work and if prices rose as wages were raised to attract people back to work? On the face of it, an unconditional basic-income scheme appears to be a formula for exploitation of the industrious by the lazy.[12] In addition, it would appear that the addition of some significant percentage of people to the list of those receiving income without making a contribution in (paid) work or taxes would reduce the pool of funds available for redistribution to the most needy.[13] Would it be fair to reduce spending on public schools, or special education, or hospitals in order to make possible the freedom not to work for capable people who otherwise would (if grudgingly) take paid employment?

Van Parijs and van der Veen have a fairly convincing rejoinder to the first of these moral concerns. From a purely formal point of view, everyone has the freedom not to work, those who continue to work and pay taxes, as well as those who do not. In fact, everyone would receive the BI grant as a right of residence. So in this respect, there is no unequal treatment involved in a basic-income scheme.

Jon Elster's argument that "it is unfair for able-bodied people to live off the labor of others" presupposes that the income paid to wage workers is proportional to their labor.[14] But wages are also a function of capital intensity, labor-market conditions (that is, scarcity of certain skills), and luck, and to that extent they are not deserved by the workers in the amounts delivered by the market. With technological progress the claims based on desert weaken. (This is not to deny that people develop expectations and a sense of entitlement based on custom and agreements, but these must be at best prima facie bases for distribution.)

Elster's position also ignores the current exploitation of unpaid labor, notably child care, which would receive some remuneration and recognition in a basic-income scheme. (Admittedly, if this were the only goal, there are more efficient ways to reach it—direct child-care allowances and parental leave for parents, for example.) Moreover, in an economy with 10 percent or higher official unemployment (as in many European countries), access to paid labor is now a privilege. As Van Parijs argues elsewhere, the division between those who have access to steady jobs and those who do not is a class division that rivals that between workers and owners.[15] Granting this, those who have full-time, secure, well-paying jobs enjoy an "employment rent" akin to the rent enjoyed by those who own scarce land and other assets. (The concept of jobs as assets is developed by Philippe Van Parijs in *Real Freedom for All*, as part of his case for a basic income.) These rents can legitimately be taxed to compensate those who are excluded from the scarce assets—jobs—in the form of an unconditional basic income.[16]

Finally, the issue of privilege can be formulated in Lockean terms: There is no longer "enough left and as good" of the commons, whether of property or of accessible jobs, for those not fortunate enough to have stable work. Some appropriate compensation is thus due to those unable to find work. This argument certainly justifies unemployment compensation. But it also justifies compensation to those able to find only less attractive, less skilled, less well-paying work by those enjoying the privilege of occupying scarce jobs.

If, after all these arguments, one still finds repugnant the idea of Malibu surfers living off a basic income derived from taxation of working people, preferring instead to attach a work or participation requirement for those able to work as a condition for receipt of BI, consider the following disadvantages cited by Barry: "Participation income . . . would require a large and expensive bureaucratic apparatus to target a relatively small number of people . . . [and] a great deal of highly discretionary decision-making to be done by low-level officials in determining whether some voluntary work was to be approved. . . . Statistically speaking, the typical surfer caught in the toils of participation income will be a housewife whose children have grown up."[17] As in the debates in the United States over welfare reform in which attention was perversely focused on the 1 percent of the federal budget going toward Aid to Families with Dependent Children, ignoring a bloated military budget, so in the basic-income debate there can be a perverse fixation on the statistically and financially unimportant problem of the free rider, the proposed solution for which would, as in past welfare policy, come down hard on women.

## CAPITAL FLIGHT

The issue of whether a BI scheme would provoke capital flight or a capital strike is debated extensively in responses to van der Veen and Van Parijs's "A Capitalist Road to Communism."[18] Any increased cost of BI could be covered by taxes on income, not on profit, so in principle it need not be seen as an assault on profits. (Remember, it was Richard Nixon who proposed a guaranteed minimum income, albeit not unconditional, and the opposition he faced came from liberal Democrats.)[19] On the other hand, financing the BI out of income taxes alone might threaten its political support.

I am inclined to agree with Erik Wright that in order to prevent a flight or strike of capital it would be necessary to regulate investment flows fairly extensively, so that "something like socialism is necessary" for Van Parijs and van der Veen's transition to "something like communism," in which the basic-income proportion of one's income grows until it reaches 100 percent—from each according to his or her abilities, to each according to his or her needs.[20] "Something like socialism" must include social controls over capital flows strong enough to prevent the flight of capital from the BI regime to a foreign country with lower taxes and strong enough also to guarantee investment in conditions in which capitalists would be inclined to strike. If investment funds were generated through a tax on the capital assets of socially owned enterprises and disbursed out of regional investment banks accountable to the citizens, as called for in economic democracy, there would be no danger of capital flight on account of BI arrangements. On the other hand, if investment funds were generated entirely through private savings and invested wherever they would yield the highest return, it is hard to see how capital flight and capital strikes could be avoided with a high basic income (especially given the increasingly global nature of capital flows). One can imagine many possibilities in between socialist investment and private capitalist investment, in which capital flight out of the country would be prohibited, freedom to disinvest restricted, and public funds would kick in when private funds were wanting. But the closer such arrangements get to solving the potential conflict so as to deliver the economically feasible highest basic income (the highest one a society can have without self-defeating disincentives to productivity), the closer they will be to "something like socialism."

But what kind of socialism? To be just, and compatible with a basic income at least as high as the highest feasible under capitalism, socialism must respect basic liberties and other prior principles of justice and be efficient enough to deliver a basic income as high as the available capitalist alternative. Note that socialism need not be as efficient as capitalism to meet these criteria. The highest economically feasible basic income under capitalism may not be politically feasible. Even if a somewhat less efficient socialism delivered a lower economically feasible basic income, if it made politically feasible a basic income higher than that under capitalism, it would be preferable. But again, what kind of socialism?

I have argued for worker management on grounds of justice. Now it is relevant to add that worker-managed enterprises are not prone to capital flight. However, if they were to borrow their capital from private investors who were free to invest elsewhere, they could find themselves capital starved in a BI regime and consequently unable to deliver the highest return on investment. If they were to invest their own residuals in their enterprise, as worker-*owned* firms are free to do, they might be less prone to capital strike than a capitalist firm, because the future of their jobs would depend upon maintaining the competitiveness of their firms. But they might take profits beyond those necessary for upgrading and invest them abroad, as a capitalist firm would do (or as union pension funds currently do). Thus, in order to secure the political feasibility of BI, worker self-management needs to be complemented by a social investment fund as in economic democracy.

We now have the four essential elements of the model here recommended:

- worker self-management of socially owned enterprises
- a market in goods and services
- a democratic investment fund generated through a tax on the capital assets of enterprises
- a highest-sustainable basic income as the key element of a social incomes policy

The first three constitute what David Schweickart calls "economic democracy." Both self-management and BI are independently supported by a left-Rawlsian theory of justice. A basic-income scheme requires socialist investment, because of the likelihood of capital flight and capital strikes under capitalism. Self-managed market socialism promises enough efficiency to surpass capitalism in delivering the maximum feasible basic income, all things considered economically and politically, and has its own built-in resistances to capital flight or strike.

There remains one question about the compatibility of BI with economic democracy: The former weakens the link between income and work. The latter puts at the center of the economy, as the "residual claimants" of the product of all economic activity, the workers; people come far closer in economic democracy than in capitalist society to being paid according to their work. Are these two socially compatible? Can citizens be committed deeply, as a matter of justice, to both worker self-management and the highest sustainable basic income? I take up this question in more detail below; but as a first pass at the problem, consider the following response of Herbert Simon, 1978 Nobel laureate in economics, to the objection that it would be unfair to tax everyone in the United States at a flat rate of 70 percent and use half of it to give each inhabitant, as "patrimony," about eight thousand dollars per year: "I observe that any causal analysis explaining why American GDP is about $25 thousand per capita would show that at least two-thirds is due to the happy accident that the income recipient was born in the United States (hence the 'patrimony')."[21] Simon's remark illustrates the kind of gestalt switch that is required to get beyond the impression that BI is unfair to workers. A large part of our income is attributable not to our individual work but to inheritances of land, technology, organization, skill, and culture. For that reason, there is a strong prima facie reason to distribute such income on an egalitarian principle, such as the difference principle.

Having said that, adoption of a maximum BI does not sever the link between work and income altogether. All income above the level of the basic income would, in a self-managed market socialist society, be available for distribution according to work. Thus, we must envision a basic-income floor, which could be quite generous but on top of which there would be distribution according to work, merit, contribution, or what have you.

The differentials that might thence emerge, owing to differences in skill, effort, market position, or the relative capital intensity of one's job, might be seen to be matters of justice (or injustice), but from the perspective of maximizing the basic income, they would be warranted on the basis of efficiency, as when higher wages are offered as an incentive to take a particular job or to work harder at one's present job. It is important not to confuse differentials appropriate for the sake of *efficiency* with unequal shares on grounds of *justice.* The considerations here for delinking income and work at least weaken, if they do not abolish, claims for higher shares purely on grounds of justice. A weakening is all that is required to render worker self-management and BI compatible as two aspects of a just society. Self-management and basic income are the first two pillars of the kind of market socialism I advocate. But these two, *in principle,* are compatible with a worker-ownership system that falls short of socialism. The decisively socialist pillars, social ownership of enterprises and democratic control of investment, are not defended directly on grounds of justice but rather as necessary conditions, *in practice,* for achieving the egalitarian goals of effective self-management and the highest sustainable basic income and have other advantages as well.

In chapter 9, I will return to the question of the compatibility of BI and economic democracy and also argue for the relevance of BI to the problem of long-term high unemployment, particularly noticeable in European countries. A preliminary task is the exploration of the features and problems of self-managed firms and the development of the case for social ownership and democratic control of investment. In chapters 4 through 6, I defend the thesis that a viable socialism must be a market socialism. The efficiency advantages of market economies (and also worker-managed firms) acquire added force from the requirement to deliver the highest sustainable basic income. In the next chapter, I respond to some objections to the left-liberal framework I have adopted to defend self-management and the basic-income arrangement.

## NOTES

1. This is Philippe Van Parijs's formulation in *Real Freedom for All: What (If Anything) Can Justify Capitalism?* (Oxford: Oxford University Press, 1995). Brian Barry argues that there is no reason to exclude nonresident citizens, but I will pass over this technical detail. See Brian Barry, "Survey Article: Real Freedom and Basic Income," *Journal of Political Philosophy* 4, no. 3 (1996): 242–76. Examples of low-level basic

incomes exist already. For example, since 1987, residents of Alaska have received an annual unconditional dividend from state oil revenues, the amount of which varies with the funds generated and the number of people applying in a given year. The dividend for 1998 was $1,541 per person; "Permanent Fund Dividend Division's Yearly Dividend Amounts," updated 12 January 1999, <http://www.revenue.state.ak.us/pfd/YEARAMOU.htm> ( 9 March 1999).

2. Brian Barry distinguishes "pragmatic" or consequentialist justifications for BI from "principled" arguments such as the Rawlsian argument sketched later, endorsing the former and criticizing the latter; "Survey," 243.

3. Robert E. Goodin, "Towards a Minimally Presumptuous Social Welfare Policy," in *Arguing for Basic Income: Ethical Foundations for a Radical Reform*, ed. Philippe Van Parijs (London: Verso, 1992), 195–214.

4. Philippe Van Parijs, "The Second Marriage of Justice and Efficiency," in Van Parijs, *Arguing for Basic Income*, 233.

5. "Assuming that sharp conflicts of interests are with us forever, the only option to forestall economically damaging chaos consists in reducing what is at stake in the market game—that is, in making an increasing part of people's material welfare depend on society's overall productivity, rather than on their individual contribution"; Van Parijs, "Second Marriage of Justice," 233. To underscore this last point some advocates use the term *social dividend* to describe the basic income.

6. Robert J. van der Veen and Philippe Van Parijs, "A Capitalist Road to Communism," *Theory and Society* 15, no. 5 (1986): 635–56.

7. Philippe Van Parijs, "Competing Justifications of Basic Income," in Van Parijs, *Arguing for Basic Income*, 3–43; Bill Jordan, "Basic Income and the Common Good," in *Arguing for Basic Income*, 155–77.

8. Van Parijs, "Second Marriage of Justice," 229.

9. Van Parijs, "Second Marriage of Justice," 229.

10. Adam Przeworski, "The Feasibility of Universal Grants under Democratic Capitalism," in *Theory and Society* 15, no. 5 (1986): 695–707.

11. A. B. Atkinson, "The Case for a Participation Income," *Political Quarterly* 67, no. 1 (January–March 1996): 67–70, 69–70. In addition to taxation there are other ways a basic income could be financed. For example, if corporate and noncorporate wealth had been nationalized, and dividends paid (roughly) equally to all adult citizens, as in the market socialist model of John Roemer (discussed in chapter 8), each adult citizen in the United States would have received a dividend averaging at least twelve hundred dollars per year in the 1980s. This estimate excludes the financial sector and farms. John Roemer, *A Future for Socialism* (Cambridge: Harvard University Press, 1994), 133–43. The most liberal estimate I have seen of the maximum basic income possible in the United States (calculated for 1990) is thirty thousand dollars per year per adult person (and smaller amounts for children), if all unearned income were distributed equally. Unearned income includes profits, rent, royalties, interest, inheritance, and unearned income paid in wages (which is estimated at 60 percent of wages). Leaving out the last component, unearned annual income would total more than sixteen thousand dollars per person; see Robert Schutz, *The $30,000 Solution* (Santa Barbara, Calif.: Fithian Press, 1996), 37–87. Schutz does not explore possible disincentives to work or misallocations of labor that might diminish over time the total available for distribution, other than to point out that people

work for many reasons besides money and that automation can replace the more expensive and undesirable jobs (14–15). Thus, his estimate is probably excessively optimistic.

12. Jon Elster, "Comment on van der Veen and Van Parijs," *Theory and Society* 15, no. 5 (1986): 709–21.

13. Brian Barry, "Equality Yes, Basic Income No," in Van Parijs, *Arguing for Basic Income*, 128–40; Joseph H. Carens, "The Virtues of Socialism," *Theory and Society* 15, no. 5 (1986): 679–87. Barry later reverses his position and supports a basic income, in "Survey."

14. Elster, "Comment on van der Veen and Van Parijs," 719.

15. See Philippe Van Parijs, *Marxism Recycled* (Cambridge: Cambridge University Press, 1993), chapter six.

16. Although the prospect of long-term high levels of unemployment such as those in France or Germany gives special urgency to the topic of basic income, the case for it does not rest entirely on this prospect.

17. Barry, "Survey," 245. The surfer image is introduced in John Rawls, *Political Liberalism* (New York: Columbia University Press, 1993), 182–83, and graces the cover of Van Parijs's *Real Freedom for All*. See also Atkinson, "The Case for a Participation Income."

18. In particular, see Erik O. Wright, "Why Something like Socialism Is Necessary for the Transition to Something like Communism," *Theory and Society* 15, no. 5 (1986): 657–72; Carens, "The Virtues of Socialism;" and Przeworski, "The Feasibility of Universal Grants."

19. Daniel P. Moynihan, *The Politics of a Guaranteed Income: The Nixon Administration and the Family Assistance Plan* (New York: Random House, 1973).

20. This is all the more evident when one notes with van der Veen and Van Parijs that the problem from the point of view of capital is not just the tax rate but the tax incidence. Even if taxes on profits were unchanged, "the fall in net wages together with the availability of a substantial unconditional grant may well depress the supply of labor and thus induce a rise in gross wages. . . . The tax incidence on capital income may well be considerable"; see Robert J. van der Veen and Philippe Van Parijs, "Universal Grants versus Socialism: Reply to Six Critics," *Theory and Society* 15, no.5 (1986): 723–57. Inefficiencies that might arise from the tax incidence on capital may be offset by some of the economic advantages of BI listed at the beginning of this chapter.

21. Herbert Simon, interview by Philippe Van Parijs, in *Basic Income* 29 (Spring 1998), <http://www.econ.ucl.ac.be/etes/bien/previous_newsletters.html> (4 April 1999).

# 3

# Liberalism and Group Difference

One proposition for which it is easy to gain general assent in almost any group, except among philosophers, is that there is not and never will be a shared conception of justice. Philosophers are initiated into a practice in which, since the time of Socrates, despite its relentless questioning, or perhaps because of it, we regard anything that hints of relativism as the antithesis of philosophy, against which it is our a priori duty to find arguments. The lack of any existing consensus is no deterrent. As Rawls has put it, public reason "describes what is possible and can be, yet may never be, though no less fundamental for that."[1] Nonetheless, it is not without reason that Marx, some contemporary Marxists and feminists, and postmodernists are suspicious of the task of liberal theory and worry about its ideological function.

In the history of liberalism since the Enlightenment, ideals of universal natural rights and universal citizenship have coexisted with the exclusion of workers, women, native populations, and slaves. Even when included, subordinate groups have been entitled to equal formal liberties only to find the means for the meaningful exercise of those liberties very unequally distributed. In such situations, universalistic ideals can legitimate oppressive regimes and, highlighting the ways in which everyone is free and equal, mask the oppression.

Nor has the gap between ideal and reality been closed in recent years. After the abolition of slavery, the institution of universal suffrage, the civil rights and women's movements, and affirmative action, oppression persists in subtler forms. For example, though women may now have more equal opportunity in employment, many with children experience a "double day" of paid work plus housework, and the lack of public support for child care together with persisting labor-market inequalities constitute obstacles to career development and political participation. Thus, the ideology of equal opportunity masks unequal capacities to seize opportunities.

On a theoretical level, the freedom and equality of parties in Rawls' original position, as "heads of households," masks inequalities in the family, the injustice of which is not a subject of Rawls' theory of justice.[2] The liberal response to such examples is to go back to the drawing board and do it better, revising theories so that they are inclusive where before they were exclusive and addressing dimensions of oppression, domination, and inequality that have been ignored or occluded.[3] Do we have any reason to be suspicious of this new and improved liberalism? Is there anything to be said for theorizing that is deliberately partial and particularistic? In this chapter I examine two examples of such a position: Iris Young's postmodern feminist politics of difference and Milton Fisk's Marxist approach to justice.

Iris Young's *Justice and the Politics of Difference* is filled with insights and a concern with problems not to be found in the writing of Rawls and many other figures at the center of debates on the theory of justice: the dynamics of power, cultural imperialism, the ways a distributive metaphor of justice and impartiality serve ideological functions, and analysis of the peculiar possibilities and injustices of city life, to mention a few. Thus, I open myself to the charge of pouring new wine into old bottles in defending some version of the distributive paradigm against her criticisms of its alleged narrowness and defending the ideal of impartiality against the more partial version of discourse ethics she proposes as an alternative. I do this somewhat at cross-purposes with myself, in that at first glance the rejection of impartiality seems to open a more direct route to justification of workplace and economic democracy or participatory democracy more generally.[4] Nevertheless, I think that, properly understood, the distributive paradigm and impartiality are needed to support the most cogent claims in Young's politics of difference. In particular, the values of self-determination and self-development on which the critiques of domination and oppression rest beg for justification that can only take us back to a moral framework similar to those Young attempts to discard.

## THE DISTRIBUTIVE PARADIGM

Young defines *social justice* as the elimination of institutionalized domination and oppression.[5] She argues that the "distributive paradigm"of social justice, of which Rawls' theory is an example, is too narrow to capture important cases of domination and oppression. In particular, "It tends to focus thinking about social justice on the allocation of material goods such as things, resources, income and wealth, or on the distribution of social positions, especially jobs. This focus tends to ignore the social structure and institutional context that often help to determine distributive patterns . . . [especially] issues of decision-making power and procedures, division of labor, and culture."[6]

Although she acknowledges that theorists such as Rawls also include power, opportunity, and self-respect among the goods distributed, Young thinks that the distributive metaphor misrepresents these as "static things, instead of [as] a function of social relations and processes."[7]

First, I fail to see how the concept of distribution ties a theory to material things or states rather than to processes. In speaking of a distribution of opportunities, for example, we do not imply that these are a zero sum or can be hoarded like coins but simply that there is some pattern (distribution) of opportunities for various people to do various things. Nor is the distribution necessarily static. Opportunities can evolve, come and go, and be contingent on a variety of changing factors. The same is true of power.

It is also unclear how talk of the distribution of power necessarily obscures the fact that power is a relation. If one accepts the quite plausible view that a person's power is constituted by a web of relations with other persons, then to identify an existing distribution of power is to understand this web and how, given it, some have more power than others in particular ways. If a theory of justice calls for equal distribution of power but fails to take into account the power that a person has by virtue of the intentions and actions of others, then the problem is in the empirical application of the theory, not in the concept of distribution.

Furthermore, I see no problem with the idea of rights being distributed. The notion does not imply that distribution is a zero sum game or that one person could collect all rights together and then parcel them out like eggs. A distribution of rights is simply a specification of who has what rights.

Consider each of the issues—decision-making power and procedures, the division of labor, and culture—Young claims the distributive paradigm fails to address:

1. If the subject of a theory of justice is, as Rawls takes it, the basic structure of society, then the structures of decision making are as much on the table as are the positions (jobs) that might be defined within a given structure. Far from taking, say, bureaucratic hierarchies of power as a given, the theory lays down criteria for permissible inequalities of power to which any institutional bureaucracy would have to conform. Given the level of abstraction on which Rawls' theory operates, it is easy to conclude that he has nothing to say about decision-making structures and processes, but this is to mistake abstraction from decision making for presupposing some existing structure of decision making. In fact, as the previous two chapters have shown, Rawlsian principles have implications, when conjoined with various empirical claims, for decision-making structures and processes.

2. Rawls makes only brief reference to the division of labor. He says that in a just society, "the worst aspects of this division [of labor] can be surmounted:

No one need be servilely dependent on others and made to choose between monotonous and routine occupations which are deadening to human thought and sensibility."[8] Nonetheless, as I have argued elsewhere, this can easily be foregrounded in the theory of justice if it unacceptably reduces one's power or undermines one's self-respect.[9] Young's remarks do raise an important issue: It is tempting to focus, as Van Parijs does, only on bargaining power in the market, which is a function of one's income, wealth, and natural or acquired talents. A just division of labor is, then, whatever division people decide upon among themselves, given a just distribution of rights and opportunities. The problem with this is that given a particular structure of occupations, labor markets, and organizations, power will be already structured in certain patterns, only partially alterable through changing the distribution of wealth, income, and opportunities. There seems in this case no reason not to attempt to evaluate the justness of the division of labor alongside these distributions and prescribe change on grounds of justice. However, the salient question will still be what is a fair distribution of power, and that is clearly within the purview of the distributive paradigm.

3. Culture, including "the symbols, images, meanings, habitual comportments, stories, and so on through which people express their experience and communicate with one another," is not among the goods considered for distribution in the distributive paradigm. Yet cultural imperialism is one form of oppression. Consider, for example, the policy of "English only" in government proceedings and in public education being debated at various levels in the United States. This may well disadvantage cultural and linguistic minorities, deprive them of an essential source of meaning in their lives, and undermine their self-esteem. But for these very reasons the cultural dimensions of the basic structure of society—especially language—can and should be included in the distributive paradigm. The absence of such considerations in the work of Rawls or Ronald Dworkin does not mean that distributive justice is too narrow a paradigm with which to address cultural imperialism. Rather, it means that among the goods each person must be entitled to is access to one's own cultural heritage, including significant structures of group self-determination. As Will Kymlicka has shown, a case can be made for group rights on such a liberal foundation.[10]

Affirmative action affords another example in which cultural imperialism operates and the distributive paradigm is nonetheless adequate to the subject. The case for affirmative action can be made on the basis of a principle of equality of opportunity grounded in the distributive theory of justice.[11] Certainly among the factors creating the discrimination against women and minorities is the hegemony of white-male-privileging norms of goodness, etiquette, and appropriateness. These need to be challenged in educational and interpersonal contexts. Yet it seems difficult to conceive of any basic structural changes directly relevant to cultural factors in this case. Rather, indirect policies such as affirmative action, which alter decision-making processes and structures by introducing criteria of selection formerly considered irrelevant, are what justice requires. One might object, as Young does, to defenses of affirmative action that appeal to impartiality, but that is a different issue from the adequacy of the distributive paradigm.[12]

In all three cases, a point in favor of articulating issues within the distributive paradigm is that it preserves the interconnections between material and nonmaterial goods. Cultures can atrophy when groups are deprived of income, wealth, and other resources. The division of labor does alter as the relative power of actors in the labor market changes (or as markets are abolished). Decision-making structures reflect as well as determine power relations and depend upon as well as determine certain patterns of resource allocation. By separating "distributable" from "nondistributable" goods, as Young does, one risks ignoring these interconnections.

At the conclusion of her critique of the distributive paradigm, Young affirms a conception of social justice as supporting the institutional conditions necessary for the realization of self-development and self-determination. Oppression and domination, respectively, are the injustices consisting in the denial of these. These are values that beg for elucidation. Is self-development the vague and open idea of having a rational plan of life and being able to carry it out—or is there a more determinate and perfectionist ideal intended? Self-determination, similarly, is open to a variety of interpretations, as discussed in chapter 1. But the relevant point here is that a conception of justice erected on this foundation need not depart from the distributive paradigm. Rawls, for example, offers one interpretation of the principles that any society must conform to if the two moral powers—rationality and a sense of justice—are to flourish. Other distributive theorists develop similar theories starting from some conception of autonomy of the person.[13] Spelling out what self-development and self-determination involve will lead us back once again to the concerns of the distributive paradigm, which, as I have tried to show, do not exclude decision-making processes, the division of labor, or culture.

## IMPARTIALITY

The deeper challenge to liberalism is Young's critique of impartiality. I am more sympathetic to (but not ultimately convinced of) the charge that impartiality, such as that invoked by Van Parijs and Arneson and which is the aim of Rawls' original position, is impossible. In an earlier article, I have tried to show that Rawls' argument for the principles of justice is not, in fact, neutral between "consumerist" and what are currently called civic humanist conceptions of the good life but rather that one or another of these positions needs to be taken if determinate results are to be inferred from the original position.[14] I now think that more recent work by Rawls and Charles Larmore clarifies a sense of neutrality that remains robust enough to yield determinate conclusions yet is in some intelligible sense neutral or impartial. Moreover, it is precisely the affirmation of difference that supports such a position, so that a politics of difference should not reject but should, rather, embrace some version of impartiality or neutrality.

The appeal of a position that rejects the ideal of impartiality is that it affords a kind of defense of participatory democracy that could include workplace and economic democracy: "If we give up the ideal of impartiality, there remains no moral justification for undemocratic processes of decision making concerning collective action. Instead of a fictional contract, we require real participatory structures in which actual people, with their geographic, ethnic, gender, and occupational differences, assert their perspectives." In contrast, the ideal of impartiality serves to justify allegedly impartial judges, allegedly universalistic bureaucracies, allegedly scientific experts, and the possibility of administered distributive justice, while in fact masking the power of particular classes and their partial interests.[15]

Young claims that impartiality is impossible, that it always serves such ideological functions, and that commitment to it, often asserted by those who recognize that existing states and theories have fallen short, itself "makes it difficult to expose the partiality of the supposedly general standpoint, and to claim a voice for the oppressed"[16] Impartiality is impossible because:

1. "feelings, desires, and commitments do not cease to exist and motivate"
2. "no one can adopt a point of view that is completely impersonal and dispassionate, completely separated from any particular context and commitments";
3. reasoning about substantive moral issues "always presupposes some particular social and historical context"; and
4. if the outcome matters, "one has a particular passionate interest in the outcome."[17]

Young does not rule out a relative distancing of oneself from one's own immediate interests but does exclude adoption of "a point of view emptied of particularity."[18] The inclusion of multiple particular points of view in a "dialogical," versus monological, view of moral deliberation implies that there is no single standpoint from which moral rightness is judged but only multiple standpoints that might converge on principles and actions.

This criticism may fit some versions of impartiality, but it does not undermine the "political liberalism" of Rawls and Larmore. Concerning the first and last objections, neutrality or impartiality should not be thought of as a psychological state. Rawls makes it clear that the motivation to support political liberalism springs from particular feelings, desires, and commitments, including commitments to particular conceptions of the good. This is why he thinks his conception of justice can be defended on the basis of an "overlapping consensus" of such conceptions of the good. The "neutrality" of the theory lies in its not aiming to advance any particular comprehensive conception of the good. (It will unavoidably have the effect of favoring some over others, but such neutrality of effect is not that defended by Rawls.)[19] The theory is neutral, but none of its adherents are impartial. Yet each can recognize in the theory some common ground that they all can share, despite their differences. Endorsing such a theory does not require the abandonment of one's feelings, desires, and the like but only a desire to reach an understanding.

As to Young's second and third objections, the precise elements that define such a construction as Rawls' original position are dictated by the particular context and commitments of the political community or communities to which it is applied. In particular, Rawls assumes, as a peculiar feature of modern societies since the time of the Reformation, an ineradicable plurality of reasonable conceptions of the good.[20] It is this peculiar context that propels us into strategies of dialogue that involve abstracting from certain differences. This abstraction is not absolute but is a relative matter. We abstract from particular differences, such as incommensurable conceptions of the good, only to the extent that a common political culture requires it.[21]

Thus, it does not appear to me that neutrality of this sort is impossible. Nor, if it happens in practice to be serving an ideological function, is it beyond correction. Whether it is the preferable response to the fact of difference is another question. Young proposes, in place of the construction of a neutral theory, the process of "participation and inclusion of everyone in moral and social life."[22] Just principles are not those chosen by parties behind a veil of ignorance or bound by neutral rules of dialogue but rather those chosen by actual people engaged in the expression and interpretation of needs in democratic dialogue. Following Hannah Pitkin, Young recommends that people be forced "to acknowledge the power of others and appeal to their standards, even as we try to get them to acknowledge our power and standards. We are forced to find or create a common language of purposes and aspirations."[23] There is no universal standpoint here: "They only move from self-regarding need to recognition of the claims of others. . . . Those claims are normatively valid which are generalizable in the sense that they can be recognized without violating the *rights* of others or subjecting them to domination."[24]

Two things appear to be going on here. First, actual dialogue is replacing hypothetical reasoning. The problem with this move is that it builds into the process of arriving at just principles all the inequalities and injustices that are supposed to be subject to criticism from the perspective of justice. To require the worker to "acknowledge the power" and "appeal to the standards" of the capitalist is to concede in the terms of dialogue what ought to be the central object of scrutiny. Contractualist, ideal speech and other hypothetical reasoning models are designed precisely to avoid setting up, as a process for arriving at justice, a dialogue that takes for granted existing unjust structures. Because a dialogue involving everyone concerned in which all are actually free and equal is not possible in an unjust society, we can only imagine what the outcome would be. Such imagining, call it utopian if you will, is what separates political philosophy from shoddy compromises. It is what gives us, if not an absolute, at least the relative distance from our own immediate interests and the status quo that Young sees as the object of moral reflection.[25] Positing such theorizing as monological mistakes the style of presentation with its ultimate political fate. The theorist is but one additional actor in the political struggle, one whose theory is put forward as an attempt to articulate some common principles that all or most can agree upon, on grounds that all or most will find reasonable. The political engagement of the theory is unavoidably dialogical.

Young has, of course, interjected that claims are valid if they can be recognized without violating the rights of others or subjecting them to domination. Although possibly saving her position from my first criticism, this move opens it to another: by invoking rights and absence of domination as constraints on what can count as a valid claim, Young presupposes criteria of justice that should be the outcome of the dialogue. In spelling out what the rights are that precede democratic dialogue, it is hard to see how hypothetical reasoning of some sort can be avoided. It is this work that contract theories of justice attempt to do and that Young is taking for granted. The conditions for a truly democratic dialogue are those identified as distributive justice.

## IDEAL JUSTICE *AND* RADICAL JUSTICE

Iris Young, as I have just shown, presupposes some univeralistic elements in her account of justice: ideals of self-development and self-determination, acceptance of at least a relative distancing from one's immediate interests to arrive at justice, and an appeal to "rights" and freedom antecedent to democratic discussion. Only by failing to provide full definition of these key terms can Young appear to have dispensed with the need for a distributive theory of justice that rests on at least a relative impartiality. In calling attention to these terms I have argued for the assimilation of Young's arguments within a theory of distributive justice.

In rejecting any ideal theory at all and defending a kind of relativism, Milton Fisk appears to go beyond Young. His materialist conception of justice ties an account of justice to an analysis of the state and the state's relation to the economy and to social actors. Part of the appeal of his theory is that it does not divorce explanation from prescription or what ought to be done from a clear understanding of the way the world is. It promises to bring the theory of justice down to earth and connect it with actually existing struggles.

The state, in Fisk's view, is not merely an instrument for advancing the economy or promoting the dominant group or bringing about technological change, as in some reductionistic Marxist theories; nor is it merely an agent of legitimation. The state both supports an economic structure, operating within its limits, and promotes a pattern of justice. Justice—official state justice—originates from the requirements of ruling: maintaining an existing mode of production or structure of class domination but putting limits on that domination by acceding to pressure from oppressed groups. Fisk claims that no state can rule without encouraging a pattern of justice. States reproduce the economy by ruling on the basis of justice. The relative autonomy of the state derives from the possibility that its economic function can conflict with its political form of rule. Official state justice is a compromise that fails to satisfy anyone. But it will particularly fall short of satisfying the interests of dominated groups. Moral outrage, modified by consideration of what elements of a group's interest would need to be compromised in order for it to rule, results in radical justice.[26]

Both official and radical justice are contrasted with ideal justice, which Fisk thinks he can do without. Ideal justice arises not from the requirements of governability but from consideration of what is needed for individuals to advance "toward their realizations"—"general social improvement"—or from what would be chosen in an ideal-choice situation, or from conformity with Platonic forms, or from an ideal of autonomy. Fisk focuses on the first of these. He argues that ideal justice rests on a false assumption "that the capacities characteristic of humans in different groups are complementary rather than conflictive."[27] If, on the contrary, capacities are conflictive, then any pattern of justice will be at best accepted by some groups but not considered acceptable. Rather, these groups will envision an alternative order in which their interests are better served but to which other groups would give only a grudging acceptance. Fisk is not positing fundamental conflict as a universal human condition but only as a feature of societies with antagonistic groups, such as capitalism or any imaginable alternative as it emerges from capitalism.[28] He seems to entertain the possibility of a "genuine unity of the groups of a society, as opposed to a forced truce between them."[29] But even radical justice is not ideal justice, because its view of the whole reflects the bias of the dominated group.[30]

Fisk defends his rejection of the compatibility assumption with an example of justice in education. If the aim of education is to enable each person to realize his or her human potential, educational reform can follow three routes: discriminatory tracking, a common curriculum, and pluralist education. The first rests on a false assumption that there is a correspondence between jobs and abilities. The second "runs against the inability of the schools to transcend social difference."

The third "intensifies the divisions in society" and so is incompatible with a coherent conception of justice.[31]

Fisk argues that Rawls' position also presupposes this assumption insofar as his ideal justice is supposed to enable people "to express their nature as free and equal moral persons." Fisk argues that if everyone's advantage were served, those advantaged in the implementation of justice would come into conflict with privileged groups, and "class hostility" rather than a just society, would result.[32]

In response to this, Rawls could say that he envisions a shared conception of justice in a well-ordered society, not in capitalism as we know it. But this is to acknowledge that in such a society the compatibility of capacities is presupposed. I do not see why this should be a damning admission, however. The aim of the theory is to project an ideal in terms of which the existing order, and the way people therein define their interests, can be criticized. It leaves us with a gap between ideal and reality and lots of questions about how to get from here to there and how to connect the perspective of justice with the motives of social actors. But such questions are not unanswerable. They are the concerns of political strategy and political rhetoric, which depend for their integrity on a theory of ideal justice. I support this claim through a critique of Fisk's attempt to do without ideal justice.

Fisk is not a radical relativist, insofar as he acknowledges an "underlying dimension of moral awareness, which tells us that social existence imposes some restraints on those within it." He holds that there is an inevitable gap between abstract moral principles that everyone might agree with and a political morality: "Neither radical nor state justice is ever simply an application of a pure morality to politics. Abstract moral principles are conceptually incapable of antecedently determining the context of political morality, even when we add in facts about existing conditions. It is only after the fact of the formation of a political morality that conceptual connections are drawn with abstract principles."[33]

On reflection, this characterization of political theorizing, though it may well describe the work of ideologists, is inadequate for a purpose Fisk must acknowledge as important: articulating an alternative to official state justice. I argue that "radical justice" depends on ideal justice and can not do without it.

The concept of interests bears all the weight in Fisk's theory of the state and justice. Official state justice makes concessions to the interests of dominated groups in order to make rule possible, but it is biased toward the interests of dominant groups. Radical justice springs from outrage at the limits on the interests of oppressed groups, modified in the direction of compromises needed for these groups to rule but with a bias toward their interests: "Both radical justice and state justice claim to fit different interests together, so that no one's interests are totally neglected, but they fit them together with a different bias."[34]

How are we to identify peoples' interests? Fisk assumes "without argument that within historical materialism the economic framework plus the interacting roles of the various groups provide a basis for picking out the fundamental interests of those groups without recourse to an a priori humanism."[35] That is an assumption that needs a lot of support. I will not attempt to defend it here but only raise some questions that call it into doubt.

First, is one's interest determined from one's preferences? If so, then radical justice will easily collapse into state justice, because preferences typically are adapted to what is possible in a given regime. As the oppressed limit their horizons to those deemed permissible by official justice, there will be no scope for alternatives. If interests are not the same as preferences, then it becomes possible to have preferences at odds with one's "real interests."[36] How are these "real interests" to be identified? An analysis of the existing economic structure and roles within it is compatible with an attribution of interests to agents compatible with official justice. Official justice works to legitimate a system of rule precisely because such an attribution is possible. My point is not that empirical analysis *may* reveal in the end that there is no conflict between a group's fundamental interests and official justice, and hence that there is no oppression; Fisk would be untroubled by this possibility and would even welcome it as an empirical check on theorizing. Rather, my point is that one can *too often* (I am tempted to say, always) describe the interests of groups in terms compatible with official justice, where nevertheless a critique is warranted. For example, consider the question of whether contemporary workers in the United States have a fundamental interest in self-management. According to official justice, they are currently free to form cooperatives, if they are willing to undertake the necessary risks and sacrifices. But normally, except in extreme cases where necessity forces ownership upon them, such as impending plant shutdowns, workers prefer to let others take the financial risks and the management headaches. They would rather diversify their savings, or spend it on consumer goods, and avoid the extra meetings that economic democracy would require. Hence, they have no fundamental interest in self-management. It is unclear how an analysis of economic structure or workers' roles can counter this sort of analysis. The alternative, I submit, is to appeal to a moral point of view that is not relative to the socially defined roles or the actual stated interests (preferences) of particular groups. There are many ways to articulate such a moral point of view, but among the most familiar and effective is the contractualist or counterfactual ideal of what people would agree to if certain prevailing inequalities, dependencies, and adaptive preferences were set aside.

Fisk explains in a more recent essay how a social theory that relativizes morality to social positions might address adaptive preferences and the like: A "social theory can interpret moral cultures associated with a given social position as either *coerced* because of a need to cope with desperate circumstances or *manipulated* by agencies outside that position. Such an interpretation . . . is a critique of [those moral cultures] if it can be assumed that those in the given social position *would* not adopt any of those moral cultures on their own *in the absence* of desperate circumstances or manipulation."[37] Note that Fisk here alludes, if only sketchily, to a counterfactual choice situation of freedom from domination and ideological manipulation. How is this different from a contractualist theory, other than that the latter attempts to be more explicit about the conditions for choice in the absence of unfair constraints?

It is true that contractualist theories can be used to support a pattern of official justice; but they can also be used to articulate alternatives. In fact, articulating an alternative requires such a theory. Fisk almost acknowledges this when he notes "the paradox that the state extends equality and liberty on the real basis of class, race, gender, or national solidarity while justifying itself on the unreal basis of universal solidarity."[38] Ironically, radical justice can only get beyond the instrumental expression of group interest to a viewpoint that has a chance of being accepted willingly by others (and grudgingly by a few) if it is articulated in universalistic terms. Group interests, which may indeed be the starting point of moral reflection, need to be moralized. But this moralizing needs the framework of a theory. In deferring always to group interests and rejecting ideal theory, Fisk deprives us of the very theoretical apparatus we need to put flesh on the bare-bones idea of radical justice.

Yet another way to see this is to consider how thin the idea of "radical justice" is. Oppressed groups are not so defined relative to a standard of inequality or disadvantage as might be specified in a theory of (ideal) justice. Rather, they are among the nondominant groups whose interests are compromised by state justice. Radical justice is an alternative conception in which this group imagines itself ruling, having compromised its interests only as far as is necessary to rule. Now, consider that among the dominated groups in the United States today are poor white Christian fundamentalists who oppose abortion. This group is repressed by the state and has its own version of radical justice, which is certainly not a conception Fisk or I would endorse. Yet it would appear to fit his formal criteria. The group rejects official justice, which respects a woman's right to choose to have an abortion. Moreover, it rejects it much more vehemently than its opponents, who also find the state not going far enough in protecting the right in dispute. The outrage, if articulated into a view of the whole that attempts to appeal to all, will produce an alternative form of radical justice, "with a different bias."

Fisk does say that his concern "is only with those rejections of state systems of justice that are built upon by an alternative conception of justice reflecting the fundamental interests of the groups rejecting state justice." Thus he might reject a Christian fundamentalist conception of justice as a form of radical justice, just as he rejects "Nazi myths and attempts to act on them" as "only a surrogate for, rather than a satisfaction of, the fundamental interests."[39] In his discussion of the abortion problem, he regards the fundamental interests at stake not as the interests of the fetus versus the interests of women in controlling reproduction but rather as the interests of male heads of households versus the interests of women in controlling the reproductive process. The interests of the fetus he construes to be a product of the struggle between these groups.[40] Although I sympathize with Fisk's analysis of the origin of the controversy, an antiabortionist could charge him with the genetic fallacy: that the interests of the fetus were first articulated in the context of struggle over control of reproduction does not imply that such interests are reducible to the interests in that struggle.

In sorting out which interpretation of "fundamental interests" is correct, the antiabortionist's or Fisk's, it is clear that some strong normative foundation is needed. It is not at all clear, however, how this can be derived merely from one's position in the mode of production (and reproduction), because conflicting interpretations will assign a different significance to that. Rather, a moral theory is needed. But that is just what Fisk says we can do without.

The problem of defining radical justice is not limited to the question of how to exclude right-wing radicals.[41] There is also the problem of how to sort through the variety of alternatives on the left. Even if we agree that workers' fundamental interests lie in the abolition of capitalism and its replacement with socialism, it will be necessary to spell out whether this is the worker-managed market socialism of David Schweickart, or the managerial market socialism of John Roemer, or the participatory planned socialism of Albert and Hahnel, or some other sort.[42] Radical justice does not favor any one of these over any other, unless we have some clearer idea of what "fundamental interests" are. If the goal of a theory of justice is to articulate and defend principles that should prevail over our more personal, idiosyncratic, and group interests, when there is conflict, such a theory is what is needed to define fundamental interests.

In conclusion, I should say that I conceive of my own project as an effort to develop a conception of radical justice counterposed to prevailing conceptions of justice that support gross inequalities of wealth and power and undemocratic social institutions. Where I differ with Fisk is on the place of ideal justice in this project. Ideal justice can and must be put in the service of this radical project. The result will not be a theory that in practice will persuade everyone. It will be fiercely resisted by many whose wealth and power would be threatened by justice.

It is important that the oppressed be able to defend the claim that it is justice—not just a masquerade of justice—that they are advancing. This can best be done on the terrain of a theory of justice in which it is theoretically possible to defend capitalism but on which the arguments against it are stronger and can persuade most people who do not have an interest in maintaining injustice. One only weakens the case for the oppressed by building in a bias for the conclusion one hopes to defend. On a playing field already tipped to the advantage of the wealthy and powerful, to argue that justice is, in effect, not an independent force but a reflection of power relations and interests is to deprive the oppressed of one of the few countervailing advantages they have.

## NOTES

1. John Rawls, *Political Liberalism* (New York: Columbia University Press, 1993), 213.

2. Susan Moller Okin, *Justice, Gender, and the Family* (New York: Basic Books, 1989).

3. In addition to Okin's work, see Rodney Peffer's left-Rawlsian theory in *Marxism, Morality and Social Justice* (Princeton: Princeton University Press, 1990).

4. Iris Young, *Justice and the Politics of Difference* (Princeton: Princeton University Press, 1990), 116.

5. Young, *Justice and the Politics of Difference*, 15. She shares with Thomas Simon and Judith Shklar the idea that we should begin theorizing about injustice rather than justice. I must confess that I have never felt the force of this point, *justice* and *injustice* being mutually interdefined. Any charge of injustice implicitly refers to some notion of justice. Any ideal of justice will single out injustices and typically is motivated by reflection on paradigmatic injustices (for example, slavery, gender inequality, capitalist exploitation, or imperialism). The difference seems more a matter of style. See Judith N. Shklar, *The Faces of Injustice* (New Haven: Yale University Press, 1990); Thomas W. Simon, *Democracy and Social Injustice: Law, Politics, and Philosophy* (Lanham, Md.: Rowman & Littlefield Publishers, 1995).

6. Young, *Justice and the Politics of Difference*, 15.

7. Young, *Justice and the Politics of Difference*, 16.

8. John Rawls, *A Theory of Justice* (Cambridge: Harvard University Press, 1971), 529.

9. Michael W. Howard, "Worker Control, Self-Respect, and Self-Esteem," *Philosophy Research Archives* 10 (1984): 455–72.

10. Young, *Justice and the Politics of Difference*, 23; Will Kymlicka, *Multicultural Citizenship: A Liberal Theory of Minority Rights* (Oxford: Clarendon Press, 1995).

11. Thomas Nagel, "A Defense of Affirmative Action," in *Values and Public Policy*, ed. Claudia Mills (New York: Harcourt Brace Jovanovich, 1992).

12. Very briefly, a shift in the defense of affirmative action, from the heritage of past injustice to the celebration of difference, has the advantage of dodging the charge of "reverse discrimination." Standards are denormalized, and more and more-varied people qualify for positions that have hitherto been the preserve of white males, but the latter are not discriminated against. However, the celebration of difference risks leveling the very palpable and morally relevant differences between others who are simply not white males and others who labor under deep prejudices and a legacy of slavery. An adequate defense of affirmative action should favor African Americans, Native Americans, and other groups with a history of oppression over groups without such a history, *because* they have been oppressed, not just because they have interesting styles or perspectives. Moreover, class differences should be factored in so that it is not primarily middle-class white women and middle-class members of minority groups who benefit. See William Julius Wilson, "Race-Specific Policies and the Truly Disadvantaged," in *Justice*, ed. Milton Fisk (Atlantic Highlands, N.J.: Humanities Press, 1993), 240–54.

13. Joseph Raz, *The Morality of Freedom* (Oxford: Clarendon Press, 1986).

14. Michael W. Howard, "A Contradiction in the Egalitarian Theory of Justice," *Phi-*

*losophy Research Archives* 10 (1984): 35–55.

15. Young, *Justice and the Politics of Difference*, 116, 111–16.

16. Young, *Justice and the Politics of Difference*, 116.

17. Young, *Justice and the Politics of Difference*, 103–104.

18. Young, *Justice and the Politics of Difference*, 105.

19. Rawls, *Political Liberalism*, 191–94.

20. Rawls, *Political Liberalism*, 58–66, 36, 136, 216f.

21. Charles Larmore, *Patterns of Moral Complexity* (Cambridge: Cambridge University Press, 1987), 50, 67. To the extent that there is, in fact, very wide agreement on substantive ethical conceptions, the neutrality of Rawls and Larmore might shade into the more communitarian liberalism of Nussbaum and Sen, or Galston, referred to in chapter 1. Young's understandable suspicion of communitarianism should move her closer to Rawls and Larmore.

22. Young, *Justice and the Politics of Difference*, 105.

23. Hannah Pitkin, "Justice: On Relating Public and Private," *Political Theory* 9 (August 1981): 327–52, quoted in Young, *Justice and the Politics of Difference*, 107.

24. Young, *Justice and the Politics of Difference*, 107; my emphasis.

25. Young, *Justice and the Politics of Difference*, 105.

26. Milton Fisk, *The State and Justice* (Cambridge: Cambridge University Press, 1989), 71, 95, 100–101.

27. Fisk, *The State and Justice*, 69, 72.

28. Fisk, *The State and Justice*, 73.

29. Fisk, *The State and Justice*, 94.

30. Fisk, *The State and Justice*, 95.

31. Fisk, *The State and Justice*, 75–76.

32. Fisk, *The State and Justice*, 78–79.

33. Fisk, *The State and Justice*, 101.

34. Fisk, *The State and Justice*, 95.

35. Fisk, *The State and Justice*, 95.

36. Steven Lukes, *Power: A Radical View* (New York: Macmillan, 1974).

37. Milton Fisk, "Justice and Universality," in *Morality and Social Justice: Point/Counterpoint*, ed. James P. Sterba et al. (Lanham, Md.: Rowman & Littlefield, 1995), 236; my italics.

38. Fisk, *The State and Justice*, 122.

39. Fisk, *The State and Justice*, 95.

40. Fisk, *The State and Justice*, 279–80.

41. Fisk does not himself see this as a problem, acknowledging that there can be radicals of left, right, or center, depending on who has hegemony in the defining of official justice; correspondence with the author.

42. David Schweickart, *Against Capitalism* (Cambridge: Cambridge University Press, 1994); John E. Roemer, *A Future for Socialism* (Cambridge: Harvard University Press, 1994); Michael Albert and Robin Hahnel, *Looking Forward: Participatory Economics for the Twenty- First Century* (Boston: South End Press, 1991). The first two models are discussed in chapter 8 of this book, and the third in chapter 6, with occasional references to all of them in other parts of the text.

# 4

# Marx and the Market

In the first two chapters I have defended self-management on the basis of a liberal theory of justice. Because historically liberalism has been closely linked with capitalism, whereas the most influential arguments for socialism have been developed in Marxist terms, such a defense may arouse suspicion that something important from the Marxist tradition is being lost. This chapter is intended to allay such suspicions.

In the more than forty volumes that make up the collected works of Karl Marx and Friedrich Engels the pages devoted to socialism could be assembled in a fairly slim volume. Marx was mainly concerned with understanding and criticizing capitalism and preferred not to prescribe "recipes for the cookshops of the future."[1] But the brief sketches of socialism and communism he and Engels provided have been enormously influential within the Marxist and socialist traditions and are indispensable points of reference in any discussion of market socialism and its relation to Marxism. Three positions of interest can be taken:

1. Market socialism is incompatible with Marxism, and Marx was not a market socialist
2. Market socialism is compatible with Marxism, but Marx was not a market socialist
3. Market socialism is compatible with Marxism, and Marx was a market socialist

In plausible interpretations of the key terms *Marxism* and *market socialism* there are defenders of each of these views.[2] In this chapter, I defend the second thesis very briefly, and without extensive exposition of Marx's critical theory or his writings on socialism and communism.[3] My purpose here is only to make clear how one can accept Marx's critique of capitalist society and also see some kinds of market socialism as acceptable alternatives to capitalism.

## MARX ON COMMODITY FETISHISM AND THE MARKET

One finds in Marx's writing two contrasting models of postcapitalist classless society: Those models of "communist" society found in the *Critique of the Gotha Program* and *Capital* are of classless societies without commodity exchange. That is, they have replaced markets in capital, labor, goods, and services with government planning. In the *Critique,* Marx further distinguishes communist society into a lower and higher phase, on the basis of whether incomes are distributed according to work or according to need, respectively. (Following Lenin, the lower phase has come to be known as "socialism," the higher as "communism," a convention I follow in the rest of this chapter.) The higher phase is only possible, according to Marx, "after the enslaving subordination of the individual to the division of labour, and therewith also the antithesis between mental and physical labour, has vanished; after labour has become not only a means of life but life's prime want; after the productive forces have also increased with the all-round development of the individual, and all the springs of co-operative wealth flow more abundantly."[4]

Abundance and radical change in the division of labor and human motivation are not within close reach, making this model seemingly not very relevant to a discussion of feasible alternatives to capitalism. Its importance has more to do with the way in which one understands the trajectory of socialism: Is it a transition to communism or not? One of the chief dividing lines between communists and socialists through most of the twentieth century has been the commitment to this goal on the part of communists and the abandonment of the goal by socialists.[5] One argument against the market in socialist society has been that it blocks progress toward full communism (or even leads back to capitalism—see the following chapter).

Earlier, in *The Communist Manifesto*, Marx himself put forward a model of socialism as a classless society, but one with commodity exchange. Some capitalist enterprises survive. There are markets for means of production, labor, and consumer goods. Socially owned enterprises also operate through these markets. In preserving commodity exchange, such a market socialism has greater continuity with the society it displaces than does nonmarket socialism, and thus it is more likely to emerge from capitalism as a result of tendencies generated within it. Nonmarket socialism may better fit the moral ideal in Marx's philosophical communism, but it is detached from the historical tendencies to be found in the real world. Some have interpreted Marx as having left behind moral prescription in favor of historical description, particularly after developing the theory of historical materialism in the late 1840s. Thus, historical materialism might be thought to favor the market-socialist model.[6] Yet Marx later consistently favors the nonmarket models of the *Critique* and *Capital*.

The reason for his abandonment of markets is to be found in Marx's philosophical communism, a commitment to the transcendence of commodity exchange grounded in a theory of human nature according to which our human existence in capitalist society is alienated from our human essence, or "species being." Our essential nature as social beings can be glimpsed in precapitalist forms of community in which the good of the individual is more closely identified with the general good. The division between individual interest and general interest sharpens with the emergence of commodity exchange in the market, a sphere of profit-seeking egoism. The emergence of the state, as distinct from the market, and as the (illusory) embodiment of the general interest, coincides with the emergence of the market (or civil society). The state is only an illusory embodiment of the general interest because in reality it has an interest of its own (including that of the bureaucracy) and because it is dominated by the dominant class of civil society, the capitalist class.

The capitalist class is the personal embodiment of a more fundamental alienation of labor. The worker, in exchanging his labor power for a wage, alienates himself from his producing activity and his product (both the artifact and the value it yields in exchange, and hence from capital as the ever increasing accumulation of such value). The worker is accordingly alienated from other human beings—notably, the capitalist, but also workers competing in the labor market and consumers seeking lower prices—and from his social being, in that he has no part in the planning of production or affairs of state, no part in matters that would bring him to identify with a universal interest and perspective.

His species being—free, creative activity in cooperation with others who share a universal outlook—can only be realized through a radical transformation of this system that goes to the very root of the problem: exchange of commodities, the articulation of human social relations as material relations among things exchanged in an impersonal market.[7]

A socialist society that did away with the capitalist class—for example, through either state ownership of the means of production or cooperative ownership—might end exploitation, but it need not end commodity exchange. Consequently, a society of worker-owned cooperatives, exchanging their products in a market, could still be an alienated society. The workers might still be egoistic, mainly concerned with profit and consumption, alienated from other cooperatives and from the general interest, relating to each other indirectly through a direct relationship to things, commodities exchanging for prices in the market. In *Capital*, Marx calls this condition the fetishism of commodities.

Whence, then, arises the enigmatical character of the product of labour, so soon as it assumes the form of commodities? Clearly from this form itself. The equality of all sorts of human labour is expressed objectively by their products all being equally values; the measure of the expenditure of labour power by the duration of that expenditure takes the form of the quantity of value of the products of labour; and finally, the mutual relations of the producers, within which the social character of their labour affirms itself, take the form of a social relation between the products.

A commodity is therefore a mysterious thing, simply because in it the social character of men's labour appears to them as an objective character stamped upon the product of that labour; because the relation of the producers to the sum total of their own labour is presented to them as a social relation, existing not between themselves, but between the products of their labour. . . . In [the religious] world the productions of the human brain appear as independent beings endowed with life, and entering into relation both with one another and the human race. So it is in the world of commodities with the products of men's hands. This I call the Fetishism which attaches itself to the products of labour, so soon as they are produced as commodities, and which is therefore inseparable from the production of commodities.[8]

Moreover, this fetishism is not dispelled merely by understanding the analysis just given. Agents in commodity exchange experience the market as an encounter with things and their prices that appears to have a life of its own. "These qualities vary continually, independently of the will, foresight, and action of the producers. To them, their own social action takes the form of the action of objects, which rule the producers instead of being ruled by them."[9]

What would it mean for producers to rule their product and to relate to each other not indirectly, through the exchange of commodities, but directly? Examples of modes of production not based on commodity exchange include serfdom, patriarchal household production, and self-sufficient production like that of Robinson Crusoe, who kept a ledger of his products and the time needed to produce them. The former two precapitalist societies are characterized by relations of dependence, but because there are direct transactions in kind of services for goods, the social relations are not transformed into relations between commodities. In a postcapitalist society, we are asked to imagine

a community of free individuals, carrying on their work with the means of production in common, in which the labour power of all the different individuals is consciously applied as the combined labour power of the community. All the characteristics of Robinson's labour are here repeated, but with this difference, that they are social, instead of individual. Everything produced by him was exclusively the result of his own personal labour, and therefore simply an object of use for himself. The total product of our community is a social product. One portion serves as fresh means of production and remains social. But another portion is consumed by the members as means of subsistence. A distribution of this portion among them is consequently necessary. The mode of this distribution will vary with the productive organization of the community, and the degree of historical development attained by the producers. We will assume, but merely for the sake of a parallel with the production of commodities, that the share of each individual producer in the means of subsistence is determined by his labour time. Labour time would, in that case, play a double part. Its apportionment in accordance with a definite social plan maintains the proper proportion between the different kinds of work to be done and the various wants of the community. On the other hand, it also serves as a measure of the portion of the common labour borne by each individual, and of his share in the part of the total product destined for individual consumption. The social relations of the individual producers, with regard both to their labour and to its products, are in this case perfectly simple and intelligible, and that with regard not only to production but also to distribution. . . . The life-process of society, which is based on the process of material production, does not strip off its mystical veil until it is treated as production by freely associated men, and is consciously regulated by them in accordance with a settled plan.[10]

Thus we see that for Marx, rational planning is essential for the overcoming of commodity fetishism and the alienation of human beings from one another and from their own natural productive powers. How, then, could one be a Marxist— be committed not only to ending exploitation and inequality (the more limited goal of social democrats) but also to ending alienation, estrangement from labor, egoism, collective irrationality, and the dominance of humanity by the blind forces of the market—and still be a market socialist?

## STRUCTURAL FETISHISM WITHOUT PSYCHOLOGICAL FETISHISM

To answer this question, it is essential to make a distinction between structural and psychological fetishism. Commodity fetishism is, structurally, the organization of society such that no one is responsible for the determination of exchange values. Rather, exchange values are determined not by a conscious decision on the part of the producers to regard products as the emblems of the social labor put into them but by the mechanism of supply and demand in the market, "behind the backs of the producers." To use Friedrich Hayek's phrase, exchange value is the result of human action but not of human design.[11] To this we might add other things in market society that are the products of human action but not of human design: pollution, unemployment, inequalities resulting from the extraction of surplus value, and so on. Psychologically, fetishism is the egoistic disposition not to acknowledge or assume responsibility for the unintended consequences of human action in the market but to be concerned only with exchange values. For example, both the CEO of a corporation, a worker employed therein, and a customer buying the corporation's product exhibit structural commodity fetishism as they seek the highest profits and wages and the cheapest prices. To do otherwise could be to depart from their roles in the market. The CEO might strive to offer decent wages and working conditions and quality goods at competitive prices, the worker may strive to do a good job, and the customer may scrutinize the label to determine whether the product was made with sweatshop labor. Still, such ethical concern is within the parameters established by the market.[12]

Structural commodity fetishism is, as Marx puts it, "inseparable from the production of commodities." We behave as though we are utility maximizers whenever we play the market game. If, in addition, the CEO believes that profits are more important than people, the worker can not imagine an alternative to the "natural price" of wages in the market, and the customer values lower prices, regardless of the social cost, and if all cast their votes accordingly in the next elections, they exhibit a consciousness shaped by the market game, fetishism in the psychological sense. It is evident that in a society in which an increasing proportion of social life takes the commodity form, agents will not only exhibit the behavior that is rational in market roles but will also tend to think like market transactors. But is the link between structural and psychological fetishism inevitable?

Imagine a society of commodity producers who have recognized the true nature of the commodity and its fetishism. Without abandoning commodity production, they seek to correct some of its consequences. Labor power continues to be bought and sold as a commodity, but restrictions are placed on minimum prices, labor income is supplemented with unemployment and old-age benefits, and laborers within the factories are endowed with various rights (such as election of their managers) that belie their fictitious existence as commodities. Moreover, those engaged in socially useful, if unprofitable, activities are subsidized by transfer payments taxed from those who profit excessively in the market. All these restrictions on the free play of the market are recognized as desirable, because everyone sees through the limitations of the "market game." Producers will produce for profit in the market, but they realize that production for profit is just one of the rules of the game, kept intact to promote increased productivity of labor and optimal allocation of resources and to provide for "consumer sovereignty," which is one of the requirements for "free individuality." Moreover, in forming the state that imposes these restrictions, the producers are meeting each other in capacities other than as exchangers of products.

They are no longer "ruled by their products" but have agreed to let their products rule them within a limited domain, in that they are still engaged in commodity production. They have agreed not to agree beforehand on a central plan about such things as prices of products or labor or types of goods to be produced. Thus, the discipline of the market is a self-imposed one. In so far as it is undesirable, it is altered by other more *directly* agreed-upon restrictions and plans (for example, pollution control laws and unemployment compensation).

One will immediately protest that this picture is a distortion of what actually happens, that in practice the state is an instrument of the dominant class, that the market permits exploitation of the propertyless by those controlling the means of production. These objections can be met by stipulating in our model that no one will be entitled to own more than is justified by considerations of distributive justice (such as Rawls' difference principle or some more egalitarian theory), that restrictions be imposed upon anyone in a position of control over means of production to prevent abuse of power (for example, that he or she be elected and recallable by those who work under him or her). In other words, eliminate the class divisions of market society and one is left with a society of commodity producers for whom the state is not so much an agent of their oppression as an instrument of their freedom: it is through the state that they overcome the fetishism of commodities, not just in thought but in practice.

Such is the ideal of present day democratic market socialism. In this ideal, one must admit, commodity production continues, but commodity fetishism in the psychological sense is overcome. One has maintained not only free choice in consumption but also a relative autonomy of the enterprises for those who work in them. However, this autonomy is understood by all to be subordinate to requisite limitations by the state, so that personal or group particularism is transcended.[13]

## MARKET SOCIALISM AND COMMUNISM

What I have suggested is the possibility of a model of socialism like that presented in the *Manifesto*, but which has nevertheless overcome fetishism in the psychological sense. What would be the relationship between such a socialist society and communism? Assuming that production for the sake of exchange continued merely as a kind of bookkeeping device and not as a psychological disposition, such a society could very well evolve into communism, given the prerequisites mentioned in Marx's *Critique*. But, assuming that the tie had been broken between fetishism in the psychological sense and fetishism in the structural sense, the community of producers could well decide to preserve the appearance of material incentives, wages, and the market economy for the sake of convenience, efficiency, and personal freedom. This would not prevent them from instituting substantial welfare measures and forms of collective consumption that distributed some social benefits, not according to work but according to need. Over time, the principle of need could eclipse the principle of work, or not. Imagine, for example, a steadily rising unconditional basic income, which could eventually exceed income from wages, or not, as the citizens would decide.

In either case, the ideals of philosophical communism would have been reached: a new community, fully self-conscious and self-managing, would have replaced not only the exploitation but also the egoism and estrangement of capitalism. There are numerous ways in which a market society might compensate for commodity fetishism in the structural sense. The democratization of productive enterprises, from the shop floor to the boardroom, and democratic planning of investment could provide the basis for the development and exercise of a sense of justice that could counter the psychological aspect of commodity fetishism.

The Yugoslav worker-managed market economy provided an imperfect approximation to this way of compensating for structural commodity fetishism. Moreover, it showed that such an economy is capable of growth and efficient production and can emerge as a transitional form from socialist planned economies. (Whether self-management can emerge as a transitional form from capitalist economies remains to be seen.) Evidence for the existence of commodity fetishism in the former Yugoslavia would seem to refute my conjecture that commodity fetishism in the psychological sense can be overcome in a market economy through the institution of self-management. But the adherence to a traditional hierarchical division of labor within the firm, the failure to extend democracy from the particular firm to the economy as a whole, and the suppression of political freedom in Yugoslavia require us to regard the Yugoslav case as an imperfect example of self-management, and inconclusive as a test of my thesis.[14]

My hypothesis is that the widespread overcoming of psychological commodity fetishism—that is, the achievement of a more universal, dare I say moral, consciousness—depends upon substantial opportunities for meaningful democratic participation. Such opportunities are highly restricted in capitalist market societies, where decisions about production, the division of labor, and investment are made by corporate elites. They were also restricted in state socialist societies in which analogous decisions were made by central planners and state-appointed managers. Self-management and democratic planning of investment together constitute the alternative to both of these demoralized elitist systems. Although no social system can guarantee participation by all of its members, not to mention moral conscientiousness, economic democracy comes much closer to providing the necessary arenas for the exercise of citizen capacities and virtues.

In the next chapter I defend economic democracy against the criticism that, as a market society, it must inevitably fall prey to commodity fetishism (and exploitation). In chapter 5, I argue that decentralized democratic planning as an alternative to markets is not feasible or desirable. If these arguments are sound, there is still hope for Marx's aspiration to a public-spirited, egalitarian, self-governing community, a hope that today must be targeted on self-managed market socialism.

## NOTES

1. Karl Marx, Afterword to *Capital*, vol. 1, trans. Samuel Moore and Edward Aveling (Moscow: Foreign Language Publishing House, 1959), 17, quoted in Steven Lukes, *Marxism and Morality* (Oxford: Clarendon Press, 1985), 36.

2. It seems one can hold any of these interpretive positions regardless of one's politics. For pro-capitalist, market socialist, and antimarket socialist defenses of the first

position, see respectively, N. Scott Arnold, *Marx's Radical Critique of Capitalist Society* (Oxford: Oxford University Press, 1990), and *The Philosophy and Economics of Market Socialism* (Oxford: Oxford University Press, 1994); Stanley Moore, *Marx versus Markets* (University Park: Pennsylvania State University Press, 1993); and the contributions of Bertell Ollman and Hillell Ticktin, in *Market Socialism: The Debate among Socialists*, ed. Bertell Ollman (New York: Routledge, 1998). For a defense of the third position, see James Lawler "Marx as Market Socialist," "Criticism of Ollman," and "Response to Ollman," in Ollman, *Market Socialism*, 23–52, 137–47, 183–92. I defend the second position.

3. For a more extended defense, see Michael W. Howard, "From Commodity Fetishism to Market Socialism: Critical Notes on Stanley Moore," *Philosophy and Social Criticism* 7, no. 2 (Summer 1980): 186–214.

4. Karl Marx, *Critique of the Gotha Program*, in *Karl Marx: Selected Writings*, ed. David McLellan (Oxford: Oxford University Press, 1977), 569.

5. This is one important dimension of the split between Social Democrats and Communists, according to Lenin. For discussion, see Moore, *Marx versus Markets*, vii–x, 3–10.

6. Moore, *Marx versus Markets*, 43; 67–68. Some have even concluded that Marx was a market socialist, for example, Lawler, "Marx as Market Socialist."

7. For a representative selection of Marx's early writings on which this sketch of philosophical communism is based, see McLellan, *Karl Marx: Selected Writings*, 3–127.

8. McLellan, *Karl Marx: Selected Writings*, 436.

9. McLellan, *Karl Marx: Selected Writings*, 438.

10. McLellan, *Karl Marx: Selected Writings*, 440–42.

11. McLellan, *Karl Marx: Selected Writings*, 428; Friedrich A. Hayek, *Individualism and Economic Order* (Chicago: Henry Regnery, 1948), 87.

12. As Marx comments in the 1867 preface to *Capital*, vol. 1, "Here individuals are dealt with only in so far as they are the personifications of economic categories, embodiments of particular class relations and class interests. My standpoint, from which the evolution of the economic formation of society is viewed as a process of natural history, can less than any other make the individual responsible for relations whose creature he socially remains, *however much he may subjectively raise himself above them*"; McLellan, *Karl Marx: Selected Writings*, 417, my italics. To subjectively raise oneself above the social relations that shape one is to overcome commodity fetishism in the psychological sense.

13. Those familiar with Hegel's *Philosophy of Right* will recognize a similarity here with Hegel's solution to the problem of alienation resulting from the market economy or "civil society." In his *Critique of Hegel's "Philosophy of Right"* and other early writings, Marx consistently favors the abolition of the distinction between civil society and state, rather than a psychological transcendence of the division through participation as a citizen in the higher form of life that, according to Hegel, the state provides. This same abolitionist position informs Marx's preference for non-market-socialist models. My own position is distinct from Hegel's and with Marx, in favoring the abolition of class inequality. It is class inequality that corrupts the state and makes of the market economy an arena of domination and exploitation. Overcome class inequality and it is possible—just possible—that Hegel's conception of the state could be a reality. See G. W. F. Hegel, *Philosophy of Right*, trans. T. M. Knox (Oxford: Oxford University Press, 1967);

Karl Marx, *Critique of Hegel's "Philosophy of Right"* (Cambridge: Cambridge University Press, 1970).

14. Antonio Carlo, "Capitalist Restoration and Social Crisis in Yugoslavia," *Telos* 36 (Summer 1978): 83–84; Gerry Hunnius, "Workers' Self-Management in Yugoslavia," in *Workers' Control,* ed. Gerry Hunnius, G. David Garson, and John Case (New York: Vintage Books, 1973), 306–10, 316–20; Svetozar Stojanović, "Social Self-Government and Socialist Community," *Praxis* (International Edition) 4 (1968): 104–16; George A. Potts, *The Development of the System of Representation in Yugoslavia with Special Reference to the Period since 1974* (New York: University Press of America, 1996); Michael W. Howard, "Market Socialism and Political Pluralism: Theoretical Reflections on Yugoslavia," *Studies in East European Thought,* forthcoming.

# 5

## Markets without Alienation and Exploitation

One implication of the previous chapter is that a Marxist can embrace the market without abandoning the goal of a society that overcomes alienation and restores community. Market socialism and the loftier "communist" or communitarian aspiration associated with Marxism are compatible to the extent that, in practice, commodity fetishism in the structural sense can be separated from psychological fetishism and the latter can be overcome through mediating social institutions, including but not limited to the state.

In slightly different terms, my argument suggests that socialists should abandon the contrast between "production for use" and "production for exchange" as a fruitful way of contrasting socialism and capitalism. For, if central planning were abandoned in favor of the market, there is no significant way in which socialism would restore "production for use" as the predominant mode of production in the way that occurred in primitive communal, feudal, or slave societies.[1]

### MARKET SOCIALISM AND ALIENATION

N. Scott Arnold's critique of Marx's radical critique of capitalist society shares with Marx the belief I have called into question, namely, that structural fetishism leads inevitably to psychological fetishism. He maintains, for example, that "a system of widespread commodity production is inherently alienating. . . . The mystification produced by commodity production [what I have called psychological fetishism] can be dispelled only by eliminating the latter and replacing it with a consciously organized system of production for use."[2] Arnold goes on to argue that Marx's models of centrally planned economies for both the lower and higher phases of communism are unrealizable. It follows that a society without alienation is unrealizable and so is not a realistic goal of social transformation. (He makes a parallel argument about exploitation, which I address in a later section and so pass over here.)

Part of the force of Arnold's criticism rests in his focus on the "radical" aspect of Marx's critique. Marx seeks not the amelioration of evils in capitalist society but their elimination or virtual elimination. Locating the causes of these evils in certain institutions of capitalist society, he seeks not the reform of these institutions but their replacement.[3] Arnold then tries to show that the evils will survive in all of Marx's models of postcapitalist society because of central planning.

I shall for the most part pass over his discussion of the higher phase of communism, as my concern is mainly with a realizable socialism, not with an ideal in the indefinite future. The "higher phase of communist society," in which it becomes possible to adopt the principle, "from each according to his ability, to each according to his needs," is only possible, according to Marx, "after the enslaving subordination of the individual to the division of labour, and therewith also the antithesis between mental and physical labour, has vanished; after labour has become not only a means of life but life's prime want; after productive forces have also increased with the all-round development of the individual, and all the springs of cooperative wealth flow more abundantly."[4] If all these conditions are necessary, needless to say, the higher phase of communism could be realized only in the distant future.[5] I will just say in passing that I agree with Arnold that some, if not all, of his "primary evils" (such as mortality, biological frailty, intermittent stupidity, and conflicting conceptions of the good life)[6] will persist. These will make for social conflict intense enough to require principles of justice.[7] However, it is not so clear that once major inequalities of wealth and power have been eliminated, these remaining conflicts could not be adjudicated rationally by appeal to principles consented to by all. This might not be "to each according to need" or "beyond justice," but neither need it be recognizably alienated as have been capitalist and state-socialist societies.

When it comes to the lower phase of communism, Arnold makes a number of compelling points about alienation under central planning. From the worker's point of view, the arbitrariness of the plan is no less alienating than the anarchy of the market, and producing for an output target no more rational than producing for profit. Meaningful work is often in tension with efficiency; and given the empirically observed inefficiencies of central planning, there is less not more room for a trade-off in favor of meaningful work. Nor is there a real gain in collective conscious control, because central planning can never keep up with unanticipated changes.[8] Alienation between worker and capitalist is simply replaced by conflict between workers and state-appointed managers, or between firms and planning bureaucrats. The more general commercialization of interpersonal relations gives way to a dependence on connections and bribes to get around the bottlenecks of planning. The alienation between civil society and state is never really overcome because class conflict is not, and never will be, the only sort of conflict requiring adjudication. However, by concentrating economic and political power in the hands of the state, central planning risks exacerbating the alienation of the individual from the state as an oppressive power.[9]

Because the model I support does not rely on central planning, it is not encompassed in Arnold's critique. Along with Marx, though more explicitly, Arnold does hold that market socialism would fail to provide a radical alternative, one that could abolish or virtually abolish alienation and exploitation. However, his argument concerning alienation, as I have shown earlier, merely assumes that commodity production must always entail commodity fetishism. There is no reason to accept this assumption. In questioning it, I am willing to grant that commodity production generally creates tendencies toward fetishism (in the psychological sense) and hence that it might be impossible to abolish alienation entirely. But a deep, if not "radical," critique of capitalist society still stands if, in that space between capitalism and its total transcendence, alienation can be substantially reduced.

In comparison with capitalism, worker self-management in a market economy, with social ownership of the means of production and a democratically controlled investment fund, would give to workers direct control of their product. The market would place some constraints on workplace humanization, but the parameters for improvement in this situation can be narrowed or widened through the investment process. Working for a share of the residuals is arguably qualitatively different from working for wages. Whereas central planning, in its ambition to control the production process, produces absurdities and makes a mockery of rational collective control, a democratically controlled investment fund, more modest in its goals, promises a more reasonable measure of genuine collective control without denying the real contingencies and unintended consequences that attend any complex, changing economy. The very real alienation between workers and owners will be overcome, without being replaced by "state capitalism." Some degree of widespread commercialism will persist, but cooperatives are less driven than capitalist enterprises, by the growth imperative,[10] allowing a more harmonious combination with ecological and other extracommercial imperatives. A distinction between civil society and state would remain, but the major divide between classes would have been closed, allowing the state to actually become what it only pretends to be in capitalist societies, the expression of a general interest. (Consider this a concession, contra Marx on the state, to Hegel and a concession, contra Hegel on classes, to Marx.) Would this not be a transformation sufficiently qualitatively superior to capitalism to qualify as radical?

## MARKET SOCIALISM AND EXPLOITATION

There remains the question of exploitation, which Arnold takes up in *The Philosophy and Economics of Market Socialism*. He argues that a market-socialist economy similar to that defended by David Schweickart is inferior to capitalism (or "free enterprise") because the former would create greater opportunities and motives for exploitation than the latter.[11] Arnold's argument hinges on a view of the importance of the concept of exploitation in the evaluation of any society and on a particular conception of exploitation in terms of which he makes his comparison. He defines exploitation as a kind of failure of reciprocity, an unfair exchange in which the exploited party has no better alternative.[12] His discussion focuses on a contrast between capitalist and market-socialist firms. Arnold examines the structure of the capitalist firm, the way it combines the various roles of worker, capital provider, residual claimant, coordinator of inputs and outputs (entrepreneur), manager of production, monitor of laborers and other input suppliers, and ultimate decision maker. In the "classical capitalist firm," all but labor is concentrated in the figure of the capitalist. In the "open corporation," there is a split between those who are residual claimants of the firm's net income, suppliers of capital, and ultimate authorities, on the one hand, and the entrepreneur-managers, on the other. In market socialism the workers become the residual claimants and ultimate decision makers, the state is the provider of capital, and managers who monitor, direct, and coordinate inputs and outputs are accountable to the workers.

Arnold argues that capitalist enterprises afford fewer opportunities and motives for exploitation than the market-socialist arrangement. Consider first the example of exploitation by cooperative workers of those who provide capital (ultimately, the taxpayers). Because the market-socialist cooperative does not own its own capital, it will have the opportunity to degrade the capital it gets on loan from the state, even if it is legally required to pay a usage fee and maintain what it uses. Real, efficient maintenance of capital equipment is hard to identify and monitor because capital values and requirements are always changing. Moreover, no state official has a strong incentive to undertake the necessary monitoring required. The classical capitalist, or stockholders in an open corporation, have a strong motivation as owners of capital to see to its maintenance; and as ultimate decision makers, they are able to do so. In this case, the opportunity for exploitation of capital providers by ultimate decision makers does not arise, because the two roles are united in one figure.

One might object that bankers are in a position to be exploited under capitalism in exactly the same way, yet debt financing plays a prominent role in a capitalist economy. Arnold's response calls attention to the way debt is usually matched with substantial equity, such that the borrower would be injured by the same sorts of actions that might threaten the creditor. Where financing is highly leveraged—where there is a high debt-to-equity ratio—the cost of the loan reflects the increased risk for the creditor. In the market-socialist economy, it is as if all financing is through debt, and the separation of capital provision from ultimate decision making opens up the prospect of cooperatives systematically exploiting future workers, the state, and, indirectly, the taxpayers: because the workers are the residual claimants but have no stake in the long-term survival of the firm, beyond their employment life, assets are, when appropriable, apt to be converted into residuals.[13]

Consider, secondly, how workers would be exploited in a cooperative, to a greater degree than in a capitalist firm. In the market-socialist cooperative, workers are the ultimate decision makers and the residual claimants (the people who receive the net income from the firm's production). In contrast, in a capitalist firm the nonworker owners are the ultimate decision makers and residual claimants. Thus, wage differentials in a cooperative will be decided by the workers collectively (or by individuals directly accountable to the collective). One can easily imagine a majority of unskilled or less skilled workers paying skilled workers (not to mention managers) an income that is proportionately less than their contribution by reducing wage differentials in the direction of greater equality. Because, by hypothesis, all or most firms would be cooperatives, the skilled workers would have no real alternatives, they would be exploited in that they would not be paid the full value of their contribution.

Although there would be competition between firms for skilled workers and managers, so that some wage differentials would persist, Arnold argues that the labor markets would be sufficiently sluggish, compared with those under capitalism, that some egalitarian exploitation of the skilled by the unskilled would be likely. There are four reasons for this: First, a cooperative would be less inclined than a capitalist enterprise to take on additional workers, as this could reduce (or at least would not increase) the income per worker, and so a consensus would have to be reached before any action were taken. No such broad consensus is required in a capitalist firm. Second, a cooperative would be less inclined to lay off workers. Third, "it will be harder to start new firms than in free enterprise [that is, capitalist] systems because entrepreneurs who believe they see a profit opportunity will have to share any profits" with the workers. Fourth, worker income would be in the form of residuals from the firm's income, rather than fixed wages, and so a skilled (or unskilled) worker's income could fluctuate from year to year and across firms more than it would in a capitalist firm. This "will make it more difficult for workers to evaluate offers from other firms." The difficulty is compounded by the lack of a stock market, making it hard to assess a firm's financial prospects. "The relevance of all this to exploitation is that firms that pay their skilled workers less than they are worth . . . would be relatively insulated from the pressures of labor markets. . . . By contrast, in a free enterprise system this systematic problem does not arise because the four factors are absent."[14] Thus, skilled workers (and managers) are apt to be exploited more in a market-socialist than in a capitalist system.

The same four tendencies will lead to exploitation by cooperatives of their customers. For example, suppose that the demand for a particular kind of soap increases. A cooperative could decide to add more workers but, for the reasons mentioned, will be less inclined to do so than a capitalist firm. If all firms reach the same conclusion, they will simply raise prices, charging the customers—who will have no alternatives—more than they would pay in a system allowing competition from capitalist firms. The situation will not be fully corrected by the formation of new firms, because the profit incentives for entrepreneurs are so much less. Although a market-socialist system will be responsive to consumer demand, the key point is that it will be less responsive than a capitalist system, with a resulting exploitation of the consumer.[15]

These examples should suffice to illustrate the kinds of exploitation that Arnold thinks will exist under market socialism that would not exist under capitalism. In these and other cases he defines *exploitation* as a kind of failure of reciprocity, an unfair exchange in which the exploited party has no better alternative. Unfair exchange is defined with reference to a "competitively efficient" market for some good or service, one "in which there are no opportunities for price profit on either the supply or demand side."[16] Price profit is that which arises from a difference between the price in the product markets and the total of prices of the factors of production. Exchange in such markets is deemed fair, because the prices paid give to each the value of his contribution. The value of something is defined subjectively here as what anyone would pay for it in a competitively efficient market. Also considered fair are exchanges "on the leading edge of a market in transition," the idea here being that the profits earned by entrepreneurs as they introduce an initially novel or scarce commodity into a market are a fair measure of the entrepreneur's contribution. (In a competitively efficient market, such profits decline to zero.)[17]

This concept of economic exploitation is broader than Marxist conceptions in that it articulates not just the exploitation of workers but also that of other parties to exchanges, such as consumers, suppliers of capital, and trading partners. In addition, it captures ways that workers can be exploited by other workers, not just capitalists, as we saw above. It is the breadth of the concept that enables Arnold to argue that market socialism will offer more opportunities for exploitation than capitalism.

The concept is also controversial, from a Marxist perspective, in maintaining that capitalists as such make a contribution to production. (No one disputes that capital is needed for production. At issue is whether the capitalist makes a contribution that deserves a reward, and a reward proportional to the market price of capital.) One's "contribution" is simply defined as the fair price for what one contributes. One is exploited when one gets less than the fair market price for the capital (or labor, et cetera) one contributes and has nowhere else to go.

Even more startling than the idea of capitalists being exploited, for those who are familiar with Marx's analysis of capitalist exploitation of workers, is Arnold's argument that in a competitive capitalist market workers are not exploited at all and thus stand to be more exploited under market socialism. The heart of Marxist analyses of exploitation is the idea that there is a failure of reciprocity in the wage labor–capital relation, because the workers contribute more than they receive and the capitalist contributes nothing. If the second claim is true, and the capitalist appropriates any profit, then the first claim follows. Arnold argues that the second claim is false, that the capitalist does make a contribution, and that furthermore, workers tend to receive wages equal in value to their contributions. He argues that "the service the capitalist has rendered—the contribution that he makes—is to allow those who provide other factors of production to get paid 'up front.' . . . All production takes time, and time is both scarce and valuable. In effect, what the capitalist contributes is *time* in the form of command over present goods, in exchange for which he receives an interest payment."[18]

If Arnold is right and the capitalist does make a contribution, more needs to be said by the Marxist to demonstrate a failure of reciprocity in what the workers receive. Moreover, workers are not *systematically* exploited, he maintains, because they typically get the value of their contributions, and they have other options. Let us consider first the issue of whether workers get the value of their contributions.

"A worker's asset is his or her capacity to labor. Either that asset has appropriable quasi-rents attached to it or it does not." (A *quasi-rent* is the difference in the value offered for an asset in an exchange and the value it would have in the next-best use. Such rents are appropriable when there are no other exchanges available in which the rent can be realized, as when the asset is highly specialized. Thus workers whose skills are site-specific are at risk of being exploited, of having the quasi-rent value of their labor being exploited by an employer who knows that the second-best use for their labor is sufficiently unattractive that they will be willing to forgo some of their quasi-rent rather than leave the job.) If a worker's asset has no appropriable quasi-rent attached to it, "either his assets have no quasi-rents at all or the quasi-rents are not appropriable. If the former is the case, the worker would earn about the same wage he would get if that asset were deployed in its next best use; this would be the case with unskilled labor in a tight labor market. If there are quasi-rents associated with his labor assets but these are not appropriable, that means there are competitors willing to offer the worker about the value of what he is selling."[19]

To be considered exploited, workers must be given less than the full value of their contribution and also have no alternative that is not worse. Given the way Arnold defines *value* and *contribution* (one's contribution is simply the value of one's asset), "if the quasi-rents of their assets are non-existent, then they are getting the full value of their contribution [thus, unskilled workers cannot be exploited!]. On the other hand, if their assets have associated quasi-rents but they are not appropriable in the sense implied by the definition, then whether or not they are paid the full value of their contributions, the workers are not exploited."[20]

This is true according to Arnold's analysis in competitively efficient markets or on the leading edges of markets in transition. The only way most workers (including unskilled workers) could nonetheless be systematically exploited is if labor markets were always stagnant, and workers had nowhere else to go. Arnold thinks that "the fact of labor mobility refutes the idea that all, or nearly all, workers in a free enterprise system are usually in a situation where all the alternatives are considerably worse than continuing to do what they have been doing."[21]

In this analysis, and in the examples discussed earlier, Arnold assumes that the competitively efficient market price for an item—a good, a service, a wage, a rent, whatever—is a fair price. For this to be the case, given that a competitive market tends to reward in accordance with marginal product, (1) the marginal product of land, labor, and capital must genuinely reflect the productive contributions of landowners, workers, and capitalists, and (2) the norm of productive contribution must be ethically decisive—that is, what is fair is that each should receive the value of his or her productive contribution. The first premise is false, and the second is indefensible.

On the issue of contribution, Arnold aligns himself with marginalist economists who define the contributions of the various factors of production as the marginal product of each factor, the output resulting from the last (marginal) unit added of that factor, other factors held constant. As Schweickart illustrates, "the marginal product of labor, given ten workers and five acres of land, is the difference between what ten workers and nine workers would produce on those five acres."[22] Thus, the contribution of ten laborers is that marginal product times ten. The marginal product of the land is the difference between what those ten workers would produce on four acres and on five acres, and the contribution of land is five times that marginal product. The sleight of hand involved in marginalist discussions of contribution is the equation of the contribution of factors of production (which add up to the total output) and the contribution of the owners of those factors. Again, Schweickart illustrates, "In physical terms, the marginal product of the land is simply the amount by which production would decline if one acre were taken out of cultivation. It does not reflect any *productive activity* whatsoever on the part of the owner of the land. *It does not, therefore, measure his productive contribution.*"[23] The same is true of capital and its owner.

Thus, Arnold has failed to establish that the owner of capital makes a contribution, much less one proportional to returns received on capital. To think otherwise is to be committed to the view that the more one owns and the less one does, the more one contributes, a fetishistic doctrine if ever there was one.

This immediately relates to another topic, the distinctiveness of labor, for in the market returns to owners of factors of production, only the owners of labor receive returns in some way apportioned to their personal contributions. The contributors of land and capital, by contrast, receive proportionately greater returns the less they actually labor and the more they simply own. In addition, as noted earlier, unskilled workers are never exploited according to Arnold's definition, no matter how hard they work or how little they are paid and no matter how high the level of unemployment, as long as they are getting the competitive market value for their labor. The intuition is thus appropriate, in all the variants of Marxist theories of exploitation, that what is to be explained is the exploitation of labor; the theory does not artificially narrow the concept of exploitation. On the contrary, Arnold's broadening of the concept, incisive as it is for identifying potential inefficiencies and local unfairness, leads to bizarre conclusions when employed as a standard of distributive justice.

Even if we were to accept that the competitive market prices for land, labor, and capital accurately reflected the productive contributions of their owners, there would still be a problem with taking productive contributions as a standard of justice and "exploitation" as the decisive measure of injustice.[24] Arnold acknowledges that exploitation is only one aspect of distributive justice and does not claim to offer a general theory of distributive justice.[25] Yet when arguing for the importance of his position that market socialism is, on the whole, more "exploitative" than capitalism, he takes the failure of reciprocity to be an "injustice" and cites Rawls' dictum that justice is the first virtue of social institutions, and he thereby intimates that "exploitation" is akin to violations of the principles of justice.[26] Given the close connection between his definitions of *exploitation* and *efficiency*, however, this is virtually to conflate efficiency and justice. Such a conclusion, rather than closing the case for capitalism, simply sends us back to the theory of justice for a more comprehensive and adequate treatment of the topic. It is widely recognized that efficient systems can be highly unjust. A system in which one person owns everything and wallows in luxury, while every one else labors hard on the edge of starvation could be an efficient system, though it would hardly be a just one.[27]

The surface plausibility of Arnold's argument partially derives from another confusion. The idea that labor effort should be positively correlated with reward is plausible, but it needs to be distinguished from the stronger notion of strict proportionality, in which labor receives its full value. Even the laborer (not to mention the capitalist) has no strong moral claim to the "full value" (marginal product) of his or her product, for this ignores the claims, for example, on the basis of need, of other people. Although he does not condemn taxation, it would seem to follow from Arnold's definition of exploitation that whenever the state taxes workers to support disabled people, it is exploiting the workers. If so, this is a reductio ad absurdum of the notion that "exploitation" is a legitimate standard of justice.[28]

Once this is understood, all of Arnold's fine discriminations of ways that a market-socialist economy will deviate more than a capitalist economy from efficient ("fair") exchanges become inconclusive, if not thoroughly misleading, when presented with a view to an assessment of the relative justice of the two systems. That inefficient exchanges are couched in the normatively charged language of exploitation only adds to the misleading effect.

The same is true of Marx's use of the concept of exploitation. On one level, the term simply describes the process by which the product of labor is appropriated by the capitalist. Yet on another level, the term suggests that this appropriation is unjust, that workers are being coercively and unfairly treated.[29] Indeed they are, but Marx's analysis does not demonstrate this. What is needed is a further argument that the inequality of wealth and power in capitalist society between workers and capitalists (and more generally between those who are better off and the less advantaged) is greater than some other feasible arrangement that could be consented to by all under reasonable conditions. By *reasonable conditions,* I mean some suitably defined hypothetical contract situation that would screen out the obvious biases that would, for example, block the consent of a capitalist to any reduction of his or her wealth.

If—and it is a big *if*—some form of capitalism, undoubtedly one with strong redistributive institutions and wide dispersal of ownership and control of wealth, could deliver a better life for the less well off than any feasible socialist alternative, then the transfer of wealth from workers to capitalists would not be unjust. But if a feasible socialist alternative could make the least advantaged better off (not just in material terms), capitalist exploitation must be judged unjust. Analogously, if the forms of exploitation Arnold identifies as more likely under market socialism than under capitalism are nevertheless an ineliminable part of a package in which, on the whole, the least advantaged are better off under market socialism, the exploitation would not be unjust.

The terms of comparison in the capitalism–socialism debate need to be shifted onto the terrain of the theory of justice. There, Arnold's analysis has a modest place, showing the probable sources of inefficiencies in a market-socialist system (and opportunities for the emergence of inequality).[30] Socialists do need to be concerned about efficiency. A system that is so inefficient that the least advantaged (and, if everyone were equal that would be everyone) are worse off than the least advantaged under a capitalist system will be comparatively unjust, other things equal. But justice allows for some losses of efficiency for the sake of justice. The burden of proof is thus on Arnold to show that the inferior incentives under market socialism vis-à-vis capitalism for managers, monitors, providers of capital, and others to do their jobs would result in inefficiencies so massive as to result in a system more unjust, on balance, than capitalism.

## NOTES

1. N. Scott Arnold, *Marx's Radical Critique of Capitalist Society* (Oxford: Oxford University Press, 1990), 150.

2. Arnold, *Marx's Radical Critique of Capitalist Society,* 158–59. It should be noted that "commodity fetishism" refers not to a preoccupation with consumption, as the term is sometimes loosely used, but rather to the mystification surrounding the origin of the value of commodities, as analyzed in chapter 4.

3. Arnold, *Marx's Radical Critique of Capitalist Society,* 3–27.

4. Karl Marx, *Critique of the Gotha Program,* in *Karl Marx: Selected Writings,* ed. David McLellan (Oxford: Oxford University Press, 1977), 569.

5. For another view, not premised on all these conditions, see Robert J. van der Veen and Philippe Van Parijs, "A Capitalist Road to Communism," *Theory and Society* 15, no. 5 (1986), 635–55.

6. Arnold, *Marx's Radical Critique of Capitalist Society,* 227 ff.

7. See Allen Buchanan, *Marx and Justice* (Totowa, N.J.: Rowman & Littlefield, 1982) for a similar argument.

8. Arnold, *Marx's Radical Critique of Capitalist Society,* 275–78.

9. Arnold, *Marx's Radical Critique of Capitalist Society,* 278–79.

10. Because a self-interested cooperative seeks to maximize income per worker, not total profits, nothing is gained by expanding production and taking on new workers, ceteris paribus; David Schweickart, *Against Capitalism* (Cambridge: Cambridge University Press, 1994), chapter four.

11. N. Scott Arnold, *The Philosophy and Economics of Market Socialism* (Oxford: Oxford University Press, 1994); Schweickart, *Against Capitalism.*

12. Paul Warren has argued that the stipulation that there be no better alternative is too restrictive. If workers are in a relationship of unequal power with those who own capital and, as a result, perform uncompensated labor, one wants to say that they are exploited, even if they have alternatives. For purposes of my argument, I will not press this point against Arnold. See Paul Warren, "Should Marxists Be Liberal Egalitarians?" *Journal of Political Philosophy* 5, no. 1 (March 1997): 47–68, 64.

13. Given his definition of exploitation, there could never be a market economy free of exploitation. Thus, the question becomes how to minimize it. Arnold goes on to argue that the opportunities for exploitation in market socialism surpass those under capitalism.

The types of exploitation Arnold discusses are the following:

- exploitation among and by the residual claimants in the cooperative (compared with the residual claimants in capitalist enterprises; this comparison is assumed throughout)
- exploitation by opportunistic workers and monitors
- exploitation of and by the firm's managers
- exploitation of the capital providers
- exploitation along the firm-market boundary
- exploitation through the state, through valuation of assets and through state control of new investment

14. Arnold, *The Philosophy and Economics of Market Socialism,* 181–83.

15. Arnold, *The Philosophy and Economics of Market Socialism,* 185–87.

16. Arnold, *The Philosophy and Economics of Market Socialism,* 74.

17. Arnold, *The Philosophy and Economics of Market Socialism,* 77.

18. Arnold, *The Philosophy and Economics of Market Socialism*, 68. See Schweickart, *Against Capitalism*, 20–29, for a refutation of the justification of capitalist profit and interest with reference to time preference. He points out that the supplier of capital only *influences* the allocation of labor, which could be shaped in other ways, but in no credible way supplies "time." In any case, the reward to capital is out of proportion to any labor the capitalist contributes.

19. Arnold, *The Philosophy and Economics of Market Socialism*, 154.

20. Arnold, *The Philosophy and Economics of Market Socialism*, 155.

21. Arnold, *The Philosophy and Economics of Market Socialism*, 163.

22. Schweickart, *Against Capitalism*, 6.

23. Schweickart, *Against Capitalism*, 10.

24. Arnold implicitly acknowledges that his concept of exploitation is not morally decisive in a critique of market socialism when he includes the elimination of exploitation as only one of the several ends to be achieved by the institutions of market socialism. The others include (1)"the achievement of a reasonable standard of living"; (2)"the end of alienation in the workplace"; (3)"the collective control of the rate and direction of economic growth and development"; (4)"the prevention or correction of the social irrationalities that would otherwise arise from the operation of the market"; and (5)"the achievement of (relative) equality of material condition"; Arnold, *The Philosophy and Economics of Market Socialism*, 61–64. Market pricing serves the first of these, self-management the second, state control of investment supported by a capital usage fee the third and fourth, state ownership and self-management the fifth, and the combination of self-management and the capital usage fee serve to end exploitation. I think few market socialists would quarrel with these as the main ends or with the relation of means to ends.

It is odd, however, that Arnold then focuses almost his entire book on the topic of exploitation, employing a conception of exploitation that no socialist could agree with and that cannot bear the normative weight he places upon it. He explicitly acknowledges that exploitation is not equivalent to injustice; see 90 and 157.

25. Arnold, *The Philosophy and Economics of Market Socialism*, 90.

26. John Rawls, *A Theory of Justice* (Cambridge: Harvard University Press, 1971), 3; Arnold, *The Philosophy and Economics of Market Socialism*, 233, 259.

27. Rawls, *A Theory of Justice*, 67–75.

28. Philippe Van Parijs, *Real Freedom for All: What (If Anything) Can Justify Capitalism?* (Oxford: Clarendon Press, 1995), 169: "Proportionality between income and effort is, therefore, fundamentally incomplete as a specification of distributive justice. It needs to be supplemented with a fair division of opportunities." Even if the initial distribution of assets were fair and we then considered competitively efficient market transactions to be just, the fairness would last only for a generation, as the inheritors of inequality would start from initially unequal, hence, unfair positions. Of course, in any known capitalist society, the initial distribution of assets is not fair.

29. It is clear from his *Critique of the Gotha Program* that Marx did not accept productive contribution as a standard of justice. There he explicitly repudiates the Lasallean principle that workers should receive the "undiminished proceeds" of their labor; *Critique of the Gotha Program*, in *Karl Marx: Selected Writings*, ed. David McLellan (Oxford: Oxford University Press, 1977), 566–70.

30. Arnold, *The Philosophy and Economics of Market Socialism*, 259. Although, as I argue, Arnold's conception of exploitation leaves much to be desired as a principle of

justice and so does not settle the question of the comparative merits of capitalism versus market socialism, still the problems he identifies in the working of a market-socialist economy are well worth studying and ought to concern socialists and merit a more considered response than I can offer here. The reason for this is that "exploitation" as he defines it is possible in any market economy meeting four plausible conditions:

> (1) assets that support many exchanges are specialized and thus have quasi-rents associated with them; (2) these assets get locked into transactions in the sense that they are costly to redeploy once they are committed; (3) the owners of these assets suffer from bounded rationality and make agreements in an environment in which not all future contingencies can be foreseen, and (4) transactors are sometimes given to opportunism on behalf of themselves or on behalf of others. . . . This penchant for opportunism is variable across individuals and is not easily knowable. (Arnold, *The Philosophy and Economics of Market Socialism*, 169)

Arnold thinks that market socialists might be reluctant to grant that propensities toward opportunism would be as great under market socialism as under capitalism. But otherwise, these are reasonable assumptions. Even the assumption about opportunism allows scope for altruism in human affairs. The socialist theorist must be wary of wishing away problems by appeal to the character-transforming potential of egalitarian institutions or revolutionary solidarity.

Having said that, it is perhaps one of the strongest virtues of Arnold's analysis to have identified those problem areas in which individualistic opportunism may undermine the socialist project and a credible theory of collective action and supervenient solidarity is needed to save socialism, even market socialism, from the charge of utopianism. Arnold has shown the ways in which such solidarity is not apt to be generated within the economic institutions per se—quite the contrary. Thus, what is needed is a more comprehensive moral sociology, making credible the ways in which opportunistic economic motives could be overridden by political, social, and moral concerns. (Once again, this represents a kind of move from Marx to Hegel, from the obliteration of the division between civil society and state to a reiteration of the "higher" corrective and redemptive role of the state and extraeconomic institutions and associations in civil society.)

# 6

# A Critique of Participatory Planning

Before I turn to a detailed discussion of models of market socialism, it is necessary to address a question that will certainly be raised by some on the Left: Why give up on planning just because of failures experienced with the Soviet model? That model was compromised by one-party dictatorship and bureaucracy. Could it not be the case that a democratic and participatory planning process could take the place of the market yet avoid the inefficiencies and irrationalities of Soviet-style central planning?

Let us first be clear about what these latter are and why they are thought to have occurred. The brief sketch provided here of a vast literature should suffice, if not to justify, at least to render plausible my assumption of a market economy in goods and services in the models discussed in chapter 8. Some of the difficulties encountered in planned economies will also provide a backdrop for some of my hesitations about investment planning.

## CENTRAL PLANNING

In the two decades after World War II the economies of Eastern Europe achieved respectable growth rates by anyone's measure. Central planning facilitated rapid industrialization, full employment, and stability. The Soviet Union was able to keep up with the United States in the arms race despite an economy half its size. Though marked by inequality, its income differentials were significantly less than in capitalist countries.[1] The economy that went furthest toward market coordination, that of Yugoslavia, also experienced growing inequalities between rich and poor regions and substantial unemployment, only partially alleviated by

worker migration to Western Europe. So it is understandable that many socialists are still skeptical about the socialist potential of a market economy: planning seems necessary to avoid the inefficiency of unemployment—a massive
underutilization of human potential—and unjust widening of income differentials. Later I argue that at least two variants of market socialism promise greater
equality in comparison with capitalism and that through investment planning—
not detailed planning of production—the problem of unemployment may be addressed well enough to tip the balance against central planning.

On the other hand, centrally planned economies failed to provide an adequate
supply of consumer goods. Shortages were chronic, and the planning process
produced irrational mismatches with consumer needs (as when a chandelier factory responded to a production target in tons by producing heavy chandeliers).
Market externalities, such as pollution, were not internalized. It also failed to
institutionalize technological innovation.

John Roemer discusses two types of explanations of these failures. The first
focuses on principal–agent problems, problems rising from an inability of one
party, the principal, to get the other party, the agent, to do what it has agreed or
is supposed to do. The lack of incentives (or of disincentives, such as fear of being
fired) for workers is a problem for managers. Managers' failing to eliminate inefficiencies is a problem for state planners who lack the knowledge or political
will to identify and close down inefficient enterprises. The planners' failing to
respond to consumer demands is, in turn, a problem for the public. The last of
these might be thought to be rectified, to some degree anyway, through political
democracy. But the former two (lack of incentives for managers and workers)
would seem to require the discipline of competition between enterprises and the
possibility of bankruptcy. Competition also links consumers to producers through
the market. Despite much evidence to support the principal–agent explanation,
Roemer considers it inadequate, given the rates of growth achieved in planned
economies for several decades in spite of such problems. Roemer's preferred
explanation for the failure of central planning is that, again because of a lack of
competition, there was insufficient incentive to innovate. After the postwar re-
construction ended, technological innovation became increasingly important for
economic development, but command economies slipped further and further behind.[2]

On either account, a market economy, institutionalizing competition among
enterprises in the production of consumer goods and services, is the key to any
viable future socialism. Not everyone has accepted this verdict that there is no
"third way" between market economies and the failed socialist planned economies.[3] (Note, I say "market economies," not capitalism, for it is a central thesis
of this book that, in opposition to apologists for capitalism such as Scott Arnold,
varieties of market socialism are, indeed, third ways between capitalism and centrally planned socialism.)

Let us assume that the planning process could be democratic and participatory, as advocated by Albert and Hahnel. Workers participate in producer councils, consumers give input concerning their needs through consumer councils or by means of their own personal computers. The process is open, and it allows for public discussions at different levels and multiple iterations before decisions are made.[4] Can this be done without markets *and* without central planning? As Alec Nove has written, "the resultant production and allocation decisions must reflect the priorities decided (by whatever means) by 'society' or its representatives. Decisions once made must be implemented, which involves the commitment of resources produced in many parts of the country or outside it. . . . Some body (somebody) must allocate resources between alternative uses."[5]

The complexity of such an allocation, when not left to market exchanges, is evident from the following questions Nove poses:

How by this route can one discover the relative intensity of people's wants, which is signaled (however imperfectly) by willingness to pay? How is one to deal with the predictable outcome—that total desires exceed the means of satisfying them? How about quality: who will opt for the cheaper cuts of meat, for instance? Finally, what remedy is available to those citizens who find that what they ask for is not supplied? And what powers are available to the planners to ensure that what they have decided is in fact implemented?[6]

Diane Elson has also asked how planning will accommodate the unexpected, both at the outset, when households must estimate their needs in advance, and as patterns of income distribution and technology and production costs change, which would ordinarily bring about shifts in demand.[7] These questions admit of answers. But Nove remains skeptical—as do I—that any planning process, democratic or otherwise, with or without the aid of computers, can handle the complexity of meeting consumer needs and demands with anything approximating the efficiency of markets.

## PARTICIPATORY ECONOMICS: A THIRD WAY?

Albert and Hahnel offer a description of a possible economy that is decentralized and nonmarket, designed to promote "equity, solidarity, variety, and collective self-management." Markets and central planning are both opposed because they "deny workers information about the situation of consumers and other workers and subordinate workers to powers beyond their reach. Both divide the workforce into task makers and task doers and rely on material incentives and coercion. Both create competition, regimentation, inequality, coercion, experts, and instrumental decision making."[8]

One of the complaints about market prices is that they misrepresent true social costs and benefits. What comes to mind are familiar externalities, such as pollution, not reflected in the cost of production. Centrally planned economies also fail to circulate the information planners have.[9] Even if such externalities were internalized, Albert and Hahnel would object to (1) the reduction to quantitative measures of the human costs and benefits, (2) the reduction of motivation to material incentives, which is hard to avoid when all that consumers and producers encounter are prices, and (3) the opportunities for accumulation that money affords and the resulting skewing of demand toward the wealthy.[10]

In place of markets and central planning they propose a decentralized, "social, iterative procedure" for creating a plan for production and consumption.[11] Individual consumers would, once a year, feed into their computers an account of their wants for the coming year. Workers would individually propose the type and quantity of work they would do (subject in later iterations to coordination with co-workers). After these first proposals—which Albert and Hahnel acknowledge would not result in a coherent match of supply and demand—successive iterations would bring wants and production plans into alignment. Prices figure into these calculations, starting with estimations based on the previous year, then adjustments up or down by Iteration Facilitation Boards (IFBs) based on initial and subsequent input by consumers, workers, and councils at various levels addressing collective consumption.

Albert and Hahnel claim that "nothing about this approach compels actors to change proposals at all. . . . On the other hand, there is pressure on workplaces to propose at least average amounts of productive labor and on consumer councils to limit consumption to roughly average per capita value."[12] They never say what this "pressure" comes to in the final analysis. If a workplace refuses to work the average, or a community insists on receiving what others judge to be more than its fair share, it is unclear how the plan will be enforced. The potential for dissension will certainly require a significant policing apparatus, which is never explicitly discussed in the model.

Although they claim that the IFBs make no decisions, they have enormous power in the later rounds, in constructing "their best estimates of (say) five feasible plans" and, after a round or two, of voting a comprehensive plan.[13] Though it builds upon local initiatives, this is, in the end, centralization, and it could well displease everyone, as voting paradoxes easily illustrate.[14] Whether a given participant has a principled commitment to the outcome of the process depends upon the importance and intent of the issue and the participant's commitment to the democratic process per se. Nothing about the process itself can provide the commitment, and if the outcome is irrational for an individual, compliance may require coercion. Yet Albert and Hahnel claim that their scheme does away with coercion.

Take, as one example, allocation of work. Albert and Hahnel advocate the restructuring of "job complexes," which are roughly equally desirable with respect to danger, unpleasantness, challenge, and the like. This might entail restructuring many jobs or sharing more of the dirty, hard, dangerous, and boring work. A worker in a dangerous and dirty steel mill might spend only twenty hours a week there and the rest of his or her time working in a day-care center or a museum. The goal here is not only to produce equitable sharing of the undesirable and desirable work but also to break down the patterns of domination arising from unequal skill and authority. The goal is admirable, but it may carry a high cost in efficiency. Leaving that aside, there is also a conceptual difficulty: how to compare incommensurable qualities like dangerousness and pleasantness. A labor market can do this, once participants are equally positioned, by the possibility of exit. (My proposal for a basic income would enable exit and so remove the coercion that now forces many into dangerous and otherwise undesirable work for low pay.) In participatory economics, however, someone has to pass judgment on the equivalence of different job complexes. Albert and Hahnel assume this enormous task to have been completed before the much easier accounting in terms of hours is done. But suppose a grave digger proposes that he work fewer hours at the same income because of the emotional distress connected with the work, on top of its dirtiness, exposure to disease, and so on. Others are not persuaded; the grave digger must then accept his lot or—lose his full income? lose his job? The sanctions for noncompliance are unclear.

The main point is that there is substantial room not just for attempts to cheat or take advantage, which Albert and Hahnel address, but for honest and profound disagreements about what is reasonable and fair. For this, peer pressure not to be a free rider is beside the point. In politicizing the consumption process—each person's plan is subject to criticism and rejection by the neighborhood and, indirectly, by higher levels—it is ironic that Albert and Hahnel give an account that appears devoid of politics and power. In this respect their vision of civil society has not gone beyond Engels's idea of politics' being replaced by the "administration of things."

I leave to the reader the exploration of the details of decision making in Albert and Hahnel's account. I find that, apart from their conjecture that the iterative process will bring about an equilibrium between supply and demand—in the end, no doubt, with the very visible hand of the IFB—none of Nove's or Elson's questions are satisfactorily addressed. What happens after the plan is produced, and what is done when producers comply in perverse ways or when goods are of uneven quality, is left to the imagination.

Without embracing egoism, one can also doubt whether there would be any incentive to innovate. Because job complexes are to be kept roughly equal, groups of workers will not reap great benefit from labor-saving devices, as they would in a market economy. Such innovations will force them to restructure their job complexes to take on other work. At the same time, "in a participatory economy innovations in thousands of plants change the *overall societal average work load and work quality norms* and . . . those changes redound equally to *everyone's* benefit."[15] The trouble is that each person experiences only a tiny fraction of the benefit of each innovation and suffers little or no benefit, and perhaps much disruption and anxiety, for his or her own innovations. There is every incentive to not innovate or to conceal innovations.

Albert and Hahnel allow for a time lag to provide some material incentive for innovation to be decided by "job-balancing committees." These committees, like the IFBs, have enormous discretion over very complicated issues concerning the comparability of different sorts of work and take much of the freedom of job design out of the hands of those engaged in the work. In addition to these practical difficulties, I find the vision of participatory economics that Albert and Hahnel offer to be undesirable compared with market socialism, with respect to work and income equality and consumption planning.

## COMPARABILITY OF JOBS AND EQUALITY OF INCOMES

As should be clear from chapter 1, I do not think that justice requires equality to the degree called for by Albert and Hahnel. Distribution of wealth and power must be sensitive to inequalities of power flowing from job complexes and the kinds of learning and behavior associated with them; Albert and Hahnel allow departures from equality only for the sake of need, savings, or borrowing. I see no reason not to allow greater departures from equality when everyone would benefit. If this Rawlsian formulation seems too inegalitarian, the concern with domination is captured by the Rousseauian principle that no one should be so rich that he can buy another and no one so poor that he can be bought; yet this is still less egalitarian than the proposal of Albert and Hahnel.

## CONSUMPTION PLANNING

Perhaps I am committing the "fallacy of unimaginative projection," but I cannot foresee being able to rationally predict my consumption of everything I consume for an entire year in advance, except for a few necessities such as heat, housing, and electricity.[16] The scheme allows for changes in one's consumption, but one has to appeal these. A moment's reflection on how one consumes in a market reveals how much one relies on the general availability of goods for needs that arise spontaneously and unpredictably and also how great a role perception plays in the selection of goods. The computer-guided planning process makes no room for me to hand-pick my tomatoes or to shop elsewhere when the quality is bad. As long as the producers have fulfilled their quotas, I must take what I get.

Even if I could rationalize my consumption in this way, why should I want to make my choices subject to the veto of a consumer's council? I acknowledge the desirability of getting everyone to be more thoughtful in their consumption, about the ways in which goods are made and the effects of using them. But I doubt that this would happen to any appreciable degree in the process described, because the volume of information confronting each individual would be too overwhelming.

Albert and Hahnel claim that the allocation system "promotes solidarity by providing information necessary for people to empathize with one another and by creating a context in which people have not only the means to consider one another's circumstances but also the incentive to do so."[17] The information is necessary but not sufficient. In the process, individuals will be most anxious to get their requests approved. To come to the point of empathizing, they would need to seek out the information provided by every producer—that is, they must already have the motivation that is supposed to be an outcome of the process. They would also have to trust the information provided; and in the qualitative dimension needed for empathy, there is no effective check on the accuracy of the information forthcoming from people in whose interest it is to present themselves in the best light possible. Although market prices often conceal externalities, they are also often relatively accurate reflections of social costs and benefits. The virtual prices in the participatory planning process will tend to predominate, just as market prices do in markets despite the availability of information on boycotts. To attend to anything else, except in egregious cases (like General Electric or Nestle, subjected to boycotts because of their nuclear weapons production and sale of dangerous infant formula in impoverished countries, respectively), makes consumption too complicated and time consuming. In the end, my objection is that the process would make us all preoccupied with petty details that rightly should be more marginal in our consciousness than creative work, beauty, love, friendship, discovery of truth, and other high values that we should strive to keep out of the market, out of the state, and also impervious to participatory planning.

Albert and Hahnel claim that their proposal would preserve privacy in that consumer requests would be made anonymously, but it is hard to see how this anonymity could be preserved at the level of neighborhoods. I am sure my neighbors could rather quickly identify who it was that thought it so important to purchase the collected works of Marx. In comparison, the anonymity of the market appears liberating and worth the risk of some irresponsible consumption, the most egregious sorts of which can be regulated or taxed or challenged in the forum of civil society.

The decentralization of decisions in a market economy is further desirable for the scope it affords for enterprise self-management. In even a democratically planned economy enterprises are largely restricted, after having only a small fraction of the input, to plan fulfillment on the output side, and the central authority has all the familiar principal–agent problems in getting enterprises to fulfill their parts of the plans.

It may be objected here that I am assuming an individualistic or small-group concept of freedom, ignoring the collective freedom of the society in determining its own destiny that planning makes possible. (I, after all, make a similar criticism of Van Parijs's individualism in chapter 1.) I am not against all centralization. Along with Nove, I would favor centralization of power generation and mass transportation, for example.[18] I would add that in some circumstances scarcity could warrant the administered allocation of certain basic necessities—basic health care, or milk for children, as is done in Cuba, for example, in accordance with priorities generally agreed upon. (No child should be allowed to go hungry.) Furthermore, I support democratic planning of investment (see chapter 8) precisely because it enables the community to address problems that face the whole community but no particular individual in it, such as provision for future generations, global pollution, and systematic unemployment. But here we are talking about planning of production and consumption, the coordination of inputs and outputs, and in this area, it seems, markets function better than the best-made plans could ever do—to enable agents to find the inputs they need, at costs they are willing to incur, in order to produce outputs that, from their own experience, they think will meet a need at a cost others are willing to incur.

## BEYOND WORKER OWNERSHIP

Where does this critique of planning leave us? Must we accept as the only feasible alternative a mixed economy, consisting of worker cooperatives, some state-owned enterprises, and a state with the regulatory and redistributive functions familiar in social democracy? If that were the case, we would be placing a heavy burden on workplace democracy to bring about the desired level of equality, work humanization, participation, and transcendence of alienation. In chapter 7, I examine the extent to which this has been accomplished in the Mondragon cooperatives. For now, I will only assert that such a system might better be called worker capitalism than market socialism and will point toward additional measures that would be needed to complement workplace democracy as thus far sketched.

## INVESTMENT PLANNING

Democracy in the workplace is only one dimension of economic democracy, and by itself it is misleadingly called socialist. Enterprises would still act in isolation from all other actors, and public goods and bads would remain "external" to decision making, unless they were addressed by the government. Inequalities of incomes as a result of differential capital intensity and other morally irrelevant factors would continue, mitigated only by lower differentials within enterprises. Unemployment could be expected, without collective measures to promote full employment.

For these reasons, among others, economic democracy should include a second dimension: democratic investment planning. Such planning still leaves to the market and to individual enterprises the setting of prices and decisions about what and how to produce. Investment funds are accumulated through taxation (as in Schweickart's proposal for a charge on capital assets). They are then disbursed to regional or local banks (in Schweickart's proposal, with an equal amount per capita) and loaned on the basis of democratically established criteria. These would obviously include the normal concerns with efficiency but could also address directly in the investment process—rather than indirectly through regulation—environmental concerns, employment creation, and other common interests external to profit maximization. I discuss the pros and cons of investment planning in greater detail in part 2.

## SOCIALIZATION OF THE MARKET

Investment planning opens up a space for democracy alongside the political system and the workplace; but it still leaves entirely private and atomized both consumption and the relationship between households and the market. There is reason to expect tendencies toward concentration in a market economy and thus a predominance of large firms. Diane Elson asks, "What is to impede the interests of producing enterprises dominating over those of households both as consumers, and as sellers of labour power?"[19]

One key problem is the isolation of consumers from one another, such that they not only choose independently of one another but also in ignorance of what others are choosing.[20] This could be remedied by planning but also by creating institutions that provide information about the producers and other consumers and by strengthening informal networks based on trust that are mediated by neither market nor state. In this context a basic income would strengthen the household vis-à-vis the labor market, as no one would be forced into work out of poverty. It would also acknowledge the reality of household work without commodifying it and lessen the dependence of women on men.[21]

Consumers' organizations would also enable households to hold enterprises more accountable. "A fully open information system between enterprises is . . . a key feature of socialized markets. . ." Markets themselves, rather than being created solely by enterprises, would be partially structured by public agencies. The latter would promote a greater flow of information, countering the concealment that is characteristic of profit-seeking enterprises, collecting information on quality, costs and prices, and establishing price norms to guide the formation of prices and wages. The information thus generated would, in turn, facilitate indicative planning on the Japanese or French model, or investment planning as advocated by Schweickart, and would help to reduce unemployment through matching of job seekers to vacancies, as well as enforcing minimum standards.[22]

Thus,

> Open access to information is the key to conscious control of the economy. There has been a tendency among Marxists (beginning with Marx) to interpret conscious control in terms of gathering all relevant information at one decision-making point and of taking decisions with full knowledge of all inter-connections and ramifications. That is an impossible, and an undesirable goal. Conscious control is better interpreted as open access to all available information concerning the product and its price so that any decision-maker has access to the same information as any other.[23]

I return to the theme of open access to information in chapter eleven, in which I explore ways in which the media might be democratized. It should be clear initially that it would not be enough to make the media accountable to media workers. Beyond that, and to some extent in conflict with it, is the need to provide wider access to the media and, more generally, to provide access to many sources of information now private and inaccessible. By such measures the atomizing tendencies of the market can be overcome, without the elimination of commodity production.

## NOTES

1. Michael Ellman, "Changing Views on Central Economic Planning: 1958–1983," *ACES Bulletin* 25, 1 (Spring 1983): 11-29, 12–13, 19.

2. John Roemer, *A Future for Socialism* (Cambridge: Harvard University Press, 1994), 37–45.

3. This is the thesis of Nove's *The Economics of Feasible Socialism Revisited* (London: HarperCollins, 1991).

4. This is the model presented by Michael Albert and Robin Hahnel, *Looking Forward: Participatory Economics for the Twenty-First Century* (Boston: South End Press, 1991).

5. Alec Nove, "Markets and Socialism," *New Left Review* 161 (January–February 1987), 98–104, 100.

6. Nove, "Markets and Socialism," 100.

7. Diane Elson, "Market Socialism or Socialization of the Market?" *New Left Review* 172, (November–December 1988): 3–43, 24–27.

8. Albert and Hahnel, *Looking Forward*, 67.

9. Albert and Hahnel, *Looking Forward*, 68.

10. Albert and Hahnel, *Looking Forward*, 69–70.

11. Albert and Hahnel, *Looking Forward*, 70.

12. Albert and Hahnel, *Looking Forward*, 87.

13. Albert and Hahnel, *Looking Forward*, 86.

14. A prefers golf to swimming and swimming to baseball. B prefers swimming to baseball and baseball to golf. C prefers baseball to golf and golf to swimming. What does the majority rank at the top? Two-thirds prefer golf to swimming. Two-thirds prefer swimming to baseball, and two-thirds prefer baseball to golf. Two-thirds will be unhappy with any first choice.

15. Albert and Hahnel, *Looking Forward*, 98.

16. Albert and Hahnel, *Looking Forward*, 67.

17. Albert and Hahnel, *Looking Forward*, 129.

18. Nove, "Markets and Socialism," 100.

19. Elson, "Market Socialism or Socialization of the Market?" 9.

20. This is Elson's interpretation of "commodity fetishism"; Elson, "Market Socialism or Socialization of the Market?" 13.

21. Elson, "Market Socialism or Socialization of the Market?" 28–29.

22. Elson, "Market Socialism or Socialization of the Market?" 28, 32, 33, 35.

23. Elson, "Market Socialism or Socialization of the Market?" 43.

# Part 2

## Institutions of Self-Managed Market Socialism

# Introduction to Part 2

The collapse of the socialist economies of Eastern Europe, including those experimenting with novel forms of ownership, management, and markets as in Hungary or Yugoslavia, has sharpened the institutional crisis of socialism: Is there any feasible socialist alternative to capitalism? Fortunately for the socialist project, not all possibilities have been tried. Some of these possibilities, variants of "market socialism," are examined in chapter 8. To further motivate the discussion, I begin with a chapter on worker ownership. Some might think of a cooperative as socialism in microcosm, and in many respects it is. However, a society of cooperatives in and of itself falls short of a just society. It also runs into difficulties of sustainability and replicability that, together with concerns about justice, will lead us to consider the more thoroughly socialist models in chapter 8. Because not everyone is a paid worker, the ideal of self-management is incomplete and needs to be complemented by institutions that address the situation of nonpaid workers. The basic-income proposal defended earlier fits this need. Chapter 9 makes more explicit how basic income would benefit unemployed and marginally employed workers and also how it might reinforce and be reinforced by economic democracy.

# 7

# Worker Ownership: Socialism in Microcosm?

If a picture is worth a thousand words, a successful experiment is worth a thousand blueprints. For those convinced that only capitalist enterprises are viable, with their wage labor, their extraction of surplus from workers for nonworking owners, their authoritarian work relations, their hundred-to-one (or larger) salary differentials, their employment insecurity, their dehumanizing labor process, their relentless pursuit of growth, their propensity toward capital flight, their resistance to environmental regulation, unions, and sometimes even political democracy—for those resigned to all that, the worker cooperatives of Mondragon, in the Basque region of Spain, provide an arresting counterexample.[1] Although, as I argue, worker ownership by itself is inadequate as a just alternative to contemporary capitalism, the cooperative enterprise form exemplified in Mondragon is a key part of such an alternative.

Since the mid-1950s, when the first Mondragon co-op was founded by a Catholic priest and graduates of his technical school, a network has unfolded of more than one hundred cooperatives, many of them capital intensive (making machine tools, for example), competing on the world market, employing more than thirty thousand workers. There have been only three business failures in the history of the group.

The co-ops have weathered bad economic times by sharing work, transferring members from one firm to another. They are remarkably productive and profitable. At the same time they have given embodiment to participatory, egalitarian democracy and community. Managers are hired by a board of directors elected by the workers, on the basis of one person, one vote. Workers own shares in their firms but get no extra voting rights for greater shares, and the cost of buying into a co-op is never prohibitive. Labor relations are far less conflictual than in capitalist firms, and there has been only one strike in the history of the group. Income differentials do not exceed seven to one.[2] A portion of co-op income goes to support various social services, pensions, a technical school, and social security.

At the heart of the group is a co-op bank, the Caja Laboral Popular, governed in part by its workers, in part by representatives from the co-ops. It is responsible not only for providing loans but also for ensuring that the affiliated co-ops adhere to the cooperative guidelines. The bank created an entrepreneurial division to promote and support new cooperative ventures, which partly explains the success of the network in generating new jobs and starting enterprises that succeed. It is living proof that workers can govern their own business, hold managers accountable, and operate as efficiently as capitalist firms, if not more so.

Given the economic and social success of the Mondragon co-ops, it is tempting to predict that the model will eventually displace capitalist firms. Who would not prefer to work in a cooperative?[3] If they are at least as efficient as capitalist firms, why wouldn't they drive capitalists out of the market by underselling them and stealing their best workers? It is also tempting to project the just society as one in which all enterprises have been converted into Mondragon-style cooperatives or co-op networks. Nevertheless, there are problems with this prediction and projection. In this chapter, I address four questions:

1. Why, given the economic success of Mondragon in competition with capitalist enterprises, have we not seen a wider proliferation of co-ops?
2. Could an entire economy be organized as a system of cooperatives, and would this be desirable? The desirability of economic democracy was a theme of part 1. But here I am concerned with the much more specific question of the desirability of cooperative enterprises, only one aspect of the idea of economic democracy, and possibly not a necessary aspect, in that many models of socialism do not provide for worker self-management but seek to equalize economic power in other ways.
3. Overlapping somewhat with the first question, if a society were organized as a system of worker cooperatives in a market economy, would they tend to degenerate into capitalist firms?
4. Should the promotion of cooperatives be an important part of a program for a transition from capitalism to socialism? The concern here is with the possibility that even if worker-managed market socialism is a desirable idea, worker cooperatives in the context of capitalism could have counterproductive effects for the larger goal of bringing about such an ideal, such as promoting enterprise consciousness at the expense of class consciousness.

## DOES REPLICATING THE MONDRAGON MODEL REQUIRE REVISING IT?

The desirability of worker cooperatives on the Mondragon model is a familiar theme in the literature on alternatives to capitalism. I will not belabor the point here but only note the proven record of worker ownership with respect to efficiency, job creation, fairer income distribution, egalitarian work relations, entrepreneurship, overcoming the alienation of labor and the dominion of capital, and cultivating stable local communities. So successful has been the Mondragon experiment and other cases of worker ownership that support for worker ownership is once again part of the strategy of the labor movement (in the United States), and a good case can be made for government policies supporting cooperative development.

The puzzle is, first, why cooperatives have not spread more widely (the theme of this section) and, second, whether an entire society organized cooperatively is feasible (the theme of the next section).

To the first question there are several proffered explanations. The first, and weakest, explanation appeals to contingent factors in the failure of cooperatives: the prejudice of bankers, predatory pricing and raiding of managers by capitalist competitors, and degeneration of co-ops into capitalist firms.[4] Cooperatives that are successful businesses should be able to overcome all of these, with the possible exception of capitalist degeneration. But even this problem has been overcome for a forty-year period by the Mondragon cooperatives through their distinctive ownership structure, a mix of collective and individual ownership.

A second factor is a tendency of cooperatives to invest less than capitalist firms.[5] This tendency will vary depending on the way ownership is structured, along a continuum from fully collective ownership to fully individual ownership of shares. (The Mondragon model falls in the middle.) The tendency is most pronounced in co-ops with fully collective ownership. Let us assume for simplicity that the capitalist firm tends to maximize profit and the worker-owned firm to maximize income per worker. I recognize that this is a gross over-simplification: Many co-ops seek to maximize employment, for example. But the assumption of maximization of income per worker will serve to highlight a tendency that no doubt comes into play in some circumstances. We will also assume for purposes of comparison that everyone has a "time discount" of 5 percent. (For example, one would set aside one hundred dollars from current consumption per year if, at the end of the year, one's savings appreciated by at least five dollars. Time discount is a measure of the value of immediate, in preference to deferred, consumption.) On these assumptions, the capitalist will invest whenever the return on investment in the future compensates for his or her deferral of income in the present, discounted at 5 percent per year. In the collectivized cooperative, the co-operator must have a much higher rate of return, because there is no personal equity in the firm. If workers were to remain in the firm for only one year, an investment would have to yield an annual return of 105 percent to be attractive. Even if all workers stayed twenty years, the investment would still need to yield a return of 8 percent per year. Assuming that on average a worker will remain with the firm ten years, the return would need to be 13 percent. Thus, "The cooperative is likely to invest a good deal less than its capitalist counterpart."

This tendency can be overcome with fully individualized capital accounts, but this will raise the problem of risk diversification, a third possible reason that cooperatives are not more widespread. As James Meade explains, "While property owners can spread their risks by putting small bits of their properties into a large number of concerns, a worker cannot put small bits of his effort into a large number of different jobs. This presumably is a main reason why we find risk-bearing capital hiring labour rather than risk-bearing labour hiring capital."[6] Moreover, the undiversified risk is borne by the workers in the firm, and for many if the firm fails, they stand to lose their life savings.[7]

Fourth, the problem of risk diversification can be overcome through external financing, but external financing brings with it several problems. Perhaps chief is the danger of loss of control. A classic example is the way in which self-management was undermined in Algeria through centralized control of the banks.[8] Loss of control would defeat a major goal of cooperatives, at least as an alternative to capitalist authoritarianism. If externally financed firms manage to keep control over their management and investment decisions, then the problem is an unreasonable "moral hazard" for the creditor. In enterprises with very high capital intensity—Jacques H. Dréze gives the example of a dozen workers on an oil tanker—there will be the need for very substantial external funding.[9] What reason could one give to a creditor to advance the necessary capital with no control rights, at least of an informal nature? This may be one reason, aside from prejudice, that bankers are reluctant to loan to cooperatives. Jon Elster and Karl Ove Moene note an additional problem with "heavy reliance on borrowing": "The workers would bear the full brunt of market fluctuations," because relatively small decreases in market prices could require relatively large percentage cuts in income available for distribution to workers.[10]

Fifth, Justin Schwartz and David Schweickart trace the paucity of cooperatives to collective action problems arising variously from (1) ignorance of the cooperative option, (2) the difficulty of getting many individuals to pool their resources, and (3) lack of extrainstitutional support.[11] The first and third of these problems are soluble even in a capitalist context. Education and publicity can raise awareness of the cooperative option. Political support can lead to the creation of cooperative banks, tax advantages, and other enabling legislation. The growth of employee stock ownership plans (ESOPs) in the United States is a response in large part to legislation granting them tax breaks, and many worker-owned firms now exist under the rubric of ESOPs. Getting many individuals, particularly workers without much capital, to pool their resources is apt to be a problem in a capitalist context but would be less of a problem if the cooperative form were the only employment option. In such a context, the same entrepreneurs who might create capitalist firms in a capitalist context might take the lead in organizing cooperatives.

Finally, there is a utilitarian argument, assuming some combination of the above listed difficulties, that the lack of cooperatives in an allegedly neutral free market reflects the preferences of workers and consumers. Put bluntly, we do not see more co-ops because people do not want them, all things considered. Robert Nozick has argued that if cooperatives were more efficient than capitalist firms they would displace them. Because that has not happened, there must be a trade-off between efficient production, investment, and innovation, on the one hand, and democracy, humanized work, and equality, on the other hand. If workers have not been willing to pool their resources, assume risks, take less income, or whatever the trade-offs must be to work in co-ops versus capitalist firms, they must, all things considered, prefer capitalist firms.[12] One could grant this pessimistic conclusion and still invoke Elster's principle of "endogeneity of preferences" to keep open the possibility that in another society, with different patterns of socialization, people might come to prefer cooperatives.[13] But this is a weak line of defense, and more importantly, it concedes too much.

Nozick's argument has been successfully refuted by David Miller, who also, in the course of his refutation, identifies an additional problem of collective action that cooperatives face. Miller shows that the market is not neutral: even if workers were to prefer cooperative organization to capitalist organization, they might end up choosing to work in a capitalist firm, in a capitalist environment. But it does not follow that we should forsake collective action—such as legislation—to alter the environment so as to favor cooperative firms.

Let us suppose that workers prefer a co-op organization, for both the income and the nonmaterial benefits. Suppose also, for reasons just discussed, that co-ops tend to fail in a capitalist environment. Then, in a capitalist environment, workers might elect to work in a capitalist firm—despite their preference to the contrary—and the outcome would, thus, be suboptimal for all workers. Miller has represented their choice as a version of the Prisoner's Dilemma. (The larger numbers represent more highly ranked preferences, and $x$ represents the variable ranking of workers' inclination to work in a capitalist firm within a cooperative economic environment.)

|  | Other Firms | |
| --- | --- | --- |
| Our Firm | Cooperative | Capitalist |
| Cooperative | 1 | −1 |
| Capitalist | $x$ | 0 |

If $x$ is less than one, "workers will opt for the cooperative system if and only if they expect other workers to do likewise."[14] In this case, everyone would benefit from the legal imposition—or financial and other support—of cooperative property relations for everyone, or at least for those wanting such relations, just as everyone benefits from the provision of other public goods like clean air and highways. Nevertheless, in a competitive capitalist market, people will behave individually and rationally in such a way as to bring about a suboptimal outcome. So the market is not neutral in selecting against cooperatives and does not automatically produce the optimal preference satisfaction.

If $x$ is greater than one, each worker will find it more rational to be in a capitalist firm, whether the competition is capitalist or cooperative. But the result when such choices are aggregated is an economy in which almost all firms are capitalist, a state of affairs inferior to both the optimal, but unstable, choice of being in a capitalist firm in a cooperative environment and also the choice of being in a cooperative in a cooperative economy. (This is the classic Prisoner's Dilemma.)

This analysis refutes the claim that the market is neutral with respect to the choice of cooperative versus capitalist firms. It does not, of course, *show* that workers would in fact prefer to be in a cooperative firm in a cooperative economy over a capitalist firm in a capitalist economy. To do that, we would need a combination of empirical evidence and arguments for the superiority of cooperatives.

## CAN MONDRAGON BE REPLICATED?

Given that a number of problems cooperatives have faced are a function of the surrounding capitalist environment but not necessarily of the superiority of the capitalist firm, what are the prospects for success of generalizing the Mondragon model? Several features of the Mondragon cooperative model make it difficult to generalize as the dominant form of workplace organization for an entire economy.

Keith Bradley and Alan Gelb argue that two features that are key to the success of Mondragon also limit its replication: strong linkages with the local community and limited labor mobility. These features contribute to consensus building, insulate the co-ops from competitive pressures, especially in the labor market, keep capital within the region, and prevent excessive loss of capital owing to departure of worker owners.

However, "cooperative survival may not be easy in a fluid labor market with technology change and general labor mobility." One possible solution to this problem would be inconsistent with the Mondragon model. "Communal, rather than individual capital holdings may reconcile equity maintenance with labor mobility—but at a high cost." First, most workers see their investments as a major factor in their motivation to work well. Second, "divorcing rewards from returns to cooperative capital provides a strong incentive for decapitalization."[15] (We will return to these points later, when discussing economic democracy.)

Another problem of replication derives from the screening of job applicants to select those who are best disposed to work in a cooperative setup. As long as cooperatives are islands in a capitalist sea, workers joining co-ops will differ in attitudes, prior employment status, and motivation for joining from workers being hired in conventional firms. This at least was true of the Basque case. Bradley and Gelb argue that screening is less effective the greater the proportion of employment in co-ops. In a system of co-ops, the cooperative educational process would be strained to the breaking point in the effort to educate workers to the cooperative ethos.[16]

Assuming that investment is not socialized (as proposed, for example, by David Schweickart), it seems unlikely that cooperative development would spontaneously generate enough jobs to achieve full employment. An exacerbating factor is the lack, in comparison with a capitalist firm, of an inherent tendency to expand. This lack is mitigated by a tendency, during recession, not to lay off workers. But the real problem concerns the relation between workers in co-ops and those outside. The stability of employment in co-ops may have as its counterpart a secondary labor market of part-time and temporary workers, which, as Bradley and Gelb observe, would absorb fluctuations in employment. Even the Mondragon network has not resisted the temptation to hire some wage workers in recent years. (I discuss this further below.)

Add to these certain moral reservations, such as an inequitable distribution of wealth owing to unequal distribution of profits across workers and differences in capital intensity.[17] These might be correctable through taxation and may be worth accepting, for the sake of democracy, if the alternative is some form of managerial or state socialism; they may even be justifiable in egalitarian terms. For example, if worker-managed firms are sufficiently more efficient than managerial firms that everyone is better off, one might justify the inequalities to the least advantaged by appeal to Rawls' difference principle.

Finally, democratic theory, although providing support for self-management in some cases, can be invoked against it in others. Robert Dahl and Michael Walzer have made perhaps the strongest arguments for democracy in the workplace based on a strong analogy between the workplace and the state or city.[18] The argument is compelling for industrial, commodity-producing enterprises. But when a firm or organization must be accountable to other groups besides customers, or when its clientele can not be adequately characterized as customers, the lines of accountability may warrant qualifying or even overriding the claims for worker self-management—for example in, education, health care, the media, public transportation, and government agencies.[19]

## DOES MARKET SOCIALISM INEVITABLY REVERT TO CAPITALISM?

N. Scott Arnold has argued that market socialism in the form of a system of cooperatives is an unstable system.[20] The effects of competition in the market are a loss of control by workers over both production and income and the restoration of capitalism, or something very much like it. Thus the market and worker control are incompatible. Arnold's argument can be summarized as follows: To compete effectively, firms need to exercise entrepreneurship. To exercise entrepreneurship they need to hire managers as entrepreneurs. These managers will press for greater autonomy and authority to enable them to devise and carry out their entrepreneurial ideas. To this extent, workers lose control over the production process. Both to attract competent managers and to provide an incentive to take responsibility for the success or failure of the firm, the profits of the firm will tend to take the form of bonuses, both for the manager and for the more skilled workers. For the latter, this amounts to a recreation of the labor market. With respect to the former, this amounts to a loss of control by the workers over the firm's income. What results is what Arnold calls "imitation market socialism," not importantly different from capitalism, where workers have some control over production and some access to profits, through collective bargaining.

In support of Arnold's claims there is substantial evidence that managers controlled decision making in Yugoslav self-managed firms.[21] Increasing hierarchy and decreasing worker participation were traced to the 1965 reforms placing firms in a more competitive market environment.[22] At the same time, managers were reportedly "deeply discontented with their jobs," complaining of a high level of responsibility but low level of authority, lack of recognition for enterprise success, and inadequate rewards and job security, and it was "increasingly more difficult to attract qualified people to the position" of director, suggesting that pressures for greater management authority persist.[23] Nevertheless, Arnold overstates the necessity of the slide from worker to manager control. Even if we grant his argument, he ignores some important differences between "imitation market socialism" and capitalism that would remain. To take the last point first, consider an analogy: In capitalist society the state is formally democratic: that is, each person has a right to vote, and the citizenry controls the government by means of periodic elections. But in reality elites control the government, by selecting and promoting candidates, staging elections, buying media space, and preventing certain basic questions from arising on the political agenda. Let us call this "imitation democracy." Does it follow that there is no difference between imitation democracy and oligarchy (such as that of Francoist Spain)? Clearly not. Limited as it is, the check on tyranny afforded by universal suffrage is significant. It is, moreover, an achievement, in part, of the struggles of those very people— workers, women, minorities—who continue to be oppressed within contemporary capitalist societies, an achievement that has served to mitigate that oppression.

Analogously, a formal constitutional accountability of managers to workers would be compatible with elitism of various kinds—managerial, technocratic, or partisan—and to that extent would indicate incomplete democracy. Nonetheless, we should not be led to conclude that formal accountability is insignificant or that it does not provide a new arena in which struggles for democracy can be carried out more effectively. At the very least, self-management "opens the books" of the enterprise to public scrutiny in a manner uncommon in mere collective bargaining contexts, providing a check on corrupt or self-serving management practices.[24] Job security, always in danger in capitalist firms, even those with strong unions, would be much greater in worker-controlled firms. Extreme disregard of workers' interests, as in shutdowns of viable firms, would be unthinkable. Importantly, the workers would always have the power to remove a director.[25] Although industrial democracy might not have arrived, industrial tyranny would have been brought to an end. Thus, it is erroneous to equate the truncated democracy of "imitation market socialism" with the much more limited power workers normally have in collective bargaining.[26]

Arnold considers four countertendencies to the slide from self-management to something like capitalism. First, when firms are failing because of competitive pressure, the state can intervene and bail them out. However, Arnold argues, such measures lead by degrees to state control, which brings with it bureaucratic abuse and inefficiency—precisely the kind of socialism that the introduction of the market was designed to avoid.[27] Second, the state can take charge of investment planning. Although this may reduce some intersectoral competition, competition between firms is likely to be encouraged, with all the effects Arnold discusses. A third strategy, indicative planning, is too weak to rein in the forces of competition: such planning outlines goals and provides information but provides no basis for directives to firms. This leaves us with the fourth countertendency: ideological commitment, in particular, an unwillingness to trade off control of the firm for higher incomes. Arnold maintains that short-term interests of firms will lead to deviations from this principle. If such deviations are regulated by the state, we are back to bureaucratic socialism. Moreover, in the face of bureaucratic socialism, some firms will fight for an extension of the market to serve their short-term interests.

I want to concentrate my attention on the fourth of these countertendencies, ideological commitment to cooperative values and institutions. We can find evidence that this countertendency is effective in the Basque cooperatives of Mondragon, where managers work for about half what they could earn in other firms, showing that an egalitarian ideology can effectively resist the pressure toward management appropriation of profits, even in a capitalist market economy. Although in Mondragon there is not a lot of shop-floor participation, there is "an unusual degree of coherence and trust between co-operators, from shop floor to management."[28] This egalitarian structure in the Mondragon cooperatives appears relatively stable: income differentials are held way below those of capitalist firms;[29] the network of cooperatives remains committed to job creation and formation of new cooperatives;[30] average income is kept approximately the same across firms, and does not exceed by much the average incomes for the region, thus avoiding the formation of an elite of co-operators; and no cooperatives have degenerated into capitalist firms. Such consequences are not automatic. They result, first, from the influence of the Caja Laboral Popular (CLP), a cooperative bank that since its founding has had a mandate to promote cooperatives, and second, from ongoing discussions within the cooperatives about all of these issues.[31] The Mondragon network is able to resist the tendencies toward degeneration into capitalism—in spite of its interdependence with the world market[32]— precisely because of its history of commitment to cooperativism. (There is a lesson here for those who seek surreptitiously to lay the material foundations of socialism: Socialism must be made by socialists.)

Thus, it appears, contrary to Arnold's claim, not only that ideological commitments can counter the tendency toward degeneration but also that they are not necessarily undermined by the pressure of short-term economic interests. Bureaucratic planning need not be among the institutions necessary for the support of these commitments, though they do involve public discussion, planning, and agreements.

As for failing firms that turn to the state for protection, the option of bailout by the state is simply not available in Mondragon, although because the CLP is controlled in part by the cooperatives themselves, it could conceivably become involved in such activity. Failures are remarkably few, a result of the effective socialization of the entrepreneurial function.[33] The CLP, a major source of investment funding, through its entrepreneurial services division, carefully researches proposals for start-ups of cooperatives and provides careful training for prospective managers, with the result that only three cooperatives have failed in the more than forty-year history of a movement that has spawned more than one hundred cooperative enterprises and created in excess of thirty thousand jobs.[34] The socialization of entrepreneurship also precludes the necessity of hiring professional managers on the market on their own terms. In pitting self-management against entrepreneurship, Arnold seems not to have considered that the entrepreneurial function could itself be socialized and integrated into an egalitarian ethos.

My thesis here may be challenged in two ways. First, there is some evidence that managers of the Mondragon cooperatives have had strong nonideological reasons for being willing to accept lower pay than they could receive in a capitalist firm. Unlike their Spanish capitalist counterparts, the Mondragon firms offered managers many opportunities for professional development, traveling to other parts of Europe for seminars and consultations with other firms.[35] To the extent that Spain's full participation in the European Community diminishes the differences between Spanish and other European management opportunities, the relative advantage for a manager of working in a cooperative could disappear. I have no way of factoring out the weight given to professional development over ideological commitment to egalitarian differentials. But the evidence for professional development as a motive to remain in a co-op does weaken the thesis that the Mondragon differentials can be fully explained by egalitarian commitments. Second, over time the wage differentials in the Mondragon group have widened from three to one, to four-and-a-half to one, and now seven to one, with the freedom of each cooperative to set its own differential.[36] In a few cases the differential has widened significantly, to as much as fifteen to one, as a new generation of top managers, and, more significantly, technical experts is being recruited for the first time from the market.[37] A more detailed analysis is needed to determine the precise causes of this gradual departure from egalitarianism. On the surface at least, it seems to support the claim that cooperatives in a capitalist context will tend over time to degenerate toward a capitalist model. This impression is confirmed by three additional trends:

1. The member co-ops have consolidated under a centralized management structure for the entire group, with vice presidents over industrial, financial, and distribution divisions. There are still individual firm presidents chosen by the workers, but they have far less control over long-term strategy, which has moved up the corporate ladder. A general assembly is sovereign for the entire group, elected by the workers, and in this respect the workers retain final authority. But the idea of a loose network of autonomous firms is giving way to that of a diversified multinational corporation (the new name is now Mondragon Cooperative Corporation).

2. The Mondragon Cooperative Corporation (MCC) has begun building plants in foreign countries, and these plants are not cooperatives. The only explanation offered for this during my visit to Mondragon in 1995 was that it was difficult to export the co-op form of organization. Further research is needed to determine to what extent the MCC has made or intends to make co-operation an option for its foreign subsidiaries in Mexico, Morocco, and elsewhere.[38]

3. The MCC has begun hiring temporary workers who are not members. These have included wives of male workers, as well as women performing janitorial services. Single women (not receiving a husband's benefits) who pressed for co-op membership and benefits lost their jobs.[39] The hiring of wage workers is a departure from cooperative principles. That many of these workers are women is part of a wider pattern of gender discrimination from which the cooperatives have not escaped, although their record is somewhat better than that of their capitalist counterparts. Women are in the minority in most co-ops, except a few that specialize in traditional and low-paying women's work, such as sewing. A higher percentage of women members than men are in the lower-paying jobs, and a lower percentage are in managerial positions. Inadequate child care ensures that women with children carry a double burden.[40] Nonetheless, with respect to percentages of women employed, pay, and benefits, women fare better in the Mondragon cooperatives than in comparable private Basque firms.[41] The basic-income pro-

posal will partially rectify gender inequality, in a way that should have positive repercussions within cooperatives—and other enterprises as well.

Three caveats need to be made to this picture of regression to capitalism. First, such evidence does not tell us what to expect in a worker-managed economy, in which the competition with capitalist firms has been replaced by competition with other cooperatives and market pressures have been countered by egalitarian institutions and culture. The MCC operates not merely in a capitalist context but in one of increasing globalization. In anticipation of Spain's entry into the European Community, the co-ops expected the loss of state export subsidies and import tariffs. The new organizational structure, rather than representing an abandonment of cooperative values, was undertaken as a necessity for survival.

Similarly, the hiring of temporary workers needs to be seen in the light of the MCC's increasing integration in the world market. It exports 70 percent of its appliance components and 60 percent of its machine tools and faces severe cost-cutting pressure from its customers. This has meant the elimination of thousands of jobs, particularly in the industrial sector, and reliance on temporary nonmember workers for 10 to 12 percent of its jobs. Yet it is remarkable that total membership in the MCC continues to rise despite such restructuring. (The biggest growth is in the distribution division, a kind of microcosmic reflection of the restructuring of core capitalist economies worldwide.) The turn to temporary workers, though not to be condoned, needs to be seen against the backdrop of a continuing commitment to retraining and relocating members and creating more jobs.[42]

Second, even with widened salary differentials, after forty years there are still major differences between the Mondragon group and capitalist firms. Each cooperative and the group as a whole are still governed by the principle of one member, one vote. Job creation is still a major goal, and indeed in the two years previous to my visit in 1995, employment continued to grow by one thousand or more jobs per year, a rate of job growth more than double that of the Basque country as a whole. A conventional capitalist firm would simply have downsized.[43]

Third, the persistence of the cooperative ethos among the workers is a basis for resistance to these disturbing trends. Evidence for this is the protest document unanimously approved, in February 1997, by the social council representing the six thousand members of the FAGOR group of cooperatives, the industrial core of the MCC. In this document the FAGOR workers accuse the MCC of fading from cooperativism by abandoning incomes solidarity, introducing waged temporary workers, neglecting the industrial sector in favor of finance and real estate, and adopting a strategic planning process that is obligatory and controlled from above.[44]

Thus, despite trends toward capitalist degeneration in the MCC under the pressures of globalization, a cooperative spirit survives. But is that enough to recommend cooperative development as part of a strategy for the transition from capitalism to a more egalitarian and democratic society (what some still call "socialism")?

## COOPERATIVE DEVELOPMENT IN A TRANSITION TO SOCIALISM

Some have argued that cooperatives, by making workers into owners, foster a kind of "enterprise consciousness" or small-business mentality that conflicts with trade-union consciousness and working class consciousness. Co-ops, it is said, stand outside the labor movement, lower labor standards, direct resources into risky and usually failing enterprises, and thus weaken and divide the labor movement.[45]

Furthermore, it is puzzling that even in countries with strong left-wing parties and strong cooperative sectors, cooperative development does not figure prominently in political strategies. Have socialists in those countries realized something we have overlooked?

Finally, it should make any socialist suspicious that some of the strongest supporters of worker ownership are from the political Right. The worker buyout of United Airlines (discussed below) was praised profusely by conservative columnist George Will because he thinks it will make the workers think and act like capitalists.[46] As David Ellerman has noted, "The original architect of the ESOP was a corporate and investment banking lawyer, Louis Kelso, who has co-authored books entitled *The Capitalist Manifesto* and *How to Turn Eighty Million Workers into Capitalists on Borrowed Money.* The conservative but populist aspects of the Kelso plan appealed to Senator Russell Long, who pushed the original ESOP legislation through Congress."[47] With union involvement, ESOPs have been used to bring about significant benefits for workers and shifts in the balance of power within firms. But whatever their progressive potential under certain circumstances, they can also provide corporations with a method for raising capital, averting hostile takeovers, co-opting their workers without giving them any real control over the company, and reducing the security of their pension benefits. There can be no doubt that the political significance of worker ownership is highly ambiguous.

The argument against worker ownership is supported by numerous cases. The plywood cooperatives in the northwestern United States enriched their worker-owners to the point that many of the firms were sold to capitalist investors. Moreover, as Edward S. Greenberg has observed, these co-op members tended to "support systems of hierarchical social relations, and identify themselves as Republicans and members of the middle class."[48]

Even the Mondragon cooperatives, considered by many as the model of what cooperatives can be, have been criticized for dividing the labor movement in the

Basque country and fostering a middle-class identity. Such criticism surfaced among a few radical nationalists in the Basque country three decades ago, but the thesis has been explored and documented recently by Sharryn Kasmir.[49]

Situating the Mondragon cooperatives in the context of Basque working-class daily life and nationalist politics, Kasmir argues that the creation of the cooperatives was the result of an effort, in line with the right wing of Basque nationalism, to create middle-class alternatives to class conflict, in which workers and managers share a common interest and ideology, enjoy egalitarian work relations, and manage to avoid entanglement with party and union conflicts. Kasmir's study provides an important corrective to earlier studies of Mondragon, which have tended to neglect the cultural and political context and the perspectives of ordinary workers. She shows convincingly that a majority of workers, particularly manual workers, do not feel that the firm is theirs or that they are a part of the firm. Workers perceive clear lines of division between those above and those down below. Conflicts erupt over job classifications, pay differentials and control of the work process. The social council, the closest thing to an institution representing members in their capacity as workers, is widely viewed by workers as ineffective.[50]

Ironically, workers in a private firm were found to have more effective leverage through their union over labor process issues, and cooperative managers can change working conditions in ways not tolerated in private firms.[51] In the 1990s co-ops began to introduce shift work, just-in-time production, the hiring of temporary workers, and other efficiency innovations that increased stress and disrupted patterns of social life. For example, managers attempted to reduce the month-long vacation in August, traditional throughout the Basque country, to two weeks, adding a two-week vacation at times of lower demand, but this was defeated by workers in the General Assembly, as have been repeated attempts to raise the salary differentials.[52] There has been an increase in the use of temporary workers, mentioned earlier. Also worrisome is the creation by the MCC of a private holding company that has purchased outside firms, making the MCC the employer of two thousand nonmember workers in Basque firms.[53] More recently, through the purchase of non-co-op supermarkets, particularly in France, about 30 percent of the workers in the MCC are now nonmembers. Overseas investment is even more extensive.

These and other trends support the unsettling verdict that the MCC, rather than offering an alternative to capitalism, is actually a good example of the sort of firm needed to survive in the global marketplace. "Lacking syndical representation, not bound by the metal-sector contract, able to transfer workers between factories, and permitted to have thirty percent of the work force on temporary contracts (as of 1993), the cooperatives had perhaps the most flexible labor force in the region."[54]

What we see here is the pattern, employed in many capitalist firms throughout the world, of a dual labor market. On the one hand are workers whose loyalty and participation are cultivated, who earn decent incomes and enjoy job security and other benefits. On the other hand, there is heavy reliance on temporary and part-time workers, who are poorly paid, and outsourcing to smaller, less secure firms, including overseas firms with cheap labor and poor working conditions. Thus, it is not surprising that Basque syndicates and informal groups within the MCC have begun to call for syndicalization (unionization) of the cooperatives.[55]

In conclusion, Kasmir suggests, "Perhaps cooperative workers (once disillusioned and apathetic) will begin to utilize the democratic organs within the cooperatives to exercise meaningful control and ownership over their firms. In so doing, perhaps they will transform the structure of those institutions to make them more democratic. Perhaps, too, co-op workers will determine that they need syndicates to press their claims and, in the process, maybe they will build a new kind of model in Mondragon."[56] Kasmir pessimistically assimilates the MCC to other large multinationals pursuing strategies for labor-management cooperation combined with flexible production. But her evidence also supports the thesis that the co-op form can accommodate, better than a capitalist firm, a more democratic model.

Although worker members were apathetic and cynical about the alleged egalitarianism of the co-ops, as the crisis deepens they begin to appeal to that very ideology to resist management that moves away from cooperativism.[57] Their votes in the General Assembly effectively blocked efforts to raise salary differentials, an issue that would never arise in a capitalist firm. Although the Third Cooperative Congress voted to allow individual cooperatives to set their own differentials, the issue of differentials is far from dead, as is evidenced in the protest of the FAGOR Social Council mentioned earlier. In fact, that document makes it clear that support for cooperative principles is very much alive among the cooperative workers, even as they are being violated.

Unlike the plywood co-ops in the United States, which had less linkage to unions or political movements, the Mondragon co-ops have sought to keep member salaries pegged to the going rates in the market so as not to undermine union contracts. Although there is a perception that cooperatives have been less involved in political and solidarity strikes, Kasmir's evidence of co-operator participation versus participation by workers in private firms does not unambiguously support this.[58] Her conclusion that cooperativism can divide workers[59] can easily be turned around to say that, with more integral union involvement, worker ownership can be a vehicle for greater worker control and democracy.

In general, the outcome of worker ownership is highly dependent upon its social and political context. The point Kasmir is driven to, that even the Mondragon cooperatives need to be supported, restrained, and challenged by labor and other social movements, is similar to conclusions others have drawn with respect to worker ownership in the United States. When asked by *Changing Work* magazine how he would "answer those labor critics of ESOPs who claim that worker-owners will become small-scale capitalists, that their consciousness will be cut off from its labor roots or from any broad-based solidarity and become fixated on the profit margins of their enterprises," labor consultant Michael Locker responded, "Here's where the union can make all the difference. The traditional mission of unions is to develop precisely that kind of solidarity to identify and meet common or industry-wide needs." In particular, unions can provide "exact, independent research," legal resources, and education so that "individual workers within individual plants will not see themselves as isolated, but as one of many fragile enterprises connected and supported by the traditional vehicle of labor solidarity." In an expression of "a willingness to 'recycle success,' some percentage of a plant's surplus earnings might be placed in a fund to support other [worker] takeovers."[60]

This kind of mutual aid among firms, which Locker imagines the union might facilitate, is exactly what the Mondragon co-ops have done for themselves through the medium of the Caja Laboral.[61] Can unions rise to the challenge? Should they? One can understand the initial reluctance, given the history of unions and worker ownership in the United States. Some of the earliest American unions adopted a strategy of support for worker cooperatives; both the National Labor Union (formed in 1866) and the Knights of Labor (1869) aimed for a system of producer and consumer cooperatives. The Knights supported the creation of "some 135 producer and consumer cooperatives, all of which ultimately failed because of underfunding and cut-throat competition."[62]

The failure of those early experiments contributed to the marginalization of cooperatives in the United States labor movement for most of the twentieth century. During the last couple of decades of downsizing and plant shutdowns, worker ownership has gradually emerged as an option to save enterprises and workers' jobs. Coincidentally, during this same period, legislation promoting employee stock ownership plans has made it financially advantageous for lenders, owners and workers to transfer ownership to workers. Some unions, notably the United Steel Workers of America, have come around to the idea, and by the end of the 1980s, steel workers owned, in whole or in part, more than fifteen companies, some employing several thousand workers. They are now the largest single group of stockholders in the United States steel industry.[63]

In 1990, the AFL-CIO established the Employee Partnership Fund to support worker buyouts. The United Auto Workers, the Amalgamated Clothing and Textile Workers Union, the United Food and Commercial Workers, the International Association of Machinists, and the Airline Pilots Association, among others, have been interested in worker buyouts. In some cases, the firms were marginal and have since failed, but there is a growing trend toward proactive involvement in ownership and management by workers in successful companies.[64]

This sea change in attitude among the unions is born of economic necessity in an era of plant closings, buyouts, and downsizing.[65] But it has been ushered along by some success stories. Acquaintance with the Mondragon experience has spread, with the aid of a BBC video and recent research. On United States soil, successful worker buyouts in steel, textiles, airlines, and other industries serve to temper the skepticism of the doubtful.

## WORKER OWNERSHIP IN THE UNITED STATES

I now want to broaden the focus from these union reactions and initiatives to the wider field of worker ownership in the United States, in order to assess the extent and significance of the increasing percentage of corporate stock owned by employees through employee stock ownership plans and other forms of worker ownership.[66]

In what follows, I provide an overview of current trends in worker ownership in the United States, and try to assess whether these developments represent a significant democratization of economic power, or at least open up prospects for such democratization, or instead are a thin veneer over business as usual, perhaps even weakening prospects for economic democracy. After an overview I provide a more detailed look at the worker buyout of United Airlines, one of the more promising cases of worker ownership on a large scale.

Let us start with a look at employee ownership in its broadest sense. If one counts all those firms owned at least in part by their employees, the last two decades have witnessed a phenomenal fiftyfold growth of employee ownership, such that today there are more than ten million workers—more than 12 percent of the private-sector workforce—in companies where employees own more than 4 percent of the company. This exceeds the number of private-sector workers in unions.[67] In many of these companies the percentage of worker-held stock is small; only salaried employees are included, and there may be no voting rights attached to the stock they own. In some cases an ESOP has been introduced in place of a more diversified pension plan, putting workers' pensions at risk, or has been set up in exchange for union concessions or to avoid unions altogether.[68] Because ESOPs can be a way of raising capital—and, under United States law, provide tax advantages for the firm, the lending agency, and the employees and are often administered by trustees unaccountable to the employees—workplace democracy is usually an irrelevant factor in their origin, and they may provide no avenues for worker participation or control. Thus, we need to discriminate carefully within this broad field to weed out the positively harmful and irrelevant cases and to find those that exemplify, or at least open the possibility for, greater workplace democracy.

## Dispelling Some Myths

First, the relatively good news: ESOPs are not usually set up to rescue failing companies.[69] Nor do they usually replace a pension plan,[70] nor are they typically the result of concession bargaining, nor are they usually introduced to avoid unionization (8 percent, 4 percent, and 8 percent of the cases, respectively).[71] Corporations do not set up ESOPs only for tax advantages or for the employee benefits, though these are reasons in more than 70 percent of the cases.[72] Employee stock ownership plans have only a small positive effect on corporate performance. In combination with worker participation, however, they produce "significant improvement in growth and productivity."[73]

For all the hype about worker capitalism, the bad news is that ESOPs have not made a dent in the inequality of wealth. Most of the wealth is still owned by rich households.[74] Although wealth owned by households is declining as a percentage of the total, households still owned 60 percent of corporate stocks in 1991 (down from 88 percent in 1960), while the percentage owned by pension funds and other institutional investors has increased. Although in the late 1980s, ESOPs accounted for less than 1 percent of all corporate stock in the United States, in the late 1990s stock owned through ESOPs and other forms of employee stock ownership accounted for 9 percent of the total.[75] But this is still less than 1 percent of the total *wealth* in the United States.[76] Most of the stock has gone to the wealthiest employees.[77] Nor have ESOPs had much effect, overall, on corporate control. Only one in six ESOP companies have non-managerial employee representatives (though this is up from less than 3 percent in 1985).[78] Studies of firms with employee board representation show no appreciable effects on job satisfaction, commitment to the company, attitude toward ownership, or corporate performance. "Eight-five percent of private ESOP firms do not provide full voting rights, and in the forty percent of majority-owned ESOPs that do, such employees seldom vote in concert."[79] Although improving productivity is listed as a reason for the formation of 70 percent of ESOPs, only a small percentage of firms had significant worker participation a decade ago. On the other hand, the percentage of ESOP firms using labor–management teams or self-managing work teams has doubled since 1986, to more than 20 percent.[80]

Joseph Blasi stresses that for ESOPs to become part of a strategy to make the United States economy more democratic, four conditions must be satisfied: "Extensive labor–management cooperation, short-term profit sharing, and shop floor reorganization so that work itself is not alienating and draws on our hearts and heads as well as our hands. . . . Beyond this, a broad political movement is needed."[81] Viewed from this angle, the phenomenon of meaningful workplace democracy through employee ownership is quite small. The ICA Group publishes a directory of worker-owned cooperatives on the Mondragon model, democratic ESOPs that allow "shareholders to vote in elections for boards of directors on all major shareholder issues," and majority-owned ESOPs, with or without full voting rights. This more limited list includes "304 firms owned by a total of 102,343 workers, of whom at least 90,624, or eighty-nine percent, represent their own economic interest through democratically elected boards of directors."[82] The cooperatives average 43 members, the largest having 450 members. The ESOPs tend to be larger, including United Airlines, with 85,000 employees. As a proportion of the ESOP phenomenon, we are talking about 3 percent of the number of firms and less than 2 percent of the number of workers, and an even tinier fraction of American business as a whole.[83] Most have formed since the 1960s, with growth accelerating in the late 1980s.[84]

Thus, measured by standards of meaningful participation, real control, and stable and egalitarian ownership structures, workplace democracy is a marginal even if growing phenomenon. Does this mean that we should write off the wider ESOP trend as irrelevant for economic democracy? I want to suggest that we view the growing field of employee ownership as "contested terrain" on which the ultimate outcome—either business as usual or economic democracy—depends upon the actions of unions, management, government, new forms of organization of nonunion workers, and other agents.

Blasi and Kruse offer another way of analyzing the ESOP picture that is helpful for estimating the potential for more-radical transformations of enterprises. After summarizing their findings, I discuss some leading examples of union-led worker buyouts in order to illustrate the scope and limits of some current struggle on this contested terrain. In *The New Owners*, Blasi and Kruse concentrate on what they call the Employee Ownership 1000, the one thousand companies whose stock is publicly traded in a stock market, in which more than 4 percent of stock is held by employees. Why concentrate on public corporations in which, almost by definition, there is the possibility of diluting any worker ownership through selling to outsiders and when 85 percent of all ESOPs are in private companies?[85] The authors explain,

> Despite the fact that they are less than one-fifth of a percent of the total businesses, they are the flagship business sector. Public corporations make up 60 percent of the market value, 50 percent of the jobs, and are estimated to command a wide majority of the sales in the nation. . . . They are where the big money of capitalism is given to the key managers to make the big profits. . . . The significance of the Employee Ownership 1000 is that these companies, in which employees are substantial and often top shareholders, now include almost a third of the market value and sales of the entire publicly traded corporate sector! The transformation of ownership in this sector has reached the center of the economy.[86]

Although the portion of worker-owned stock in some companies on the list is as little as 4 percent, "the average holding is about 12.2 percent and employees are the top shareholder in almost half of the Employee Ownership 1000." From the mid-1970s to the mid-1980s, the number of companies with more than 20 percent employee ownership increased 2,000 percent. In six companies employee ownership exceeds 50 percent, and in fifty-four it is more than 25 percent. Already "41 percent of these public corporations either have 15 percent or have said that their employee plans are the dominant holder."[87] Although Employee Ownership 1,000 companies constitute only 10 percent of all the companies with 4 percent or more employee ownership, they account for 40 percent of the employee stockholders. Hence, growth of employee ownership in this sector is particularly significant for the future of employee ownership as a whole.[88] Moreover, employee ownership is expected to grow. "By the year 2000 . . . more than a quarter of all public corporations will be more than fifteen percent owned by their employees, and a quarter of private-sector employees will be in such companies."[89] What accounts for this growth? Where is it headed? Is it fertile soil for economic democracy?

## The Growth of Employee Ownership

The substantial tax advantages and employee benefits are a factor in most ESOPs. But companies have other options for conferring benefits and saving on taxes; why do they choose ESOPs? Blasi and Kruse identify four "engines propelling" the growth of employee ownership as a preferred way to save on taxes and compensate workers:

1. Corporate financing: ESOPs are attractive to companies in a wide range of transactions, including "stock buybacks, cashing out large holders, selling new shares, going private and going public, spinning off units and restructurings, recapitalizations, and bankruptcies."[90]
2. Restructuring employee benefits (70 percent of cases): The trend is away from expensive defined-benefit programs. ESOPs are an option that, although riskier for workers, is better than losing pensions altogether. Here, it is restructuring that is driving ESOP formation, not the possibility of ESOPs that is leading to restructuring.[91]
3. Defending against takeovers (11 percent of cases), and giving employees a voice in governance: ESOPs are involved in more than 40 percent of companies "going private." Building a stockholder group with a stake in the long-term health of the company, to resist hostile takeovers, is another strong reason companies can be expected to introduce ESOPs.[92]
4. Encouraging labor–management co-operation and improving company performance (a motive for formation in 70 percent of the cases):[93] The actual record falls far short of the intent. According to Blasi and Kruse, "less than

5% of the companies . . . are actively finding ways to encourage participation. . . . Less than 1 percent . . . have non-managerial workers serving on their boards."[94] Thus, although the motivation is there and many companies may enjoy a modest increase in profitability with the ESOP "simply because of the subsidy's effect,"[95] most are not taking advantage of the productivity improvements that are possible from combining ownership and participation.[96]

For all these reasons, we can expect employee ownership to grow, not least in the core public companies of the economy. As this happens, we can expect to see more companies in which employees are the largest shareholder, as well as more majority worker-owned companies.[97] Unions will be involved in some cases, and in many they will not, but new forms of worker organization may emerge, perhaps eventually forming links with unions or modeling their institutions on those in unionized firms.

Still, for any significant change in inequalities of wealth and power, ESOPs must be extended to lower-paid workers, full voting rights secured, the capacity to vote the shares in a bloc made easier, and further incentives for ESOPs of this sort written into law. Even then, we must not lose sight of where we are beginning: ESOP assets represent less than 4 percent of total corporate stock[98] and less than 1 percent of total wealth, and favor the better-paid employees. We must also not lose sight of the limited horizons of even some of the most incisive critics of current ESOP practices: Blasi and Kruse are against the goal of complete employee ownership of all corporations "because a vibrant competitive capitalism requires flexible access of those companies to equity and bond markets and the pressure of investors on corporate managers." The principle here is akin to the Italian Lega's proposal to open co-ops to outside investors and the movement in the same direction in the Mondragon cooperatives, not to mention the decision of Weirton Steel, temporarily 100 percent worker-owned, to sell some of its shares on the stock market. The ESOP phenomenon, even at its best, with the success of struggles to protect workers' rights and benefits, vigorous shop-floor participation, and adequate representation, would result in "entrepreneurial capitalism, capitalism with a human face."[99] At that point, will we have opened up new prospects for more-radical transformations of capitalism into economic democracy, or will we have co-opted the better-situated workers into the iron cage of a new, more fiercely competitive global capitalism in which the only agents with a motive for democratization are those on the margins of the system of production?

Employee ownership is part of a larger shift in the structure of ownership in the United States. "Households still own a good chunk of these public companies, but their holdings are declining significantly. . . . Pension funds and employee holdings are visibly increasing. . . . Their ownership is substantial and neatly organized into one bloc, often the dominant bloc, but in most companies, these new owners have not yet begun to exercise their ownership interest in any coordinated way."[100] Employee owners can team up with other institutional investors. Their position as the dominant bloc of owners may make up for the relatively small percentage of shares they own, particularly if their shares can be voted as a bloc and they can win board representation, as in the United Airlines or Weirton Steel cases. However, I know of no cases where this has occurred with less than majority employee ownership.

## The United Airlines Buyout

In 1994, the workers of United Airlines launched an experiment with one of the largest majority worker-owned companies in history.[101] Fifty-five percent of the stock of UAL was purchased by its machinists, pilots, and unrepresented workers, who made up three-quarters of the eighty-four-thousand-person workforce. (The flight attendants have so far declined to join the ESOP.) The workers also received three of the twelve seats on the board of directors and chose the company president[102] and the vice president for people, and the two union-nominated directors got virtual veto power over key decisions such as mergers and acquisitions.[103] This package they got in exchange for a 15 percent cut in wages. Although the arrangement was born of a need for survival, the results in the first three years, helped along by a boom in the airline industry, were spectacular. The unions negotiated 10 percent wage increases over the next two years. The company adopted a no-layoff commitment to the workers and hired seven thousand new workers, at a time when competitors were cutting back. It started gaining market share, its operating margins increased, productivity went up, and grievances declined. The value of its stock rose after the buyout and rose more than that of the rest of the industry.[104] Although worker concessions contributed heavily to United's success, an important part of the story is the commitment and participation of workers on cost-cutting task forces that saved twenty million dollars in fuel costs, reduced the sick time and worker compensation claims by 17 percent, and introduced greater flexibility in technology and schedules.[105]

That workers exercise some real control over major decisions is exemplified in an unusual buyout negotiation with USAir, which, unlike most such deals, which are worked out in secrecy, was conducted with information to and input from employees. Their opposition put an end to the deal.[106] "It's absolutely out of the ordinary for such a large company as United to consult its employees so publicly, in such detail, for such a long time and so decisively," according to Joseph Blasi.[107] It is true that the informal power of the workers in this instance is not a right but rather the result of a decision of the president, Gerald Greenwald. But the president, who once organized garment workers before a career as an auto industry executive, was chosen with the support of the unions and was committed to government by consensus: "I think the day is gone when an adversarial relationship between labor and management worked for both sides in some productive way. In the 1990s it's just not healthy anymore. The inefficiencies such wrangling causes make it that much more difficult for companies to compete in the world."[108]

Although the biggest majority-owned ESOP in history, United is not the only airline to experiment with worker ownership, nor is it the first.[109] What is noteworthy, apart from its size, is its structure, in which the unions choose two of the three seats reserved for workers.[110] This structure, together with new top management supportive of participation, is the key to United's success as a form of worker control so far and may provide a check against the slide back toward majority external ownership that has happened often in the history of worker ownership, both successful and unsuccessful. (Some of the highly successful plywood cooperatives of the Pacific Northwest became privately owned when the price of shares for potential new members became too high. John Roberts Clothing, a worker-owned company in Maine, sold out when it fell into financial difficulties. In both cases, financial considerations were pivotal for the change to private ownership. In the case of John Roberts, a strong union-supported climate of support and enthusiasm for worker ownership existed, but the company was overwhelmed by lack of financial resources.) By contrast, some of the other airlines seem not to have undertaken the same commitment to a change in corporate culture and so drift in and out of employee ownership.[111] It remains to be seen how lasting the United plan will be and how deeply it will alter the corporate culture in the direction of workplace democracy and worker participation. In the meantime, one can make certain observations and reflections:

1. United still has a long way to go toward a democratic participatory culture, even by ESOP standards. One barometer of this is the "rather modest" cost savings attributed to participation and improved attitudes of workers noted earlier.

2. The airline pilots, the most enthusiastic of the union supporters of the deal, are perhaps the most highly paid unionized workers in the world, with average salaries of $100,000 (and top salaries of $180,000–200,000).[112] One cannot help but wonder whether worker ownership here represents an alignment of elite workers and managers over against much of the rest of the union movement, nonunionized workers, and poorer people generally. To the extent that the United case is typical of a trend, is worker ownership to be a phenomenon of a worker aristocracy, and if so, is this an undesirable trend from the point of view of the least advantaged in our society? (This issue is taken up again later, in the context of a discussion of basic income.) Some forces countering the worker aristocracy dynamic are the history of militancy of the airline pilots' union (ALPA);[113] a wider commitment to ownership among industrial unions such as the United Steel Workers of America and the International Association of Machinists, whose relatively less privileged status may temper self-aggrandizing positions that might be

taken by the pilots; and the possibility of a broad political alliance between unions and other progressive forces that would include worker ownership as one among many measures to reduce inequalities of wealth and power. Because unions in 1998 represented less than 10 percent of private-sector workers (and less than 15 percent of all workers), they need to be concerned about their long-term survival, and not merely short-term gains achievable through strategic alliances with management. A closer study is needed to assess whether this is an outcome it is reasonable to work for or if, on the contrary, the more likely survival strategy will be a circling of the wagons by the most privileged primary-sector workers together with investors and managers, in a new ownership culture that leaves 80 percent of the population outside the circle.

## ITALIAN COOPERATIVES AND THE LEFT

If worker ownership really does have the potential to democratize workplaces and form part of a wider democratization of the economy, why is it so marginal in the strategies of left-wing parties around the world? In England, the Labour Party has not been a strong supporter of cooperatives. Rather, such support as exists has come from the centrist Liberals. This situation might be chalked up to the influence of the Webbs, early Fabian opponents of cooperatives, and might lend support to Kasmir's thesis that cooperatives tend to be middle-class institutions that divide the working class. The same cannot be said of Italy, which has the most developed cooperative sector in Europe and more worker cooperatives than any of the other member countries of the Organization for Economic Cooperation and Development.[114] Eight million members and forty thousand co-ops are divided into three associations. The Confederation is a Christian co-op network formed in 1919 in opposition to the League of Cooperatives (Lega delle Cooperative), which was Socialist and Republican, and, later, Communist. A smaller third association was formed by Republicans and Social Democrats splitting off from the Socialists during the Cold War. The first two, roughly comparable in size, make up the bulk of the cooperatives (ignoring banks and temporary housing cooperatives). In the Lega the largest member sector is that of consumer co-ops, though it is not the largest sector in terms of numbers of co-ops.[115] Housing and agriculture are also large, along with social insurance and welfare. In terms of annual turnover in lira, the largest sectors are, in declining order, agriculture, production and labor, consumer goods, services, housing, and retailing.[116] Altogether the firms in the Lega have an annual turnover comparable to that of Fiat, the largest private group in Italy.[117] Given its size and success and its long affiliation with left-wing parties, one would expect to find the Lega guided by a vision of cooperativism as an alternative to capitalism, and correspondingly some prominent place in the strategies of left-wing parties for the promotion of cooperatives.

How far the Lega is from conceiving of itself as an alternative to capitalism is perhaps evident in John Earle's interview with its president, Onelio Prandini, who was also on the Central Committee of the PCI (Italian Communist Party). He stresses the importance of innovation to meet competition, seeking new markets, providing financial services on a large scale,[118] and expansion, in the face of private competition, in the direction of large shopping centers. Prandini says, "I am not for a cooperative republic." Rather, he favors a pluralism of cooperative, private, and public firms. The aim is to decrease the strength of multinationals while increasing the strength of small and medium-sized businesses and to modernize the public sector. The only non-business parameter in his concerns was a prohibition of the export of military technology. The succeeding president, Lanfranco Turci, announced that "the Lega has exited the era of Brezhnev and has inaugurated glasnost." Under the new regime, efforts would be made to expand financial services, including the creation of a bank and selling shares in the stock market.[119]

In the early 1990s proposals were debated within the Lega itself to enable risk capitalists to purchase nonvoting shares, short of a majority, in cooperatives, thus opening up new sources of financing, and to open Lega membership to other forms of participatory and democratic enterprise, such as ESOPs.[120] Such measures, to be sure, have been promoted with a view to strengthening the co-op movement. But they are also motivated by the pessimistic fear that economic democracy must be justified primarily by its efficiency. "The social and cultural attraction of the cooperative formula itself has lost much of its appeal. This is the real problem to be faced. And it must be faced with no illusions as to the possibility of recovering the utopian and romantic attraction of 'self-management' that for so long after 1968 underlay the decision of many to set up cooperatives. The appeal of the cooperative movement today must rest above all upon its entrepreneurial incisiveness."[121]

My own visit in 1991 to the regional headquarters of the Lega in Emilia-Romagna suggested some hypotheses as to why a "cooperative republic" is not on the agenda of the Left. First, the intersectoral linkage of consumer, producer, housing, marketing, and other cooperatives that is a strength of the Italian cooperative movement also results in political inertia. Cooperators, so broadly and heterogeneously defined, are not easily mobilizable politically, in contrast with members of a union. Second, people from all parties participate in the cooperatives themselves, and they tend to set aside their political differences and concentrate on business concerns.

Both hypotheses are illustrated by the example of Riunite, the winery organized as a cooperative of three thousand growers, exporting 65 percent of its wine. The three-hundred-plus workers in the plant are not members but belong to a union. The thirty-five delegates who constitute the board of directors include Communists, Socialists, Christian Democrats, and others—"as it should be," according to the company's vice president, if politics is not to get in the way of business. This opinion was echoed by the president of the regional Lega, a Socialist, who thought that ideology should not enter into the work of the Lega and considered its political independence a strength. I asked him about wage differentials, making a comparison with Mondragon. On the one hand, he said that if managers are not paid comparably to those in capitalist firms, businesses will fail. But when I pointed out that differentials in the successful Mondragon co-ops had been held to 4.5 to 1, he replied that the rewards of working in a co-op where one is less servile are very attractive and might be worth a lower income. Concerning the first hypothesis, one has only to imagine the task of trying to mobilize thirty-five hundred independent farmers or small farms—some employing seasonal workers—to see how far Riunite, as a cooperative, differs from a union as a solidary social institution.

Thus, like the MCC, only more so, the Italian cooperative sector, immense in size and complexity, seems detached from radical politics, moving away from cooperative forms and principles. Its very success seems to have brought with it an inertia that raises doubts about its viability as a vehicle for social change. What I have offered in this section is little more than some initial observations. The status of the Italian cooperative movement and its potential as a third way, and not merely a third sector, merit further study.

In this chapter I have examined the worker cooperative as a kind of embryonic socialist institution. I have argued, first, that many of the problems cooperatives face are rooted in the surrounding capitalist context, not intrinsic difficulties with the cooperative form as such. Second, I have raised some questions about the desirability of generalizing the Mondragon model without revising it. A national economy must either restrict labor mobility or design enterprises that can accommodate more labor mobility than co-ops normally experience. Job creation, equitable distribution of wealth and income, and attention to the complex constituencies of work in the media, health care, and other non-commodity-producing domains will require institutions distinct from the Mondragon-style cooperative. As we shall see in the next chapter, social ownership and social investment should address all but the last of these problems. Self-management, in the long run, requires socialism. Later I examine the media and propose a mixture of institutions appropriate to the complexity of functions the media serve.

Third, I have argued that cooperatives in a market economy need not degenerate into capitalist firms, although the challenges in preventing this are formidable, particularly in a capitalist context. Finally, I have cautiously endorsed a union and left-wing strategy for worker ownership, recognizing that without a broad political movement including unions, worker participation, and linkage of worker ownership with measures favoring nonworkers and marginal workers (notably, a basic income), worker ownership could result in a privileged-worker aristocracy opposed to justice for the less advantaged. As the evolution of the MCC, the Italian cooperative sector, and ESOPs in the United States illustrate, a democratic, egalitarian outcome of the worker ownership movement is by no means guaranteed.

## NOTES

1. For detailed accounts, see William Foote Whyte and Kathleen King Whyte, *Making Mondragon: The Growth and Dynamics of the Worker Cooperative Complex* (Cornell University Press, 1988); Roy Morrison, *We Build the Road As We Travel* (Philadelphia: New Society Publishers, 1991); Henk Thomas and Chris Logan, *Mondragon: An Economic Analysis* (London: Allen and Unwin, 1982); and Greg MacLeod, *From Mondragon to America* (Sydney, Nova Scotia: University College of Cape Breton Press, 1997).

2. Exceptions are noted below.

3. Only 10 percent of workers surveyed in a Mondragon cooperative said they would prefer to work in a capitalist firm; Sharryn Kasmir, *The Myth of Mondragon: Cooperatives, Politics, and Working-Class Life in a Basque Town* (Albany: State University of New York Press, 1996), 165.

4. See Justin Schwartz, "Where Did Mill Go Wrong? or If Market Socialism Is So Wonderful, Why Doesn't It Already Exist?" Paper presented to the American Philosophical Association, Central Division, Kansas City, Missouri (May 1994), 11.

5. This paragraph is mostly a précis of Miller's argument. See David Miller, "Market Neutrality and the Failure of Cooperatives," *British Journal of Political Science* 11 (1981): 309–29.

6. James Meade, "The Theory of Labour-Managed Firms and of Profit-Sharing," *Economic Journal* 82 (1972): 402–428, quoted by Jacques H. Dréze, "Self-Management and Economic Theory: Efficiency, Funding, and Employment," in *Market Socialism: The Current Debate*, ed. Pranab K. Bardhan and John E. Roemer (Oxford: Oxford University Press, 1993), 258.

7. Benedetto Gui, "Basque versus Illyrian Labor-Managed Firms: The Problem of Property Rights," *Journal of Comparative Economics* 8 (1984): 168–81.

8. Ian Clegg, *Workers' Self-Management in Algeria* (New York: Monthly Review Press, 1972).

9. *Moral hazard* is "the presence of incentives for individuals to act in ways that incur costs that they do not have to bear," as when insured homeowners neglect to protect their property; Graham Bannock, R. E. Baxter, and Evan Davis, *The Penguin Dictionary of Economics* (London: Penguin Books, 1992), 295; Dréze, "Self-Management and Economic Theory."

10. See Jon Elster and Karl Ove Moene, introduction to *Alternatives to Capitalism* (Cambridge: Cambridge University Press, 1989), 33.

11. David Schweickart, *Against Capitalism* (Cambridge: Cambridge University Press, 1994), 293; Schwartz, "Where Did Mill Go Wrong?" 11–12.

12. Robert Nozick, *Anarchy, State, and Utopia* (New York: Basic Books, 1974), 232–75.

13. Jon Elster, "Self-Realization in Work and Politics," in Elster and Moene, *Alternatives to Capitalism,* 127–58.

14. Miller, "Market Neutrality," 323; the table is also Miller's.

15. Keith Bradley and Alan Gelb, "The Replication and Sustainability of the Mondragon Experiment," *British Journal of Industrial Relations* 20 (March 1982): 20–33, 31.

16. Bradley and Gelb, "The Replication and Sustainability," 31.

17. On the latter see D. M. Nuti, "Socialism on Earth," *Cambridge Journal of Economics* 5 (1981): 391–403. On the former, see John Roemer, "Can There Be Socialism after Communism?" in Bardhan and Roemer, *Market Socialism;* I discuss Roemer's non-worker-managed market socialism in chapter 8.

18. Robert Dahl, *A Preface to Economic Democracy* (Berkeley: University of California Press, 1985); Michael Walzer, *Spheres of Justice: A Defense of Pluralism and Equality* (New York: Basic Books, 1983); see also Samuel Bowles and Herbert Gintis, "A Political and Economic Case for the Democratic Enterprise," in *The Idea of Democracy,* ed. David Copp, Jean Hampton, and John E. Roemer (Cambridge: Cambridge University Press, 1993), 375–99; Carol C. Gould, *Rethinking Democracy* (Cambridge: Cambridge University Press, 1988); and Carole Pateman, *Participation and Democratic Theory* (Cambridge: Cambridge University Press, 1970). For criticism of these arguments, see Richard Arneson, "Democratic Rights at National and Workplace Levels," in Copp, Hampton, and Roemer, *The Idea of Democracy,* 118–48; and my reply in chapter 1.

19. For discussion of the media, see Michael W. Howard, "Media Democratization: Access or Autonomy?" *Socialist Forum* 20 (1993): 53–57; Michael W. Howard, "Self-Management, Ownership, and the Media," *Journal of Mass Media Ethics* 8, no. 4 (1994): 197–206; and chapter 11.

20. N. Scott Arnold, "Marx and Disequilibrium in Market Socialist Relations of Production," *Economics and Philosophy* 3 (1987): 23–48. See also the lively exchange over this article between Arnold and David Schweickart, in the subsequent issue of the journal.

21. Saul Estrin and William Bartlett, "The Effects of Enterprise Self-Management in Yugoslavia: An Empirical Survey," in *Participatory and Self-Managed Firms,* ed. Derek Jones and Jan Svejnar (Lexington, Mass.: Lexington Books, 1982), 86; Harold Lydall, *Yugoslav Socialism: Theory and Practice* (Oxford: Clarendon Press, 1984), 114.

22. Andrew Zimbalist, Howard Sherman, and Stuart Brown, *Comparing Economic Systems: A Political Economic Approach* (Fort Worth, Tex.: Harcourt Brace Jovanovich, 1989), 433–38. The problem is not just that enterprises must compete in a seller's market for managers. Because of the "need to make more rapid responses to the unstable market and the effort to influence actual market conditions," decision making is shifted to middle management in marketing.

23. Lydall, *Yugoslav Socialism,* 248–49. For an argument that the collapse of the former Yugoslavia should not be blamed on self-managed market socialism, see my "Market Socialism and Political Pluralism: Theoretical Reflections on Yugoslavia," in *Studies in East European Thought,* forthcoming.

24. This right to see company documents is "often practiced" in United States plywood cooperatives, according to Edward S. Greenberg, *Workplace Democracy: The Political Effects of Participation* (Ithaca: Cornell University Press, 1986), 50.

25. This was the case in the former Yugoslavia, where the power of the party considerably qualified self-management powers of workers. This leads one not very sympathetic commentator to distinguish Yugoslavia from "totalitarian" socialist states; Lydall, *Yugoslav Socialism*, 131. The change in social relations within a firm, which often accompanies these formal powers of self-management is evident in the plywood cooperatives described by Greenberg.

26. Judgments about relative power are complicated and must be carefully qualified. Thus, one could argue that Swedish workers, though not entitled to self-management rights, nevertheless have more power over their firms than Yugoslavian workers did over theirs, because of the power of the Swedish unions and the extensive rights, won through collective bargaining, over factory health conditions, job security, hiring and firing, work organization, and labor-market conditions versus, in Yugoslavia, the de facto control by local Communist Party organizations over the appointment and removal of directors, diminishing the accountability of the director to the workers. On Sweden, see Martin Carnoy and Derek Shearer, *Economic Democracy* (White Plains, N.Y.: M. E. Sharpe, 1980), 261–63. On Yugoslavia, see Lydall, *Yugoslav Socialism*, 119, 122–23, 246–47.

27. Most commentators on the Yugoslav economy note how rare it was for a firm to go bankrupt, because of bailouts by banks and government authorities. Another response to insolvency was mergers, with a resulting high concentration of industries and reduced competition.

28. Thomas and Logan, *Mondragon*.

29. The differential from highest- to lowest-paid in a Mondragon cooperative was, for a long time, 4.5 to 1; it has since widened somewhat, to 7 to 1, but still is substantially lower than what one might find in a capitalist firm in the United States (more than 400 to 1) or in many Yugoslav firms (20 to 1); Mark Lutz and Kenneth Lux, *Humanistic Economics: The New Challenge* (New York: Bootstrap Press, 1988), 262; Zimbalist, Sherman, and Brown, *Comparing Economic Systems*, 31–32. Pay differentials have widened dramatically in the United States in the last two decades, with the ratio of the pay of the average CEO to the average factory wage rising to 419 to 1 in 1998, compared with 42 to 1 in 1980, according to *Business Week*; quoted by the AFL-CIO, "How Much Would You Be Making if Your Pay Had Grown As CEO Pay Has?" <http://www.aflcio.org/paywatch/ceou_compare.htm> (12 May 1999).

30. Between 1975 and 1983, when the Basque economy lost sixty thousand jobs, the Mondragon group continued to expand, albeit more slowly with the depression of the Spanish economy in the early 1980s; Lutz and Lux, *Humanistic Economics*, 268.

31. Thomas and Logan, *Mondragon*, 142.

32. Exports made up 18 percent of aggregate sales in 1979, according to Thomas and Logan, *Mondragon*, 103. The percentage has increased in subsequent years.

33. Thomas and Logan, *Mondragon*. See also David Ellerman, "The Socialization of Entrepreneurialism: The Empresarial Division of the Caja Laboral Popular" (Somerville, Mass.: Industrial Cooperative Association, 1982).

34. The entrepreneurial services division split off to become an independent "second-tier" cooperative, that is, a cooperative that, like the bank, is controlled partly by its workers but also by representatives of the cooperatives it serves; Lutz and Lux, *Humanistic Economics*, 263 ff.

35. Comment by sociologist Peter Heisig, on a paper given by the author, at a meeting of the International Institute for Self-Management, Dubrovnik, Yugoslavia, 28 May–8 June 1990. Set against this observation is evidence from a recent survey of Spanish economics and business students that the MCC is the place where they most want to work, despite managerial and professional salaries 25 percent to 30 percent lower than those in other firms; National Center for Employee Ownership, "Companies," *Employee Ownership Report* 19, no. 2 (March–April 1999): 14.

36. Koldo Gorostiaga, a researcher on the Mondragon cooperatives from the University of the Basque Country, reported in conversation with the author in July 1998 that the MCC in its Third Congress had abandoned the long-standing requirement that individual cooperatives adhere to a differential established for the entire group.

37. Mark Lutz, in conversation, based on a research trip to Mondragon in the fall of 1996.

38. "By the end of 1994 [the MCC] had set up seven plants abroad" in Mexico, Thailand, Taiwan, China, Egypt, and Morocco, and it "intends to have twenty-two such plants open by the end of the century." None of these are cooperatives. Although "there are plans for at least considering implementation of profit sharing and a possibility of conversion into co-ops in the long run," the general manager of the Mexico plant had never heard of such plans as of summer 1997, though he thought it would be a good idea; Mark Lutz, "The Mondragon Cooperative Complex: An Application of Kantian Ethics to Social Economics," *International Review of Social Economics* 24, no.12 (December 1997): 1404–21; personal correspondence, 9 July 1997 and 20 July 1997.

39. Sally Hacker, *Pleasure, Power, and Technology* (London: Unwin Hyman, 1989), 108.

40. Hacker, *Pleasure, Power*, 129. Hacker notes that women are also enrolling in engineering courses in higher percentages (128).

41. Hacker, *Pleasure, Power*, 105.

42. Even the temporaries are referred to as *eventuales*, indicating some prospect of their becoming members at a future date; Lutz, "The Mondragon Cooperative Complex."

43. Greg MacLeod reports that even in the dynamic retail division, where much of the change—and employment growth—is occurring, the stores in and around Mondragon are cooperatively run; noncooperative stores elsewhere sell 8 percent of the shares to the supervisory staff; and locally produced products are promoted, all in contrast with the multinationals; e-mail correspondence, 6 May 1997.

44. "Fagor acusa a MCC de alejarse del co-operativismo," *Egin*, 28 February 1997, 25, translated by the author with assistance from José Guzman. The response of management has been to adopt a new policy that extends to temporary workers some of the rights of members—inadequate, but indicative of a shared acknowledgment of the problem; Mondragon Cooperative Corporation, "Temporary Members: Key Points," <http://www.mondragon.mcc.es./tu/english/9703/art2.htm> (18 July 1997).

45. Greenberg, *Workplace Democracy*; Mike Slott, "The Case against Worker Ownership," *Labor Research Review* 1, no. 6 (Spring 1985): 83–98.

46. George Will, "A New Chapter in Capitalism," *Boston Globe*, 6 December 1996.

47. David Ellerman, "ESOPs and Co-ops: Worker Capitalism and Worker Democracy," *Labor Research Review* 1, no. 6 (Spring 1985): 55–69, 59.

48. Quoted in Slott, "The Case against Worker Ownership," 87. For a case study of what can go wrong even in a union-organized worker buyout, see Gene Redmon, Chuck Mueller, and Gene Daniels, "A Lost Dream: Worker Control at Rath Packing," *Labor Research Review* 1, no. 6 (Spring 1985): 5–23.

49. Kasmir, *The Myth of Mondragon*, 86–87.

50. Kasmir, *The Myth of Mondragon*, 195, 161–63.Kasmir found that there was actually less participation in the social council of the cooperative she studied than there was in the workers' council of a comparable private firm. Less paid time was set aside for the council work, no independent union expertise could be called upon, and the council was compromised by serving a dual function, not only representing the workers' interests but also representing management concerns to workers (133–41).

51. Kasmir, *The Myth of Mondragon*, 190.

52. Kasmir, *The Myth of Mondragon*, 184, 38, 190.

53. Kasmir, *The Myth of Mondragon*, 180-81.

54. Kasmir, *The Myth of Mondragon*, 184.

55. Kasmir, *The Myth of Mondragon*, 190–91.

56. Kasmir, *The Myth of Mondragon*, 192.

57. Kasmir, *The Myth of Mondragon*, 189.

58. Kasmir, *The Myth of Mondragon*, 164.

59. Kasmir, *The Myth of Mondragon*, 198.

60. Quoted in "Unions and Worker Ownership," in *When Workers Decide*, ed. Len Krimerman and Frank Lindenfeld (Philadelphia: New Society Publishers, 1992), 172–73.

61. If unionized, the Mondragon cooperatives' solidarity with the labor movement might be strengthened.

62. Ronald L. Filipelli, *Labor in the USA: A History* (New York: Knopf, 1984), 64, 83, 130.

63. Lynn Williams, "Worker Ownership: A Better Alternative for the United Steel Workers: Interview with Lynn Williams," in Krimerman and Lindenfeld, *When Workers Decide*, 174–77; see also 207.

64. Krimerman and Lindenfeld, *When Workers Decide*, 71, 180–81. Of course, not all worker buyouts are cooperatives or involve worker participation in management.

65. According to Corey Rosen, only rarely are ESOPs used to prevent a hostile takeover or to make a publicly traded company private; "ESOPs: Hype or Hope?" in Krimerman and Lindenfeld, *When Workers Decide,* 185. Referring to downsizing, Joan Suarez, the key union organizer for the worker-owned textile firm, Colt Enterprises, said, "I just got tired of dealing with plant after plant closing"; Jackie Van Anda, "Colt Enterprises, Inc.: Union-Based Self-Determination in Texas," in Krimerman and Lindenfeld, *When Workers Decide*, 32.

66. Besides ESOPs, which account for about 40 percent of the assets and 58 percent of the seventeen million employee-owners, the most significant plans are 401(k) plans with assets invested in employee stock (more than two hundred and fifty billion dollars in assets per two million workers) and broad stock option plans (i.e., plans providing stock options to most employees—roughly $200 billion per seven million workers). Worker cooperatives make up an interesting but small slice of the worker ownership pie; National Center for Employee Ownership, "A Statistical Profile of Employee Ownership," updated January 1999, <http://www.nceo.org/library/eo_stat.html> (24 March 1999).

67. Blasi and Kruse predict that "by the year 2000, there will be more employees in firms that are *more than 15 percent employee held* than in the entire private sector trade union movement"; Joseph Blasi and Douglas Kruse, *The New Owners: The Mass Emergence of Employee Ownership in Public Companies and What It Means to American Business* (New York: HarperCollins, 1991), 12. Blasi claims that the prediction is proving to be accurate; personal correspondence, 25 March 1999.

68. Blasi and Kruse note that "the total employee-ownership sector is largely a nonunion sector, because over 87 percent of the private sector work force is already nonunion and because . . . [union members] are generally excluded from the employee-ownership plan", *The New Owners*, 12. For a short summary of data on ESOPs and a discussion of some of the main issues, see Krimerman and Lindenfeld, *When Workers Decide*, 186–92, 286–89. For lengthier treatments, see Joseph Blasi, *Employee Ownership: Revolution or Ripoff?* Cambridge: Ballinger Publishing, 1988); and Blasi and Kruse, *The New Owners*, see also chapters five through seven of David Ellerman, *The Democratic Worker-Owned Firm; A New Model for the East and West* (Boston: Unwin Hyman, 1990), for a critical evaluation and analysis of democratic ESOPs. For overviews and up to date information, visit the National Center for Employee Ownership web site (www.nceo.org). Electronic references to NCEO below are to documents available at this site.

69. Only 2 percent of cases fall into this category, according to Corey Rosen, "ESOPs: Hype or Hope?" in Krimerman and Lindenfeld, *When Workers Decide*, 184–87.

70. Although in public corporations, ESOPs "usually replace a company contribution to a 401(k) or profit-sharing plan"; National Center for Employee Ownership, "An Overview of ESOPs, Stock Options, and Employee Ownership," <http://www.nceo.org/library/overview.html> (20 July 1997).

71. Rosen, "ESOPs: Hype or Hope?" 184–87; Blasi, *Employee Ownership*, 101; Blasi and Kruse, *The New Owners*, 109. There is a trend toward companies eliminating defined-benefit plans, but few such eliminations involve substituting ESOPs, so ESOPs are not the cause of the trend but may be one of the better outcomes. The bottom line is that "it's better to get employee ownership instead of zero in return." It is estimated that overall compensation increased in 48 percent of cases and did not in 40 percent. "Workers are not getting ripped off by any stretch of the imagination"; Blasi and Kruse, *The New Owners*, 111, 130–31. They are, however, incurring risk, but Blasi and Kruse resignedly conclude that retirement plans invested in company stock are the wave of the future (132).

72. Blasi and Kruse, *The New Owners*, 28; Blasi, *Employee Ownership*, 101. "Although taxes may be a relevant factor, the corporate finance uses of employee ownership (such as cashing out a large shareholder) are motivated mainly by the ability of employee ownership to make possible financial transactions, which corporate boards of directors wish to complete"; Blasi and Kruse, *The New Owners*, 28.

73. Rosen, "ESOPs Hype or Hope?" 186; see also Blasi and Kruse, *The New Owners*, 228; National Center for Employee Ownership, "Employee Ownership and Corporate Performance," <http://www.nceo.org/library/corpperf.html> (10 March 1999).

74. Ninety percent of corporate wealth owned by households is owned by the richest 10 percent; Blasi, *Employee Ownership*, 17.

75. National Center for Employee Ownership, "ESOPs, Stock Options, and 401(k) Plans Now Control 9% of Corporate Equity," <http://www.nceo.org/library/control_eq.html> (20 July 1997).

76. Blasi, *Employee Ownership*, 114; other forms include real estate, bonds, business assets, etc.

77. Joseph Blasi, "Are ESOPs Part of the Problem? Interview with Joseph Blasi," in Krimerman and Lindenfeld, *When Workers Decide,* 188–90; Blasi, *Employee Ownership*, 114–15. In ESOPs all full-time employees with a year of service must participate, but allocations are usually proportional to wages and salaries, according to Corey Rosen (personal correspondence, 4 August 1997).

78. National Center for Employee Ownership, "Excerpts from *Employee Ownership and Corporate Performance*," <http://www.nceo.org/nceo/perf.html> (18 July 1997).

79. Rosen, "ESOPs Hype or Hope?" 187. More recent evidence suggests that more ESOP companies are giving full voting rights. National Center for Employee Ownership, "A Statistical Profile."

80. National Center for Employee Ownership, "Excerpts."

81. Blasi, "Are ESOPs Part of the Problem?" 188.

82. Frank Adams and Michelle Siegal, introduction to *Directory of Workers' Enterprises in North America*, (Boston: ICA Group, 1991). The Industrial Cooperative Association Group numbers worker cooperatives at five hundred; ICA Group, "Some Common Questions about Employee Ownership," <http://members.aol.com/icaica/ICAPAGE.htm> (29 April 1999). Blasi estimates that there are one thousand producer cooperatives; Blasi, *Employee Ownership*, 115. His criteria for what counts as a cooperative may be less exacting.

83. The National Center for Employee Ownership's estimate of three thousand majority employee-owned companies still puts the figure at less than 30 percent of the number of ESOPs of any significant size, and these are mostly in private companies, where numbers of employees and capital assets are smaller.

84. Adams and Siegal, *Directory of Workers' Enterprises,* 6–7.

85. National Center for Employee Ownership, "A Statistical Profile."

86. Blasi and Kruse, *The New Owners*, 8.

87. Blasi and Kruse, *The New Owners*, 242, 11.

88. Another reason for taking seriously the Employee Ownership 1,000 is Bennett Harrison's argument that it is big firms, not small firms, that are reorganizing global capitalism, creating new jobs, innovating, and developing flexible production networks. Some have argued that flexible manufacturing networks of small firms of highly skilled workers adapting rapidly to changing market demands, exemplified in Emilia-Romagna and other parts of northern Italy, are part of a "new industrial divide" away from "Fordist" mass manufacturing by large firms. Harrison's study suggests that the success of the "Third Italy" may have been an episode containing the seeds of its own demise and thus not particularly fertile soil for the emergence of a cooperative economy; Charles F. Sabel, *Work and Politics* (Cambridge: Cambridge University Press, 1982); Charles F. Sabel and Michael J. Piore, *The Second Industrial Divide: Possibilities for Prosperity* (New York: Basic Books, 1984); Bennett Harrison, *Lean and Mean: The Changing Landscape of Corporate Power in the Age of Flexibility* (New York: Basic Books, 1994) especially chapter four, 75–105; Robert Fitch, "In Bologna, Small Is Beautiful," *Nation*, 13 May 1996, 18–21; Robert D. Putnam, *Making Democracy Work: Civic Traditions in Modern Italy* (Princeton: Princeton University Press, 1993). For a more positive assessment of flexible manufacturing networks in the United States see Amy Borgstrom Somers, Jim Converse, Cathy Ivancic, and Ray West "Grassroots Economic Networking in Ohio,"

*Grassroots Economic Organizing Newsletter* 7 and 8 (January–February and March–April 1993).

89. Blasi and Kruse, *The New Owners*, 242.

90. Blasi and Kruse, *The New Owners*, 2, 28, 243.

91. Blasi and Kruse, *The New Owners*, 125, 132–33.

92. Blasi and Kruse, *The New Owners*, 125, 57, 243.

93. Blasi, *Employee Ownership*, 101.

94. Blasi and Kruse, *The New Owners*, 216. A study of Ohio ESOP firms shows significant improvement in participation since 1986. According to a report from the National Center for Employee Ownership, "One in six firms had nonmanagement employees on boards of directors or has had them in the past five years. . . . In 1986, 28% of the companies said employees wanted to participate more in decisions since the ESOP; in 1992–3, 63% said they did. . . . The incidence of various kinds of participation programs doubled or more since 1986. For instance, 42% of the companies had problem solving groups, compared to 20% before; labor–management teams grew from 11%–25%; self-managing work teams from 11%–21%. . . . The incidence of sharing financial information has increased 50% to 100%"; National Center for Employee Ownership, "Excerpts."

95. Blasi, *Employee Ownership*, 231.

96. Rosen, "ESOPs: Hype or Hope?" 186; but the Ohio study suggests a trend toward greater participation.

97. The percentage of private-company ESOPs with more than 50 percent of the company's stock will grow to 30 percent in the next five years; National Center for Employee Ownership, "A Statistical Profile."

98. Nine percent in conjunction with other forms of employee stock ownership; National Center for Employee Ownership, "ESOPs, Stock Options."

99. Blasi and Kruse, *The New Owners*, 254, 255; Weirton Steel is now less than 30 percent worker-owned, according to Corey Rosen, e-mail correspondence, 7 August 1997.

100. Blasi and Kruse, *The New Owners*, 35. The percentage of stock owned by households declined from 83 percent in 1960 to 59 percent in 1990; pension-fund ownership rose over the same period from 3.8 percent to 13.7 percent. Other institutional investors such as insurance companies and mutual funds have increased, but not so dramatically as pension funds, which now account for about 25 percent of corporate stock. About a third of corporate stock is now owned by these and other institutional investors, 36; Blasi, *Employee Ownership*, 15–17.

101. United Parcel Service, with 315,000 employees, and Publix Supermarkets, with 95,000, are larger employee-owned companies, but some or all of the stock is acquired through vehicles other than an ESOP; National Center for Employee Ownership, "The Employee Ownership 100," *Employee Ownership Report* 17, no. 4 (July–August 1997): 8–9. Most of the employee-owned stock of UPS is owned by managers and was not available to nonmanagerial or part-time workers until 1995, which may explain in part why workers at this worker-owned company struck against the company in 1997; United Parcel Service, "UPS Extends Stock Ownership to Nonmanagement Employees," <http://www.ups.com/news/950828stock.html> (6 August 1997)

102. Susan Chandler, "United We Own," *Business Week*, 18 March 1996, 96–100.

103. Susan Carey, "As UAL, USAir Talk, They Let World Overhear," *Wall Street Journal*, 10 November 1995; and "UAL Appoints a Mediator Head of Human Resources," *Wall Street Journal*, 3 March 1997.

104.  Chandler, "United We Own."

105.  Robert Oakeshott judges the $60 million in savings to be "rather modest," being less than one-half of one percent of United's annual cost base, a significantly smaller percentage than other majority employee-owned businesses in the United States and the United Kingdom have achieved. Oakeshott qualifies his criticism by noting that the experiment is only two years old and that cost savings may be more difficult in the airline business than in manufacturing; Robert Oakeshott, *Majority Employee Ownership at United Airlines: Evidence of Big Wins for Both Jobs and Investors* (London: Partnership Research, 1997), 53–54.

106.  Carey, "As UAL, USAir Talk"; Kenneth Labiche, "When Workers Really Count," *Fortune,* 14 October 1996, 213–14; Chandler, "United We Own."

107.  Quoted in Carey, "As UAL, USAir Talk."

108.  Quoted in Labiche, "When Workers Really Count," 214. James E. Goodwin succeeds Gerald Greenwald as chief executive officer of UAL effective July 1999; <http://www.ual.com/airline/default.asp?SubCategory=our_company> (10 May 1999).

109.  "Defunct Eastern Airlines Inc. and other carriers had great success with the idea in the mid-1980s—only to see it fizzle when fare wars hit." More recently, "Northwest Airlines Inc. and Trans World Airlines Inc. have sold 30 percent stocks to employees," and in February 1996, "Delta traded two percent cuts for a non-voting board seat and stock options on nineteen percent of the company"; Chandler,"United We Own," 96–100; see also Blasi and Kruse, *The New Owners,* 102–4, for earlier cases.

110.  Christopher Mackin, "Will United Buyout Get Off the Ground?" *Los Angeles Times,* 11 July 1994.

111.  Chandler, "United We Own," 100.

112.  Oakeshott, *Majority Employee Ownership,* 12.

113.  Oakeshott, *Majority Employee Ownership,* 15–19. Of course, a militant union may still be unwilling to support wider solidarity with other oppressed groups. I have seen no statement of the unions' positions on the issue, but United has fought a San Fransisco ordinance requiring companies doing business with the city to extend to employees' domestic partners those benefits afforded to employee's spouses—hardly a gesture in support of gay rights. See Jessica Champagne, "Boycott Action News," *Co-op America Quarterly* 48 (Summer 1999): 29.

114.  Edwin Morley-Fletcher, "The Cooperative Movement and the Left in Twentieth Century Europe (with Special Reference to Some Suggestions Arising from the Current Italian Debate)," paper presented at a conference of the International Institute for Self-Management, Ariccia, Italy, 26 October 1992.

115.  This fact reflects a trend toward concentration, particularly in retail trade. Interestingly, it is the Christian Confederation, not the secular Left, that has sought to preserve a small scale, to facilitate the social values of cooperatives, face-to-face membership, et cetera.

116.  John Earle, *The Italian Cooperative Movement* (London: Allen and Unwin, 1986).

117.  Paulo Pilati, "Lega di Denari," *L'Espresso,* 20 September 1987, 243–44.

118.  Here the plans and existing institutions (Fincooper, Unipol) invite comparison with Mondragon's Caja Laboral.

119.  Pilati, "Lega di Denari," quotation translated by the author.

120.  Morley-Fletcher, "The Cooperative Movement and the Left in Twentieth Century Europe."

121. Morley-Fletcher, "The Cooperative Movement and the Left in Twentieth Century Europe." He defends his proposal for a capital fund generated from a percentage of the profits of cooperatives by appeal to an egalitarian ideal of a "right to enterprise" made general, rather than the privilege of those who inherit wealth, but otherwise his perspective is one of aggressively molding cooperatives to the requirements of the market.

# 8

# Models of Market Socialism

In the previous chapter, which examined the theory and practice of cooperatives, I argued that cooperatives left to themselves cannot be expected to displace capitalism. They encounter technical limitations to their expansion, such as limited labor mobility and insufficient diversification of risk, connected with their private property bases. They also experience collective action problems, particularly in a capitalist context. Even developed cooperative networks, such as the Mondragon cooperatives or the Italian Lega, can not through their own resources fully address the challenges of job creation and the equitable distribution of income, wealth, and power.[1] Although the alienation of labor in the workplace is attenuated to some degree in a worker-owned cooperative, the commodity fetishism of the market remains intact to the extent that enterprises are autonomous and no countervailing social and political institutions exist to address common problems such as environmental devastation and the pace of growth.

For all these reasons, some form of socialism is still on the agenda, specifically, some model of social organization that seeks systematically to rectify the inequality of capitalism and to counterbalance the anarchy of the market. For reasons offered in part one, replacing the market with central planning, even of a democratic sort, is undesirable. Thus I turn to two models of market socialism.

The first, advocated by John Roemer, gives primacy to the problem of inequality but makes no space for self-management. It also takes to heart efficiency arguments for private property but seeks to keep ownership widely dispersed through citizen shareholding. Because of the centrality of a kind of socialist stock market in this model, I call it "coupon socialism." This model has much to recommend it, both in terms of efficiency and equality; however, I argue that it abandons too much of what is appealing in the socialist project.

The second model, economic democracy, tries to combine public property with worker self-management and comes closer to capturing what is appealing in the Mondragon model in a way that can be generalized. But it may not meet the efficiency challenge of socialism's critics as well as does coupon socialism, and it may allow more unjust inequality than coupon socialism.

## COUPON SOCIALISM

Why did socialism fail? Are there any feasible models for a comeback? John Roemer sheds light on the first question and answers affirmatively the second. But what he offers is an iconoclastic, minimalist socialism that shares the following with capitalism: wage labor, property income, a stock market, hierarchical work relations, and a sharp separation of the economic and political spheres.[2]

One argument in support of this form of market socialism in contrast with other models such as economic democracy, not to mention proposals for democratic planning that abolish the market, is that it is more likely to be as efficient as capitalism, because it departs least from it. The importance of this point emerges in Roemer's discussion of why centrally planned socialism failed. Part of the failure he attributes to principal–agent problems—difficulties in successfully monitoring and motivating managers and other agents to do what they are supposed to do.[3] But more important was the failure, from the 1970s onward, sufficiently to innovate in competition with capitalist countries. The only way systematically to promote innovation, Roemer argues, is through firms competing in a market.[4]

The challenge, then, is how to structure ownership and the monitoring of firms and distribution of profits to ensure efficiency and innovation comparable to that of capitalism, while at the same time moving closer to the egalitarian goals of socialists, namely, "equal opportunity for: (1) self-realization and welfare, (2) political influence, and (3) social status."[5]

The key to achieving these goals, according to Roemer, is not public ownership, of which "socialists have made a fetish,"[6] but whatever forms of ownership promote socialist goals. The most important short-term goal on the way to equality is some form of market socialism, "any of a variety of economic arrangements in which most goods, including labor, are distributed through the price system, and the profits of firms, perhaps managed by workers or not, are distributed quite equally among the population."[7] Although inequality stemming from differences in wages will remain, the much larger property income inequality will be abolished. This, incidentally, at least partially solves the question of how to finance a basic income. Each American adult citizen's share of profits annually (in the 1980s) would have amounted to about fifteen hundred dollars, according to Roemer (see chapter 2).

Roemer's own preferred model of market socialism retains the profit-maximizing firm (PMF) versus the labor-managed, worker-income-maximizing firm

(LMF) favored by some other market socialists, including this author; small private firms could exist; firms would be financed through bank loans, but profits could be distributed to individual shareholders. However, unlike shares in the capitalist stock market, these shares could not be bought or sold for cash. The government would issue coupons to citizens when they reached adulthood, and citizens would purchase stock with the coupons, which could, in turn, be sold for other coupons. At death each citizen's shares or coupons would revert to the state for redistribution. The trading of shares in pursuit of the highest profits would result in price differentials for the stock of different firms, reflecting their profitability and efficiency, and would thus discipline firms, in much the same way as a capitalist stock market, to economize and innovate.[8]

However, capital would be raised not by firms issuing new stock to purchasers with cash but rather through borrowing from publicly owned banks. These banks would, moreover, be the principal monitoring agents of firms' performance, having an interest in the ability of firms to repay their loans. Roemer acknowledges that one of the central unsolved problems is how to ensure that the banks perform this function and not, as public institutions, cave in to the soft-budget constraint, the tendency to abandon economic discipline in the face of political pressure, which has been the Achilles' heel of socialist economies. He and Pranab Bardhan propose a number of reasonable measures to insulate banks from such pressure and cite as successful models the Japanese *keiretsu*, clusters of firms organized around and monitored by a bank.

(Some of these measures may run counter to socialist goals: if bank management were evaluated only on economic criteria, it would result in bank and firm practices oblivious to externalities, such as unemployment or pollution; international competition could imperil the ability of a community to regulate its own environment, working conditions, and the like—as critics of NAFTA have pointed out. But, as we shall see, in a market-socialist society there may be stronger political forces to counter these market tendencies.)

So much for the market part. How is this socialist? "Because money cannot be used on the coupon stock market, the small class of wealthy citizens will not end up owning the majority of shares."[9] There would evidently be wealthy citizens, for several reasons: wage differentials; successful trading in the coupon market resulting in higher returns on one's shares; and perhaps more profoundly, entrepreneurs accumulating wealth through the sale of small private firms when they reach a certain size. Roemer repeatedly reminds us that he has no opposition to conventional social-democratic redistributive measures, so perhaps the wealth differentials arising from such entrepreneurial activity could be kept within bounds through taxation and redistribution, balancing the social utility of encouraging innovation against the evils of inequality. In any case, the main effects of the coupon economy would be a radical and permanent deconcentration and diffusion of profits throughout the economy and the elimination of a class of big capitalists.

Such a reform would also serve to eliminate a number of "public bads" that arise in capitalism because they enhance profits for wealthy owners. Small shareholders would not have so much incentive to generate pollution or to start wars to lower oil prices; "there would exist no small, powerful class of people deriving gargantuan amounts of income from profits, hence no class would have an interest in fighting for large levels of public bads."[10]

The extent to which public bads would be eliminated in a market-socialist society would depend on the character of politics in the society. Although the banks and firms would, by design, be constrained to profit maximization and as institutions would probably behave like their capitalist counterparts, individuals would no longer divide into classes, with a capitalist class having a stronger interest in public bads and possessed of the means to exert greater political influence. Thus in this environment, though there might still be economic motivation for pollution, imperialism, and so forth, the political playing field would be more even, and environmentalists and other groups could exert proportionately greater influence in public affairs.[11]

How much greater is hard to gauge. The society would still be competitive and individualist. Indeed, one of the virtues Roemer claims for his model is that it would function with people as we know them today. It would not require a new, cooperative, altruistic "socialist man." There can be little doubt that such a socialism would be a significant step toward a more egalitarian society. It may well be the only feasible alternative available in the former socialist countries or in developing countries, where socialism is likely to be politically possible.

But should socialists scale down their expectations and concentrate their efforts on some variant of profit redistribution? Why, for example, should democratization of production, through worker self-management, not also be on the agenda, both as a laboratory for developing cooperative abilities within capitalism and as a key part of the alternative to capitalism?

Roemer acknowledges the principal weakness of his model to be that firms are not democratic, but he has reservations about worker self-management. Foremost among these is that labor-managed firms may be too risk averse and thus not sufficiently innovative.[12] The innovation exhibited by the Mondragon cooperatives would presumably not count as counter-evidence, because they operate in a fiercely competitive environment competing with managerial firms. Roemer's fear is that without the managerial firms the pressure for innovation would slacken and socialism would once again lose ground in comparison with capitalism. Thus, he suggests, it might be desirable, even in an economy with a large co-op sector, to have a critical mass of managerial firms setting the pace of innovation. (Even if we grant Roemer's argument, this critical mass could also be provided by foreign competition, as long as markets remained open. At some distant future point when the whole world was cooperativized, the invidious comparisons would no longer be relevant.)

Roemer's second reservation about self-management is that, assuming firms are not self-financing, self-management in LMFs would be compromised by control exerted by external sources of financing, whether banks or stockholders. Because of this, the significance of self-management in such an environment may be overrated. However, the Mondragon case is a good example of bank-financed cooperatives. Yet here it would be wrong to conclude that self-management was insignificant.

Roemer's third concern is that managerial market socialism, being closer to capitalism than self-managed market socialism, has a greater likelihood of being as efficient as capitalism. The trouble with this conservative position is that it ignores all the arguments for the efficiency advantages of worker self-management stemming from greater worker commitment and participation.[13] Add to these the arguments for democratizing firms on grounds of justice—a core concern for socialists—and the case for the self-managed variant becomes even stronger.[14]

Furthermore, a troubling feature of Roemer's model is the maintenance of the labor market. The argument for this is that the labor market is necessary to insure efficient allocation of labor.[15] Won't this perpetuate the condition of workers being coerced into labor, and thus in a relation of antagonism with employers?[16] Won't such a labor market also result in unemployment, favored by profit-maximizing firms insofar as it exerts a downward pressure on wages?[17]

The labor-managed variant, granted, will have something like a labor market, insofar as firms compete with one other for members and establish wage differentials within the firm reflecting the cost and scarcity of skills. But becoming a member of a self-managed firm, is qualitatively different from being hired as a wage worker, because of the democratic rights attached to membership. The LMF can be expected to have a flatter hierarchy with lower wage differentials and greater security of employment. Most importantly, the capacity of workers to fire the manager is a fundamental shift from capital hiring labor to labor hiring capital. It is difficult to estimate a priori, but it could be that more egalitarian differentials within LMFs would result in more equal distribution overall than equal distribution of profits generated in profit-maximizing firms. Perhaps even more importantly, democratic control of managers by workers would be a more effective safeguard against managers' becoming a new class than anything available in coupon socialism without LMFs. So let us turn now to a model of socialism that features worker management of firms, as in the cooperative society, but without some of the self-limiting features of the Mondragon model.

## ECONOMIC DEMOCRACY

Recall that in David Schweickart's model, called economic democracy (ED), all firms above a certain size are worker managed, buying and selling in the market and deciding how to distribute the net proceeds among themselves (after subtracting depreciation and capital costs, including a tax on capital assets). But the firms are not worker owned. They are the collective property of society. Workers only use them, pay a tax for the use, and are obliged to maintain them. Hence, they have no incentive—and are not allowed—to invest profits in the firm except to cover depreciation costs. Investment is financed entirely externally, by a national investment fund, which is financed by the tax on capital assets. The fund is dispersed to regions (perhaps on a per capita basis), and regional or local communities, in turn, dispense funds to local banks on the basis of past success in making profitable investment, creating jobs, and possibly other criteria (for example, environmental). Any excess funds are returned to the fund for reallocation.

I have already written at length on worker management in the previous chapter; what I want to focus on here are the particularly socialist aspects of ED: collective ownership of enterprises and the public investment fund. Before addressing problems with this public ownership scheme, let us consider the reasons for it:

- In contrast with self-financing by labor-managed firms, risk will be socialized, so LMFs will not be risk averse. (The problem, as we shall see, is that investment managers may not be sufficiently risk averse to avoid bad investments.)
- Merging public and private investment will lead to more balanced growth (for example, transportation policy could coordinate investment in public versus private means of transportation). More generally, democratic priorities can be built into the investment process itself. Another important example is the capacity to promote full employment.
- The distribution of investment to regions could be on a per capita basis, evening out inequalities and thus raising overall welfare.
- Destructive export policies—for example, export of food together with destruction of subsistence agriculture—can be curbed directly.
- Capital will not flee localities with strong environmental and workplace protection or flow out of the country.
- The pace of growth can be set democratically by deciding on the tax rate on capital assets.
- There will be a limit to inequality of wealth. Small-scale entrepreneurs can become wealthy, but they cannot turn their purchasing power into capital and hence control over the labor process and the social surplus. Particular cooperatives may reap windfall profits from advantageous positioning in the market, and members may enjoy enhanced incomes, but in a competitive environment such gains will be short lived and, again, can not be transmitted into capital wealth. No one will make money simply from having money. From the standpoint of political equality, no one will have so much that he or she can dominate others, or so little that he or she can be dominated.

- Also worth mentioning is that private investors will not be able to hold the state hostage through threats of an investment strike.

A common objection to any system of public ownership is that it falls prey to the soft-budget constraint:[18] it is unable to replicate successfully the incentives for profitable and efficient investment provided by private ownership and capital markets. The key problem has to do with the centralization and diffuseness of ownership. As Aristotle long ago observed, if everyone owns property in common, no one has a large enough stake to care for it.[19] Nowadays the argument is described as an agency problem, with the public as principal and the investment fund managers as agents. In economic democracy, these managers are responsible for

- assessing the value of capital assets of thousands of firms
- disbursing (at a local level) the funds to banks, after
- determining the success of these banks in making profitable grants, generating employment, and possibly meeting other political objectives, and
- making reallocations after assessing the comparative success of different banks and enterprise groups.

Each bank is responsible for assessing the success of its own grants, that is, the financial health of firms in its group, for example, monitoring balance sheets and manager performance.

In short, local banks monitor firms, regional communities monitor local banks, the central bank monitors regions, and the public monitors the central bank through the political process.

According to Louis Putterman, the weakness in such a system is the last of these, the relationship between the public and the investment fund managers.

There are limits both on the public's *ability* to evaluate bureaucratic and government performance and on its *motivation* to engage in the research activity necessary to such evaluation. With respect to the difficulty of assessment, not only are the targets of evaluation numerous, but also the ability to form judgments will be hampered by the dearth of alternative or counterfactual information. Whereas an investor has simple criteria at hand when choosing between a bank paying 6 percent and another offering 5.5 percent interest on its savings accounts, or between a mutual fund that has achieved returns of 8.5 percent and another that has achieved returns of 7.5 percent in a given period, if the state is the only investor and achieves a return of 8 percent on the public portfolio, it may be difficult for a citizen to judge whether it would have been possible to achieve 8.5 percent through a more careful choice of projects.[20]

Putterman's argument is that the breakdown in monitoring at the top filters all the way down. Because the central bank is not held to the fire by the owners of the collective capital, regional banks can be assured of their per capita allotments, regardless of performance, at least within certain broad parameters. I think, however, that Putterman's worries about the national level are exaggerated. Although it is true that the per capita funds will roll in to communities regardless of their subsequent allocation, everyone in the regional community will have a stake in wise investment of these funds. The numerous local banks and enterprise groups will compete vigorously for these funds, and gross misallocations by fund managers can be sure to provoke public criticism and political challenge. Putterman's objection would have more weight for a scheme in which investment allocations to individual enterprises was made by a central bureaucracy rather than a regional or local community.

On the other hand, the regional bank or community, in monitoring local banks and enterprise groups, has relatively weak incentive to impose hard-budget constraints, whereas pressure to subsidize ailing firms will be strong. The problem is compounded by the difficulty of getting accurate information about firm performance (short of catastrophic failure) and the incentives to do so. Local banks might compete for public funds, as contractors bid for public contracts, where ability to return appropriate taxes in the long run would be one of the salient criteria. But this seems a very weak test of profitable investment. The community officials will have no strong incentive to monitor banks carefully, because their incomes are independent of the success of the banks they finance.

One microincentive solution would be to tie the income of the community fund managers to their success in monitoring local banks—that is, to the ultimate success of the investment projects. For this to work, enterprises would need to return a proportion of their net profit—not just a tax—to the bank, and a sizable part of this would go to the bank manager. It is unclear how large a chunk of the profit would have to be passed upward for this incentive to be effective. The larger the chunk, the more this solution represents a capitulation to capitalist relations (and the more the workers' residual claimancy is reduced to profit sharing). There is reason to think that a relatively small chunk would not suffice to provide a substitute for effective supervision of the managers.[21]

To these macro problems of public ownership may be added certain difficulties at the level of the firm in ED: In ED, firms are financed entirely externally, from the investment fund. This makes the firm more like a Yugoslav self-managed enterprise than a Basque cooperative. The latter is distinguished by substantial equity financing through worker membership fees, internal capital accounts, and a collective capital account. Opponents of internal financing fear an inefficient allocation of capital and labor. Some, such as Jaroslav Vanek, propose complete external financing as the solution.[22]

But, as Benedetto Gui notes, complete external financing brings with it the "serious moral hazard resulting from the possibility of bankruptcy."[23] This hazard is unlikely to be undertaken by lenders in a capitalist capital market (hence one reason for the relatively small number of cooperatives, given the paucity of capital in workers' hands). In ED, the hazard is born by society, as risky ventures are funded, at little cost to the workers or agents making the grants. The safest solution, in the case of bad investments, will generally be to keep providing grants even when a firm has difficulty paying its capital tax, on grounds of employment creation.

There may also be a high cost in X-efficiency from external financing, in terms of loss of personal commitment to the firm on the part of its workers. *X-efficiency* is the benefit derived from the organizational structure of the firm, such as the higher level of worker motivation that might result from worker control of the firm, compared with control by managers and nonworking stockholders.[24] As Bradley and Gelb note, in the Mondragon cooperatives, most workers see their investments as a major factor in their belief that they and their co-workers will work well. Moreover, "divorcing rewards from returns to co-operative capital provides a strong incentive for decapitalization." In ED, laws would forbid depletion of operating capital and mandate depreciation funds for replenishment, but de facto decapitalization would be difficult to monitor.

The relatively low labor mobility characteristic of the Mondragon co-ops, and necessary for their success, would be less characteristic of firms in ED, because the loss of a worker would not mean the loss of invested capital. This is an advantage, on the one hand, in that worker management can thus be adapted to situations of higher labor mobility, and firms would not face a capital loss crisis when a generation of workers retires. But by the same token, no worker has an incentive to stay with a firm, particularly when it is going through economic difficulties. Additional financial incentives will need to be offered, and this will further reduce the efficiency advantage of the co-op form.

All these considerations raise doubts about the capacity of undifferentiated public ownership to counter the agency problem and overcome the soft-budget constraint. They argue for a model that allows for a degree of private ownership (as in the Mondragon co-ops) or simulates more closely the financial or capital markets in a capitalist economy.

Thomas Weisskopf proposes allowing self-managed firms to acquire assets in four ways:

1. leasing
2. borrowing from self-managed banks
3. selling nonvoting tradable shares
4. investing some net returns in nonvoting nontradable shares (akin to the internal capital accounts)

The internal capital accounts would be a fairly widely dispersed form of property, linked to work and available to most workers, and would not compromise the democratic governance of firms. But the first three allow for pure property income: some firms or individuals would collect leasing fees or rent on capital goods, and cooperative banks would earn income on financial transactions. The buying and selling of shares allows additional income on property. External shareholders would have no formal control rights, but Weisskopf readily admits that such financial power would lead to de facto control over some firms, probably explicitly agreed upon in financial contracts.[25]

To prevent concentration of such equity in a few hands, the tradable shares could be organized in mutual funds and, as in Roemer's model, not convertible into cash. At the initiation of the scheme each citizen would be issued coupons (or "clam shells") tradable for stocks. The stocks could be traded only for coupons, and vice versa. Upon death a citizen's portfolio would revert to the community for redistribution. But during a person's lifetime a personalized portfolio reflecting the person's risk aversion and judgment as to the profitability of enterprises could be developed. More plausibly, mutual funds would compete for investments from coupon holders, earning a percentage of the dividends. (These mutual funds could be organized as service cooperatives.)

Roemer and Bardhan have described how stockholding groups could be formed around monitoring banks, with the aim of mutual monitoring, motivated by the shareholding of each in the others. The risk would ultimately be borne by the citizen shareholders, who in the worst case would stand to lose all their property income. But unlike in the undifferentiated public ownership system, their holdings would be focused in particular firms or mutual funds and would be shifted to the investments offering the higher returns.[26]

In correspondence with the author, Schweickart has argued that this synthesis of ED and coupon socialism will not function to provide additional sources of capital to firms. "If firms can't sell shares for cash—not coupons—then they won't get any capital. But if people have to pay cash for these shares, they would certainly expect to be able to sell them for cash, not coupons. If the shares aren't liquid, they're not going to be a significant source of new capital for firms."[27] However, the coupon–share system can provide new capital in other ways. Banks could issue equity in the form of coupons, as well as loans and grants. As in ED, the state provides capital, collected through taxation, but in addition to (or even instead of) outright capital grants that are vaguely socially owned, the banks could simultaneously issue cash to the firm and claimancy rights to the bearers of shares purchased with coupons. The firm does not issue the shares, the state does. But as new social wealth emerges, its owners can as easily be identifiable shareholders as society at large.

This seems to me the best proposal to date for meeting the soft-budget constraint while maintaining an egalitarian distribution of wealth. What is lost? And is the loss worth the gain? The flip side of a financial system modeled on stock markets and profit-maximizing banks is that noneconomic imperatives become marginalized from the investment and production process. Shareholders will seek maximum return on investment and, hence, will invest in the most rapidly growing firms. To attract such investment, firms will need to adopt the most efficient work method and give priority to growth. The rate of growth will be the unintended effect of thousands of small decisions rather than the result of conscious democratic deliberation. Trade-offs between work and leisure and humanization of work will not be given scope. Environmental concerns will continue to fall outside the economic domain and clash with the decisions of enterprises. Self-management will be weakened by the financial control of outside investors and by competition from small businesses.[28] There will be a corresponding weakening of the advantages of self-management.

Thus, I think it safe to say that there is no easy synthesis of ED and coupon socialism. The efficiency advantages of the latter come at a price: many of the goals motivating socialism in the first place become marginalized. But coupon socialism offers a more plausible solution than ED to the agency problem associated with public ownership, and so a model incorporating some elements of coupon socialism may stand a chance of gaining acceptance in the competition with capitalism, among those most concerned with allocational efficiency. On the other hand, economic democracy extrapolates from existing trends toward worker ownership and participation, in effect strengthening the power of workers while weakening that of outside stockholders, and promises numerous other ends marginal to coupon socialism, and so may stand a better chance of gaining acceptance among those strongly supporting these ends.

A final consideration that tips the balance toward ED has to do with the political transition to socialism. No model of socialism will come into existence without the self-conscious movement of a large part, if not a majority, of the population of capitalist society. The high degree of political consciousness, commitment, and solidarity necessary for such a transition might be expected to lay to rest concerns about principal–agent problems. If the people can get its act together to overthrow capitalism, surely it will be vigilant and informed enough to monitor and discipline corrupt or inept bankers. As Schweickart confessed to me in correspondence, "I don't see any way around the principal–agent problems you point to, apart from open books, democracy, and a culture that values and promotes responsible behavior." Exactly. It may be that what separates socialists from nonsocialists, more than anything else, is our conviction that such a culture is possible. The blind spot in Roemer's allegedly more realistic reliance on material incentives is that he neglects the question of how coupon socialism could ever be brought into being with people as economically self-interested as they appear in capitalist society (or economists' models thereof). If people became public-minded enough to make such a revolution, why would they fail, subsequently, to monitor the banks?[29]

## UNEMPLOYMENT UNDER ECONOMIC DEMOCRACY

For all its faults, one of the strengths of centrally planned socialism was its ability to provide full employment and in so doing to avoid the often unmeasured social costs of unemployment: unjust inequality, poverty, crime, drug abuse, and despair. The inefficient allocation of labor in such a system and poor labor discipline nevertheless ultimately argue for the introduction of markets, at least in products and material inputs, if not in labor and capital. All the evidence on labor productivity improvement resulting from worker participation, particularly when coupled with profit-sharing and job security suggests that worker-managed firms, in which each worker gets a share of the profits (or losses), should provide sufficient incentives for efficient production at the level of the firm.

Schweickart has argued that such a system, when combined with public allocation of investment funds, could achieve full employment. The inability of any known market economy to achieve full employment should make us pause. But then no market economy has incorporated this mechanism for investment. To be fair, the criterion we should use to evaluate ED is not ideal full employment but rather superior employment creation in comparison with other models.

Consider first the worker-management dimension. On the one hand, a worker-managed firm will be less expansionary than a capitalist firm. Like a capitalist firm it can be expected to expand in response to substantial and seemingly permanent increases in demand or significantly increasing returns to scale. Either the long-term viability of the firm or the income per worker would be enhanced in these cases.

But a worker-managed firm, in contrast with a capitalist firm, will not typically expand when returns to scale are constant or when cost reductions make possible price reductions and increased production. It might prefer instead to reap more income at a steady price or reduce necessary labor time. This flexibility, spread over the economy, is itself an advantage not to be lightly dismissed. The reduced growth imperative takes on added importance in the context of the ecological crisis: an economy that, unlike capitalism, does not need to grow may be our best hope for sustainable development.

The down side is that, if additional employment is needed, the impetus will not come from enterprises. It will have to come from would-be managers, banks, or groups of workers. Groups of workers will always face a collective action hurdle. That applies to some degree to the would-be manager as well, to the extent that he or she is but one of the group, would not stand to gain exorbitantly by the undertaking, and would be bearing a rather large risk, in terms of time and possible lost opportunities for more stable employment. Thus, a lot of the initiative would fall back on the bank.

The bank managers could be induced to make employment creation a major criterion in the funding of enterprises. Indeed, Schweickart gives this criterion almost equal weight with efficient investment. But here we encounter the soft-budget constraint head on. The pressure to fund employment and keep enterprises going regardless of performance will be difficult to resist, particularly when taxation guarantees a steady flow of investment funds. Banks will be competing with one another for these funds, but there is no more a guarantee that the "hard" constraints of market viability will win out over the "soft" continuing employment concerns in this economy than in socialist experiments we have seen.

Let us assume, nevertheless, that a way is found to impose a limit on the funding of unprofitable ventures, a "three strikes and you're out" rule for failing enterprises. Can the economy achieve full employment better than capitalism? One factor in its favor is the tendency of worker-managed firms to retain workers during economic downturns and share the burden of lost sales. This amounts to a shifting of risk to workers, to the extent that their incomes are a proportion of net proceeds rather than a fixed wage. It will also be unequally distributed to workers in some firms or industries more than others. But these inequities may be warranted for the sake of efficiency, particularly if the minimum income and benefits are set sufficiently high.[30]

Still, the economy will probably not spontaneously generate demand for new workers sufficient to meet the supply. This is where investment planning comes in. Information on unemployment will be one important signal to those responsible for making loans to set the cost of loans at a level designed to stimulate new initiatives from would-be producers.

But this alone may not be enough to bring about the desired level of employment. In economic democracy, just as in a capitalist economy, investment does not respond automatically to lower interest rates if the effective demand is missing. (The fact that fewer workers will have been laid off will not improve effective demand in comparison with a capitalist economy, if these workers have agreed among themselves to work less and reduce their incomes.) To generate the requisite employment, short of unprofitable public works projects, it may be necessary to set the cost of loans below the level required to sustain real capital growth—in effect subsidizing producers to invest. (On the other hand, given the collective action problem, banks might find themselves confronted with more requests from "small businesses" than from cooperatives and end up financing more of these than a balanced self-managed economy could permit.) Once banks cross the line from supporting profitable investments to subsidizing much riskier initiatives, on balance unprofitable, the state will face either a political crisis or the ramifications of the soft-budget constraint familiar in the planned economies.

Perhaps this case is overstated. One problem in a capitalist economy is the lack of coordination between public and private investment, with the former usually starved below socially optimal levels—witness the potholes in the roads and the poor state of public transportation or the low level of research into sustainable energy alternatives. A national investment fund could more easily shift available funds into worthy public projects and at the same time generate additional demand for products from the self-managed sector. Although this flexibility raises significant risk of allocational inefficiencies, it may more than compensate for these in Keynesian efficiencies (generating effective demand) and provision of needed public goods.

My point is not to make a case for the superiority of capitalism in efficient employment creation but simply to raise some questions about how much better ED could be expected to be, given the persistence of potential effective demand failures and the lowered tendency to expand of self-managed firms. To the extent that it falls short, we will need a liberal welfare state to provide a "safety net" (perhaps including a guaranteed basic income) and thus continue to be faced with trade-offs between these expenditures, on the one hand, and investment and consumption, on the other.

## NOTES

1. David Ellerman's defense of worker ownership is vulnerable to similar objections, if it is taken as a natural-rights alternative to a Rawlsian theory of justice; Ellerman, *Property and Contract in Economics: The Case for Economic Democracy* (Oxford: Blackwell, 1992). For a critique, see Michael W. Howard, "Worker Ownership and Wage Slavery," unpublished manuscript, 1999.

2. John E. Roemer, *A Future for Socialism* (Cambridge: Harvard University Press, 1994).

3. Roemer, *A Future for Socialism*, 34.

4. Roemer, *A Future for Socialism*, 46.

5. Roemer, *A Future for Socialism*, 11.

6. Roemer, *A Future for Socialism*, 20.

7. Roemer, *A Future for Socialism*, 27. Those familiar with Roemer's *General Theory of Exploitation and Class* will recognize here the emphasis on differential ownership of assets as the root of exploitation versus control over the production process. It is the unequal bargaining capacity conferred by unequal ownership of capital, skills, and the like that enables some to exploit others and to enjoy superior life prospects. What justice requires, then, is an end to the relevant inequalities. Full justice can only be approximated in stages. Thus, a socialist abolition of exploitation based on ownership of capital will still be afflicted with exploitation based on unequal skills, what Roemer elsewhere has called "socialist exploitation." Such a society is nonetheless an improvement over capitalism, which compounds inequality of skills with unequal property ownership; Roemer, *A General Theory of Exploitation and Class* (Cambridge: Harvard University Press, 1982).

8. According to David Schweickart, Roemer has admitted, in conversation, that this efficiency effect is highly dubious; e-mail correspondence with the author, 30 November 1994. For a critique of management oriented toward enriching outside stockholders, see Doug Henwood, *Wall Street* (New York: Verso, 1998).

9. Roemer, *A Future for Socialism*, 50.

10. Roemer, *A Future for Socialism*, 57.

11. John E. Roemer, "The Possibility of Market Socialism," in *The Idea of Democracy*, ed., David Copp, Jean Hampton, and John E. Roemer (Cambridge: Cambridge University Press, 1993), 347–67.

12. Jon Elster and Karl Ove Moene remark, "It could well be that a low rate of innovation, and hence, of economic growth would be the Achilles' heel of a market socialist

system"; introduction to *Alternatives to Capitalism*, ed. Jon Elster and Karl Ove Moene (Cambridge: Cambridge University Press, 1989), 31. They define market socialism as a system of worker cooperatives.

13. These arguments are well summarized by David Schweickart, *Against Capitalism* (Cambridge: Cambridge University Press, 1994), chapter three.

14. Roemer, *A Future for Socialism*, 20.

15. See Roemer, "The Possibility of Market Socialism," 361.

16. If a high basic income were added to Roemer's model it could mitigate the coercive effects of the labor market. See chapter 2 for my argument for basic income.

17. On this, see Roemer, "The Possibility of Market Socialism," 362.

18. Janos Kornai, "Market Socialism Revisited," in *Market Socialism: The Current Debate*, ed. Pranab K. Bardhan and John E. Roemer (Oxford: Oxford University Press, 1993), 42–68.

19. Aristotle, *Politics*, trans. Ernest Barker (Oxford: Clarendon Press, 1968), 48–55 (1262b37–1264b25).

20. Louis Putterman, "Incentive Problems Favoring Noncentralized Investment Fund Ownership," in Bardhan and Roemer, *Market Socialism*, 159.

21. Putterman, "Incentive Problems," 160–61.

22. Jaroslav Vanek, *The General Theory of Labor-Managed Market Economies*, (Ithaca: Cornell University Press, 1970).

23. Benedetto Gui, "Basque versus Illyrian Labor-Managed Firms: The Problem of Property Rights," *Journal of Comparative Economics* 8 (1984): 168–81.

24. Schweickart, *Against Capitalism*, 81.

25. Thomas E. Weisskopf, "A Democratic Enterprise-Based Market Socialism," in Bardhan and Roemer, *Market Socialism*, 120–41.

26. Pranab K. Bardhan and John E. Roemer, "Market Socialism: A Case for Rejuvenation," *Journal of Economic Perspectives* 6 (1992): 101–16. In addition to (1) these independent groups of equity-holding firms coordinated around a monitoring bank, Bardhan proposes the following mechanisms for tackling the soft-budget constraint:

2. the bank manager's reputation
3. payment schemes rewarding effective monitoring
4. international competition to further depoliticize production and investment decisions
5. constitutional barriers against political intervention in investment decisions
6. well-publicized liquidation precommitments
7. diversification of ownership of the main bank, even if the state owns a majority of shares

Pranab K. Bardhan, "On Tackling the Soft Budget Constraint in Market Socialism," in Bardhan and Roemer, *Market Socialism*, 145–55. The first and last of these seem not only absent from but inconsistent with economic democracy, as Schweickart envisions it. Insofar as he favors protectionism and the building of noneconomic considerations into the investment process, the fourth and the fifth mechanisms are also difficult for him to accommodate with ED.

27. David Schweickart, e-mail correspondence, 30 November 1994; *Against Capitalism*, 323.

28. Small businesses, assuming they have the same access to financing as LMFs, can actually loom quite large, as nominally small contractors can organize through subcontracting rather large undertakings—perhaps less efficiently than a capitalist firm, but possibly more efficiently and with much larger financial incentive than LMFs.

29. Schweickart, e-mail correspondence, 30 November 1994; Milton Fisk, in conversation, Havana, Cuba, June 1993, made an analogous point against not just coupon socialism but all kinds of market socialism: if there were enough solidarity to create market socialism, then there would be enough solidarity and cooperation to plan production cooperatively without markets. I think, however, that he underestimates the informational advantages of markets, discussed in part 1. Against Fisk, and also in response to my own rhetorical question, it should be noted that the solidarity needed for a revolution may not give rise to postrevolutionary solidarity for many reasons: lack of confidence and expertise to plan production or monitor banks, lack of interest in the same, lack of institutional channels and training, and emergence of conflicts that remain latent as long as people are united against a common enemy.

30. In chapter 2 I argued for a basic-income scheme as a necessary complement to ED to lighten the risk burden on individuals. For skepticism about such a combination, see Maurice Glasman, "The Great Deformation: Polanyi, Poland, and the Terrors of Planned Spontaneity," *New Left Review* 205 (May–June 1994): 59–86.

# 9

# Basic Income and Economic Democracy

Now that many of the particular features and problems of cooperatives and economic democracy have been discussed, it is possible to pursue further an issue raised in chapter 2, the compatibility of economic democracy (ED) and basic income (BI). There I defended BI on grounds of justice, argued that it would probably require some kind of market socialism to achieve the highest sustainable level, and showed that, despite an initial appearance of incompatibility, it is conceptually coherent with self-management as defined and defended in chapter 1. In this chapter I argue further that BI and ED (which includes self-management) are mutually supportive. Basic-income schemes can address some problems arising for ED, and vice versa. There is also political merit in combining the two objectives in a common strategy under capitalism rather than pursuing one to the exclusion of the other. I begin with a brief survey of employment trends, showing why BI has rightfully emerged on the political agenda in Europe and could in the United States, as well. The guiding idea is that with seemingly permanent high levels of unemployment (as in Europe) or an increasing proportion of part-time, temporary, or poorly paid work (as in the United States), the prospects and desire for self-management would seem to be on the decline for all but an elite of workers.

Identifying the ways ED and BI can be mutually supportive is key to putting both on the agenda and avoiding a division between an elite of worker owners and a large population dependent upon an inadequate welfare state. Along the way I respond to one moral objection to BI from a socialist perspective, which points toward work-time reduction and job sharing, and I note some difficulties with these. In the last section I show why a return to something like the Swedish model of social democracy is not possible, thus reinforcing my case for the alternative ED–BI model as a long-term goal.

## FEWER JOBS OR FEWER GOOD JOBS?

Consider the prospect of rising levels of unemployment and underemployment. Although unemployment in the United States, at less than 5 percent in 1999, is significantly lower than in many European countries (where it is in double digits), the long-term trend before the 1990s is striking: Average unemployment in the United States has risen from 4.5 percent in the 1950s to 4.8 percent in the 1960s, 6.2 percent in the 1970s, and 7.3 percent in the 1980s, falling slightly in the early 1990s to 6.6 percent. When we factor in the discouraged workers and the underemployed, the figure for 1993 rises to 13 percent of the labor force.[1] There has been significant job growth in the United States since 1993, but the majority of the new jobs are poorly paid, nonunionized service jobs.[2] Thus, as good jobs are eliminated fewer Americans are unemployed, but more are overworked, trying to make ends meet with marginal jobs.[3]

One cause of this long-term trend toward higher rates of unemployment or marginal employment is automation, particularly that brought about through computerization and particularly in the 10 percent of big United States companies (employing five hundred or more workers) that employ 41 percent of all workers in the private sector. Downsizing has been most dramatic in manufacturing, but it is going on in the service sector, as well. "In just one service industry, commercial banking and thrift institutions, re-engineering will mean a loss of 30 to 40 percent of the jobs over the next seven years. That translates into 700,000 jobs eliminated."[4]

The numbers of new "symbolic analysts'" jobs that former secretary of labor Robert Reich thinks we need to train people for, in "science, engineering, management, consultancy, teaching, marketing, media, and entertainment . . . will remain small compared to the numbers of workers displaced by the new generation of 'thinking machines,'"[5] or in poorly paid low-skill service jobs.

This new "knowledge class" partly accounts for growing inequality in the United States. The upper echelons—4 percent of the working population—earn "as much as the entire bottom 51 percent of American wage earners." Their incomes, along with those of another 16 percent of second-tier knowledge workers, continue to rise while the rest of the labor force suffers losses of real income, benefits and jobs. The total income of the top 20 percent of the workforce exceeds that of the other 80 percent combined.[6]

Some tend to blame the growing inequality on tax breaks to the wealthy during the 1980s. However, less than 10 percent of the increase enjoyed by the richest 10 percent of families from 1980 to 1988 resulted from tax changes.[7] Thus, we need to focus on the deeper structural changes in the economy if we want to come to terms with the growing inequality. The knowledge class can command high salaries in the labor market and can coerce governments to keep taxes down because of their monopoly on knowledge and skills and their mobility: information technology enables them to operate from anywhere. This, combined with declining trade barriers and rising capital mobility, places an upper limit on taxation even in countries like Sweden with strong social democratic traditions.

Thus we see in country after country fiscal crises and cutbacks in government services and loss of public-sector jobs, adding to the unemployment from private-sector downsizing. We also face the prospect of increasing polarization, not only in the United States but globally, between the knowledge elite and the wealthy, on the one hand, and the rest of the population marginalized in varying degrees, on the other, increasing numbers of whom will have no hope of steady full-time jobs at livable wages.

What place is there for worker self-management and cooperatives in such a world? The skeptic will argue that trends toward greater worker participation and worker ownership represent in many cases an assimilation of privileged workers into the wealthiest 20 or 30 percent of the population, leaving the rest out in the cold. How shall we answer the skeptic?

## JOB CREATION AND SOCIAL INVESTMENT

A society of cooperatives in the global economy is not likely to solve this problem. Each cooperative, even if supported in one country by ED, will face the job-cutting pressures that the Mondragon Cooperative Corporation has experienced, despite an internal dynamic to preserve jobs (see chapter 7). The socialization and democratization of investment would yield some additional tools for fighting unemployment; however, it is hard to see how investment, if it is to create competitive enterprises, can outpace trends toward elimination of the better jobs. At the end of the previous chapter I expressed other doubts about reaching full employment under ED. The United States could, of course, pull out of NAFTA and the GATT (General Agreement on Tariffs and Trade), throw up trade barriers, and focus on an internal market. But I wonder whether we are not already too far enmeshed in a global web for that to be economically or politically feasible. There are also issues of international distributive justice that such a strategy raises, particularly in a country that controls so much of the world's capital and resources. So I turn next to the question of how basic income, a universal measure but one particularly valuable for those needing income support, could also strengthen ED economically, ecologically, and morally. After that, I examine a major moral objection to BI from a socialist perspective, which points toward work-time reduction and job sharing. After noting some difficulties with work-time reduction and job sharing, I then show what ED can add to a BI strategy for social justice, compared with BI in a capitalist context. Finally, I argue that returning to something like the Swedish model of social democracy is not a viable alternative.

## WHAT THE BASIC-INCOME SCHEME ADDS TO ECONOMIC DEMOCRACY

Basic-Income arrangements add six elements to economic democracy, that strengthen it economically, politcally, and morally.

1. Labor market flexibility: The BI scheme, by providing all workers—and nonworkers—with an unconditional income floor, will give to ED greater labor-market flexibility. Workers could leave co-ops without fear of catastrophic loss of income, and co-ops could work out more flexible work-sharing arrangements among their members.[8]

2. Lessening of risk aversion: The risk associated with a capital stake in the firm would be minimized, because a portion of each member's income would be independent of the success or failure of the firm. This could be expected to encourage risk taking, a desirable thing, given that co-ops tend to be too risk averse.[9]

3. Greater innovativeness: For similar reasons, firms could be expected to innovate, and introduce new technologies, with less fear of job or income loss. Part-time employment, self-employment, and career shifts would be underwritten by the BI.[10]

4. Hard-budget constraints: With BI, the pressure on investment funds to compromise efficiency for the sake of job creation would be reduced. We would not need to fear that economic democracy would go the way of Eastern European Communist states that have maintained full employment at the expense of massive inefficiencies.

5. Slower growth: To the extent that both ED and BI make possible economies that are less growth- and consumption-oriented and so ecologically more attractive, they are mutually supportive. The way in which ED is less growth oriented is spelled out in chapters 8 and 12. With BI, individuals would be able to withdraw periodically from the labor market in varying degrees to live a more modest life.

6. Social justice: Adding BI to ED should help ED to meet Rawlsian objections from the standpoint of the least advantaged. Politically, this might translate into support for ED from unemployed people, homemakers, and other beneficiaries of BI, who might otherwise regard ED as a system benefiting mainly privileged workers. But here we must note that much depends on claims by Schweickart and others for the superior efficiency not only of worker management but also of socialized investment. A society that aims to maximize the minimum basic income, subject to preserving freedom and equal opportunity, could conceivably favor capitalism over socialism. The specific efficiency advantages of worker cooperatives could be had in a system of worker-owned enterprises on the Mondragon model, under which

firms would have the right to make their own investment decisions and socialized investment would not be required.

In general, a basic-income scheme alters the economic and social environment in which ED would operate, bettering the chances of ED's being both more just and more efficient than capitalism. ED with a basic-income scheme will also have a wider political base than ED alone.

## BASIC-INCOME APARTHEID?

André Gorz fears that BI, particularly in a capitalist society (but, we may add, also under economic democracy), could lead to a decline of the work ethic and a division of society into two classes, with deleterious effects on the integrity of the political community. Although BI may facilitate participation in "micro-social communities such as a family, a club, a co-op, a self-help network, a neighborhood association for mutual aid," Gorz stresses that participation at this level is insufficient for full citizenship in the larger social system, including the institutions of the market and the state: "To feel anyone's equal, you also need to feel that you are useful to that society as a whole, and that it needs whatever skills or capabilities you may have. In other words, you need a job and, what is more, not any kind of casual job like walking someone's dog, shoe-shining, or selling flowers at street corners." In language that echoes Hegel's and Marx's analyses of the transition from feudalism to modernity, Gorz stresses the difference between these sorts of "services you render others as private persons," implying "personal submission to personal demands," and the more formalized work in the public sphere, measured by public standards and governed by a regime of rules applying equally to each.[11]

Resisting what he calls the "South-Africanization" of society—the continuing segmentation of the population into a "working-class aristocracy" and a "growing proletarian underclass of expendable unskilled workers," the growth of menial, servile services for the rich at very low wages, all furthered by the underpinning of a basic income[12]—Gorz nevertheless sees a way in which basic income could have a more positive outcome: "It could help to spread socially useful work more evenly across the working population as a whole, and between men and women in particular, instigate shorter working hours, make skilled jobs accessible to everyone, and open up new unlimited opportunities for unpaid community work."[13] For this more egalitarian outcome, Gorz identifies three conditions:

- reduction in work time without loss of income
- work sharing, supported by education and training
- promotion of unpaid community work

In this scheme, work becomes intermittent for everyone, and "the income paid during the interruptions to or intermissions in work, then, must be seen as the deferred or anticipated payment of your share of the socially produced wealth: as an income you have earned and which is owed to you, not granted to you, by society for the basic amount of work you are committed to do. . . . You cannot become a member of any community if you have no obligation whatsoever towards it. Being a member of a group means that you can rely on the others, but also that they can rely on you."[14]

Gorz's proposal has the advantage of preserving the link between income and socially useful work. However, any systematic enforcement of a participation requirement will run into the problems that Barry raises, cited earlier in chapter 2. Furthermore, Gorz assumes dubiously that reduction in work time would involve no loss in productivity. Van Parijs identifies three dilemmas that a work-sharing strategy will encounter, with respect to earnings, skill, and self-employment: (1) Either the reduction in earnings is not differentiated according to pay levels so that the lowest ranking jobs fall below the level of entitlement to social benefits, or there is differentiation, in which case the relative cost of unskilled jobs rises, hastening their elimination through automation. Either way, people in unskilled jobs suffer. (2) If work-time reduction is undifferentiated according to skill, bottlenecks will occur in certain skilled trades and regions, as well as high training costs; but if not, then the unskilled will unfairly bear the burden of reduced work time and highly skilled people will be able to work long hours at higher pay. (3) The self-employed will either be treated like waged workers, and a difficult and costly need for monitoring will arise, or they will be exempted from time reduction, resulting in more "falsely self-employed" subcontractors and "victimizing those who have no option but to be and remain salaried employees."[15] (Additional problems arise in the United States where health and pension benefits are not universal but are part of the cost per worker for an employer.)[16]

## WHAT ECONOMIC DEMOCRACY ADDS TO BASIC INCOME

Economic democracy can help a BI scheme bring about the outcome Gorz desires better than can capitalism. First, making firms worker-managed is an effective way to control the unemployment that results in a capitalist society from the squeeze on profits exerted by wages.[17] Second, to the extent that worker control would make work in ED more attractive than it is in a capitalist economy, the price of labor could be reduced, and more people could be hired, or the numbers opting out of work because of the BI would be reduced.

Third, and most important, the socialization of investment decisions would prevent capital flight and capital strikes, two limitations on the maximum sustainable BI under capitalism. As long as investment depends upon private savings, the maximum sustainable BI is limited by the possibility of investors pulling out their money and reinvesting it in other countries where it would bring a higher return than in the country where it is taxed to support the BI. If a socialist society can sustainably provide a higher level of BI than capitalism can, it is to be preferred, even if it involves some loss of efficiency through soft-budget constraints. Fourth, the socialization of investment makes it possible to build into the decision-making process the support of socially valuable work, such as the kinds of community work Gorz envisions, but which is marginalized in a strictly profit-oriented economy and costly to administer as a condition for a participation income. Thus, ED promises to limit, to a greater extent than capitalism, the numbers of unemployed, reducing the strain on the work ethic, and to pitch the BI at the highest sustainable level.

One final comment on the introduction of BI in a capitalist society: In the transition from capitalism to a more just society, BI also gives each worker, and thus workers in unions, more bargaining power, in that the threat of unemployment loses some of its sting. This should, in turn, pave the way for the emergence of genuine democratic firms. The trade-off for workers in such firms is that they must be prepared to pay their share of the taxes necessary to support an adequate basic income. One overriding political question is whether an alliance can be forged between the "worker aristocracy" in such firms and those workers not so fortunately positioned, united by a shared conception of justice. Such an alliance is possible to the extent that the former feel increasingly insecure and thus more akin to the latter and to the extent that a plausible comprehensive conception of justice can be articulated. Such an alliance is by no means inevitable. One alternative is an alliance between owners and better-paid workers against the remaining 70 or 80 percent of the population. The political dilemma is that one of the trends that can favor economic democracy, namely, movement toward worker ownership, can also favor this more reactionary political alliance. It can be countered only by sustained political work and pushing for economic democracy, through avenues additional to stock ownership.

## WHATEVER HAPPENED TO SOCIAL DEMOCRACY?

Some will argue—particularly as the official unemployment rate in the United States drops to less than 5 percent (in 1999), that my case for a basic income on the basis of permanent high levels of unemployment rests on excessive pessimism. If full employment is recoverable,why bother with basic income? I have already expressed some doubts about the capacity of economic democracy to generate full employment. What about social democracy on the Swedish model, which for years seemed to maintain virtually full employment? Furthermore, might not a revitalized social democracy pave the way for economic democracy?

**From Social Democracy to Economic Democracy?**

One scenario of social progress envisions economic democracy and self-management as the next stage after social democracy. In Sweden, for example, uninterrupted Social Democratic governments in the postwar period succeeded in maintaining full employment and constructing a cradle-to-grave welfare system in health care, education and other areas. To cite one example illustrating the generosity of the Swedish model, all Swedish workers are entitled to a year's paid parental leave. The major union federation, the LO (Landsorganisationen), adopted a solidaristic wage policy designed to raise the wages of the least well paid, reduce wage differentials, and establish wages in accordance with work rather than the profitability of the firm.[18]

The policy also had the goal, while aiming at full employment, of avoiding inflation by restraining wage increases. The less profitable firms would be pushed out of the market if they could not pay the standard scale. Labor-market policy would aim at retraining and relocating displaced workers. The more profitable firms would reap windfall profits, because workers' wages therein would be held down. On the one hand, this tended to plow investment back into the most profitable firms, so that productivity gains would keep pace with wage increases and inflation would be avoided. On the other hand, large firms seemed the major beneficiaries, and they began investing abroad. To address the latter concern, the LO proposed skimming off the excess profits into wage-earner funds, which over time would become the principal owners of capital in Sweden. Thus economic democracy, though emerging in response to concrete problems within the labor movement, would be the logical next step beyond social democracy.

During the 1970s both blue- and white-collar unions pushed for industrial democracy as well, succeeding in getting a number of labor laws passed "including minority representation on company boards, enhanced powers for safety stewards, and much tighter rules on layoffs and firings . . . and requiring management to negotiate with the unions over any corporate decisions that would affect the workplace."[19] In these ways, labor was going beyond the labor–capital compromise in which workers received high wages and social benefits while capital retained ownership and control; the wage-earner funds challenged capitalist ownership and investment prerogatives, and workplace legislation encroached on capitalist control of production.

This momentum was lost and never regained in the middle to late 1970s, epitomized by electoral defeats of the Social Democrats in 1976. The consensus between labor and capital broke down as employers went on the offensive, campaigning heavily against the idea of the wage-earner fund and later pushing for neoliberal policies and privatization of much of the public sector. Wage-earner funds were finally introduced, but they were much watered down and only "symbolic" in character.[20]

Had the Social Democrats succeeded in establishing the wage-earner funds as originally conceived, and had they gotten some control over investment decisions, another major problem undermining social democracy itself might have been averted: the flight of capital from Sweden.[21] The very firms benefiting from Sweden's solidaristic wage policy (and favorable tax policies) began investing profits abroad and closing plants in Sweden.[22] With only minuscule control over investment decisions, there was little the government or unions could do to resist this loss of jobs and the consequent strain on the social budget. Much of this investment went into financial and real estate speculation,[23] the losses of which have contributed to the state's fiscal crisis (along with rising import costs, depressed international markets for exports, and "increasing popular resistance to higher taxes").[24] Thus, the failure to advance to economic democracy has, in a way, contributed to a retreat from social democracy.

Some are hopeful that the labor movement in Sweden will regain its hegemony and restore the Swedish model, but there are serious obstacles in its path. Sweden's entry into the European Community will subject it to anti-inflation policies inconsistent with full employment and render banks independent of parliamentary control.[25] The only hope is for a Social Democratic alliance within the European Community, modifying the rules in favor of national sovereignty and greater democracy within EC institutions.[26] In the meantime, the continuing internationalization of capital works against the reviving of social democracy, not to mention economic democracy.

Why did the labor movement in Sweden fail to move forward in the 1970s when a third of the population and a majority of Social Democratic voters favored the wage-earner funds? Jonas Pontusson suggests several reasons: the fundamentally defensive posture of the Social Democrats whenever right-wing parties accused them of socialism; the political resources of business, especially its control over the media; influence over workers by corporate management; the lukewarm or even hostile attitude of Social Democratic leaders toward wage-earner funds; and, perhaps most importantly, the failure of the unions to "engage in a full-scale popular mobilization."[27] When one reads the account by Rudolf Meidner—one of the LO's architects of the plan for the wage-earner fund (often called the Meidner Plan)—of the failure of the Swedish model, it is clear that he conceived of it as a solution to specific problems of trade-union strategy, in particular, how to get workers in the more profitable firms to adhere to wage solidarity, rather than as the key to a transition from capitalism to socialism. But the structurally transformative character of the plan did not escape him, and the plan received enthusiastic support among shop stewards and others at the grass roots.[28]

What ultimately has done in not only the radicalization of social democracy but social democracy itself in Sweden, in addition to the external factors mentioned, are the internal divisions in the country's Left. According to Pontusson, "the principal cleavage . . . followed a vertical line, with the LO and union activists on one side, and the SAP [the employers' organization] leadership and the majority of Social Democratic voters on the other . . . [creating] a basic tension between the logic of unionism . . . and the logic of electoral competition."[29] In this cleavage, it has been the unions that pushed the Social Democrats toward more-radical reforms of ownership and industrial relations.

Pontusson plays down the division between labor rank and file and the leadership, but he suggests that "the centralization and bureaucratization of the postwar labour movement has weakened its capacity to engage in popular mobilization, and more importantly, that participation in corporatist structures has restricted labour's conception of politics."[30] We have here the makings of a dilemma. It was the very centralization of union bargaining that made possible the solidaristic wage policy and gave to Swedish unions a power to be envied by labor movements in most countries. Yet the concomitant bureaucratization and narrow focus on trade-union problems contributed to the unions' failure when it came to major reforms.

The situation of the LO is complicated by its relationship to the smaller, mostly white-collar federation, the TCO (Tjanstemannens Centralorganisation). This organization was never an enthusiastic supporter of wage-earner funds, retreating in 1979 and then withdrawing support altogether in 1981.[31] This suggests a difference in interest between blue- and white-collar workers over the question of control of investment, a difference that was not unbridgeable, perhaps, but which the LO failed to bridge.

Pontusson notes, on the other hand, that the impetus for "industrial democracy"—greater workers' rights and control in the workplace—originated in the TCO, was picked up by the LO in the interest of strengthening ties, and resulted in successful passage of labor law reforms.[32] Thus, there was some common ground for encroaching on the rights of the owners at the level of the workplace. But the wage-earner funds, as designed, were arguably not the most effective vehicle for socializing capital. The complicated scheme promised at best an indirect avenue for workers to participate in investment decisions, vesting power in the union bureaucracy, instead.

The failure to establish a substantial wage-earner-fund scheme (a much-watered-down version was finally passed, with assurances to business from the Social Democratic leadership that reforms would go no further) may account in part for the further disintegration of the Swedish labor movement. With no clear solution to the problem of excess profits, and economic crisis turning the sharing of wage increases into the sharing of wage losses, it is not surprising that employers succeeded in decentralizing the bargaining process, beginning with the Metalworkers Union in 1983.[33] Thus the Swedish labor movement is more divided and in a much weaker position vis-à-vis capital today to strengthen social democracy, not to mention to advance radical reforms.

As David Vail has commented, "The Social Democrats cannot return to power and govern effectively unless they broaden their base of support beyond the mix of blue collar workers, public employees, and pensioners who have been their core voters in recent elections."[34] There is a ray of hope in the rebound in union membership (from a low of 80 percent in the late 1980s to 84 percent by 1993), a movement in which women are prominent.[35] This may provide an opening for strategies that link together the immediate concerns of these workers with broader social issues (in particular, those concerning working women and families) and an overarching egalitarian vision.

One thing seems clear: The balance of power over the last decade has tipped decisively toward capital in Sweden and elsewhere. Whether this could have been averted does not alter the fact that now full employment is further out of reach, corporations backed by international lending agencies and supranational bodies like the European Community can pressure governments to cut expenditures in the public sector, and, following the abandonment by corporations of their national moorings and commitments, unions have lost patience with social contracts and are scrambling to survive.[36]

New strategies are needed that take this new situation as a given. The worsening situation of workers and others who have benefited from the social budget may create an opening for more-radical challenges to the prerogatives of capital. But the prospects for social democracy look much worse now than when Sweden and other Social Democratic countries were at the peak of their performance. Some of the objective conditions favoring social democracy have weakened, perhaps irreversibly. The demand for export goods will probably never equal the post–World War II demand. The flight of capital cannot be recalled. Still, it might be possible, economically if not politically, to place controls on the outward flow of capital. It might bepossible for a block of Social Democratic European countries to alter the policy of the European Community to allow this. But these measures alone seem insufficient to restore the economy to a state in which capitalism generates jobs and income sufficient to spin off taxes for the welfare state and active labor-market policy.

## A Basic-Income Strategy with Economic Democracy

A more plausible restoration of social democracy would involve a takeover of investment by the state, along the lines described in the model of economic democracy. Investment could then be steered toward job creation and would not be held hostage to international financial markets. But note what a radical decoupling from international financial institutions this would involve. The greatest challenge for this strategy is finding the popular base and political will for such moves, which are bound to be resisted fiercely not only by local capitalists but also by international financial interests. Assuming some way around these difficulties can be found, the problem I have posed would be solved if full employment could be restored and each worker guaranteed a good job in a democratically governed workplace.[37] As we have seen in chapter 8, there are serious doubts about the capacity of economic democracy to generate full employment without creating other undesirable effects.

The basic-income strategy, by contrast, is more pessimistic. It takes as a given the split between primary and secondary labor markets, employed and unemployed, and may even favor greater mobility of capital.[38] In these respects, it is easier to imagine going from where we are to the adoption of this strategy. Moreover, it admits of degrees, and so could be phased in over time, allowing its effects to be observed in practice, whereas gradual inroads on the control of private investment are likely to provoke even greater capital flight or even a capital strike. Of the different elements of my proposal, it is easier to envision basic income, and worker control in the form of ownership or participation, in the short run. The combination of both would tend to mitigate the more undesirable tendencies of each in isolation. A democratic investment fund, essential for all the reasons canvased earlier as well as in later chapters, must be a long-term goal, although expansion of government-funded loans to small businesses emphasizing cooperatives would provide a laboratory for exploring ways to manage such a fund successfully.

## NOTES

1. Jeremy Rifkin, *The End of Work* (New York: G. P. Putnam's Sons, 1995), 10–11.

2. Doug Henwood, "Talking about Work," *Monthly Review* 49, no. 3 (July–August 1997): 18–31. It should also be noted that official figures underestimate the actual unemployment by ignoring discouraged workers and others not actively seeking work, not to mention the disproportionately high percentage of the population in prison. Adjusting for the "larger share of the United States population that is in prison (in relative terms, about ten times the share in Germany)" adds a percentage point to the unemployment rate for 1996, according to Jeff Faux, "The 'American Model' Exposed," *Nation*, 27 October 1997, 18–21. In 1996, more than 30 percent of jobs paid less than poverty-level wages, defined as "the hourly wages that a full-time worker would need to keep a family of four above the poverty level"; John Schmitt, Lawrence Mischel, and Jared Bernstein, "Dangers for European Workers in the United States Economic Model," *WorkingUSA* (May–June 1998): 73–85, 85.

3. Juliet Schor, *The Overworked American: The Unexpected Decline of Leisure* (New York: Basic Books, 1991).

4. Rifkin, *The End of Work*, 9.

5. Rifkin, *The End of Work*, 35.

6. Rifkin, *The End of Work*, 197. The percentage of workers whose condition is improving substantially may be even lower than Rifkin's data shows. "The decades-long shift into white-collar occupations actually ground to a halt in the early 1990s. . . . Corresponding to this slow growth are historically high rates of white-collar job displacements from downsizing and greater job instability and insecurity among college-educated men. . . . Wage trends for white-collar and college-educated workers have not been especially favorable in the 1990s"; Lawrence Mischel, Jared Bernstein, and John Schmitt,

*The State of Working America 1998–99* (Ithaca: Cornell University Press, 1999). This is bad news for college-educated and white-collar workers. But it means that the danger of an alliance between the "knowledge class" and capital, the elitist alternative to an alliance of all workers and unemployed, may be less likely than it earlier appeared.

7. Mickey Kaus, "For a New Equality," *New Republic*, 7 May 1990, 18–27.

8. This idea was suggested to me by David Schweickart, personal correspondence.

9. Philippe Van Parijs, *Real Freedom for All: What (If Anything) Can Justify Capitalism?* (Oxford: Clarendon Press, 1995), 42.

10. Van Parijs, *Real Freedom for All*, 223.

11. Andre Gorz, "On the Difference between Society and Community, and Why Basic Income Cannot by Itself Confer Full Membership of Either," in *Arguing for Basic Income*, ed. Philippe Van Parijs (London: Verso, 1992), 178–84, 178, 180–182.

As Hegel recognized early on, whether they receive public assistance or charity, "the needy would receive subsistence directly, not by means of their work, and this would violate the principle of civil society and the feeling of individual independence and self-respect in its members." What is now called "workfare" is no solution, because "the evil consists precisely in an excess of production"; G. W. F. Hegel, *Philosophy of Right*, trans. T. M. Knox (Oxford: Oxford University Press, 1967), 150. The danger is not only dependence but moral disintegration: "When there is [following a decline in the standard of living below subsistence] a consequent loss of the sense of right and wrong, of honesty and the self-respect which makes a man insist on maintaining himself by his own work and effort, the result is the creation of a rabble of paupers" (150). Some of what Hegel describes here is the result of poverty, but important for our purposes is the part owing to dependence and lack of work:

Poverty in itself does not make men into rabble; a rabble is created only when there is joined to poverty a disposition of mind, and inner indignation against the rich, against society, against the government, etc. A further consequence of this attitude is that through their dependence on chance men become frivolous and idle, like the Neapolitan *lazzaroni* for example. In this way there is born in the rabble the evil of lacking self-respect enough to secure subsistence by its own labour and yet at the same time of claiming to receive subsistence as its right. (277)

Here are the seeds of Nietzsche's analysis of *ressentiment* and Marx's view of the lumpenproletariat. Read through a Marxist lens, Hegel's formulation sounds like a sort of apologetic for class differences. But substitute "skilled workers" or "the employed" for Hegel's "rich," and you have the makings of profound resentment, even in a market-socialist society, if there is a sharp division between those who work for their subsistence and those who do not.

Hegel also recognized that, particularly in a modern state where the scope for political participation of the individual citizen is restricted, "it is essential to provide men—ethical entities—with work of a public character over and above their private business. This work of a public character, which the modern state does not always provide, is found in the Corporation" (278). In Hegel's not yet industrialized Prussia, the "corporation" was akin to a medieval guild. In contemporary industrialized societies, belonging to a firm is one important way—perhaps the most important, next to the care for others one takes from family life—one acquires a sense of belonging, of contributing to the well-being of others, not only one's fellow workers but the wider society. This is true for many even under conditions of alienated labor.

12. Gorz, "On the Difference between Society," 180–82.

13. Gorz, "On the Difference between Society," 183.

14. Gorz,"On the Difference between Society," 184.

15. Philippe Van Parijs, "Basic Income: A Green Strategy for the New Europe," in *Green Light on Europe*, ed. Sara Parkin (London: Heretic Books, 1991), 170–71.

16. If such job-linked benefits were universalized and their cost socialized, as one would expect in a socialist society, this would remove some of the pressure on employers to hire as low a number of regular workers as possible, as the cost of the job would be primarily the cost of wages plus hiring and training costs but not necessarily the cost of insurance and other benefits. In France employers and employees each pay a share into a social security fund, which includes health benefits as well as pensions available to everyone regardless of employment status. If a worker's income is one thousand dollars, the company will pay six hundred dollars into social security. (These figures are illustrative, not precise.) Thus, the cost of benefits attaches to the employment of workers even when the benefit is detached from one's employment history or status.

But if the cost is proportional to the wage paid, rather than being a fixed cost per worker, the effect on the number of workers hired overall is neutral. If more workers are hired to work fewer hours with no net change in the wage fund, the same percentage of income can be taxed; it will just be spread out over a larger number of workers. Thus, an important obstacle to work sharing in the United States is the current linkage of health, old age, and disability insurance with particular jobs.

Even removing this last obstacle would not eliminate the pressure on particular employers to reduce the absolute number of labor hours compensated, in that however these are distributed across the workforce, they carry the cost of benefits as well, which are not required for robots and computers. Whether the French employer hires one worker at forty hours per week for one thousand dollars a month or two workers for twenty hours per week at five hundred dollars a month, he still must pay six hundred dollars a month in benefits.

There is thus the danger of a downward spiral resulting from work-time reduction (at least under capitalist conditions): as workers are laid off through automation, the cost per working hour of social benefits rises, creating further pressure either to replace workers with machines or to cut an increasingly necessary social budget. Economic democracy could be better expected to resist this downward spiral, because each firm will seek to maintain its current level of employment, and investment policy can aim for job creation. The conjunction of ED and BI takes some of the pressure off ED to produce more employment than is compatible with efficiency. Economic democracy also provides more-stable investment conditions for BI, since it removes the threat of capital flight. Thus it would seem that in the postindustrial economy, ED has a future when supplemented with a basic-income scheme.

17. Van Parijs, *Real Freedom for All*, 206–10. The theory of unemployment here is that crisis arises when workers are strong enough to win wage increases high enough to reduce profits, thus provoking a loss of investor confidence. In a worker-owned economy with a capital market, workers would restrain themselves in ways that they would not if they were not residual claimants interested in attracting capital in the form of loans and

nonvoting shares held by outside investors. In ED, the rate of investment does not depend on the profit motive of private investors at all, so unemployment from this cause will not arise.

18. Rudolf Meidner, "Why Did the Swedish Model Fail?" *Socialist Register* (1993): 211–28; Jonas Pontusson, "Radicalization and Retreat in Swedish Social Democracy," *New Left Review* 165 (September–October 1987): 5–33.

19. Pontusson, "Radicalization and Retreat," 12.

20. Meidner, "Why Did the Swedish Model Fail?" 223; Pontusson, "Radicalization and Retreat," 19–20.

21. Kenneth Hermele, "The End of the Middle Road: What Happened to the Swedish Model?" *Monthly Review* 44, no. 10 (March 1993): 14–24.

22. Hermele, "The End of the Middle Road"; David Vail, "The Past and Future of Swedish Social Democracy: A Reply to Kenneth Hermele," *Monthly Review* 45, no. 5 (October 1993): 24–31.

23. Hermele, "The End of the Middle Road."

24. Vail, "The Past and Future of Swedish Social Democracy," 25.

25. Kenneth Hermele, "A Response to David Vail," *Monthly Review* 45, no. 5 (October 1993): 32–37, 36.

26. Vail, "The Past and Future of Swedish Social Democracy," 30.

27. Pontusson, "Radicalization and Retreat, 19, 29–31.

28. Meidner, "Why Did the Swedish Model Fail?"; Pontusson, "Radicalization and Retreat," 13–14.

29. Pontusson, "Radicalization and Retreat," 30.

30. Pontusson, "Radicalization and Retreat," 31.

31. Pontusson, "Radicalization and Retreat," 10.

32. Pontusson, "Radicalization and Retreat," 12.

33. Pontusson, "Radicalization and Retreat," 17, 23.

34. Vail, "The Past and Future of Swedish Social Democracy," 26.

35. Vail, "The Past and Future of Swedish Social Democracy," 29.

36. See David Moberg, "War Zone," *In These Times* (24 July–6 August 1995): 12–16, for a relevant example of labor management struggles in the United States.

37. The Labor Party in the United States favors a constitutional guarantee to everyone of a job at a living wage; *Labor Party Press* 4, no. 1 (January 1999): 2. For a critique of the idea that there should be a right to work, where this means more than aiming for a goal of full employment, see Jon Elster, "Is There (or Should There Be) a Right to Work?" in *Democracy and the Welfare State*, ed. Amy Gutmann (Princeton: Princeton University Press, 1988), 53–78.

38. Philippe Van Parijs, *Marxism Recycled* (Cambridge: Cambridge University Press, 1993), 146–48. Brian Barry takes a position similar to mine, seeing basic income as a second best to a no longer available Swedish model, in "Survey Article: Real Freedom and Basic Income," *Journal of Political Philosophy* 4, no. 3 (1996): 242–76.

# Part 3

## Socialist Practice in a Changing Capitalist World

# Introduction to Part 3

Socialist practice is currently confronted with many challenges generated by the changing character of capitalism. Three of these are addressed in part 3, with particular attention to the degree to which self-managed market socialism could respond to these challenges. The first is that generated by the increasingly global marketplace, resulting in capital flight, deindustrialization in the core capitalist countries, and a decline in unions, and yet also, movements toward more "communitarian" workplaces in some of the larger enterprises. How might the Left respond to these changes? The previous chapters examined some aspects of globalization. Chapter 10 will focuses on "communitarian" workplaces and union responses to them and asks whether the discourse of liberal theory provides adequate terms for articulating the needs and objectives of the inhabitants of a global marketplace.

The second challenge is that posed by the shift from an industrial to a service and information economy. This is particularly a challenge for the worker-managed socialism favored in this book, as the paradigm of worker self-management has traditionally been located in factories. Does worker self-management have a future in growing sectors such as education, health care, or the media? Chapter 11 on the media provides a cautiously positive answer to this question but also underscores the complexity of self-management in such spheres, in comparison with self-management of commodity production.

The third challenge is that of new social movements. Socialism has always encompassed more than the labor movement, but for the better part of the socialist movement's existence the labor movement has been its heart and soul. As industrial production shrinks as a proportion of the economy and as new social movements (particularly the women's and environmental movements) assume greater political significance, will socialism go into decline? Or is there hope for a revived socialist movement that incorporates these social movements with as much success as earlier, in some countries, it embraced the labor movement? These questions are explored, with particular reference to market socialism, in chapter 12.

# 10

# Cooperation between Union and Management in the Global Marketplace

In chapter 7, I argued that without other aspects of socialism (public ownership and social control of investment), worker-managed enterprises are likely to regress to capitalist firms and to leave many injustices intact. However, if integrated with other strategies for a just society (such as a basic income) in a movement uniting workers and nonworkers, worker ownership can have long-term positive effects and can resist degenerative tendencies. Unions will have a key role to play in the outcome as they decide whether and how to promote worker ownership and with whom to ally themselves.

I also noted the evidence supporting the claim that worker ownership when combined with worker participation, produces striking improvements in efficiency, whereas either one in isolation has, at best, modest results. In this chapter, I shift the focus to worker participation in order to evaluate trends toward union-management cooperation. First, I examine the emergence of what Ronald Dore calls the community-model firm, in the context of globalization, and in contrast with the company-law model more traditional in the United States and Great Britain. The community model opens possibilities for self-management, but it also heightens the need for something like basic income, as well as socialization of capital. In the second half of the chapter I consider what Charles Heckscher calls associational unionism and his thesis that unions should support cooperation with management. I then identify some limits to associational unionism and argue for a broadened discourse of economic rights that includes, but is not limited to, employee rights.

The conclusions of this chapter give some added support to the left-liberal defenses of self-management and basic income in chapters 1 and 2, insofar as they support a liberal discourse of rights versus a communitarian discourse. This is somewhat surprising, given some communitarian themes associated with the community-model firm.[1]

Recent trends in enterprise management toward Japanese-style communitarian firms and away from firms characterized by conflict between managers and workers might be thought to be better supported by communitarian political and moral theory than by a liberal theory of justice. A move from enterprises characterized by profit-seeking, egoistic agents contracting with one another for each other's advantage, but otherwise in an antagonistic relationship, to enterprises in which all are presumed to share a consensus about justice and about common aims of the firm would seem to signify a move away from liberalism at the level of the firm.

Upon reflection, the communitarian firm, particularly if it is democratic rather than authoritarian as are most Japanese firms, can be better articulated with movements for workers' rights (including the rights of other groups such as women and minorities), and by a theory of justice defending those rights, than with communitarian moral theory.

## THE ECONOMIC CONTEXT OF CHANGING ENTERPRISES

The world economy is undergoing profound changes, only some of which can be mentioned here. Perhaps the most relevant for its implications for the way enterprises are managed is the shift from Fordist mass manufacturing—which is increasingly being exported overseas to lower-wage economies—to "flexible specialization," a form of manufacturing suited to specialty markets in which quality counts more than quantity and which require rapid changes and high levels of flexibility.[2] Some related trends, which in part explain this "second industrial divide" and also in part complicate its effects, are the opening of international markets; internationalization of capital markets; greater capital movement within countries, resulting in mergers and plant closings; technological change, especially that resulting from computerization; and the shift from manufacturing to services.[3] It would be hard to overemphasize the significance of these changes. Among other things, they have provided the conditions for the culture of postmodernism.[4] At the enterprise level, they have provoked much rethinking of management theory and practice and have given rise to a crisis for unions.[5] Many on the management side have turned to the Japanese enterprise for a model of how to cope with the challenges of the world economy.

## COMPANY-LAW MODEL VERSUS COMMUNITY
## MODEL ENTERPRISES

Let me begin by clarifying Dore's distinction between Japanese-style "community-model" enterprises and the "company-law" model more common in the United States or Great Britain. There are three major dimensions along which these models can be contrasted: (1) who constitutes the firm, (2) the status of shareholders, and (3) the relationship between managers and workers. In the company-law model, "the firm is primarily defined as the property of shareholders whose rights [for example, to sell the firm] are paramount"; "The management are the *trusted* agents of the shareholders. . . . The management hires workers. The wage-effort bargain is struck in what is inevitably an adversary relationship in which each side seeks continuously to improve its position" and in which there is a relatively low level of trust.

In the Community Model, by contrast: (1) The firm is primarily defined as a social unit made up of all the people who work full-time in it. . . . (2) The shareholders are, like customers and suppliers and local authorities, one group of outsiders who have to be satisfied if the firm is to prosper. . . . (3) Every member of the firm can act on the assumption that other members share a desire to make the firm prosper, and this gives enough fellow-feeling for those who have less than a full understanding of the accounts to trust managers not to conceal things from them for manipulative purposes. They are likely to believe that the distribution of rewards is what it appears to be and is fair.[6]

Closely connected to this contrast in types of firm is a contrast in types of employment patterns. Western economies tend to be market oriented, whereas Japan's is organization oriented. For example, there is more mobility from one firm to another in the West, whereas lifetime careers are more the norm in Japanese firms.[7] Wages are market oriented in the Western firm, reflecting a norm of equal pay for equal work, but in the Japanese firm wages are incremental within the firm and conform to the principle of equal shares of shared effort, with considerable differentials for work of the same sort from one firm to another. In Japan this is an outcome of bargaining at the enterprise level, by company unions. Trade and industrial unions are more the norm in the West.[8]

The community-model firm has attracted much attention among management theorists and companies in the West because, as Dore argues, it is superior in comparison with the company-law model in innovativeness, efficiency, and competitiveness and in quality of life and satisfaction for its members.[9] But this is, of course, only one side of the picture. What companies gain in competitiveness through a stable and loyal workforce they lose in flexibility to hire and fire at will. Hence, it is not surprising that side by side with internal labor markets is a trend toward subcontracting and hiring of part-time workers and a "secondary labor market" for the more market-sensitive sectors of the economy or of large enterprises, in which workers are dispensable, are paid less, and receive less in benefits.

These changes pose a complex challenge not only to unions but also to political parties that have traditionally sought to advance the interests of working people. Workers in Japan and the United States are increasingly and more sharply divided into two classes, those within the elite, and perhaps increasingly com-munity-model firms and those in the competitive labor market, increasingly in-secure and marginalized.[10] If wage differentials tend to correspond to firms more than to trades and skill levels, one would expect to find changing patterns in both "trade-union consciousness" and "working-class consciousness," as commonali-ties shift from occupation or class to the enterprise level.[11]

## SOME TENDENCIES OF THE COMMUNITY MODEL

To understand the limits of the community model and to perceive the need for additional supporting institutions, it is helpful to think about where community-model enterprises might lead in the absence of an organized socialist movement, that is, within the parameters laid down by and serving the interests of capital. After completing his largely positive assessment of the community model as embodied in the Japanese enterprise, Dore asks how such firms might be pro-moted in the West. In general, he proposes legislation to shift the balance of power from shareholders to employees. In particular, this could include tighter regula-tion of corporate takeovers so as to build in regard for the fate of workers, pro-motion of profit sharing, and worker ownership of shares, but most importantly it involves industrial democracy. For, barring a massive transfer of capital wealth from current shareholders to workers or the state, the only other way to effect a shift in power is to empower workers within firms by virtue of their status as members. One might think of this as a strategy for developing self-management, that this is an alternative, and complementary, to the strategy of expanding worker ownership.

Among other things, Dore proposes that, in order to signify that workers are participating members of firms, they ought to be allowed as much say in deter-mining managers' salaries as managers do in determining theirs.[12] He proposes setting up Fairness Councils in each enterprise, which would work out a consensus on salaries and wages, on the premise that all should get a fair share of the prod-uct of their shared efforts. Such enterprise-level bargaining would ideally occur in the context of incomes policy at the national level, designed not only to keep inflation under control but also to establish consensual norms concerning what is a fair distribution of incomes.[13] (Others propose empowering workers to hire and fire management, as well, but in so doing they move beyond capitalism, be-cause it would be difficult to accomplish this without abolishing shareholder ownership or transferring it to workers or communities.) I do not wish to chal-lenge the claim that such institutions could be made to work in the very differ-ent cultural context of Great Britain or North America. (Dore is much more skep-tical about transplanting Japanese models to the United States than to Great Britain.) My concern is with the problems that would remain even if such insti-tutions were successful.

One problem, perhaps the major one, is that the community model would lead to a sharpening of the division between workers in the primary and secondary labor markets.[14] To provide secure employment for some workers, companies will need to differentiate them from those vulnerable to layoff. There are difficulties with this strategy.[15] Nonetheless, it is not too difficult to imagine a simultaneous strengthening of the position of permanent workers and a weakening of the position and conditions of temporary workers or those in subcontracting firms. This is, indeed, the situation of Japanese workers.[16]

With this division we can expect changes in class configurations. Enterprise-level bargaining for the elite workers will result in growing differences between similarly skilled workers across firms and a decline in the norm of equal pay for equal work that has informed trade union and industrywide bargaining. Thus, to a division between permanent and part-time or temporary workers we must add a division among permanent workers corresponding to the better- and worse-placed firms.[17] As Dore notes, the new corporatism will rest less on class interest than on sectional interest.[18] The permanent workers will also have more in common with their employers than with workers in other firms or in the secondary labor market.

A second problem has to do with meritocracy. Dore describes Japan as the most meritocratic of societies. Testing and tracking in education are highly developed, and educational performance is a critical determinant of entrance into the prestigious universities and firms. The community model, to the extent that it calls for reduced labor mobility, requires "more careful checking of ability potentials for recruitment purposes" and, hence, more reliance on educational performance and testing.[19] The greater egalitarianism of universal educational opportunity under those conditions may thus have the paradoxical result of a new hierarchy of educational achievement.[20]

Dore himself notes two dangers in such a meritocracy, concerning unemployment and citizen equality. Assuming that the skill level of jobs is rising, there is, particularly in times of recession, a tendency in such a meritocratic system for those higher in the hierarchy to bump those lower, so that those at the bottom of the employment ladder tend to coincide with those at the bottom of the merit hierarchy. Although a welfare minimum may be maintained at a decent level, the "dignity minimum" plummets.[21] Dore, following James Meade, proposes to create a new basis for the dignity minimum, a guaranteed minimum income, as a matter of citizenship right.

As with all other proposals for a substantial guaranteed basic income, there is a question of how it is to be financed. A digression here on the topic of basic-income funding will also serve to reveal affinities between Dore's proposals and the models of socialism discussed in chapter 8. Dore proposes a social dividend to each citizen, financed through state acquisition of a sizable share of capital, itself a growing proportion of the value of products. Dore describes a scheme for transferring half the national wealth to such a fund within a generation. Without spelling out the organizational details, this amounts to a gradual transition toward Roemer's coupon socialism and would have the effect of universalizing and equalizing the profit share of national income, even as wage and salary differentials widened. This might appear to be mere resignation to the growing inequality stemming from differences in skill and market position and, in particular, to a growing division between paid workers and others who get by on their basic income. But one common argument for a basic-income strategy is that it would enable people to price themselves into a job, because under BI, workers' incomes are not so dependent upon their wages.[22] Thus, dignity is supported in two ways: an entitlement to basic income (along with basic liberties) affirms the intrinsic worth of the life of each person, regardless of paid work performed, and wider opportunities for paid work (not to mention citizen participation and child care) better enable each person to contribute to society.

On the funding question, basic income does not mesh quite so neatly with economic democracy as it does with coupon socialism. The aim in economic democracy is to abolish property income, not to distribute it equally. Hence, short of full employment, in ED the gap between workers and the unemployed may pose a need for basic income that will need to be funded through income tax or by use of a portion of the investment fund for income support. The former could cause political battles. On the other hand, BI funded through income tax might be higher than that yielded through a social dividend and at the same time lower the meritocratic hierarchy resulting from wage inequalities. Funding basic income from the tax on capital assets would muddy the fund's transparency as an investment fund and complicate the debate over its use. The danger here is widespread inefficient allocation of the fund and ultimately a shrinking (relative to the capitalist alternative) of the total social wealth available for any purpose.

Economic democracy meshes very well, on the other hand, with the community-model firm. The worker-managed firm corresponds to the first and third of the defining dimensions of the community model: the firm is defined as the association of the people who work full-time in it, and there is cooperation and trust among managers and workers in making the firm prosper and sharing the rewards equitably. With respect to the second dimension, in a worker-owned or self-managed firm, the shareholders are the workers, but in contrast with the community model, there is a much-reduced role for other stakeholders. The bank that allocates investment funds is the only outsider that would normally exercise indirect control over decision making. If this were thought to be a weakness, it could easily be addressed by making space for other relevant outsiders on the governing board. (The Caja Laboral Popular, the cooperative bank of Mondragon, is a second tier cooperative, its board including not only representatives of bank workers but also representatives from the co-ops in the group, to ensure accountability to the cooperative network. If there were compelling reasons for doing so, all cooperatives could be similarly "second-tiered.")

One might wonder, after a decade of corporate raiding and downsizing in America, including many corporations that had historically offered something approaching community-model job security, whether there is much room left for the community model. Perhaps the disasters resulting from those years will actually leave some people more receptive to the community model.[23] But a more secure and likely wellspring for community-model firms is worker ownership. As we have seen in chapter 7, worker ownership is steadily growing in both "publicly traded" and private firms, and it can yield efficiency advantages when combined with the sort of participation characteristic of the community model. If the logical end point of expanding worker ownership is economic democracy (rather than coupon socialism), this is another point in favor of economic democracy as the ultimate preferred environment for the community model.

## ASSOCIATIONAL UNIONISM

Most unions in the United States have been resistant or ambivalent toward elements of the community model, such as shop-floor participation and joint labor–management committees, for three reasons: (1) they threaten the unity of the union through the proliferation of representative bodies and the possibility of splits over key issues; (2) they call into question contractual rigidities concerning work rules and pay scales; and (3) in general, they undermine the "balance of power" model of union–management relations in which powerful corporate bureaucracies are countered by powerful union bureaucracies.[24] Many suspect that what I have been calling the community model and other management trends that seek to blur the lines between managers and workers and win workers' commitment to the company are merely rhetorical tricks to break unions or keep them out in the first place. Some of the clearest examples of "managerialism," the idea that every employee is a manager, have been in nonunion companies such as IBM.[25] There are also many examples of the rhetoric of participation being used in entirely cynical ways, with no real change in management practice behind it.[26]

But the crisis that unions face is deeper than new forms of union busting. Although the decline in union membership in the 1980s, in absolute as well as relative terms, was no doubt accelerated by a hostile administration in Washington, a National Labor Relations Board that was openly anti-union, and an owning class thus encouraged to go on the offensive, the decline of unions is a long-term trend that has been under way for more than a quarter of a century. Union membership has declined from 35 percent of workers in 1954 to 14 percent in 1998. Half the membership of the AFL-CIO is in the declining manufacturing industries, whereas 90 percent of all new jobs are in service industries and organizations in which less than 10 percent of workers are organized. But the decline is not an outcome simply of such sectoral shifts, for the percentage of workers organized has declined in every sector of employment. An increase in the number of part-time and temporary workers and "independent contractors," who are difficult to organize, also weakens the relative strength of organized workers.[27]

Nor are new trends in management unique to nonunion companies. Some of the most innovative reforms have been introduced in companies such as General Motors, Ford, and AT&T, which have long recognized unions. What is driving management reform is not so much short-term battles against unions as long-term adjustments to an increasingly competitive international market and the desire for increasing flexibility. The trend seems to be widespread: a quarter of the companies on the New York Stock Exchange claim to have shifted their basic approach to management.[28]

In the absence of unions, such "managerialism" runs up against limits:[29] (1) there is no check against cynical uses of participation rhetoric to disguise abuses of power; (2) in the absence of any system for representing workers, it is hard to identify disaffection among workers; (3) managerialist companies tend to be closed communities, failing, on the one hand, to legitimate themselves in the face of political challenges from diverse environmental and other social movements outside the company and relying, on the other hand, on a "buffer" of part-time, temporary, and subcontracted workers to shore up their programs of long-term job security for full-time employees inside the firm.[30]

Traditional industrial unions, Charles Heckscher argues, are unable to transcend these limits. Collective bargaining, if limited to issues of wages, benefits, and working conditions, can not address the complexity of issues that workers face (job restructuring, company strategy, job creation, mobility, discrimination). Industrial unions have tied "their members closely to the fortunes of a particular employer by negotiating non-portable benefits, strong seniority provisions, and rules for advancement within the firm."[31]

Heckscher envisions a "new unionism," which would aim for portable benefits, retraining, and job creation, focusing on *employment* security rather than *job* security, which would provide representation that could check arbitrary abuses of management flexibility but at the same time make possible representation of the complex concerns of workers. In other words, representation will need to be plural, local, and decentralized in many ways that are not possible within the framework of industrial unionism. Second, representation would be secured through rights of individual workers in addition to collective rights of the union. Finally, the new unionism would incorporate representation of outside interests and resolve disputes through multilateral negotiation.

Their efforts to institute representation of "employee groups in shifting combinations rather than insisting on two-party confrontation," taking on concerns that have more to do with careers than with jobs, and undertaking study and strategy concerning the long-term trends in the industry are among the trends that make unions appear more like professional associations, such as associations of doctors, professors, or engineers. Hence, Heckscher calls these "associational unions." For example, the CWA (Communications Workers of America) has moved in this direction by shifting away from the "master contract," focusing on employment (versus job) security, and establishing strategy centers.[32] Some professional associations are also taking on the union role of collective bargaining while preserving their associational functions and methods. The NEA (National Education Association), for example, remains relatively decentralized, and in addition to engaging in collective bargaining it provides lobbying and public appeals.[33] The strike is used only as a last resort, with great reliance on publicity and on enforcement of civil rights through the courts.[34]

Thus, unions responding proactively to managerialism would push for a new system of labor–management relations grounded in employee rights, new forms of representation, and multilateral conflict resolution. They would thus have more to offer their members in the new forms of enterprise that are likely to continue to emerge. The rights that form the bedrock of such a system would include protection from discrimination against women and minorities, rights to comparable worth, pregnancy leave, and privacy; rights to know about unsafe workplaces, materials, and products and about planned plant closings and other strategic matters; freedom of speech, including protection for whistle-blowers, and rights of association that include other groupings besides collective-bargaining units.[35] Some of these currently exist; others are being contested in legislatures and courts. Heckscher envisions this new framework of rights as providing a basis of power from which to resist abuses of managerialism. The most important fact to keep in mind about these emerging employee rights is that many of them have come about not primarily as a result of action by unions alone but rather because of the pressure of other social movements of women, environmentalists, and minorities.[36]

## THE LIMITS OF UNIONISM

The limits of associational unionism concern (1) the basis of power, (2) those outside the margins of unions, and (3) the nature of consensus in the context of multilateral negotiation. Heckscher rightly observes that large union bureaucracies and strikes are not sufficient responses to the challenges of the contemporary world market and management innovations. New forms of association are needed, as are new weapons of struggle. But the idea that a new system of employee rights can serve something like the same function that union bureaucracy has served in countering the power of management is problematic. Whether such rights will come into being and how well they will be enforced depend upon the power of the social movements that are pushing for them. Once established, they do indeed provide an institutional power basis, the courts, for pressing claims. But the courts are a far less certain ally of workers than their own organizations, as evidenced by anti-union court decisions of political appointees of the 1980s.

Associational unionism goes further than industrial unionism in incorporating outsiders, those members beyond the confines of the workplace. Lane Kirkland, when he was president of the AFL-CIO, proposed creating an "associate membership" for "workers who want access to collective action . . . but where the exigencies make it impossible to establish a contractual relationship with the employer."[37] Such membership is important for addressing the needs of the unemployed, part-time and temporary workers, and others who fall outside the collective bargaining units of industrial unionism. But can unions, even associational unions, accommodate all those who fall outside the boundaries of corporations? Even if a change in self-conception is in the offing, the limited resources of unions suggest that the needs of such workers (for retraining, for example) are better met by governmental agencies and public policy measures such as basic income. Even associational unionism is more apt to accommodate itself to a growing trend toward an elite of workers in community-model firms and an underclass of part-timers, who are, in addition, marked as failures in a meritocratic competition for membership.[38]

Associational unionism in the context of community-model firms involves a shift away from adversarial relations to consensus. This alone should occasion the suspicion that consensus is being achieved only because an elite of workers is being co-opted by the most privileged companies and the two constitute an interest apart from the rest of society. However, associational unionism also involves opening up the negotiating process in such a way that it is no longer bilateral but multilateral. This opens the possibility that other groups could claim the right to participation in negotiations over such matters as technological innovation and long-term industry strategy. Heckscher identifies the key problems in establishing a new system of negotiations as who has *standing*, and what constitutes a *fair procedure*. Heckscher is concerned with how associations might gain standing within a firm, by virtue of having some of their members employed. For example, "any association with at least ten percent of a unit would have rights of representation."[39] This would certainly open up firms to representation by a variety of associations. But it does not address the issue of representation of nonemployees, such as affected community members or environmental groups, except insofar as the associations would be rooted in movements outside the firm and would "bring the outside in."[40]

Heckscher thinks *fair procedure* consists in involving all groups with standing, their accepting the outcome, and sufficient time and resources being set aside so that informed decisions can be made.[41] These are necessary conditions of fairness, but such a conception of fairness does not account for the effects of unequal power in the bargaining process. Nor does it take account of the effects of ideology. Workers will consent to negotiations arrived at under such a "fair" procedure without the outcome being genuinely fair. This is evident once we consider the bases of consent to the political system of capitalism, which apply with added force to cases of consent to agreements between workers and managers.

Without invoking "false consciousness" or fear of violent repression, Joshua Cohen and Joel Rogers explain how capitalist democracy is limited by the unequal distribution of resources and by the way capitalist democracy directs the exercise of political rights to the satisfaction of some interests but not others. Taking the second of these first, "Capitalist democracy is in some measure capable of satisfying the interests encouraged by capitalist democracy itself, namely, interests in short-term material gain."[42] Because capitalists control investment, the satisfaction of their interests is a necessary condition for the satisfaction of all other interests in the system, including interests in higher wages or increased state revenues. Combined with the material uncertainty workers face in the labor market, this structural constraint impels workers to struggle to increase wages and, in general, to improve their short-term material condition. Schooled in economic calculation, they will reject radical long-term struggle to abolish capitalism. Short-term struggles are easier to coordinate and are recognized and licensed by the state. Individual workers contemplating long-term struggle are likely to succumb to the free-rider problem because of the cost of information gathering, the personal risks involved, and the losses likely to result even if they succeed—capital strikes, economic chaos, and the like.

Capitalists, on the other hand, have enormous and mutually reinforcing advantages with respect to assets, knowledge of their industry and economic situation, the number of units they need to coordinate politically, and their access to key decision makers in government and business. The free-rider problem is less serious for capitalists because they are smaller as a group, and their stakes and the likelihood of success are both high. The result of these unequal advantages will be a bias in public expenditures and benefits toward capitalist interests, a bias to which workers nevertheless consent for the reasons sketched.

What goes for workers' consent to the capitalist system goes doubly for their consent to agreements negotiated within the parameters of capitalism. Thus, any "fair procedure" or negotiation that presupposes the inequalities of resource distribution, the uncertain labor market, and capitalist property rights must be suspect, along with any consensus that is the outcome of such a procedure.

It has long been recognized that unions occupy an ambivalent position in the struggle between capital and labor. On the one hand, they defend the immediate interests of workers, particularly concerning wages and working conditions. On the other, and partly to better serve the first aim, they make compromises with management and government and, in general, accommodate themselves to the capitalist system. Associational unions as envisioned by Heckscher would define the immediate interests of workers somewhat differently, but in their accommodation with capitalism they would appear to fit the pattern of earlier unionism. Hence, the need continues for some organization or movement to criticize the basic structural conditions of exploitation and oppression to which unions accommodate. This other ranges from isolated critics engaged in the "diffuse dissemination of insights individually gained in the style of the eighteenth-century Enlightenment" (as Habermas described Theodor Adorno) to tightly organized radical parties with strategies (whether reformist or revolutionary) for transcending capitalism.[43] I will not try to specify the appropriate organizational form or vehicle for today's "Left." I limit my concern here to the discourse that the Left might embrace in response to the deeper structural transformations that have given rise both to the community model, or managerialism, and to the seeds of associational unions.

## RIGHTS TALK AND COMMUNITY

The analysis so far suggests that the community-model firm and associational unionism involve, on the one hand, a shift from adversarial to more communitarian or consensual relations within firms. On the other hand, if fully developed, such firms would have to recognize rights of individuals within firms. Hence, the new developments include both more-communitarian and more-liberal elements than industrial unionism. The shift from a focus on wages and working conditions to issues of work structure and enterprise policy and industrial policy also suggests that analysis of the issues would benefit from a shift away from the exclusive focus on the problem of exploitation. Hence, Marxist analysis of exploitation needs to be broadened if it is to prove useful in theorizing contemporary struggles for social justice.

It is clear that some form of associational unionism is emerging in response to new needs of workers, needs of new groups of workers, and new challenges of international competition. At the same time we can anticipate a new thrust toward meritocracy and a growing marginalization of groups not employed in primary-sector firms. This opens up the possibility of new movements of the unemployed or underemployed and raises the question of how their needs may be connected in a positive way with the needs of workers in community-model firms. As Van Parijs has noted, it is these movements, along with the Green parties, that are pressing for a right to a basic income in some European countries.[44]

Associational unionism also represents an opening up to new constituencies, such as women and minorities, and new issues, such as rights and participation. But the concerns of these constituencies are obviously not exhausted by an employee bill of rights, because they seek expanded rights of participation in the welfare state, in schools, in the media, and in other arenas of the state. Hence, what is needed is a broadened discourse of rights that includes the new unionism but links it to broader, more radical demands that could lead beyond capitalism. An "economic bill of rights" that includes the new "employee rights" but also rights to basic income and participation would exemplify the discourse we are looking for.[45]

It may appear that I am endorsing liberal capitalism by calling for a discourse of rights and thus abandoning the goal of socialist self-management. However, as Samuel Bowles and Herbert Gintis have argued, "elements of the now-dominant liberal discourse can be forged into powerful tools of democratic mobilization, a mobilization which, if successful, is almost certain in the long run to burst the bounds of the liberal discourse itself."[46] To understand their argument it is necessary to see how they characterize liberalism. It can not be understood in terms of values and commitments, because liberalism has included many conflicting strands of thinking. But what is generally common to liberal thinkers is silence on the subjects of exploitation (as Marxist critics have long pointed out) and community (as feminists have noted with respect to the family, communitarians with respect to the state, and as is evident in liberal legal theories of the corporation as a fictive private person). Following Michael Walzer, they characterize liberalism as erecting walls between the public realm of the state and the private realm of economy and family, walls that are intended to secure liberties but which also shelter domination.[47] The fault of liberalism hitherto lies in its failure to identify the roots of domination in patriarchal authority and economic dependence.[48]

In a perhaps somewhat oversimplified account of social change since the advent of capitalism, Bowles and Gintis argue that the motor of social change is the interaction of two (often contradictory) expansionary logics:

> The first is the expansionary logic of personal rights, progressively bringing ever wider spheres of society—the management of the economy and the internal relationships of the family, for example—under at least the formal if not the substantive rubric of liberal democracy. The second tendency concerns the expansionary logic of capitalist production, according to which the capitalist firm's ongoing search for profits progressively encroaches upon all spheres of social activity, leaving few realms of life untouched by the imperatives of accumulation and the market.[49]

The history of liberal democratic capitalism is a history of accommodations to the expansionary logic of capital secured in property rights by movements for expansion of personal rights and democratic accountability. But further expansion of personal rights points beyond capitalism itself:

> The presumed harmony of personal rights and property rights appears reasonable only when their permissible *range of applications* is not called into question. When the freedom of speech and press is extended to the right of equal access to education, when equal treatment before the law is extended to equal treatment before the health care system, and when freedom of association extends from political demonstrations to trade unions, we have clear-cut instances of the clash of personal and property rights. When freedom of speech is extended to workers on the job, or equal treatment is extended to women, or freedom of association is extended to gay and lesbian couples, we move toward undermining the fundamental structures of authority in economy and family.[50]

Bowles and Gintis draw a controversial implication from this analysis:

If we are to affirm the notion that the political history of the advanced capitalist societies has been etched by the collision of personal rights and property rights, we cannot avoid the implication that socialism—as a language and a program, if not as a movement—has been largely irrelevant to this evolution. Where workers' movements have mobilized more than handfuls of isolated militants . . . their inspiration and their solidarity has been based more on the demand for democracy than for socialism.[51]

Thus, they are among those recommending that the Left abandon the rhetoric of socialism for a rhetoric of rights and radical democracy. Although the direction of my argument tends to support this, I want to interject an important qualification. Democracy is a matter of degree, and it can be extended by degrees for a very long time, involving ongoing accommodations with the requirements of capitalism. The rhetoric of radical democracy, stripped of any reference to socialism, runs the risk of sliding into such accommodations. Socialism signifies, if nothing else, relentless criticism and hostility toward capitalism. More positively, it represents the overcoming of capitalist inequality of condition and inequality in control of the means of production and the means of life. I agree with Frank Cunningham that these themes should not be lost, because they are important in order to advance democracy, which itself is important to advance human freedom.[52]

The question of socialism aside, once the discourse of rights is detached from the particular accommodations with capital accumulation in which it has been enmeshed and is understood to include rights to participate in democratic decision making, it is evidently a more promising discourse for promoting a democratic version of the community-model firm than communitarian political theory. The latter is suspect from the point of view of many of the groups essential for the success of both the new unionism and for a movement that transcends it.

For example, Marilyn Friedman agrees with the communitarian criticism of the abstract individual of some liberal theories, who stands outside of society and is possessed only of an emaciated utility-maximizing rationality. But she questions the tendency of communitarians to encourage uncritical acceptance of those communities in which one finds oneself—families, tribes, neighborhoods, nations—as the sole basis for one's identity. Such communities often make illegitimate moral claims rooted in hierarchies of domination and subordination, as is evident in the oppression of women in most traditional cultures and the denigration of outsiders in many ethnic communities. Friedman argues that communities of choice, typical of urban environments and oriented less around place than around common interests and values, or common oppression, are equally important with found communities, if not for the constitution of the self then for its reconstitution.[53]

In this chapter, I have tried to show how trends toward flexible production provide an opening toward more communitarian firms, which in democratic form incorporate at least some elements of self-management. The democratic form of enterprise can only come about if unions begin to take on new roles and identities, if social movements with overlapping interests in employee rights and multilateral negotiation come together politically, and if a new discourse uniting these movements can be articulated. I have argued that communitarian discourse is not so well suited to this task as a discourse of rights. In chapter 12, I examine how economic democracy is relevant to the concerns of new social movements. In the next chapter, I explore complications that arise in the media for the democratic organization of enterprises.

## NOTES

1. For examples of communitarians, see Michael Sandel, *Liberalism and the Limits of Justice* (Cambridge: Cambridge University Press, 1982); Alasdair MacIntyre, *After Virtue*, 2d ed. (Notre Dame: University of Notre Dame Press, 1984); and Charles Taylor, *Sources of the Self* (Cambridge: Harvard University Press, 1989). For purposes of this chapter, I consider *liberalism* to be a political theory that assumes that (1) there is no consensus concerning what constitutes the good life; consequently, (2) the role of the state is to adjudicate conflict between individuals motivated by distinct and possibly incompatible conceptions of their good; (3) the role of political theory is to articulate a conception of justice consisting of principles setting the bounds of acceptable conflict. The metaphor of a social contract is well suited to the liberal theory of justice because it represents justice as the outcome of a fair bargaining process between mutually disinterested individuals, each seeking to maximize his or her good. Communitarianism is a reaction to liberalism, which (1) questions the desirability or possibility of liberal neutrality on questions concerning the good life, (2) challenges the primacy of justice as the first virtue of social institutions; and (3) questions the liberal conception of the self as an abstractly rational utility maximizer. For the communitarian the self is "encumbered" by commitments and values arising from membership in various communities and traditions. The analogue at the level of the firm is the contrast between those firms that are divided by conflict and distrust and those in which members cooperate in pursuit of commonly shared purposes.

2. Charles Heckscher, *The New Unionism: Employee Involvement in the Changing Corporation* (New York: Basic Books, 1988); see also Ronald Dore, *Taking Japan Seriously: A Confucian Perspective on Leading Economic Issues* (Stanford: Stanford University Press, 1987), 188–89. Whether the trends discussed involve, on the whole, a reemergence of artisans or global de-skilling is hard to determine. For a critical view of the thesis of the new industrial divide, see Bennett Harrison, *Lean and Mean: The Changing Landscape of Corporate Power in the Age of Flexibility* (New York: Basic Books, 1994).

3. Heckscher, *The New Unionism*, 55. See also Charles F. Sabel and Michael J. Piore, *The Second Industrial Divide: Possibilities for Prosperity* (New York: Basic Books, 1984).

4. David Harvey, *The Condition of Postmodernity* (New York: Basil Blackwell, 1989).

5. Ray Marshall, former U.S. secretary of labor, argues that the basic choice is between low wages, on the one hand, and "higher quality, productivity, and skills," on the other, if U.S. enterprises are to compete successfully; see Marshall, "Work Organization, Unions, and Economic Performance," in *Unions and Economic Competitiveness*, ed. Lawrence Mischel and Paula B. Voos (Armonk, N.Y.: M. E. Sharpe, 1992), 287–315. He adds, "Unions are an integral part of high performance companies in Germany, Sweden, and even in Japan." But to avoid weakening their own bargaining position, unions will need to integrate employee involvement strategies with more participatory "organizing approaches." This is not yet being done very much in the United States; see Tom Juravich, "Employee Involvement, Work Reorganization, and the New Labor Movement: Toward a Radical Integration," *New Labor Forum* 2 (Spring 1998): 84–91. For a debate on participation, see Andy Banks and Jack Metzgar, "Participating in Management: Union Organizing on a New Terrain," *Labor Research Review* 8, no. 2 (Fall 1989): 1–55, and critical responses in the same issue.

6. Dore, *Taking Japan Seriously*, 54.

7. Rising unemployment, deflation, and layoffs in major Japanese corporations may signal a weakening of job security in Japan. One is struck nevertheless by the degree to which layoffs are avoided in the Japanese firm compared with comparable American firms undergoing restructuring; Stephanie Strom, "Mitsubishi Electric to Cut Global Workforce by 10%," *New York Times*, 1 April 1999, and "A Revolution by Degrees," *New York Times*, 6 April 1999.

8. Dore, *Taking Japan Seriously*, 29–30.

9. Dore, *Taking Japan Seriously*, 145.

10. For future development, this hypothesis needs to be fleshed out. Valerie Carter, in conversation in 1992, suggests something like the following, using Richard Edwards' analysis of firms as either core/primary labor-market firms or periphery/secondary labor-market firms: In the primary labor-market most firms are still following the company-law model, but community-model firms are increasing. In the periphery, there are few if any community-model firms, and most fit the company-law model; see Richard Edwards, *Contested Terrain: The Transformation of the Workplace in the Twentieth Century* (New York: Basic Books, 1979).

11. This touches upon a major issue in the sociology of work, which I cannot develop further here: how to theorize social class; see, for example, Erik Olin Wright, et al., *The Debate on Classes* (London: Verso, 1989); and David M. Gordon, Richard Edwards, and Michael Reich, *Segmented Work, Divided Workers: The Historical Transformation of Labor in the United States* (Cambridge: Cambridge University Press, 1982).

12. Dore, *Taking Japan Seriously*, 160.

13. Dore, *Taking Japan Seriously*, 68-84.

14. Gordon, Edwards, and Reich, *Segmented Work*.

15. Heckscher comments, "This solution—also widely used among the large firms of Japan—is not very satisfactory from any point of view. From the public policy perspective, it simply sharpens the difference between 'stable' and 'transient' workers; the latter, who absorb the pain of economic shifts, necessarily increase claims on the public coffers. From the perspective of the business itself, it is difficult to maintain a unified culture in which significant numbers are second-class citizens," *The New Unionism*, 10.

16. Rodney Clark, *The Japanese Company* (New Haven: Yale University Press, 1979).

17. Differences between industries may be more significant in the long run than differences between firms.

18. Dore, *Taking Japan Seriously*, 62. German codetermination illustrates how it is possible to combine worker participation with strong unions, according to Lowell Turner, "Industrial Relations and the Reorganization of Work in West Germany: Lessons for the U. S.," in Mischel and Voos, *Unions and Economic Competitiveness*, 217–46.

19. Dore, *Taking Japan Seriously*, 207.

20. Dore, *Taking Japan Seriously*, 207–8. For a critique of meritocracy, see Kai Nielsen, *Equality and Liberty: A Defense of Radical Egalitarianism* (Totowa, N.J.: Rowman and Allanheld, 1985), 103–87.

21. Dore, *Taking Japan Seriously*, 211.

22. Brian Barry, "Survey Article: Real Freedom and Basic Income," *Journal of Political Philosophy* 4, no. 3 (1996): 242–76.

23. For an account of the harms of corporate raiding and a general critique of the stock market, see Doug Henwood, *Wall Street* (New York: Verso, 1998).

24. Heckscher, *The New Unionism*, 156. This should not be taken to imply that union bureaucracies are equal in power to corporate bureaucracies but only that unions have developed central bureaucracies in an attempt to counter the power of their adversaries.

25. Heckscher, *The New Unionism*, 85 ff. According to John Hanson, director of the Bureau of Labor Education, University of Maine, building and construction trade unions provide a proven alternative model, in which portable benefits accrue to workers as union members rather than as employees of a particular firm. These unions are also active in apprenticeship programs, training, and retraining; personal conversation, 8 April 1999.

26. Heckscher, 101–13, 116–17. See also David Moberg, "War Zone," *In These Times* (24 July–6 August 1995): 12–16; Steve Babson, "When 'Empowerment' Means 'Exploitation': Negotiating the Terms of Lean Production," *WorkingUSA*, (May–June 1997): 69–76.

27. AFL-CIO Committee on the Evolution of Work, *The Changing Situation of Workers and Their Unions* (Washington, D.C.: n.p., 1985); Heckscher, *The New Unionism*, 261–62, 278. It would be useful to understand why American union membership has declined so, while from 1963 to 1983, Canadian membership in unions went from 30 percent to 40 percent of the workforce.

28. Heckscher, *The New Unionism*, 89–90.

29. Heckscher, *The New Unionism*, 100–111.

30. Job security breaks down even in the largest and strongest companies, as is evident from IBM's layoff of forty thousand workers in the early 1990s.

31. Heckscher, *The New Unionism*, 106, 111.

32. Heckscher, *The New Unionism*, 180–81; personal correspondence, 16 March 1999.

33. The emphasis should be on "*relatively* decentralized," as the NEA remains quite centralized and committed to a service model of unionism, in which regional representatives of the union perform most of the grievance processing and contract bargaining and maintenance rather than enlisting the participation of the membership. The Communications Workers of America (CWA), the Association of Federal, State, County and Municipal Employees (AFSCME), and Union of Needletrades, Industrial and Textile Employees (UNITE, created in 1995 through the merger of the Amalgamated Clothing and Textile Workers Union and the International Ladies' Garment Workers' Union) of-

fer better examples of a more participatory "organizing model"; Jack Metzgar, ed., "An Organizing Model of Unionism," *Labor Research Review* 10, no.1 (Spring 1991): 1–97; personal conversation with staff of the Bureau of Labor Education, University of Maine, 8 April 1999.

34. Heckscher, *The New Unionism*, 186.

35. Heckscher, *The New Unionism*, 158–76.

36. Heckscher, *The New Unionism*, 191. As Bill Murphy, assistant director of the Bureau of Labor Education, University of Maine, noted (personal correspondence, 1 April 1999), unions have lobbied together with other social movements for many important laws such as the Occupational Safety and Health Act, the Americans with Disabilities Act, social security legislation, and the Equal Employment Opportunity Act.

37. Quoted in Heckscher, *The New Unionism*, 183.

38. Heckscher acknowledges this point and adds that "for the lower part of the wage/skill distribution a fairly traditional form of unionism is necessary. The AFL-CIO may well be moving in the direction of representing that sector primarily; and Working Today, which is an attempt to develop an associational union in practice, has trouble reaching those lower ranks and stays focussed around semi-professionals and professionals"; personal correspondence, 16 March 1999.

39. Heckscher, *The New Unionism*, 224.

40. Charles Heckscher, personal correspondence, 16 March 1999. One proposal suggested to me by Maurice Glasman derives from the German system of codetermination. The board governing a firm consists of five representatives of capital, five of labor, and the mayor, representing other constituencies. This system allows for some input directly in firm management, through the political process, but minimizes participation by those, other than capitalists, who do not work; personal correspondence, 28 October 1992.

41. Heckscher, *The New Unionism*, 225.

42. Joshua Cohen and Joel Rogers, *On Democracy* (New York: Penguin Books, 1983), 48–73, 51–52.

43. Jürgen Habermas, *Theory and Practice*, trans. John Viertel (Boston: Beacon Press, 1973), 31.

44. Philippe Van Parijs, "Basic Income: A Green Strategy for the New Europe," in *Green Light on Europe*, ed. Sara Parkin (London: Heretic Books, 1991), 166–76.

45. The Twenty-First Century Party, primarily a feminist group but with some supporters from the United Farm Workers, some Greens, and a few other left-wing groups, organized its platform around discrimination. "Sex discrimination tops the list, with racial and ethnic discrimination listed second. Abortion rights and lesbian/gay rights are also a major part of the agenda, followed by economic rights, environmental rights, the right to be free from all forms of violence, including war, the right to unionize and bargain collectively, and the right of all to participate in government"; *In These Times* (September 16–29, 1992): 6. The Fairness Agenda, an initiative of the Institute for Policy Studies endorsed by many grassroots organizations, some unions, and more than fifty members of the Congressional Progressive Caucus, is another call for economic rights, under such headings as dignified work, environmental justice, economic redistribution, democratic participation, community empowerment, global nonviolence, and social justice. "According to a report of the Institute for Policy Studies, fifty-two Congressional candidates running on explicitly progressive agendas unanimously won their sought-after seats in the

'96 November elections"; Institute for Policy Studies, "The Progressive Challenge", updated 7 April 1999, <http://www.netprogress.org/index.htm> (14 April 1999). For an argument that such economic rights need to be global in scope, see William Greider, "Why the Global Economy Needs Worker Rights," *WorkingUSA*, (May–June 1997): 32–44.

46. Samuel Bowles and Herbert Gintis, *Democracy and Capitalism: Property, Community, and the Contradictions of Modern Social Thought* (New York: Basic Books, 1987), 175.

47. Bowles and Gintis, *Democracy and Capitalism*, 15–17.

48. Bowles and Gintis, *Democracy and Capitalism*, 176.

49. Bowles and Gintis, *Democracy and Capitalism*, 29.

50. Bowles and Gintis, *Democracy and Capitalism*, 164; cf. Heckscher, *The New Unionism*, 232–33, on the opposition of the business community to new rights for workers.

51. Bowles and Gintis, *Democracy and Capitalism*, 62; see also page 33 on the importance of discourse in forging solidarity.

52. Frank Cunningham, *Democratic Theory and Socialism* (Cambridge: Cambridge University Press, 1987). In the terms of chapter 1 of this book, socialism is important for extending democracy, which, in turn, is important for ensuring the fair value of liberty.

53. Marilyn Friedman, "Feminism and Modern Friendship: Dislocating the Community," *Ethics* 99 (January 1989): 275–90.

# 11

## Self-Management and the Media

The press is not an instrument for commercial profit. It is an instrument for culture; its mission is to give accurate information, to defend ideas, to serve the cause of human progress.
The press can fulfill its mission only in freedom and through freedom.
The press is free when it does not depend either on governmental power or on the power of money, but only on the conscience of journalists and readers.
*Draft Declaration on the Rights and Responsibilities of a Free Press,*
National Press Federation (France), November 24, 1945

Regardless of what a progressive group's first issue of importance is, its second issue should be media and communication, because so long as the media are in corporate hands, the task of social change will be vastly more difficult, if not impossible, across the board.
Robert W. McChesney, *Corporate Media and the Threat to Democracy*

In this chapter I argue for worker self-management of the media, particularly the press. In the first section I discuss the problems of media concentration, commercial dominance, and journalistic bias, which self-management alone can not solve. I follow this with a more general argument for self-management of enterprises. Then I respond to objections to my proposal arising from the distinctive character of media, their social and political functions, and their legal status. I argue that not only would self-management not conflict with the function of enabling citizens to be informed and participate equally in social and political life, it would also enable media better to perform their function than when controlled by either government or concentrated commercial corporations. But self-managed media would require some rethinking of the meaning of freedom of the press, and it would itself need to be supplemented with other measures, such as rights of access, to ensure equality of freedom of expression. The concluding section discusses some of the difficulties of combining access and autonomy.


## THE MEDIA MONOPOLY

One of the least covered stories in journalism is the growing concentration of the media in profit-seeking corporations. Ben Bagdikian first documented the trend in *The Media Monopoly* in 1983, when fifty firms controlled the majority of U.S. media. In less than a decade the number shrank to twenty[1]. Robert McChesney has recently noted that as a result of mergers and acquisitions in the 1990s, "fewer than ten colossal vertically integrated media conglomerates now dominate U.S. media" and, increasingly, the world, Disney and Time-Warner being among the largest.[2] These, together with an additional forty or so second-tier corporations like the New York Times and Hearst, provide "the overwhelming majority (in revenue terms) of the world's film production, TV show production, cable channel ownership, cable and satellite system ownership, book publishing, magazine publishing, and music production. By any standard of democracy, such a concentration of media power is troubling, if not unacceptable."[3] Not only is enormous media power concentrated in a few hands, but the profit orientation of these firms ensures that low-income groups will receive little attention, news and public affairs will be underfunded and marginalized[4], and, in general, the interests of advertisers will predominate. In the words of one media-corporation CEO, "we are here to serve advertisers. That is our *raison d'etre.*"[5]

With respect to journalism, the particular focus of this chapter, the commercial funding of newspapers partially accounts for the transformation from the partisan press of the early years of the U.S. republic to the mass media, in which both news and editorials strive for an "objectivity" marked less by an aspiration to truth than by a desire to offend no one.[6] The reemergence of a "public sphere" of discussion, free from the domination of both the state and the corporations, would require "a major commitment to non-profit and non-commercial media. . . . The crucial structural factor for democratic media is to have the dominant portion of the communication system removed from the control of business and the support of advertising," subsidized instead through taxation or lease of spectrum space.[7]

Furthermore, the journalism profession will need to emancipate itself from implicit norms formulated under decades of corporate dominance, norms that may seem like rational and ethical standards but on examination are found to encode relations of power. In their "propaganda model," Noam Chomsky and Edward Herman elucidate these power relations. They identify five "filters" through which information must pass to become news in the major media:

(1) the size, concentrated ownership, owner wealth, and profit-orientation of the dominant mass-media firms; (2) advertising as the primary income source of the mass media; (3) the reliance of the media on information provided by government, business, and "experts" funded and approved by these primary sources and agents of power; (4) "flak" as a means of disciplining the media; and (5) "anticommunism" as a national religion and control mechanism. These elements interact with and reinforce one another. The raw material of news must pass through successive filters, leaving only the cleansed residue fit to print. They fix the premises of discourse and interpretation, and the definition of what is newsworthy in the first place, and they explain the basis and operations of what amount to propaganda campaigns.

The elite domination of the media and marginalization of dissidents that results from the operation of these filters occurs so naturally that media news people, frequently operating with complete integrity and goodwill, are able to convince themselves that they choose and interpret the news "objectively" and on the basis of professional news values. Within the limits of the filter constraints they often are objective; the constraints are so powerful, and are built into the system in such a fundamental way, that alternative bases of news choices are hardly imaginable.[8]

This theory is well confirmed by the evidence of double standards in media coverage of foreign policy, for example, elections in Central America.[9] Chomsky and Herman identify five basic conditions political entities must satisfy for their elections to be considered free: freedom of speech and assembly; freedom of the press; freedom of organization of intermediate groups; freedom to organize parties, field candidates, and campaign for office; and absence of state terror and a climate of fear.[10] They then carefully examine against these criteria the elections in El Salvador in 1982 and 1984, in Nicaragua in 1984, and in Guatemala in 1984–85. They conclude that

electoral conditions in Nicaragua in 1984 were far more favorable than in El Salvador and Guatemala, and the observer team of LASA [Latin American Studies Association] found the election in Nicaragua to have been "a model of probity and fairness" by Latin American standards. In El Salvador and Guatemala, *none* of the five basic preconditions of a free election was met. In both of these countries, state-sponsored terror, including the public exposure of mutilated bodies, had ravaged the civilian population up to the very day of the elections. In both, voting was required by law, and the populace was obliged to have ID cards signed, testifying that they had voted. In both, the main rebel opposition was off the ballot by law, by credible threat of violence, and by plan. Nevertheless, in exact accord with the propaganda line of the state, the U.S. mass media found the large turnouts in these countries to be triumphs of democratic choice, the elections legitimizing, and "fledgling democracies" thus created. This was accomplished in large part by the media's simply refusing to examine the basic conditions of a genuinely free election and their application to these client state elections. Only for the Nicaraguan election did the media look at matters such as freedom of the press, and they did this with conspicuous dishonesty. Despite its superiority on every substantive count, the Nicaraguan election was found by the media to have been a sham and to have failed to legitimize.[11]

To illustrate only the last criterion, in the months preceding the elections in El Salvador and Guatemala, death-squad and army violence created a climate of fear that made meaningful elections impossible. In El Salvador the "average rate of killings of civilians in the thirty months prior to the 1982 election was approximately seven hundred per month." In Nicaragua, in sharp contrast, "in 1984 its government was not murdering civilians."[12] In media coverage of these elections, violation of the basic conditions is systematically played down in the cases of El Salvador and Guatemala.

The role of the army was summarized by Warren Hoge in the *New York Times*: "Is the military playing any role in the election? Members of the military are not allowed to vote, and the armed forces are pledged to protect voters from violence and to respect the outcome of the contests." We may note that the army's mass killing of civilians and systematic destruction and demobilization of virtually all popular organizations in El Salvador over the preceding thirty months . . . is not part of the army's "role" for Hoge and the *Times*. Hoge repeats the Salvadoran army's pledge, not only taking it at face value, but never suggesting that it (and the election itself) was meaningless in a terror state where the "main opposition" was off the ballot and only the war parties were able to field candidates.[13]

Standards of reporting were very different in the case of Nicaragua. In the Salvadoran election, "rebel disruption" was centrally featured, and the large turnout was taken as a sign of electoral success—ignoring the fact that it was illegal not to vote.

In the case of Nicaragua, the propaganda format was reversed—the rebels were the good guys, and the election held by the bad guys was condemned in advance. Rebel opposition to the election—and efforts at disruption—did not make voting and a large turnout a repudiation of the rebels and approval of the Sandinistas.

The U.S. mass media once again followed the government agenda, *even though it meant an exact reversal of the standards they had applied in the Salvadoran election*. The contras and their supporters urged the public not to vote, and interfered with the election process with at least as much vigor as (and with more killings than) the rebels in El Salvador. Furthermore, voting was more assuredly secret and the citizens were not required to vote, or to have ID cards stamped indicating that they had. And the Sandinistas did not kill ordinary citizens on a daily basis, as was true in the "death-squad democracies." Thus turnout was far more meaningful in the Nicaraguan election than in the ones held in El Salvador and Guatemala—the public was free to abstain as well as to vote for opposition parties.

The U.S. mass media disposed of this problem mainly by massive suppression. They simply ignored the contra–U.S. campaign for abstention, waged with threats and attacks on polling places and election workers; and they buried the fact of an effectively secret vote and the right *not* to vote, just as, in parallel, they had inflated rebel disruption efforts in El Salvador in 1982 and 1984 and buried the voting *requirement* and other pressures to vote.[14]

This double standard was acknowledged by a "senior U.S. official": "The United States is not obliged to apply the same standard of judgment to a country whose government is avowedly hostile to the U.S. as for a country like El Salvador, where it is not. These people [the Sandinistas] could bring about a situation in Central America which could pose a threat to U.S. security. That allows us to change our yardstick."[15] What is more surprising, given a supposed journalistic code of objectivity, is the degree to which major media, notably the trend-setting *New York Times*, adhere to this double standard in reporting, as the propaganda model predicts.[16]

Any proposal for self-managed market socialism that failed to address ingrained double standards, as well as media concentration and commercialization, would be seriously flawed for four reasons. First, transferring ownership of concentrated media to media workers would merely transfer from one elite group to another a degree of power over information and agenda setting for the entire society out of proportion to their share of total capital wealth, for those workers would be in control not only of the affairs of their own firms but of a major determinant of politics and culture. Second, transfer of ownership would not begin to address the elements of the "propaganda model" entrenched in the norms of professional journalism. Third, cooperatively owned media would still be commercial media and so could be expected to exhibit most of the undesirable features of the capitalist media that flow from commercialization. Fourth, commercial media will be an obstacle to any major structural transformation of the larger society as long as other dimensions of the propaganda model remain unchallenged. Advocacy of worker control of the media without such qualifications can only serve to obscure the kind of media reforms needed as part of an egalitarian transformation of society.

Nevertheless, worker-managed media can be a part of this larger media reform. In the interest of diversity and freedom of speech, there should be a mix of private and public media, even if the public media are dominant, as McChesney advocates. Media cooperatives could be worker managed, as I argue below. Public media corporations could be codetermined by media workers, as well as representatives of communities. In the sections that follow I do not pretend to offer a systematic solution; I simply open the discussion and underscore the place for self-management of media in market socialism, while acknowledging the qualifications needed. Some recent socialist criticism of the media has emphasized the importance of citizen access to the media, to the neglect of the importance of journalistic autonomy. My aim is to rectify the balance, with self-management as an instrument of autonomy, consistent with the model advocated for other workplace settings.

## DEMOCRACY AND SELF-MANAGEMENT

One of the most persuasive arguments for worker self-management is that which is based on the value of democracy and seeks to extend democracy into areas of social life that are not, but could and should be, democratized.[17] Some maintain that the argument from democracy is defeasible, in the sense that it can be defeated by appeal to other principles in certain contexts, such as rights of ownership. I concur with Robert Dahl that appeal to rights of ownership does not necessarily defeat the argument from democracy.[18] But there are special cases in which the right of ownership acquires added importance, as in the case of ownership of media. In this case, some have argued that ownership is a necessary condition for securing the independence of the media, which is important both for individual freedom of expression and for the successful functioning of a democracy. However, discussion of ownership, although important, is beyond the scope of this chapter. Here, I can only examine ways in which self-management of the media, regardless of ownership forms, might be a key to the furtherance of democratization if instituted in a manner consistent with freedom of expression and plurality of independent voices.

In chapter 1, I argued for worker self-management as a reasonable extension of democracy and as supported by principles of justice. As Dahl succinctly put it, "*If* democracy is justified in governing the state, then it must *also* be justified in governing economic enterprises; and to say that it is *not* justified in governing economic enterprises is to imply that it is not justified in governing the state." The idea here is that corporate management constitutes a kind of private government, the decisions of which affect those who work for the corporation not in a transient but in a profound and ongoing way. The workers are the governed, and just as in a democratic state the governed should have a voice in the binding collective decisions made by their government, so, too, should workers have a voice in the corporation. "For laws cannot rightfully be imposed on others by persons who are not themselves obliged to obey those laws."[19]

The parallels between the government of a corporation and the government of a state are sufficiently strong that considerations supporting democratic rights to self-government in the latter carry over by analogy to the former. If governments have the power to punish, so too do corporate managers have the power to levy fines and to suspend or fire employees. Although governments are territorially rather than functionally defined, the pervasive importance of the governance of one's community of work is, in terms of the way it affects one's life, comparable to the pervasive importance of the governance of one's community of residence. If workers form a contract when they become employed, it is a peculiar kind of contract, with far-reaching implications for the character of their lives, more akin to the decision to reside in a particular town than to the decision to buy a car. Changing jobs can be a more significant change in a person's life than moving to a different community. For these reasons, people should have rights to self-government, or self-management in their work, just as they are entitled to rights to self-government in their communities of residence.[20]

The argument for self-management I am employing thus is an extension of democratic theory. In chapter 1, I built the case for democracy on a Rawlsian rights-based theory rather than a utilitarian argument, but my argument should be compatible with a number of different defenses of democracy. In the Rawlsian framework, basic liberties take precedence over consideration of distribution of incomes. Rawls' argument for basic equal political liberties—including those characteristic of political democracy—can be extended to make an argument for economic democracy.[21] If equal rights to participate in the political process or to exercise freedom of speech are important, so too must be equality in the conditions that make the exercise of such rights effective. If inequality in control over corporate wealth and governance of the workplace is great enough to constitute, for the more powerful, greater weight in the political process, a more egalitarian distribution of wealth and power would be called for. Such political considerations take priority for Rawls over utilitarian considerations of welfare—promoting growth or maximizing the incomes of the least fortunate. Thus, the arguments for self-management would take precedence over any utilitarian argument for private property rights. This argument is compelling, particularly in ordinary economic enterprises—commodity-producing firms—the value of whose product consists merely in its satisfaction of consumer preferences and the activity of which consists mainly in production for a profit.

But many kinds of work, and institutions supporting them, are not defined by ordinary commodity production, even when they are brought under the commodity form. Health care is an example. Health is not merely a commodity, even if substantial segments of health care have been commodified. The community as a whole has a special kind of interest in health, how it is defined and how health care is provided. Individuals have basic rights to certain forms of health care (though there is dispute about just which forms of care are covered by such rights). Individual rights and collective concerns should circumscribe the freedom of health-care providers more than that of other economic agents and may have implications for the appropriate form of organization of health-care institutions, trumping not only private property rights but also rights to worker self-management. Furthermore, central activities in health care are judged by standards independent of profit maximization. Over the long run this is not true for mere commodity production in a competitive market. But a profitable hospital that did not cure would not be judged successful. Those who have a special knowledge, as well as those who have a special interest, in health care, have a special claim to control—for example, doctors, nurses, and patients, more than the janitors or the owners.

## MEDIA SELF-MANAGEMENT AND FREEDOM OF THE PRESS

What is true for health care is true for other forms of work that resist classification as mere commodity production. At least some forms of communication have a special importance for the community as a whole, have a bearing on peculiar individual rights, and involve standards of success independent of profit maximization and consumer satisfaction. For these reasons, worker self-management in the media requires special justification above and beyond that provided by democratic theory. Because different media—print, broadcasting, and common carriers such as the telephone system—have different characteristics and different legal histories in the United States, I confine my attention to print media, but much of what is said about newspapers could be carried over to broadcasting.[22] In the media, unlike in many other forms of commodity production, the product comes under the protection of the First Amendment clause on freedom of the press. Freedom of the press is important both as a fundamental individual right and as a means for insuring the proper functioning of democracy. The problem with a legal requirement for self-management in the media is thus twofold.

First, it appears that self-management would encroach on freedom of speech in so far as this is currently guaranteed through property rights. The First Amendment, as it has been interpreted, allows owners of presses to publish what they will, without legal constraint.[23] Legally mandated worker control of the means of communication—such as printing presses and newspaper organization—inhibits the freedom of expression of any person, party, or organization that sets out to publish a newspaper (for example) on an ambitious scale. The technical requirements of some publishing include complex organization of the kind characteristic of newspaper production. It is unrealistic to expect that any individual or any organization wishing to publish a newspaper should, with a view to securing autonomy over publishing content, do all the work of reporting, editing, typesetting, and distribution themselves. They must hire others to do this. These others are subordinate to the owners in a workplace setting and by the democratic analogy would seem to be entitled to a right of self-government. It would seem in this case that there is a strong prima facie case for the right to property of the publishers overriding the right to self-government, at least if the latter right is construed in an unqualified way. (There is no reason to rule out limited rights of self-government over wages, working conditions, health and safety, and so on, but the argument we are considering definitely draws the line at control over the content of the publication.)

The second problem concerns the role of the press in a democracy. In a democracy, it is important that the press be as independent as possible from the requirements of governments or of large oligarchical interests, to be free to present the facts as they see them.[24] The truth is sufficiently elusive and, in matters of social and political importance, sufficiently value laden that it is important that there be a multiplicity of voices.[25] On the face of it, private ownership in an increasingly monopolized industry poses a threat both to the independence of journalists from the dominance of owners and from commercial considerations and to the presence of a multiplicity of voices in the media. But worker control of the media could also limit the independence and variety of journalists. Why should typesetters, clerical staff, delivery persons and janitors have a right to control the content of a newspaper or to choose an editor or those with the authority to hire an editor? Not being engaged directly in journalistic activity, they may be more apt to be concerned with the commercial success of the enterprise than with the standards intrinsic to journalism, thus perpetuating the commercial bias of privately owned newspapers. It would seem, then, that with a view to enhancing responsible and independent journalism, a strong case could be made for a narrower right to control of the work of editing and reporting by working journalists. This would include control over hiring and firing in the newsroom as well as control over day-to-day reporting and editing.[26] Let us call this narrower form of worker control "newsroom democracy" to distinguish it from the form of worker self-management that extends to all workers equal rights of self-management.[27]

The second problem, that the independence of journalists may be endangered as much by worker self-management as by private ownership, can be solved institutionally by splitting off groups of journalists as separate legal entities, with internal self-management. The workers responsible for printing, delivery, and so forth may have full self-management in their own spheres and would have what amounts to a contractual relationship with the newsroom. One model for this is the system of "basic organizations of associated labor" (BOALs) in all self-managed enterprises in the former Yugoslavia. Workplaces in large enterprises considered too unwieldy for effective democratic self-management were effectively broken up into departments, with each department essentially constituting an autonomous self-managing unit. However one wants to criticize this system from the point of view of economic efficiency, it makes sense from a functional point of view in self-managed media: it allows for full self-management in the industry and at the same time facilitates the autonomy of journalists.[28] Such autonomy would insulate the process of news production, more effectively than can now be done, from the commercial dimension of the newspaper business. Alternatively, journalists as a group would hold sufficient shares in an enterprise to enable them to block decisions that would change the information-providing, service character of the enterprise.[29]

The other problem I mentioned earlier has to do with the importance of property as a basis for freedom of the press and freedom of expression. Most such defenses of freedom of the press will be grounded in a theory of the person, and the person's inherent right to freedom of expression, together with an argument that possession of property is the only sure institutional guarantee of these freedoms. The free press is envisioned as one of the institutions supporting self-expression. But does publishing, particularly newspaper publishing, as it currently exists fit the image we have of self-expression—an individual or group using a publishing organization to advance their views?

Freedom of the press arose in the context of governmental repression of small, numerous independent publishers. A casual glance at the market in publishing suggests that, in the United States today, there still exists a large number of independent publishers. A closer look reveals the pervasiveness of monopoly, which threatens to render largely irrelevant the First Amendment as a protection of individual rights and which itself constitutes a threat to both individual freedom of expression and diversity of views. Although today there are around twenty-five thousand different daily newspapers, magazines, radio and television stations, book publishers, and movie studios in the United States, most of the business is controlled by less than two dozen corporations. This growing concentration is the result of a trend over the last fifty years in which, for example, newspapers have gone from being individually owned to being owned by corporations.[30] From 1983 to 1992, "the number of companies controlling most of the national daily circulation has shrunk from twenty to eleven."[31] Even more dramatic concentration has occurred during the same period in magazine and book publishing. Cross-media ownership is accelerating.[32] Anticipated growth in the number of available cable channels will not suffice to insure diversity against this growing media monopoly if, as is likely because of deregulation, the channel systems also use them to transmit their own programs.[33] At best, such corporate owners engage in publishing only partly for reasons of personal expression and typically for reasons of commercial gain, making journalism indirectly subordinate to advertising, tending toward a bland uniformity, and appealing to a mass audience to the exclusion of smaller groups.

Thus, added to the ever present danger of governmental censorship of the press and other media is the growing danger of censorship by a few powerful corporate oligarchies and their advertising supporters. In such a context, First Amendment protection of press freedom, although it protects publishers against governmental intrusion, also provides support for monopoly power if and when it is invoked to resist efforts to diminish that power.

At its worst, worker control of the media would only perpetuate the problems of media monopoly, with groups of workers, rather than owners, monopolizing the media. At its best, worker control can constitute a part of the solution for today's most important threat to freedom of the press. I suggest that for that part of the industry that has become monopolized—that is, for all media outlets above a certain size—we need to rethink the definition of freedom of expression and press freedom in relationship to ownership.[34] If the bearers of the right to a free press included all members of the firm rather than merely the owners, the base of accountability of media organizations would be considerably broadened. Instead of being accountable to a few owners, the chief editors controlling the content of newspapers would be accountable to all those working for them. Because it is easier to become a member of the core of journalists than to own a newspaper, press freedom opportunities would increase for the average person.[35]

Such a scheme does not address the question of how press freedom would serve every person's freedom of expression. As with private and monopolized ownership, only relatively few could ever exercise their press freedom. But autonomous groups of journalists will have freedom to be more diverse, independent, and free from commercial bias than journalists in media that are owned and controlled by private corporations oriented toward profit maximization. Consequently, more viewpoints will find expression, and thus many people's views will be expressed, even if they do not personally engage in the expression. Moreover, if the function of media is to inform citizens in such a way as to enable them better to participate in democratic self-government, more diverse and autonomous media will better serve each person's "right to know."[36]

Beyond this "virtual representation," provisions for access to media could be established, making it possible for any person to express himself or herself under specifiable conditions. Various kinds and degrees of public-access television provide examples of this. The Fairness Doctrine in the broadcast media—unfortunately, now history[37]— is another example of a qualified access right: the right of response when one has been attacked. A fairness doctrine for print media has been resisted in American courts because of the way in which it limits freedom of the press. Telling an editor to include something is as much an infringement on press freedom as censoring something out.[38] If it is desirable to preserve this kind of press freedom, it is, nonetheless, possible to establish alongside First Amendment–protected media a public print medium, that would function more like a common carrier, such as the telephone system, to which all citizens would by right have access. Such a medium could itself be self-managed, but with legal parameters guaranteeing citizens rights of access, in much the same way that a self-managed telephone system would still operate within the framework of laws governing access to the common carrier.[39] My purpose here is not to defend all these additional measures. I mention them only to acknowledge that self-management is not a cure for all problems and to show how it could be consistent with a broad program for securing not only the autonomy of journalists and diversity of media but also equality of access to means of communication for all citizens.[40]

In sum, what I am proposing is a redefinition of freedom of the press, such that the relevant bearers of rights are workers in the production of media content (and also readers and audience members, insofar as they would have access rights). This will better serve the function of the media as institutions for informing citizens in a democracy and giving voice to a wide variety of views. It will diminish somewhat the power of media monopolies, although the problem of monopoly will require other measures in addition to worker control. However, there is no reason worker control should not be among the measures designed to bring freedom of the press and freedom of expression in line with contemporary social reality.

Deciding what form of worker control of newspapers is most desirable is best done through empirical study of cases of worker control and ownership, of varying kinds and degrees, in mainstream and in alternative media, in both capitalist and socialist contexts. In this chapter, as a prelude to such an investigation, I have tried to make a qualified case for worker control of the media and of newspapers, in particular. In an age of media monopoly, arguments for private ownership of the press on grounds of freedom of the press no longer carry weight against democratic arguments for worker control, arguments for access, and concern for responsible and independent journalism. What is needed is a mixed medium, with space reserved for small-scale individual and group ownership, as well as worker-controlled media, and some public media to provide access to those lacking the resources to establish their own individual or group media. In this way freedom of expression can be enhanced without compromising freedom of the press either through governmental control or through corporate and advertising dominance.

## ACCESS OR AUTONOMY?

Some media critics from the Left, in drawing attention to the need for wider access to the media, ignore some other purposes that media must serve. We expect the media to do a lot of different things, and some choices may have to be made concerning which of these should receive higher priority. We want the media to be equally open and accessible to all, unlike the capitalist media, which are open mainly to those with money. We also want the media to perform important functions for democracy: to inform the citizenry and engage in uncompromising criticism of the government and other social institutions. A necessary condition for these latter is securing the independence of the media from government, business, and advertising control.

The goal of access and the goal of autonomy can sometimes be harmoniously combined. Douglas Kellner describes how he and others produced an alternative television program, *Alternative Views*, featuring interviews with prominent social critics on the Left, by means of resources made available through a public-access cable channel.[41] But it is not hard to imagine how at least certain kinds of access laws could conflict with autonomy and the goals it is meant to serve. If we want the mass media to provide reliable information and a broad range of critical perspectives—and it is the mass media we must talk about, because such things are available to everyone in alternative media—would it not make more sense, rather than establishing diffuse rights for all to express themselves, to secure control of the media in the hands of media professionals, working journalists, and editors and take control away from both government officials and profit-oriented owners, as I have advocated?[42] Public-access media might not necessarily provide the sort of reliable information and analysis that citizens in a democracy need, however much it might broaden each person's freedom of speech. If, as Janet Kobren and Gloria Channon suggest, "free speech implies the right to be heard, including access to *whatever* electronic and print media are out there," it might become difficult for any group, whether a group of journalists or a political party, to preserve the journalistic integrity and perspective of a publication or program. The intrusion of multiple voices in *every* medium might well undermine the public's "opportunity to hear and read what we (in opposition to the apparent mainstream) have to say."[43]

Putting the emphasis on newsroom democracy, and hence on maximizing autonomy, rather than on access has a number of advantages. It could win the strong support of workers inside media institutions. Implementing it would not require the establishment of regulatory agencies, as some forms of access would require. It is compatible with a range of financing arrangements, from codetermination with capitalist owners, as at *Le Monde*, to cooperative ownership, to various forms of foundation- or government-subsidized plans.[44]

There are some drawbacks that need to be considered. Newsroom democracy focuses rather narrowly on "the news." But the media also have a powerful impact in the sphere of culture and entertainment, not to mention through advertising. Does it make sense to call for worker control in the production of culture and entertainment as well? Who are the relevant workers—the "professionals" or all the workers involved in the creative process? Even the line between journalism and other areas is not easy to draw. Do we include film critics along with news reporters? What about writers of short stories printed in a newspaper? Do we include part-time as well as full-time workers?

There is also a problem with focusing on journalists as professionals. Problems with granting control to professionals arise in other domains, even where practitioners need specialized knowledge, must be qualified and licensed to practice, and have professional codes of conduct and professional organizations. For example, a key issue in the democratization of health care is how much participation should be opened up to patients and the community in the governance of health-care institutions. In journalism, there is no consensus on what constitutes a journalist, no system of qualifications, no generally agreed upon professional standards. Moving toward professionalization of journalism may in fact be undesirable, as it will entrench questionable norms of "objectivity" that screen out alternative perspectives and analyses from the mass media. After all, we will be dealing not with ideal journalists, but with journalists as they have been educated under capitalism; the norms of good journalism will not change simply because the structure of ownership and control is altered. For all these reasons, we should be circumspect about endorsing plans for empowering professional journalists in the name of the public interest.

A somewhat deeper problem is with the very idea of the public interest. Proposals for newsroom democracy, which emerged from the underground press of the French Resistance suppose that there is a clearly defined body of knowledge that "the public" needs to know and hence that it is possible to empower a group—professional journalists—to provide that knowledge.[45] Feminists and postmodernists have called this supposition of the universal public into question.[46] The bourgeois "public sphere" out of which freedom of the press emerged, and which is the reference point for many of our attempts to revitalize and democratize the media, was a public founded on multiple exclusions: of women, Native and African Americans, and workers. Socialists seeking transformation of the media need to recognize first of all that there is no unitary public behind the "masses" of the mass media. There are multiple publics. At the same time, democracy requires that these publics communicate with one another as well as find their own voices, and in this respect a new public has to be forged.

Will that public require mass media serving its need to be informed and to hear critical analysis? Will it, rather require a heterogeneous proliferation of diverse media, and the dissolution of mass media altogether, with the possible exception of some surviving mass entertainment? New technologies certainly open up the possibility of the latter. Ironically perhaps, it is the right-wing assault on the fairness doctrine and on public programming requirements that is leading to decline of general public-interest programming. The proliferation of media is structured overwhelmingly in accord with commercial imperatives.[47] Hence, one has to be very careful, if endorsing a postmodernist dissolution of mass media, to distinguish commercially dominated media from more pluralistic media made possible by new technologies. It would be sadly ironic if the celebration of diversity contributed to the triumph of bland uniformity.

I do not think a democracy can ever dispense entirely with some notion of the general good. There will always be issues of distributive justice that require articulation of a consensus through discussion. There are common global problems, such as environmental threats, that call for democratic responses. Consequently, we will for the foreseeable future need to aim at mass media that attempt to inform the citizenry with a view to the general good. For this reason, newsroom democracy should be among the aims of the Left. But the arguments for it, unlike those emerging in the two decades after World War II, must be sensitive to the theme of difference and circumspect about the claims of professionals.

The biggest challenge will be to synthesize in practical proposals the concerns that point toward equal access to the media with the concern for an independent and reliable news service. A combination of community and worker ownership of a newspaper would be one way to bring together and empower both readers and writers. Public-access cable channels can be funded to provide professional training for any citizen or group of citizens qualifying for access. The proliferation of media sources might be complemented by a proliferation of media criticism, and over time some would acquire a reputation for reliability and accuracy. After all, in a free society, opinion should replace regulation as the rule of life.

The most important thing is to recognize at the outset that the media must serve multiple aims in a democracy. Consequently there is no single goal, such as equal access, that can well promote a democratic media system.

## NOTES

1. Ben Bagdikian, *The Media Monopoly*, 4th ed. (Boston: Beacon Press, 1992), ix.

2. Robert W. McChesney, "The Global Media Giants," *Extra!* 10, no. 6 (November–December 1997): 18.

3. McChesney, "The Global Media Giants," 12.

4. Robert W. McChesney, *Corporate Media and the Threat to Democracy*, (New York: Seven Stories Press, 1997) 24–25.

5. Quoted in McChesney, "The Global Media Giants," 12.

6. McChesney, *Corporate Media and the Threat to Democracy*, 11–17.

7. McChesney, *Corporate Media and the Threat to Democracy*, 10; 66–67.

8. Edward S. Herman and Noam Chomsky, *Manufacturing Consent: The Political Economy of the Mass Media* (New York: Pantheon Books, 1988), 2.

9. Herman and Chomsky, *Manufacturing Consent*, 87–142; see also Edward S. Herman and Frank Brodhead, *Demonstration Elections: U.S.-Staged Elections in the Dominican Republic, Vietnam, and El Salvador* (Boston: South End Press, 1984).

10. Herman and Chomsky, *Manufacturing Consent*, 88–106.

11. Herman and Chomsky, *Manufacturing Consent*, 140–41.

12. Herman and Chomsky, *Manufacturing Consent*, 105–6.

13. Herman and Chomsky, *Manufacturing Consent*, 109.

14. Herman and Chomsky, *Manufacturing Consent*, 121–22.

15. Herman and Chomsky, *Manufacturing Consent*, 91.

16. For a response to critics of the propaganda model and application to domestic issues such as trade agreements, strikes, and health care, see Edward Herman, "The Propaganda Model Revisited," in *Capitalism and the Information Age*, ed. Robert W. McChesney, Ellen Meiksins Wood, and John Bellamy Foster (New York: Monthly Review Press, 1998), 191–205.

17. In addition to the authors cited below, some other relevant sources are David Ellerman, "Capitalism and Workers' Self-Management" (as well as essays by other authors), in *Self-Management: Economic Liberation of Man*, ed. Jaroslav Vanek (Baltimore: Penguin Books, 1975), 145–58; Branko Horvat, Mihailo Marković, and Rudi Supek, *Self-Governing Socialism* (White Plains, N.Y.: International Arts and Sciences Press, 1975), 2 vols., the first volume of which contains relevant excerpts from classical authors such as Marx, Lenin, and Gramsci; Carole Pateman, *Participation and Democratic Theory* (Cambridge: Cambridge University Press, 1970); Samuel Bowles and Herbert Gintis,

*Democracy and Capitalism: Property, Community, and the Contradictions of Modern Social Thought* (New York: Basic Books, 1987). In an earlier article, Beverly James concludes, after summarizing the case for economic democracy, that "a society characterized by inequality in either the economic or political sphere can make no claim to democracy, and attempts to alleviate inequality solely through alterations in one particular societal institution—in this case, the press—are bound to meet with failure. Suggestions for restructuring the press must be congruent with a vision of society in which democracy finds its practical definition in the participation of all men and women in decision making"; James, "Economic Democracy and Restructuring the Press," *Journal of Communication Inquiry* 6, no. 2 (Winter 1981): 119–29, 129. My goal in presenting an argument for worker control of the media in the context of more general arguments for worker control is to provide proposals that are congruent with just such a vision of society.

18. Robert Dahl, *A Preface to Economic Democracy* (Berkeley: University of California Press, 1985).

19. Dahl, *A Preface to Economic Democracy*, 111, 57.

20. Michael Walzer, *Spheres of Justice: A Defense of Pluralism and Equality* (New York: Basic Books, 1983), 295–303.

21. See chapter 1 for my argument and relevant references.

22. Douglas Kellner, *Television and the Crisis of Democracy* (Boulder, Colo.: Westview Press, 1990).

23. In the case of *Miami Herald v Tornillo*, 418 U.S. 241 (1974), the Supreme Court ruled that there was no right of reply to newspaper editorials; such a right would violate First Amendment protection of editorial autonomy; for discussion, see Judith Lichtenberg, introduction to *Democracy and the Mass Media*, ed. Judith Lichtenberg (Cambridge: Cambridge University Press, 1990), 1–20, and "Foundations and Limits of Freedom of the Press," in Lichtenberg, *Democracy and the Mass Media*, 102–35; Ithiel de Sola Pool, *Technologies of Freedom* (Cambridge: Harvard University Press, Belknap Press, 1983), 133.

24. Robert G. Picard, *The Press and the Decline of Democracy: The Democratic Socialist Response in Public Policy* (Westport, Conn.: Greenwood Press, 1985); Jean Schwoebel, *Newsroom Democracy: The Case for Independence of the Press* (Iowa City: University of Iowa Center for Communication Study, 1976), 21–23.

25. Lichtenberg, "Foundations and Limits."

26. In the words of Jean Schwoebel, foreign affairs editor of *Le Monde* and leader of the worker control movement among French journalists, "I'm for the participation of every kind of people but we don't want to put in the same basket the intellectual responsibilities and the mechanical and commercial responsibilities. If the printers have a majority they will be as tyrannical as the state or the commercial interests.

"This is not because we are salaried but because we have a responsibility to the people to tell the truth and we have to discover it. We have to deliver to the people the truth they need to survive." Quoted in Ronald Dorfman, "Toward a Noncapitalist Journalism," *Chicago Journalism Review* (December 1970): 7.

See also Schwoebel, *Newsroom Democracy*, 56–57, for an argument against a purely cooperative ownership of the press, and 62–63 for a description of the formula worked out at *Le Monde* for partial ownership with recognition of the special status of journalists; and Nanette Funk, "Reporters and a Free Press," *Journal of Applied Philosophy* 2, no.1 (1985): 85–97, for an argument for reporter-codetermined newspapers. Funk's proposal lacks Schwoebel's provisions for share ownership and restriction on the degree to which individuals can profit through speculation in information enterprises (Schwoebel, *Newsroom Democracy*, 60).

27. I take the term from the title of Schwoebel's monograph. There is, of course, nothing to prevent clerical, administrative, or production workers from sharing in ownership—as they do at *Le Monde*. The important points, as Schwoebel emphasizes, are that the journalists possess shares not on an individual basis but collectively, through their associations, and that the associations possess sufficient shares "to give them a veto in the case—and only in the case—of 'extraordinary decisions'" such as the choice of managers, large investment decisions, mergers, or liquidation; Schwoebel, *Newsroom Democracy*, 57, 62–63.

28. Stephen R. Sacks, "Giant Corporations in Yugoslavia," in *Participatory and Self-Managed Firms*, ed. Derek Jones and Jan Svejnar (Lexingon, Mass.: Lexington Books, 1982), 86. For criticism of the BOALs, see Alec Nove, *The Economics of Feasible Socialism* (London: Allen and Unwin, 1983), 140; Andrew Zimbalist, Howard Sherman, and Stuart Brown, *Comparing Economic Systems: A Political Economic Approach* (Harcourt Brace Jovanovich, 1989), 433–38.

29. Herman and Chomsky, *Manufacturing Consent*, 88–106.

30. Ben Bagdikian, *The Media Monopoly*, ix–xvi, 4; McChesney, "The Global Media Giants," 18, estimates eleven corporations in 1997.

31. Bagdikian, *The Media Monopoly*, ix.

32. Bagdikian, *The Media Monopoly*, x. See also Mark Crispin Miller et al., "The National Entertainment State," *Nation*, 3 June 1996, 3–32.

33. Bagdikian, *The Media Monopoly*, xv.

34. For very small publishing enterprises, it should be possible for individuals and groups to establish editorial lines that reflect their interests and philosophies and to hire writers and other intellectual workers who would be subject to their authority. There should not be such a thing as a crime of "clandestine publishing" applied to such undertakings.

35. As with other cooperatives, accountability of editors to journalists is compatible with the hierarchy of authority in the day-to-day operations of the newsroom. The exact mix of worker participation and editorial prerogative would have to be worked out with a view to the tasks at hand.

36. Some question whether there is really a "right to know"; John C. Merrill, *The Imperative of Freedom: A Philosophy of Journalistic Autonomy* (New York: Hastings House Publishers, 1974), 100–108. I do not wish to argue for such a right. I use the phrase as an allusion to the argument that supports press freedom by showing how it provides the flow of information and criticism necessary for democracy. See Alexander Meiklejohn, *Political Freedom: The Constitutional Powers of the People* (New York: Harper, 1960), 8–28, summarized in Lichtenberg, "Foundations and Limits," 110–12.

37. Patricia Aufderheide, "After the Fairness Doctrine: Controversial Broadcast Programming and the Public Interest," *Journal of Communications* 40, no. 3 (Summer 1990): 47–71.

38. *Miami Herald v Tornillo*.

39. For example, see Kellner's proposal for a satellite television channel "available

to various groups who want to broadcast their political views and information"; Kellner, *Television and the Crisis*, 217–19. See also Ernest Mandel's plan for socializing presses and newspapers, which various groups would be entitled to utilize on the basis of demonstrated public support through signatures or showings in elections, and which would be financed through subsidies (quoted in Picard, *The Press and the Decline*, 81–82). Social ownership opens up prospects for both self-management and access that are difficult to realize in commercial enterprises. It also can make possible the dissolution of the distinction between media professionals and audiences that is presumed in arguments for newsroom democracy such as Schwoebel's or that of this chapter. But media dependent for their financing on subsidies risk becoming dependent upon the government. Evidence suggests that the risk may not be as great as has been supposed; see Picard, *The Press and the Decline*, 111–14.

40. Merrill advocates a laissez-faire policy to support journalistic autonomy. Thus, he opposes proposals for access, fairness doctrines, and rights of reply. Although he is quite sensitive to ways in which government can restrict the autonomy of journalists, he does not address the ways in which media monopolization of the kind Bagdikian describes can restrict journalists, nor does he attend to the narrow parameters established for mass media journalism by dependence on advertising revenue. This omission is also characteristic of his later work. Yet, even he might welcome contractually devised schemes—such as that at *Le Monde*—designed to give greater control to journalists over the media enterprise. In addition to the work cited, see John C. Merrill, *Existential Journalism* (New York: Hastings House Publishers, 1977), and *The Dialectic in Journalism* (Baton Rouge: Louisiana State University Press, 1989).

41. Kellner, *Television and the Crisis*.

42. Schwoebel, *Newsroom Democracy*.

43. Janet Kobren and Gloria Channon, "Beyond Media Activism: Media Democratization," *Socialist Forum* 19 (Spring 1992): 83–90; my emphasis.

44. See Schwoebel *Newsroom Democracy,* for a discussion of *Le Monde*. For a codetermination proposal, see Funk, "Reporters and a Free Press." For a discussion of government subsidies of the press, see Picard, *The Press and the Decline of Democracy*.

45. Schwoebel, *Newsroom Democracy*.

46. Iris Young, *Justice and the Politics of Difference* (Princeton: Princeton University Press, 1990); Nancy Fraser, "Rethinking the Public Sphere: A Contribution to the Critique of Actually Existing Democracy," in *Habermas and the Public Sphere*, ed. Craig Calhoun (Cambridge: MIT Press, 1992), 109–42; also relevant is Jürgen Habermas, *The Structural Transformation of the Public Sphere* (Cambridge: MIT Press, 1990).

47. McChesney, "The Global Media Giants," 11–12.

# 12

# Market Socialism, New Social Movements, and the Socialist Vision

Readers who have persisted with me this far may be convinced that worker-managed market socialism could be efficient and just. But is this ideal able to inspire people to action? How does it fare, in this regard, in comparison with more traditional ideas of socialism? Does it address the concerns of new social movements, such as the women's and environmental movements?

Recall that my preferred model of market socialism combines the best features of the Yugoslav model and the Mondragon cooperative model: workplaces controlled by their workers on the basis of one person, one vote, coordinated by means of a market, with details of ownership, investment, and income distribution worked out with a view to efficiency, justice, and the maximization of democracy. The salient features are worker control, market coordination, and a state more closely resembling social democratic states than Soviet centrally planned economies or workers' states on the Leninist model. I occasionally refer here to Roemer's managerial market socialism, which does not include self-management. Concerns voiced here about worker-managed market socialism apply a fortiori to Roemer's model.

Market socialism thus sketched is easily developed as a kind of revision of traditional Marxism. The labor movement is still central: the movement for worker control has its expression in Poland's Solidarity (of the early 1980s) and in Western union demands for greater worker participation, worker ownership, codetermination, and the like. Moreover, the model is conceived as a solution to the central problem of capitalist exploitation in the workplace. If workers control the firm and decide on the distribution of the surplus, then there is no longer a capitalist class, no longer exploitation in the Marxist sense, no longer oppression at the point of production except that built in structurally by the necessity to labor as such. Even the last would be diminished to the extent feasible by a maximum sustainable basic income. The state can no longer be a capitalist state—at least if this system of worker control encompasses the institutions of finance and economic planning and regulation. New meaning is given to the idea of socializing the means of production. The vision is no longer one of state planning with a view to the general interest but rather one in which workers control their own work with a view to enterprise and group self-interest, within parameters established by a democratic state.

The accomplishment of such a society would be no mean achievement. Still, there would appear to be something lacking, even by traditional Marxist reckoning. What will have become of the workers' movement as a universalizing force? I have in mind here not only the workers' movement as an international movement but also the idea that people, in their capacity as workers, learn to rise above their individual or group self-interest and concern themselves with the good of the whole society. The market socialist seems resigned to a labor movement or a working class that is fragmented and concerned with narrow group interests. Concern with international class considerations would be even more remote, and the struggle against imperialism would be a struggle occurring outside the workplace, on the basis of identities grounded in something other than class. Granted, worker self-management may obviate imperialism in certain respects: there is no reason to expect capital flight in a worker-managed economy; and the struggle to bring about a worker-managed market society might require a degree of solidarity nationally and internationally comparable to that envisioned by more traditional socialist goals and strategies. Nevertheless, in the end, there is envisioned a socialist person considerably less class conscious than in traditional conceptions of socialism.

From the point of view of new social movements—feminism, ecology, disarmament, anti-imperialism, anti-racism, gay and lesbian rights—there is even more missing from the market-socialist vision described up to this point.[1] It is not merely that the model has nothing much to say about gender relations, limited growth, internationalism, and the like. The problem is that market socialism at its best retains some features of capitalism that appear to cause what these movements oppose.

The most obvious such feature is production for exchange rather than production simply for use. The market socialist might say that the phrase, "production for use," is little more than a slogan anywhere it has been employed as a guide for planning. In Soviet-type economies, production is no more for use than in capitalist economies. The operative principle is something like plan fulfillment, which is something different. The market socialist is willing to settle for a modified form of production for exchange as a concession to the intractability of coordinating production rationally on the scale of a national, not to mention an international, economy. This is not to endorse laissez-faire, however. The idea of production for human needs, not for profits, still has a role, but more indirectly— as in welfare-state capitalism—in the state redistribution of resources and in legal parameters governing production and exchange but not directly in the production process or exchange relations themselves.

In such a society, what will become of the shortening of the working day? What will be done to reorganize the relationship between the exchange economy and the household—the current patterns of which are a major basis of gender inequality? Won't worker-controlled enterprises, insofar as they are producing for profit, be as indifferent to that pollution that does not affect them directly as are capitalist firms? (Granted, they might be less disposed to pollute the local environment, but what about the towns downstream or the acid rain in the next state?)

For such questions, market socialism seems to be not the answer but, most likely, just a continuation of the problem. So it is understandable that ecologists, feminists, and others would hesitate to call themselves socialists, if market socialism is all that socialism means. Another reason can be found in market socialism's focus on production. Although questions of production— how it is done, who does it, under what conditions, and to what end—are issues that have implications for women, for the environment, for peace, and for human rights, the struggles around the latter are fought on many other, and often more salient, fronts—in households, courts, in direct confrontation with police and military, and in the media. Unless socialism is defined in such a way that it is clearly seen as the answer to the problems movements confront, social movements will not be sympathetic to socialism.

Closely related to the concern with production is self-managed socialism's concentration on the labor movement and on workers both as the agents of change and as the peculiar victims of capitalist oppression and exploitation. If one is more oppressed as a woman, a breather of the air, a gay person, a draftee, or a friend of the Nicaraguans than as a worker, the traditional Marxist critique of capitalism has less appeal. Moreover, it may be that a workers' movement is inherently nonrevolutionary. As Adam Przeworski has argued, socialist parties, identified as workers' parties, have had to choose between electoral failure, on the one hand, and class compromise, on the other, if they shunned the insurrectionary road— which they have done in most advanced capitalist countries. He concludes his study of social democracy by contrasting the limited vision of social democracy with the more deeply liberatory vision of classical socialist thinkers. Social democracy can achieve full employment, equality, and efficiency—Sweden has come fairly close to this. But it is still a society geared toward production for profit, alienation, wage labor, commodity fetishism, and the necessity to toil. Przeworski continues:

> Socialism was to be a society in which people individually would acquire control over their lives because their existence would no longer be an instrument of survival and people would collectively acquire control over shared resources and efforts because their allocation would be a subject of joined deliberation and rational choice. Socialism was not a movement for full employment but for the abolition of

wage slavery; it was not a movement for efficiency but for collective rationality; it was not a movement for equality but for freedom.[2]

Market socialism may promise both more and less than social democracy. On the one hand, and especially in conjunction with basic income, it aims at the abolition of wage slavery. This would be an important achievement, even though firms would still be competing in the market so that the forms of work and perhaps work hierarchy would be likely to be continued. On the other hand, full employment (which social democracy approximates) may be sacrificed with the introduction of the market—that has been the experience in every socialist society that has introduced market reforms, and especially in the former Yugoslavia. Market socialism promises collective rationality only slightly more than does welfare capitalism. We might expect that class relations would not distort political discourse as much as they do under capitalism, and the democratic investment fund makes possible some collective rational planning. The state might become more truly an instrument of the whole citizen population. Equality may also be sacrificed, if the former Yugoslavia is any indication. Freedom remains as elusive as ever.

If socialism is to inspire, it must not be limited in its definition to a particular way of reorganizing production nor in promoting solely the interests of the working class. As Przeworski states,

> Socialism may perhaps become possible, but only on the condition that the movement for socialism regains the integral scope that characterized several of its currents outside the dogmas of the Internationals, only on the condition that this movement ceases to make the socialist project conditional upon the continual improvement of material conditions of the working class. It may become possible when socialism once again becomes a social movement and not solely an economic one, when it learns from the women's movement, when it reassimilates cultural values.[3]

To approach the matter from the other side, social movements, to the extent that they are radical, to the extent that they identify among the root causes of oppression and degradation those that are intrinsic to capitalism as such, are in need of an economic program. Otherwise, a common bond among these movements is lost. The observations that military intervention is usually rooted in capitalism, that capitalism reinforces patriarchy, that the pursuit of profit (or at least single-minded development) is at the root of environmental destruction, et cetera, take the form of afterthoughts, if the analysis does not lead one to work for a specific type of alternative socialist system. One is left instead, in practice, working for an end to this or that intervention, this or that weapons system, working for equal pay within capitalism, day care within capitalism, a halt to pollutions of particular kinds. Meanwhile, the seeds of new interventions are being planted as capitalist development advances; new environmental disasters are in the making; socialist-feminist reforms run up against structural limits. Where in our practice are we struggling—rather than merely hoping—for a socialist alternative?

The challenge for the market socialist—for the socialist theorist generally— is to explain how a particular model of a socialist alternative can accommodate the concerns of existing social movements and then to point the way from here to there. The first is a task of connecting ideals with felt needs, the second, a question of strategy. A missing dimension in the existing literature on market socialism is how the concerns of feminists, ecologists, and internationalists will be addressed within the very institutions of market socialism. Otherwise, market socialism, for all its attractive features, looks too much like business as usual. Otherwise, the struggles for the emancipation of women, for a safe environment, and so forth appear to be struggles that go on elsewhere than in the economy, affecting people in nonworker roles, for which the labor movement is marginal and economic models irrelevant. This would be unfortunate, because given the interconnections of economic and other dimensions of modern life, given the dominance of economic thinking and economic issues in politics, the social movements will themselves be marginalized, at least in their most radical dimensions. In the following two sections, I will make an attempt to link market socialism to the concerns of women and ecologists.The concerns of other social movements, no less important, should be taken up on another occasion.

## THE WOMEN'S MOVEMENT AND SELF-MANAGEMENT

Women traditionally, and to this day, participate less frequently than men in politics and in the management of enterprises, including cooperatives and self-managed firms.[4] Two reasons for the pattern of low participation by women in politics and in democratic self-governance are the division of labor in the household and the welfare state structures that parallel this division.[5]

### Division of Labor

Women who bear a dual responsibility for paid work and for household work, including child care, lack the time and energy to serve on committees in their neighborhoods, cities, workplaces, and unions. Furthermore, women tend to be segregated into lower-wage occupations. This, coupled with a long-term decline in wages overall, so that in order to survive families now typically require the wages of two full-time workers, leaves most working single mothers in poverty. As long as women tend to be paid a fraction of what men are paid, there will be a tendency, among heterosexual couples, to favor advancement of the man's career at the expense of the woman's and to have her rather than him be the one to work part-time and take care of the children. As long as support in the form of affordable day care is not provided to parents, single or coupled, single women will face a poverty trap, losing more income by working full-time at low-wage jobs than they would have by being on welfare. Married women will tend to take on the responsibilities of household work at the expense of other kinds of social participation.[6] What does market socialism have to offer to address such issues? Schweickart's economic democracy suggests the possibility—indeed, the likelihood—that workplace reform, a democratic investment fund, and an arrangement guaranteeing a basic income would result in the relaxation of the gendered division of labor.

Self-management, especially if participatory, opens up greater prospects for job redesign. To the extent that workers have an interest in flex time, more-humanized work, and other departures from alienating work conditions, a democratic workplace is more likely to realize these interests than a workplace accountable only to outside stockholders. Job redesign, in the context of this chapter, importantly can include job sharing, flexible hours, and other features that accommodate the needs of parents. Jobs can be redesigned so that men and women have options for equal participation in child raising, which are precluded by many jobs today.

Self-managed enterprises are more likely than capitalist (or managerial socialist) firms to institute child care in the workplace, if this is a demand of the workers. Two qualifications are in order, however. First, child care, flex-time, and other innovations are possible, and occur, in capitalist enterprises where strong unions demand them. But the demands are more easily met when workers demand these things of themselves rather than of opponents across a class divide. Second, even self-managed firms are not likely to redesign work in ways that begin to overcome the gender division of labor if women are not active in decision making. This point is driven home by evidence of the conditions of women in the Mondragon cooperatives, cited earlier. Those female spouses who do piecework for the co-ops are not participating as members but are in reality second-class wage workers. Although the Mondragon cooperatives have a higher rate of employment of women and advancement of women into managerial positions than their capitalist counterparts, substantial inequalities still exist, and most senior positions are still held by men.

Self-managed firms in a market economy will find themselves under structural pressures not to redesign jobs or provide child care, to the extent that these involve some cost to the firm (assuming there is no national child-care system), if their competitors can gain a competitive advantage by not offering these benefits. Consequently, in a worker-owned economy, or in managerial socialism, the workplace changes necessary for equal participation of women will not be realized unless the market forces shaping enterprise decisions are themselves addressed.

The democratic investment fund has potential to address the market conditions themselves: investment can include provisos or advantages for firms offering child care, flexible hours, et cetera. At least some of the goals could be reached less directly through regulation of the market or legislation mandating uniform workplace rights where union power falls short. But without control of the investment fund, states will face the resistance of firms much as they now do under capitalism.

Under Roemer's managerial socialism, mutual funds are depoliticized and so are not strong levers for "socially responsible investing." On the other hand, equalization of wealth should favor mass social movements over the interests of those wealthy enough to buy their way around difficulties raised by gender inequality (such as women who can afford nannies). The elimination of a class of wealthy rentiers will level the playing field for feminist and other social movements and reduce resistance to egalitarian regulation of the market. To the extent that it is more egalitarian than Schweickart's, this consequence favors Roemer's scheme from a feminist point of view. But if economic objections to the democratic investment fund can be overcome, economic democracy is clearly preferable for the leverage it gives to the entire community to reshape the conditions of work and of social participation.

The basic-income scheme, as I noted earlier, can facilitate self-management in several ways. With respect to the gender division of labor, it simultaneously acknowledges child care and housework as work deserving of remuneration and also removes them from the commodifying market and from state intrusion. Thus it promises to help free working women from a patriarchal state,[7] and enable them (and, in principle, men) to *choose* child rearing as a vocation. At the same time, as a universal and unconditional benefit, a guaranteed basic income would enable recipients to engage in part-time work and in social and political activity. New cooperative forms of child rearing and schooling could emerge, for example. Child care as an income-earning occupation would become more feasible when remunerated on top of a basic income. Parents making use of it could, in turn, be freed to participate in the self-management of their workplaces.

But workplaces themselves would need to change if we are to avoid the disturbing spectacle of most enterprises dominated by childless or absentee-parent workers—male or female—serviced by a second tier economy of poorly paid—albeit basic-income-supported— child-care providers, a version of André Gorz's vision of basic-income apartheid mentioned earlier. Indeed, we have to move beyond the idea that the emancipated woman is simply the woman who has been assimilated into male patterns of employment: a forty-hour (or longer) workweek earning a household income. Once child rearing is acknowledged as socially valuable work that needs to be done in conditions free of economic dependence, both men and women should be free to choose a shorter waged-work week and share equally the responsibilities and personal rewards of raising *their own* children.

It is not clear that a basic income by itself would result in this cultural shift. This is where the socialized investment fund, with a mandate to favor investment

in gender-egalitarian workplaces, could provide the necessary structuring of enterprises to bring about collectively what most of us want but which we are not
able to choose when capital markets pit us against one another through the tyranny of small decisions.

Neither basic income nor a socialized investment fund with feminist priorities will come about without strong social movements pressing for legislation and
holding legislators accountable. I have not focused in this book on extrainstitutional mass mobilization as an element of democracy, concentrating instead
on questions of institutional alternatives. This should not be construed as claiming that institutional reforms alone are sufficient for democracy or that mass
mobilizations are unnecessary for the process of democratization or its maintenance under economic democracy. On the contrary, in the absence of strong feminist (and ecological) movements, economic democracy could only entrench a new,
predominantly male, technocratic ruling elite.

## Structures of the Welfare State

The welfare state in the United States reflects and reinforces the gender division of labor in the household and the workplace. As Nancy Fraser notes, women
"make up the overwhelming majority both of program recipients and of paid
social-service workers. On the other hand, they are the wives, mothers, and daugh-
ters whose unpaid activities and obligations are redefined as the welfare state
increasingly oversees forms of care giving."[8]

Hence any discussion of the democratization of work that ignores social services is, in effect, male-centered. Furthermore, the division of government programs, officially gender neutral, in fact positions men and women differently.
Programs tied to work participation and provided to individuals, such as social
security pensions, mainly benefit men. Programs oriented to households and "tied
to combined household income for example, AFDC, food stamps, and Medic-
aid" are "designed to compensate for what are considered to be family failures,
in particular the absence of a male bread winner."[9]

Fraser further observes that these programs are unequally administered, with
pensions and unemployment compensation conceived of as rights to a cash benefit earned through contributions, available uniformly throughout the country.
Welfare is administered unevenly at state levels (much more so after President
Bill Clinton's "welfare reform"); it is inadequate, conceived as noncontributory,
in kind rather than in cash, and recipients are subjected to humiliation and surveillance. The focus on family income defines women primarily as mothers and
needy clients rather than workers, rights bearers, or rational consumers.[10]

Recent trends in "welfare reform" have only made matters worse. Block grants
to states, allegedly designed to reduce bureaucracy and encourage experimenta-
tion, are really an effort to roll back income and other support to the poor, who

are increasingly female.[11] The strategy—I have never seen evidence of a conspiracy, but it seems too obvious to me not to be intended—is to make each state responsible for the level and kind of welfare provision. States will then go further down the road most are already traveling, slashing taxes and public expenditures in order to hold or attract capital from the large corporations that place them in a bidding war against one another. There is some evidence that submitting to corporate blackmail is not the only or the best strategy for economic development. Investment in education and infrastructure is a more efficient use of tax dollars than tax giveaways to corporations that are largely unaccountable.[12] Nonetheless, this is not the proverbial wisdom, and the block-grant dismantling strategy is likely to succeed in the short run. Many of the "experiments" are largely scapegoating and punitive. "Workfare," for example, will typically force welfare recipients to work for less than a going market wage, thus subsidizing employers, reinforcing the segregation of women in low-wage labor markets, maintaining dependence on and surveillance by the state, and failing to address the need for education and child care.

The one ray of hope is the possibility that on the ruins of "welfare reform" a genuine fresh start can be made. My proposal for a basic income at the highest sustainable level would establish income as an individual right. It would eliminate much of the need for means-tested benefits and so of means testing, humiliation, and surveillance. It would regard the recipients as rights bearers, consumers, workers, and citizens, not as clients (mothers). It would also be genuinely supportive of families. We should avoid Engels' dream of social equality through the abolition of the family that is accomplished by making all family functions public, wage-bearing employment. That would be destructive of the love that only families can provide. Rather, we should aim for income support and the restructuring of paid work so that, on the one hand, women are economically independent and able to earn as much as men and on the other, men have the leisure to take an equal part in the responsibilities and joys of raising children.[13]

It must be acknowledged that to the extent that basic income would eliminate much of the welfare-state bureaucracy or, in the wake of "welfare reform," not restore it, women would be the primary victims of social-services layoffs. As in any major economic restructuring, equity would require that some special provision be made to ease the transition, as is often proposed (but seldom provided) for the working-cass victims of deindustrialization or conversion of defense industries.[14]

Basic income is not likely to eliminate the need for all means-tested benefits. It is unlikely to be introduced anywhere at the highest sustainable level, and this level can only be arrived at experimentally, starting with a modest benefit and increasing it until negative incentive effects begin to arise. Even at the highest sustainable level, it is hard to disagree with opponents who rightly object that it is unjust to give everyone a high basic income that would result in people with special needs getting less than they otherwise would. Special provision at a just level for people with physical or mental disabilities must be a background condition for the calculation of the maximum sustainable basic income.[15] These special provisions will inevitably be made on the basis of need, will require means testing, and are likely to be in the form of services (or reimbursement for services), not cash.

There remains the question of how to organize social services under economic democracy. If the principle of worker self-management were to become the dominant principle governing enterprises producing for a profit in the market, it would provide strong prima facie grounds for extending similar self-management rights to workers in welfare services, health care, education, and the media, whether publicly or privately owned. If the principle is widely acknowledged that workers as a matter of right should choose their own managers, how can this right be acknowledged for steelworkers, but denied to welfare caseworkers or hospital orderlies?

One avenue of inquiry is to explore to what extent these workplaces could be organized and function well as cooperatives. On a very small scale, for example, home-health-care workers have successfully organized their work in cooperatives. The Industrial Cooperative Association together with Home Care Associates Training Institute has provided technical assistance for enterprises replicating the successful Cooperative Home Care Associates of the Bronx, involving predominantly paraprofessional health-care workers. "For the purpose of achieving community economic development (CED) goals, home care has several important industry characteristics including: rapid growth, a large number of entry level jobs, a potential career ladder, low barriers to entry, and a concentration of clients within easy reach of the potential workforce." The Industrial Cooperative Association (now called ICA Group) has also worked on a project to replicate a successful worker-owned child-care model in Philadelphia.[16] Worker ownership in a field characterized by low wages and poor benefits promises workers greater control and a share of the profits. These are worthwhile and promising developments and may help to plug a few holes in the disintegrating safety net.

But this line of inquiry misses the main point. Social services, particularly welfare benefits, are not commodities, they are entitlements of the beneficiaries. Consequently, there is an issue of accountability of the state, and its agencies, to the recipients, the citizen-beneficiaries. A strong case can be made for participation by beneficiaries on the boards of welfare agencies, hospitals and other public services in place of pure worker self-management.

The alternative to such a directly participatory process is more-conventional bureaucratic mediation of beneficiary and citizen input through the state. In this way enterprises might be worker self-managed but regulated and functioning within parameters laid down by the state and reflecting a political consensus about such matters as the interpretation of needs (which are "rights" and which are "gifts," which involve means testing, when surveillance is warranted, et cetera). Although state mediation to some degree is inevitable and necessary for determination of general standards, limiting democratic participation of nonworkers to state channels will inevitably constrict discussion, with representatives and lobbyists remaining as the principal participants. Existing patriarchal structures are more likely to give way if opened to challenge from below, through direct participation of the beneficiaries. Such participation is also more likely to pull welfare workers toward political alliances with their beneficiaries and away from a corporate or profit-oriented mentality.

My remarks are regrettably general. I hesitate to say more without further research on the current welfare system in transition, a diagnosis of the problems the system should address, and a closer "class analysis" of the potential participants in a democratically managed system. However, in chapter 11 I have attempted to sketch out what democratic media would look like. Workers in the media, like those in social services and health care, are not mere commodity producers. Serious questions arise as to whether some or all of the media should be removed from the market and organized as public enterprises—at least as far as journalism is concern. There are analogous dangers that worker self-management would only continue some of the worst problems associated with the media, such as monopolization and corporate bias. Thus, what I have to say about the media may be suggestive of more elaborate analogous treatments of welfare and health care, which I hope to pursue in subsequent work.

## SELF-MANAGED MARKET SOCIALISM AND ECOLOGY

A committed environmentalist is apt to be suspicious of worker-managed market socialism on several counts. First, as the spotted owl controversy illustrates, workers often clash with environmentalists when the issue is framed as jobs versus the environment. Wouldn't worker self-management only sharpen the conflict? Second, many environmental problems seem to arise because of the market economy: negative "externalities" like pollution and resource depletion, the relentless pursuit of growth, promotion of a consumer society, and individualism work against the environment. Won't these persist in a *market*-socialist economy? Third, and somewhat at odds with the second concern, haven't socialist economies been among the worst environmental offenders? How, then, can a market-*socialist* economy be defended on environmental grounds?

In what follows, I address these concerns, focusing on the different dimensions of the model I am defending, first on worker self-management, then on the market, then on the democratic investment fund, and finally on basic income. No one of these by itself adequately meets the tremendous ecological challenges we face; but together, they tend to correct for their various individual shortcomings, to the extent that any institutional scheme can. In the end, there will be no substitute for vigorous, independent environmental activism. My hope is that environmentalists seeking sustainability, and workers and socialists seeking social justice can join forces, mutually reinforcing one another's efforts rather than clashing. Herman Daly and John Cobb have aptly noted, "Sustainability is really justice extended to the future."[17] That such an alliance is not farfetched is the burden of proof of this section.

## Worker Self-Management

In comparison with capitalist enterprises, worker-managed enterprises have several ecological advantages. First, worker management (including, typically, in a capitalist context, worker ownership) is one way to establish local or regional control over resources and is more likely to result in more-sustainable management of those resources. Multinational corporations, as long as they have the option of moving to new locations, have no strong incentive to manage forests, land, or fisheries sustainably. An international paper company can clear-cut its land and then move on to another forest elsewhere, leaving unemployment as well as pollution, soil erosion, and habitat despoliation in its wake. A worker-managed enterprise will not wish to eliminate the resources necessary to sustain the enterprise locally, where the workers live and work. Nor will workers in such enterprises feel that they need to bend over backward in support of anti-ecological corporate imperatives just to hang on to their jobs.

Second, worker-managed firms will have strong incentives against certain kinds of pollution that do not trouble capitalist firms. Workers will not favor pollution of their own neighborhoods, towns, and workplaces. They might be as indifferent to "downstream" pollution of others as are other market-oriented producers, so acid rain, river pollution, and other forms of waste that do not show up locally will need to be addressed in other ways. But this should not blind us to the ways worker management can internalize a concern for the environment that is externalized by capitalist firms.

Of course, the possibility of conflicts between environmentalists and workers will remain, particularly when the issue is not so much sustainability of a resource base as it is conservation of habitat and other ecological concerns. But these conflicts need not be as sharp as the head-on clash between environmentalists and workers in the spotted owl controversy. There are voices within the labor movement for sustainable forestry, and some ecologists recognize the need for an ecological conversion program that would provide job training and support to workers displaced by conservation of old-growth forest or other environmentally necessary measures.[18] These voices need to be brought into dialogue and strengthened until they become dominant in their respective movements.

Third, worker-managed firms have less incentive for growth than capitalist firms, and a worker-managed economy, unlike a capitalist economy, need not grow in order to avoid economic crisis. It is the excessive growth of consumption and resource-depleting production that currently threatens the planet with global warming and ozone destruction, to mention but two of the most commonly discussed and widely acknowledged environmental dangers. To get a glimpse of the scale of the collision between economic growth and ecological sustainability, consider the growing human consumption of net primary production (NPP), "the amount of energy captured in photosynthesis by primary producers, less the energy used in their own growth and reproduction. . . . 25% of potential global (terrestrial and aquatic) NPP is now appropriated by human beings." If this appropriation were to double twice—not that remote a prospect, given that the world population has doubled in the last forty years and production and fuel consumption have quadrupled—there would be 0 percent of NPP left for all nonhuman nondomesticated species, an ecologically inconceivable outcome.[19] Consider that the United States, with less than 5 percent of the world's population, consumes roughly 25 percent of its fossil fuels and produces 20 percent of its greenhouse gases. China, with more than a billion people, is the second-largest producer of greenhouse gases. "With its immense coal reserves, huge population, and booming economic growth, China is very likely to triple its greenhouse emissions by 2020."[20]

According to the Union of Concerned Scientists, "passenger vehicles and heavy trucks are responsible for about a quarter of annual U.S. carbon dioxide emissions—more than most other countries emit from all sources combined. . . . If recent trends continue, the global automobile population will double in as little as twenty-five to fifty years. Thus, aggressive action to slow, and eventually reverse, the growth of carbon dioxide emissions from cars is a high priority."[21] If there were one automobile for every two people in China, as there is in the United States, its carbon dioxide emissions from autos could increase by seventy-five times the amount of current Chinese emissions and quadruple the amount currently emitted from U.S. cars.[22] Clearly, the level of consumption per person in the United States is not a sustainable target for all humans on the planet; as Herman Daly and John Cobb argue, "the scale of human activity relative to the biosphere has grown too large."[23] We are headed for disaster unless the major nations of the globe act on a grand scale to conserve energy, limit population growth, reduce consumption, and protect endangered species and habitat.

Capitalist economies collide with this ecological imperative insofar as they require continuous economic growth. If capitalism does not expand, then profits fall to zero, and capitalists lose their incentive to invest or to carry on production. Profit enables growth and is the incentive for growth.[24] Profit must be realized in the market and so requires ever expanding consumption. As national economies find Keynesian effective-demand policies unsupportable in a global economy—budgets must be cut to reduce taxes and inflation and to keep businesses competitive—policy makers have come to rely on exports to sustain demand. Whether this approach can succeed will depend upon whether a kind of "global Keynesianism" can underpin demand on a world scale.[25] But even if it does, the prospect of ever expanding economic growth on a world scale is an ecological nightmare.

An economy of worker-managed enterprises is not dependent upon growth and so holds the promise of a feasible, less feverish economic alternative to capitalism, more compatible in its ordinary workings with ecological imperatives.[26] The underlying reason for this is that the economic goal of a worker-managed enterprise is to maximize income per worker, not to maximize profits for the owner. This goal can function like profit in a capitalist firm to motivate efficient high-quality production. But it leads to different results with respect to expansion, as David Schweickart illustrates:

> When costs per item are constant, a capitalist enterprise can increase its net profit by enlarging the scale of its operation, and this increase accrues to the owner of the enterprise. If a hamburger stand employing twenty people nets $20,000, a second stand doing similar business will net another $20,000. So the owner has an almost irresistible incentive to expand. Under worker self-management, by contrast, doubling the size of the enterprise may double the net profit, but it will also double the number of workers who must share that profit. Two hamburger stands run by forty people will generate precisely the same per-worker income as one stand run by twenty. Thus the first stand, even if successful, has no incentive to open up another, or even to take on more workers, unless increasing returns to scale make a larger operation more efficient. (I am assuming, here, that there is no shift in demand and that all workers are paid equally.)[27]

The self-managed firm will respond to market signals and be mindful of competition. "The firm's workers do not want to lose customers, nor lose market share, but they have less to gain from an expansion. . . ." [Both capitalist and self-managed firms] will expand if there are significantly increasing returns to scale. But a capitalist firm, much more so than a worker-managed firm, is motivated to expand when returns to scale are constant and/or costs decline.[28] Moreover, worker-managed firms are content to continue production at a given level as long as prices will support their incomes. Because they are not outside investors, they require no entrepreneurial profits premised on growth. A system of such enterprises could function in a steady state, in contrast with capitalism, which is in crisis when profits fall.

### The Market

The advantages of competitive markets over centralized planning are well summarized by Daly and Cobb: their capacity to handle information and to respond to changes in demand, the way profit both signals shortages and provides incentives to correct them, and decentralization, making possible independence and participation on a human scale.[29]

Nevertheless, there are problems that markets can not solve or that they create. Most commonly acknowledged by economists are positive and negative externalities, or public goods and public bads. Public goods are goods from which many benefit, some without paying for them. A standard example is a road, from which the builder may benefit, at considerable cost, but so also do many others who pay nothing. When limiting access and charging tolls is not feasible, such goods fail frequently to be produced. Public funding provides the good by taxing everyone, and all, or almost all, benefit when the good is widely shared. Negative externalities, or public bads, are costs that fall on parties outside of market transactions and are not reflected in market prices, as when citizens downstream from a paper mill suffer the costs of the mill's pollution and the cost of the paper does not reflect this environmental and health cost.

Some see the ecological challenge for economics as consisting simply in providing communally, or subsidizing producers to provide, for public goods and internalizing negative externalities through taxation.[30] So, for example, the paper mill would be taxed for its pollution at a level sufficient to give the owner an incentive to clean it up or to compensate all those who suffer the costs. A market-socialist economy would presumably need such measures as much as a capitalist one. Such fine-tuned measures are inadequate, however, when dealing with what Daly and Cobb call pervasive externalities, in which the costs are spread over huge numbers, or a wide area, and are difficult to calculate precisely. Acid rain, greenhouse gases, and ozone depletion might exemplify such externalities and may require policy measures aimed at direct abolition or reduction.[31]

Most important, ecologically speaking, is the externalization from market transactions of any consideration of the "optimal scale of the macro-economy relative to the ecosystem."[32] Market transactors—and most economists—consider the environment to be an infinite tap and an infinite sink. Production that appears efficient when viewed with such blinders is, in fact, costly to the point of unsustainability, using up nonrenewable resources without replacing them and fouling the nest without incurring the cost. The problem here is not how to fix discrete taxes on particular enterprises but how to reduce the overall level of consumption, pollution, and growth.

Market economies tend to be self-eroding in ways that reinforce the previously mentioned problems. There is, first, the "tendency for competition to be self-eliminating" as successful enterprises grow and drive out their competitors. "Trust busting" is generally seen as the solution, but the political will for this is undermined by the second tendency, the "corrosiveness of self-interest on the context of community that is presupposed by the market."[33] A market economy of any kind—not least a highly competitive market that guards against monopolies—

requires a shared consensus in support of market institutions and sufficient political awareness and involvement to put the consensus into practice. Political economists since Adam Ferguson have noted the tendency for citizens of commercial societies to become preoccupied with their own private interest to the neglect of the public interest.[34] Although in certain respects markets are self-regulating—in competitive markets supply and demand tend toward equilibrium—with respect to ongoing support for the political community that sustains the market, the market undermines itself, because its agents have lost their public spirit. What is true of political support for the market is true a fortiori of political support for measures for regulating the market in the common interest, such as environmental regulation.

Finally, it is a common observation that the best-functioning markets, resulting in the most efficient production, do nothing to bring about just distribution of income or wealth.[35] Pareto optimality, a common measure of efficiency, is achieved if no alteration in a given allocation of resources can occur to make one person better off without making someone else worse off. But a society in which 1 percent of members own 99 percent of the wealth and live in luxury while the other 99 percent live in poverty could be Pareto optimal. Just distribution will typically require redistribution of income or wealth or limits on accumulation of wealth. The criterion of just distribution is not mere efficiency but a moral norm, such as a principle of utility or Rawls' difference principle.

The failure of markets with respect to justice has a number of environmental implications. First, on a world scale the unequal distribution of wealth and income is one of the most important factors in the growing ecological crisis. Historically, the rate of population increase has tended to decline as societies become more affluent. If the world were to raise existing poor countries out of poverty through redistribution, their rates of population increase could be brought under control, and the richer countries would not be able to continue spending all out of proportion to their share of the earth's resources. We could anticipate a future in which growth in the richer countries would moderate, the ideal of wealth would fall to a lower level (so that not all Asians would desire to own two cars per family), and the gap between rich and poor would narrow to a tolerably just level. (I do not mean to suggest here that people's aspirations can be socially engineered, but simply that if the standard set in the richer countries is moderated, those from poorer countries who aspire to it will be aiming for a lower, and more sustainable, target.)

Second, markets are blind to justice between generations. The rapid depletion of the earth's resources and habitat is an injustice to future generations of human beings, if not other species. As Brian Barry has said,

It is not simply that the more we use [of nonrenewable resources] the less they will have—which is a tautology, given the definition of "nonrenewable"—but that the more we use the fewer options they will have, other things being equal. . . . We must come up with a criterion that allows for some exploitation of nonrenewable resources even when that is going to mean that, other things being equal, future generations will be put at a relative disadvantage compared with us.[36]

Barry's solution is to compensate future generations for our use of nonrenewables, such that "the combination of improved technology and increased capital investment should be such as to offset the effects of depletion." By "off-setting" he means not maintaining the same utility but replacing "the productive *opportunities* we have destroyed by the creation of alternative ones."[37] For example, if fossil fuels enable people currently to stay warm and to travel, future generations deprived of fossil fuels should be guaranteed alternative technologies affording them similar opportunities. This criterion is compatible with the left-Rawlsian conception of justice I have defended earlier. If implemented, it would build ecological sustainability into the standard of justice, at least as far as relations among humans are concerned. (I must confess bewilderment or a lack of imagination when it comes to defining a clear conception of justice due to individual animals, other species, or ecosystems as such. If what I propose does not go far enough in the minds of some environmentalists, it surely goes far beyond what any state currently acknowledges, and it would have very substantial positive side effects for habitat preservation and reduction in animal product consumption. For example, sustainable forestry practice that will leave to future generations similar yields of wood from the forests will also involve maintaining a biologically diverse forest and will preserve the habitat of many species threatened by clear-cutting or monocultures. A more equitable distribution of income would reduce the incomes of people in richer countries and make vegetarian diets more attractive financially—resulting in a much more sustainable agriculture.)

All of these problems with the market point toward substantial state regulation, at the very least. Will it be enough, as Van Parijs argues, to adjust prices administratively, offer subsidies, and levy taxes to internalize the externalities in a capitalist economy? Will additional *socialist* modifications of the market economy be necessary, such as social ownership of capital or democratic planning of investment?

## Democratic Investment Fund

Van Parijs's defense of basic-income capitalism assumes that private property, wealth accumulation, and the possibility of wage-labor contracts is compatible with green pricing, a strongly egalitarian redistribution policy (in the form of an unconditional maximum sustainable basic income for everyone), and nurturance of a community strong enough to support such policies. The wild card in his theory is always an unspecified "exact design of . . . political institutions."[38] What is needed is an account of how a state in capitalist society could rise above class sufficiently to regulate the market with a view to both ecological sustainability and justice. Van Parijs himself suggests that though a socialist economy might be less efficient than a capitalist economy, "it may still be able to finance a higher basic income than capitalism could, thanks to its greater ability sustainably to allocate its output in the required way."[39]

A capitalist economy is constrained by the necessity for production to be profitable in order to attract investment. It is further constrained politically by the threat of capital flight or capital strike against egalitarian—or ecological—measures that threaten profits. By controlling capital through ownership and control over investment, a socialist society has greater latitude in steering investment toward egalitarian and green objectives. In particular, a democratic investment fund such as Schweickart proposes could build into its investment criteria commitments to sustainable, clean production and job creation in areas such as energy conservation and alternative energy.

Moreover, as John Roemer has emphasized, the absence of a class of individuals that profits enormously solely from income from property will give more weight in politics to the forces of ecological, labor, feminist, and other social movements. Whatever "exact design" of political institutions we desire for a capitalist economy must wrestle with the concentrated power of private capital ownership. The wide dispersal of this ownership, through socialization and worker management (in Schweickart's model) or through a socialist stock market (in Roemer's), would eliminate the central obstacle to democratic politics in any capitalist society.

But what about the poor environmental record of the socialist economies? These economies were undemocratic and allowed no scope for independent environmental activism. A democratic market-socialist economy would allow environmental challenges to unecological investment in all the ways that they occur under capitalism, including consumer activism to which market-oriented enterprises would have to respond. But, in addition, environmentalists would have a forum in the debate over the investment fund itself, a debate that does not exist in a public or democratic way in capitalist societies. Decentralization and worker self-management would work against the imposition of environmental risks and costs on unwilling local communities. Thus, there are good reasons for distinguishing the model of socialism I am advocating from those that have produced environmental disasters in Eastern Europe.

## Basic Income

Finally, the basic income, favored by some European Greens, will support ecological ends in several ways. It will support a more equitable sharing of work, and less work per person, than an economy without basic income, even without a mandated shorter workweek. The basic income will make possible the taking on of part-time work that without a basic income would be insufficient to support the worker. With less pressure to work full time, more options open up for individuals and work communities (such as cooperatives) to consume less and enjoy more leisure; such a society will be less hooked on unsustainable growth. Particularly if the basic income is tied to political or community participation, as A. B. Atkinson has proposed, it will contribute to a revitalization of the public sphere, citizen participation, and focus of attention on public matters, not least of which would include the ecological crisis.[40] Even Van Parijs's unconditional basic income would enable those so inclined to direct their energy toward the public sphere and away from production of commodities. One consequence of an unconditional basic income is to create pressure on workplaces to make work more attractive, for as the level of basic income rises, it will become harder to attract workers to dangerous, arduous, or, apropos here, dirty, unhealthy, and unecological work. By lessening the *necessity* to work, basic income will help to narrow the gap between the political self that favors justice and sustainability and the economic self that seeks employment in order to boost income.

As this last section demonstrates, the measures I am advocating can attenuate the division between civil society and state, although my support of markets means that I am abandoning Marx's goal of abolishing this division. Perhaps these measures—self-management, democratic control of investment, and basic income—will be enough to overcome commodity fetishism in the psychological sense (see chapter 4). More generally, I have tried in this chapter to show that the advocate for market socialism does not need to abandon what is inspiring and transformative in the socialist vision. Moreover, market socialism has more to offer feminists and environmentalists than appears at first glance. In fact, it provides an institutional and economic model more conducive to socialist, feminist, and environmental ends than either capitalism or centrally planned socialism. Given the right kind of coalition building, it is not unreasonable to expect a convergence of social movements around such a model.

## NOTES

1. These movements are "new" in comparison with the labor movement in their comparatively recent origin (or reemergence) in the 1960s and 1970s and in their relative importance for the Left since that time.

2. Adam Przeworski, *Capitalism and Social Democracy* (Cambridge: Cambridge University Press, 1985), 243–44.

3. Przeworski, *Capitalism and Social Democracy*, 247–48.

4. See Susan Moller Okin, "Politics and the Complex Inequalities of Gender," in *Pluralism, Justice, and Equality*, ed. David Miller and Michael Walzer (Oxford: Oxford University Press, 1995), 120–43. The percentage of female members of national legislatures in the late 1980s or 1990s ranges from less than 3 percent in Japan to more than 30

percent in the Nordic countries, the U.S. figure being around 10 percent. For discussion of women's participation in the workplace, see Carole Pateman, *The Disorder of Women* (Stanford: Stanford University Press, 1989), 166–70, 220–23.

5. Other factors include sexual objectification and gendered inequalities in communication patterns, especially in the workplace, which often effectively marginalize women in decision making. See Deborah Tannen, *Talking 9 to 5* (New York: William Morrow, 1994). See also Nancy Fraser on the complex gendering of the roles of citizen, consumer, worker, head of household, child rearer, client, and soldier, in *Unruly Practices: Power, Discourse, and Gender in Contemporary Social Theory* (Minneapolis: University of Minnesota Press, 1989), 113–43. I owe most of what follows on work and welfare in this chapter to Fraser and to Pateman, *The Disorder of Women.*

6. Although the idea of married couples' equally sharing household work is laudable, "in the USA at least, in heterosexual households where both adults work full-time, the woman does, on average, at least twice as much of the unpaid 'family work' as the man does"; Okin, "Politics and the Complex Inequalities of Gender," 137. These deep-rooted patterns are not likely to change without other social, economic, and political changes.

7. Fraser, *Unruly Practices*, 132; Pateman, *The Disorder of Women*, 202–3.

8. Fraser, *Unruly Practices*, 147. She also notes, "In 1980, 70 percent of the 17.3 million paid jobs in [the human-services] sector in the U.S. were held by women. This accounts for one-third of U.S. women's total paid employment and a full 80 percent of all professional jobs held by women" (148). See also Pateman, *The Disorder of Women*, 180–81; 200–201.

9. Fraser, *Unruly Practices*, 149. "Female-headed" households are by definition without a healthy adult male, whereas male-headed households may contain a full-time adult female wage earner (147).

10. Fraser, *Unruly Practices*, 151–53.

11. For references on the "feminization of poverty," see Fraser, *Unruly Practices*, 158–59; Pateman, *The Disorder of Women*, 205.

12. William Schweke, Carl Rist, and Brian Dabson, *Bidding for Business: Are Cities and States Selling Themselves Short?* (Washington, D.C.: Corporation for Enterprise Development, 1994); Melvin L. Burstein and Arthur J. Rolnick, "Congress Should End the Economic War Among States," *Region* (March 1995 ) (Minneapolis: Federal Reserve Bank of Minneapolis), cited with other relevant references in "Economic Development in Maine: Long-Term Growth or Short-Term Fixes?" factsheet (Bureau of Labor Education, University of Maine, Spring 1996).

13. See Pateman, *The Disorder of Women*, 202–3.

14. In 1987, "public spending on employment and retraining as a percentage of gross domestic product (GDP) was 1.7 percent in Sweden, 1 percent in West Germany, 0.7 percent in France, Spain, and Britain, and a minuscule 0.3 percent in the United States"; John Bellamy Foster, *The Limits of Environmentalism without Class: Lessons from the Ancient Forest Struggle of the Pacific Northwest* (New York: Monthly Review Press, 1993), 27.

15. I will not attempt in this book to define what justice requires for the disabled. Rawls also defers on this question, making it clear that by "least advantaged" he has in mind not the truly least advantaged but the lowest-paid class of workers; John Rawls, *Politi-*

*cal Liberalism* (New York: Columbia University Press, 1993), 20–21. For one proposal, worked out in conjunction with a basic-income scheme, see Philippe Van Parijs, *Real Freedom for All: What (If Anything) Can Justify Capitalism?* (Oxford: Clarendon Press, 1995), chapter three.

16. *ICA Bulletin* (September 1997): 1–2; *ICA Bulletin* (August 1996): 2; Frank Adams, Fred Gordon, and Richard Shirey, *Cooperative Home Care Associates: From Working Poor to Working Class through Job Ownership* (Boston: ICA Group, 1991).

17. Herman E. Daly and John B. Cobb, *For the Common Good*, (Boston: Beacon Press, 1989), 146; a propos of other concerns in this chapter, they also recognize the value of cooperatives (302).

18. Foster, *The Limits of Environmentalism without Class.*

19. Daly and Cobb, *For the Common Good*, 143.

20. Daly and Cobb, *For the Common Good*, 114.

21. Union of Concerned Scientists, "The Hidden Costs of Transportation," <http://www.ucsusa.org/transportation/index.html?hidden.html> (1 April 1999).

22. Calculations from data in Mark Hertzgaard, "Our Real China Problem," *Atlantic Monthly*, November 1997, 97–114.

23. Daly and Cobb, *For the Common Good*, 2.

24. James O'Connor, "Is Sustainable Capitalism Possible?" in *Is Capitalism Sustainable? Political Economy and the Politics of Ecology*, ed. Martin O'Connor (New York: Guilford Press, 1994), 152–75.

25. O'Connor, "Is Sustainable Capitalism Possible?" 158–61.

26. David Schweickart, *Against Capitalism* (Cambridge: Cambridge University Press, 1994), 154, 96.

27. Schweickart, *Against Capitalism*, 96.

28. Schweickart, *Against Capitalism*, 97.

29. Daly and Cobb, *For the Common Good*, 45–49. See also chapter 6 and the introduction to part 1 above.

30. Van Parijs, *Real Freedom for All*, 187, 200.

31. Daly and Cobb, *For the Common Good*, 55.

32. Daly and Cobb, *For the Common Good*, 145.

33. Daly and Cobb, *For the Common Good*, 49–52.

34. Adam Ferguson, *An Essay on the History of Civil Society* (1767; New York: Garland, 1971).

35. Daly and Cobb, *For the Common Good*, 59; John Rawls, *A Theory of Justice* (Cambridge: Harvard University Press, 1971), 67–72.

36. Brian Barry, "Intergenerational Justice in Energy Policy," in *Justice*, ed. Milton Fisk (Atlantic Highlands, N. J.: Humanities Press, 1993), 225.

37. Barry, "Intergenerational Justice," 225; my italics.

38. Van Parijs, *Real Freedom for All*, 187, 201, 228, 231.

39. Van Parijs, *Real Freedom for All*, 222.

40. A. B. Atkinson, "The Case for a Participation Income," *Political Quarterly* 67, no. 1 (January–March 1996): 67–70. For criticism of participation income, see chapter 2.

# Conclusion

## "To Win the Battle of Democracy"

I submit this book to the publisher just after the 150th anniversary of the *Communist Manifesto*.[1] Although my book is certainly no manifesto, nor is it "Communist" with all the connotations that term has acquired, I intend it as a contribution to the further development of a movement for which the *Communist Manifesto* was a founding document, a movement for the emancipation of workers and oppressed people everywhere. Emancipation from exploitation and oppression is a protracted process, with each victory immediately giving rise to new obstacles. In 1848, Marx and Engels allied themselves with the Chartists in the struggle for working-class voting rights. That struggle continues, or is only recently won, in countries such as China, Indonesia, Russia, and South Africa. It has long since been won in the United States, yet we are far from genuine democracy. The power of money in politics effectively disenfranchises workers and poor people. Growing social and economic inequality strengthens the haves and weakens the have-nots. Democracy as we know it stops at the doors of private enterprises and corporate boardrooms.

Political democracy in 1848 was only the first step, to be followed by a revolutionary transformation. In the twentieth century we have seen that transformation in process, sometimes gradual, as in the piecemeal victories to establish social welfare benefits, public education, mass transit, and more progressive tax laws, sometimes sudden and violent, as in the upheavals in Russia, China, and the former European and American colonies of Asia, Africa, and Latin America. The disappointments, wrong turns, reversals, and disasters need not be rehearsed here. It is more important to note that we have come some distance, we have learned some lessons, and we still have much to do.

In 1848 the ten-hours bill was a recent triumph. We have since seen the working day shrink to eight hours, and, as I write, the French socialist government is instituting a thirty-five-hour workweek. At the same time, we see in the United States a growing divide between fully employed workers who are often overworked (Charlie King sings, "Bring back the eight-hour day") and marginally employed people, many of whom must work several jobs to make ends meet. The economic struggles of daily life are also inevitably political struggles, struggles for control over the conditions of life and work. That end is increasingly elusive as the global market, partly structured to serve corporate interests, in turn dictates the terms to corporations, which then have been able to blackmail unions, states, and municipalities for more concessions, deregulation, and tax breaks. In this context, I trust that worker self-management, democratic control over investment, and a basic income for all will be perceived not as nostalgic daydreams but as necessary means to make good on the promise of democracy and individual freedom that is at the heart of the liberal political tradition, but which liberal politics has too often betrayed.

The small-scale but promising developments in the field of worker ownership and worker participation are evidence of interest and potential for more-extensive economic democracy, given the right political context and coalitions. The growth and political self-consciousness of the women's movement, which cuts across all dimensions of social life, is one of the most encouraging developments of the last quarter century. The looming environmental catastrophe that industrial society—now, with the collapse of the Soviet system, almost exclusively capitalist—has wrought is in a new way the grave capitalism has dug for itself. If the environmental movement, in cooperation with other social movements, does not take up the challenge to bury capitalism, we will all be buried, just as some earlier struggles have ended not with the victory of one party but with "the common ruin of the contending classes." To bury capitalism we must have something to erect in its place. I have tried to provide some feasible alternatives, grounded in real-world examples. The growth of worker ownership and participation, although sometimes conservative and apolitical in character, is nonetheless a potential vehicle for economic democracy. Whether it becomes so will depend heavily on the political context and the kinds of understandings people have of its significance. In place of Marx and Engels's glib dismissals of bourgeois ideology as the "ideas of the ruling class," I have, at the risk of tedium, devoted a major part of this book to criticism of liberal, postmodern, and communitarian theories. Such theoretical disputes are necessary for self-clarification but also to achieve intellectual and political hegemony. Although I have defended a kind of left liberalism and a market economy, I hope that the conclusions drawn and models proposed show that such a position is consistent with the deepest aspirations toward social transformation and emancipation at the heart of Marxism.

The idea of socialism, for the next generation, must be an idea of an egalitarian, sustainable society in which the levels of growth and work are collectively debated and determined by democratically organized enterprises and communities in which each person is guaranteed the rights and resources to be a free and equal participant. Although the philosophical and legal underpinnings are liberal and the market is the principal means of economic coordination, in such a society there are fewer obstacles to effective democratic politics and more avenues for association, hence greater scope for community. Community should be encouraged to the degree necessary to achieve such a state and sustain it. Whether it will be defined as a community of workers united in a workers' state is debatable. Its banner might well be a reinvigorated older slogan, "with liberty and justice for all." Whatever the slogan, the idea of self-managed market socialism is philosophically defensible, institutionally feasible, and relevant to the struggles of workers—and quite a few nonwage workers—in contemporary capitalist society. Although we may have more than our chains to lose, after 150 years, we still have a world to win.

## NOTES

1. Quotations in this conclusion are from Karl Marx and Frederick Engels, *The Communist Manifesto*, trans. Samuel Moore (Chicago: Charles H. Kerr Publishing, 1984), 42, 12, 40.

# Bibliography

Adams, Frank, Fred Gordon, and Richard Shirey. *Cooperative Home Care Associates: From Working Poor to Working Class Through Job Ownership.* Boston: ICA Group, 1991.

Adams, Frank, and Michelle Siegal. *Directory of Workers' Enterprises in North America.* Boston: ICA Group, 1991.

Adler, Paul S. "New Technologies, New Skills," *California Management Review* 29 (1986): 9–28.

_____. ed. *Technology and the Future of Work.* Oxford: Oxford University Press, 1992.

AFL-CIO. "How Much Would You Be Making if Your Pay Had Grown As CEO Pay Has?" <http://www.aflcio.org/paywatch/ceou_compare.htm> (12 May 1999).

AFL-CIO Committee on the Evolution of Work. *The Changing Situation of Workers and Their Unions.* Washington, D.C.: n.p., 1985.

Albert, Michael, and Robin Hahnel. *Looking Forward: Participatory Economics for the Twenty-First Century.* Boston: South End Press, 1991.

Arias, Oscar, Jordana Friedman, and Caleb Rossiter. "Less Spending, More Security: A Practical Plan to Reduce World Military Spending." <http://www.fas.org/pub/gen/mswg/year2000/oped.htm> (cited 12 March 1999).

Aristotle. *Nicomachean Ethics.* Trans. Martin Ostwald. Indianapolis: Bobbs-Merrill, 1962.

_____. *Politics.* Trans. Ernest Barker. Oxford: Oxford University Press, 1968.

Arneson, Richard. "Democratic Rights at National and Workplace Levels." In Copp, Hampton, and Roemer, *The Idea of Democracy.*

_____. "Market Socialism and Egalitarian Ethics," In Bardhan and Roemer, *Market Socialism.*

Arnold, N. Scott. "Marx and Disequilibrium in Market Socialist Relations of Production." *Economics and Philosophy* 3 (1987): 23–48.

_____. *Marx's Radical Critique of Capitalist Society.* Oxford: Oxford University Press, 1990.

251

_____. *The Philosophy and Economics of Market Socialism*. Oxford: Oxford University Press, 1994.

Atkinson, A. B. "The Case for a Participation Income." *Political Quarterly* 67, no. 1 (January–March 1996): 67–70.

Aufderheide, Patricia. "After the Fairness Doctrine: Controversial Broadcast Programming and the Public Interest." *Journal of Communications* 40, no. 3 (Summer 1990): 47–71.

Babson, Steve. "When 'Empowerment' Means 'Exploitation': Negotiating the Terms of Lean Production." *WorkingUSA* (May–June 1997): 69–76.

Bagdikian, Ben. *The Media Monopoly*. 4th ed.. Boston: Beacon Press, 1992.

Banks, Andy, and Jack Metzgar. "Participating in Management: Union Organizing on a New Terrain." *Labor Research Review* 8, no. 2 (Fall 1989): 1–55.

Bannock, Graham, R. E. Baxter, and Evan Davis. *The Penguin Dictionary of Economics*. London: Penguin Books, 1992.

Bardhan, Pranab K. "On Tackling the Soft Budget Constraint in Market Socialism." In Bardhan and Roemer, *Market Socialism*.

Bardhan, Pranab K., and John E. Roemer. "Market Socialism: A Case for Rejuvenation." *Journal of Economic Perspectives* 6 (1992): 101–16.

_____. eds. *Market Socialism: The Current Debate*. Oxford: Oxford University Press, 1993.

Barry, Brian. *Democracy, Power, and Justice: Essays in Political Theory*. Oxford: Clarendon Press, 1989.

_____. "Equality Yes, Basic Income No." In Van Parijs, *Arguing for Basic Income*.

_____. "Intergenerational Justice in Energy Policy." In *Justice*, ed. Milton Fisk. Atlantic Highlands, N.J.: Humanities Press, 1993.

_____. "Spherical Justice and Global Injustice." In Miller and Walzer, *Pluralism, Justice, and Equality*.

_____. "Survey Article: Real Freedom and Basic Income." *Journal of Political Philosophy* 4, no. 3 (1996): 242–76.

Blasi, Joseph. "Are ESOPs Part of the Problem?: Interview With Joseph Blasi." In Krimerman and Frank Lindenfeld, *When Workers Decide*.

_____. *Employee Ownership: Revolution or Ripoff?* Cambridge, Mass.: Ballinger Publishing, 1988.

Blasi, Joseph, and Douglas Kruse. *The New Owners: The Mass Emergence of Employee Ownership in Public Companies and What It Means to American Business*. New York: HarperCollins Publishers, 1991.

Bowles, Samuel, and Herbert Gintis. *Democracy and Capitalism: Property, Community, and the Contradictions of Modern Social Thought*. New York: Basic Books, 1987.

_____. "A Political and Economic Case for the Democratic Enterprise." In Copp, Hampton, and Roemer, *The Idea of Democracy*.

Bradley, Keith, and Alan Gelb. "The Replication and Sustainability of the Mondragon Experiment." *British Journal of Industrial Relations* 20 (March 1982): 20–33.

Buchanan, Allen. *Marx and Justice*. Totowa, N.J.: Rowman & Littlefield, 1982.

Burstein, Melvin L., and Arthur J. Rolnick. "Congress Should End the Economic War among the States." *Region* (March 1995). Minneapolis: Federal Reserve Bank of Minneapolis.

Carens, Joseph H. "The Virtues of Socialism." *Theory and Society* 15, no. 5 (1986): 679–87.

Carey, Susan. "As UAL, USAir Talk, They Let World Overhear." *Wall Street Journal,* 10 November 1995.

————. "UAL Appoints a Mediator Head of Human Resources." *Wall Street Journal,* 3 March 1997.

Carlo, Antonio. "Capitalist Restoration and Social Crisis in Yugoslavia." *Telos* 36 (Summer 1978): 81–110.

Carnoy, Martin, and Derek Shearer. *Economic Democracy.* White Plains, N.Y.: M. E. Sharpe, 1980.

Center for a New American Dream. "Towards Sustainable Consumption." <http://www.newdream.org/discuss/nas.html> (12 March 1999).

Champagne, Jessica. "Boycott Action News." *Co-op America Quarterly* 48 (Summer 1999): 29.

Chandler, Susan. "United We Own." *Business Week,* 18 March 1996, 96–100.

Clark, Rodney. *The Japanese Company.* New Haven: Yale University Press, 1979.

Clegg, Ian. *Workers' Self-Management in Algeria.* New York: Monthly Review Press, 1972.

Cohen, G. A. "Capitalism, Freedom, and the Proletariat." In *The Idea of Freedom,* ed. Alan Ryan. Oxford: Oxford University Press, 1979.

————. *Self-Ownership, Freedom and Equality.* Cambridge: Cambridge University Press, 1995.

Cohen, Joshua. "Deliberation and Democratic Legitimacy." In *The Good Polity: Normative Analysis of the State,* ed. Alan Hamlin and Philip Pettit. Oxford: Basil Blackwell, 1989.

————. "Reflections on Rousseau: Autonomy and Democracy." *Philosophy and Public Affairs* 15, no. 3 (Summer 1986): 275–97.

Cohen, Joshua, and Joel Rogers. *On Democracy.* New York: Penguin Books, 1983.

Cohen, Stephen F., and Katrina vanden Heuvel. "Help Russia." *Nation,* 11–18 January 1999, 8-9.

Constant, Benjamin. "Liberty of the Ancients Compared with That of the Moderns" (1819). In *Political Writings,* ed. and trans. Biancamaria Fontana. Cambridge: Cambridge University Press, 1988.

Copp, David, Jean Hampton, and John E. Roemer, eds. *The Idea of Democracy.* Cambridge: Cambridge University Press, 1993.

Cunningham, Frank. *Democratic Theory and Socialism.* Cambridge: Cambridge University Press, 1987.

Dahl, Robert A. *A Preface to Economic Democracy.* Berkeley: University of California Press, 1985.

Daly, Herman E., and John B. Cobb. *For the Common Good.* Boston: Beacon Press, 1989.

Daniels, Norman. "Equal Liberty and Unequal Worth of Liberty." In *Reading Rawls: Critical Studies on Rawls' "A Theory of Justice,"* ed. Norman Daniels. New York: Basic Books, 1975.

Dore, Ronald. *Taking Japan Seriously: A Confucian Perspective on Leading Economic Issues.* Stanford: Stanford University Press, 1987.

Dorfman, Ronald. "Toward a Non-Capitalist Journalism." *Chicago Journalism Review* (December 1970): 7.

Dréze, Jacques H. *Labour Management, Contracts, and Capital Markets: A General Equilibrium Approach.* Oxford: Basil Blackwell, 1989.

_____. "Self-Management and Economic Theory: Efficiency, Funding, and Employment." In Bardhan and Roemer, *Market Socialism.*

Dworkin, Ronald. "Liberalism." In *Public and Private Morality*, ed. Stuart Hampshire. Cambridge: Cambridge University Press, 1991.

_____. "What Is Equality? Part One: Equality of Welfare." *Philosophy and Public Affairs* 10, no. 3 (Summer 1981): 185–246 .

_____. "What Is Equality? Part Two: Equality of Resources." *Philosophy and Public Affairs* 10, no. 4 (Fall 1981): 283–345.

Earle, John. *The Italian Cooperative Movement.* London: Allen and Unwin, 1986.

"Economic Development in Maine: Long-Term Growth or Short-Term Fixes?" Factsheet, Bureau of Labor Education, University of Maine, Spring 1996.

Edwards, Richard. *Contested Terrain: The Transformation of the Workplace in the Twentieth Century.* New York: Basic Books, 1979.

Ellerman, David. "Capitalism and Workers' Self-Management." In *Self-Management: Economic Liberation of Man*, ed. Jaroslav Vanek. Baltimore: Penguin Books, 1975.

_____. *The Democratic Worker-Owned Firm: A New Model for the East and West.* Boston: Unwin Hyman, 1990.

_____. "ESOPs and Co-ops: Worker Capitalism and Worker Democracy." *Labor Research Review* 1, no. 6 (Spring 1985): 55–69.

_____. *Property and Contract in Economics: The Case for Economic Democracy.* Oxford: Blackwell, 1992.

_____. "The Socialization of Entrepreneurialism: The Empresarial Division of the Caja Laboral Popular." Somerville, Mass.: Industrial Cooperative Association, 1982.

Ellman, Michael. "Changing Views on Central Economic Planning: 1958-1983." *ACES Bulletin* 25, no. 1 (Spring 1983): 11–29.

Elson, Diane. "Market Socialism or Socialization of the Market?" *New Left Review* 172 (November–December 1988): 3–43.

Elster, Jon. "Comment on van der Veen and Van Parijs." *Theory and Society* 15, no. 5 (1986): 709–21.

_____. "Is There (or Should There Be) a Right to Work?" In *Democracy and the Welfare State*, ed. Amy Gutmann. Princeton: Princeton University Press, 1988.

_____. "Self-realisation in Work and Politics." In Elster and Moene, *Alternatives to Capitalism.*

Elster, Jon, and Karl Ove Moene, eds. *Alternatives to Capitalism.* Cambridge: Cambridge University Press, 1989.

Estrin, Saul, and William Bartlett. "The Effects of Enterprise Self-Management in Yugoslavia: An Empirical Survey." In *Participatory and Self-Managed Firms*, ed. D. Jones and J. Svejnar. Lexington, Mass: Lexington Books, 1982.

"Fagor acusa a MCC de alejarse del cooperativismo." *Egin*, 28 February 1997, 25.

Faux, Jeff. "The 'American Model' Exposed." *Nation*, 27 October 1997, 18–21.

Ferguson, Adam. *An Essay on the History of Civil Society* (1767). New York: Garland, 1971.

Filipelli, Ronald L. *Labor in the USA: A History*. New York: Knopf, 1984.

Fisk, Milton. "Justice and Universality." In Sterba, *Morality and Social Justice*.

————. *The State and Justice*. Cambridge: Cambridge University Press, 1989.

Fitch, Robert. "In Bologna, Small Is Beautiful." *The Nation*, 13 May 1996, 18–21.

Foster, John Bellamy. *The Limits of Environmentalism without Class: Lessons from the Ancient Forest Struggle of the Pacific Northwest*. New York: Monthly Review Press, 1993.

Foucault, Michel. "Disciplinary Power and Subjection." In Lukes, *Power*.

Fraser, Nancy. "Rethinking the Public Sphere: A Contribution to the Critique of Actually Existing Democracy." In *Habermas and the Public Sphere*, ed. Craig Calhoun. Cambridge: MIT Press, 1992.

————. *Unruly Practices: Power, Discourse, and Gender in Contemporary Social Theory*. Minneapolis: University of Minnesota Press, 1989.

Friedman, Marilyn. "Feminism and Modern Friendship: Dislocating the Community." *Ethics* 99 (January 1989): 275–90.

Funk, Nanette. "Reporters and a Free Press." *Journal of Applied Philosophy* 2, no. 1 (1985): 85–97.

Galston, William. *Liberal Purposes: Goods, Virtues, and Diversity in the Liberal State*. Cambridge: Cambridge University Press, 1991.

Glasman, Maurice. "The Great Deformation: Polanyi, Poland, and the Terrors of Planned Spontaneity." *New Left Review* 205 (May–June 1994): 59–86.

Goodin, Robert E. "Towards a Minimally Presumptuous Social Welfare Policy." In Van Parijs, *Arguing for Basic Income*.

Gordon, David M., Richard Edwards, and Michael Reich. *Segmented Work, Divided Workers: The Historical Transformation of Labor in the United States*. Cambridge: Cambridge University Press, 1983.

Gorz, André. "On the Difference between Society and Community and Why Basic Income Cannot by Itself Confer Full Membership of Either." In Van Parijs, *Arguing for Basic Income*.

Gould, Carol C. *Rethinking Democracy*. Cambridge: Cambridge University Press, 1988.

Green, Philip. *Retrieving Democracy: In Search of Civic Equality*. Totowa, N.J.: Rowman and Allanheld, 1985.

Greenberg, Edward S. *Workplace Democracy: The Political Effects of Participation*. Ithaca: Cornell University Press, 1986.

Greider, William. "Why the Global Economy Needs Worker Rights." *WorkingUSA* (May–June 1997): 32–44.

Gui, Benedetto. "Basque versus Illyrian Labor-Managed Firms: The Problem of Property Rights." *Journal of Comparative Economics* 8 (1984): 168–81.

Habermas, Jürgen. *The Structural Transformation of the Public Sphere*. Cambridge: MIT Press, 1990.

————. *Theory and Practice*. Trans. John Viertel (Boston: Beacon Press, 1973).

Hacker, Sally. *Pleasure, Power, and Technology*. London: Unwin Hyman, 1989.

Harrison, Bennett. *Lean and Mean: The Changing Landscape of Corporate Power in the Age of Flexibility*. New York: Basic Books, 1994.

Harvey, David. *The Condition of Postmodernity*. Oxford: Basil Blackwell, 1989.

Hayek, Friedrich A. *Individualism and Economic Order* (Chicago: Henry Regnery, 1948).

_____. *Studies in Philosophy, Politics, and Economics.* Chicago: University of Chicago Press, 1967.

Heckscher, Charles. *The New Unionism: Employee Involvement in the Changing Corporation.* New York: Basic Books, 1988.

Hegel, G. W. F. *Philosophy of Right.* Trans. T. M. Knox. Oxford: Oxford University Press, 1967.

Henwood, Doug. "Talking about Work." *Monthly Review* 49, no. 3 (July–August 1997): 18–31.

_____. *Wall Street.* New York: Verso, 1998.

Herman, Edward S. "The Propaganda Model Revisited." In *Capitalism and the Information Age,* ed. Robert W. McChesney, Ellen Meiksins Wood, and John Bellamy Foster. New York: Monthly Review Press, 1998.

Herman, Edward S., and Frank Brodhead. *Demonstration Elections: U.S.-Staged Elections in the Dominican Republic, Vietnam, and El Salvador.* Boston: South End Press, 1984.

Herman, Edward S., and Noam Chomsky. *Manufacturing Consent: The Political Economy of the Mass Media.* New York: Pantheon Books, 1988.

Hermele, Kenneth. "The End of the Middle Road: What Happened to the Swedish Model?" *Monthly Review* 44, no. 10 (March 1993): 14–24.

_____. "A Response to David Vail." *Monthly Review* 45, no. 5 (October 1993): 32–37.

Hertzgaard, Mark. "Our Real China Problem." *Atlantic Monthly,* November 1997, 97–114.

Horvat, Branko, Mihailo Marković, and Rudi Supek. *Self-Governing Socialism.* 2 vols. White Plains, N.Y.: International Arts and Sciences Press, 1975.

Howard, Michael W. "A Contradiction in the Egalitarian Theory of Justice." *Philosophy Research Archives* 10 (1984): 35–55.

_____. "From Commodity Fetishism to Market Socialism: Critical Notes on Stanley Moore." *Philosophy and Social Criticism* 7, no. 2 (Summer 1980): 186–214.

_____. "Market Socialism and Political Pluralism: Theoretical Reflections on Yugoslavia." In *Studies in East European Thought.* Forthcoming.

_____. "Media Democratization: Access or Autonomy?" *Socialist Forum* 20 (1993): 53–57.

_____. "Self-Management, Ownership, and the Media." *Journal of Mass Media Ethics* 8, no. 4 (1994): 197–206.

_____. "Worker Control, Self-Respect, and Self-Esteem." *Philosophy Research Archives* 10 (1984): 455–72.

_____. "Worker Ownership and Wage Slavery." Unpublished manuscript, 1999.

Hunnius, Gerry. "Workers' Self-Management in Yugoslavia." In *Workers' Control,* ed. Gerry Hunnius, G. David Garson, and John Case. New York: Vintage Books, 1973.

*ICA Bulletin.* August 1996; September 1997.

ICA Group. "Some Common Questions about Employee Ownership." <http://members.aol.com/icaica/ICAPAGE.htm> (29 April 1999).

*In These Times.* 16–29 September 1992.

Institute for Policy Studies. "The Progressive Challenge." Updated 7 April 1999. <http://www.netprogress.org/index.htm> (14 April 1999).

James, Beverly. "Economic Democracy and Restructuring the Press." *Journal of Communication Inquiry* 6, no. 2 (Winter 1981):119–29.

Jordan, Bill. "Basic Income and the Common Good." In Van Parijs, *Arguing for Basic Income.*

Juravich, Tom. "Employee Involvement, Work Reorganization, and the New Labor Movement: Toward a Radical Integration." *New Labor Forum* 2 (Spring 1998): 84–91.

Kasmir, Sharryn. *The Myth of Mondragon: Cooperatives, Politics, and Working-Class Life in a Basque Town.* Albany: State University of New York Press, 1996.

Kaus, Mickey. "For a New Equality." *New Republic*, 7 May 1990, 18–27.

Kellner, Douglas. *Television and the Crisis of Democracy.* Boulder, Colo.: Westview Press, 1990.

Khor, Martin. "Growing Consensus on Ills of Globalization." <http://www.twnside.org.sg/souths/twn/title/ills-cn.htm> (12 March 1999).

Kobren, Janet, and Gloria Channon. "Beyond Media Activism: Media Democratization." *Socialist Forum* 19 (Spring 1992): 83–90.

Kornai, Janos. "Market Socialism Revisted." In Bardhan and Roemer, *Market Socialism.*

Kraut, Richard. "Politics, Neutrality, and the Good." *Social Philosophy and Policy* 16, no. 1 (Winter 1999): 315–32.

Krimerman, Len, and Frank Lindenfeld, eds. *When Workers Decide.* Philadelphia: New Society Publishers, 1992.

Kymlicka, Will. *Multicultural Citizenship: A Liberal Theory of Minority Rights.* Oxford: Clarendon Press, 1995.

Labiche, Kenneth. "When Workers Really Count." *Fortune*, 14 October 1996, 213–14.

*Labor Party Press* 4, no.1 (January 1999).

Lappé, Frances Moore, Joseph Collins, and Peter Rosset, with Luis Esparza. "Twelve Myths about Hunger." *Food First Backgrounder* 5, no. 3 (Summer 1998):1–4.

_____. *World Hunger: Twelve Myths,* 2d ed. New York: Grove/Atlantic and Food First Books, 1998.

Larmore, Charles. *Patterns of Moral Complexity.* Cambridge: Cambridge University Press, 1987.

Lawler, James. "Marx as Market Socialist," "Criticism of Ollman," and "Response to Ollman." In Ollman, *Market Socialism.*

Levine, David, and Laura D'Andrea Tyson. "Participation, Productivity, and the Firm's Environment." In *Paying for Productivity: A Look at the Evidence*, ed. Alan Blinder. Washington, D.C.: Brookings, 1990.

Lichtenberg, Judith. "Foundations and Limits of Freedom of the Press." In Lichtenberg, *Democracy and the Mass Media.*

Locker, Michael. "Unions and Worker Ownership: Interview with Michael Locker." In Krimerman and Lindenfeld, *When Workers Decide.*

_____, ed. *Democracy and the Mass Media.* Cambridge: Cambridge University Press, 1990.

Lukes, Steven. *Marxism and Morality.* Oxford: Clarendon Press, 1985.

_____. *Power: A Radical View.* London: Macmillan, 1974.

_____, ed. *Power.* Oxford: Basil Blackwell, 1986.

Lutz, Mark. "The Mondragon Cooperative Complex: An Application of Kantian Ethics to Social Economics." *International Review of Social Economics* 24, no.12 (December 1997): 1404–21.

Lutz, Mark, and Kenneth Lux. *Humanistic Economics: The New Challenge*. New York: Bootstrap Press, 1988.

Lydall, Harold. *Yugoslav Socialism: Theory and Practice*. Oxford: Oxford University Press, 1984.

MacIntyre, Alasdair. *After Virtue*, 2d ed. Notre Dame: University of Notre Dame Press, 1984.

Mackin, Christopher. "Will United Buyout Get Off the Ground?" *Los Angeles Times*, 11 July 1994.

MacLeod, Greg. *From Mondragon to America*. Sydney, Nova Scotia: University College of Cape Breton Press, 1997.

Marshall, Ray. "Work Organization, Unions, and Economic Performance." In Mischel and Voos, *Unions and Economic Competitiveness*.

Marx, Karl. Afterword to *Capital*. Vol. 1. Trans. Samuel Moore and Edward Aveling. Moscow: Foreign Language Publishing House, 1959.

————. *Capital*. Trans. Samuel Moore and Edward Aveling. New York: International Publishers, 1967.

————. *Critique of the Gotha Program*. In McLellan, *Karl Marx: Selected Writings*.

————. *Critique of Hegel's "Philosophy of Right."* Cambridge: Cambridge University Press, 1970.

Marx, Karl, and Frederick Engels. *The Communist Manifesto*. Trans. Samuel Moore. Chicago: Charles H. Kerr Publishing, 1984.

McCarthy, Thomas. Introduction to *Legitimation Crisis*, by Jürgen Habermas. Boston: Beacon Press, 1975.

McChesney, Robert W. *Corporate Media and the Threat to Democracy*. New York: Seven Stories Press, 1997.

————. "The Global Media Giants." *Extra!* 10, no. 6 (November–December 1997).

McLellan, David, ed. *Karl Marx: Selected Writings*. Oxford: Oxford University Press, 1977.

Meade, James. "The Theory of Labour-Managed Firms and of Profit Sharing." *Economic Journal* 82 (1972): 402–28.

Meidner, Rudolph. "Why Did the Swedish Model Fail?" *Socialist Register* (1993): 211–28.

Meiklejohn, Alexander. *Political Freedom: The Constitutional Powers of the People*. New York: Harper, 1960.

Merrill, John C. *The Dialectic in Journalism*. Baton Rouge: Louisiana State University Press, 1989.

————. *Existential Journalism*. New York: Hastings House Publishers, 1977.

————. *The Imperative of Freedom: A Philosophy of Journalistic Autonomy*. New York: Hastings House Publishers, 1974.

Metzgar, Jack, ed. "An Organizing Model of Unionism." *Labor Research Review* 10, no.1 (Spring 1991): 1–97.

Miller, David. "Complex Equality." In Miller and Walzer, *Pluralism, Justice, and Equality*.

————. "Market Neutrality and the Failure of Cooperatives." *British Journal of Political Science* 11 (1981): 309–29.

Miller, David, and Michael Walzer, eds. *Pluralism, Justice, and Equality.* Oxford: Oxford University Press, 1995.

Miller, Mark Crispin, et al. "The National Entertainment State." *Nation,* 3 June 1996, 3–32.

Mischel, Lawrence, Jared Bernstein, and John Schmitt. *The State of Working America 1998-99.* Ithaca: Cornell University Press, 1999.

Mischel, Lawrence, and Paula B. Voos, eds. *Unions and Economic Competitiveness.* Armonk, N.Y.: M. E. Sharpe, 1992.

Moberg, David. "War Zone." *In These Times,* 24 July–6 August 1995, 12–16.

Mondragon Cooperative Corporation. "Temporary Members: Key Points." <http://www.mondragon.mcc.es./tu/english/9703/art2.htm> (18 July 1997).

Moore, Stanley. *Marx versus Markets.* University Park: Pennsylvania State University Press, 1993.

Morley-Fletcher, Edwin. "The Cooperative Movement and the Left in Twentieth Century Europe (with Special Reference to Some Suggestions Arising from the Current Italian Debate)." Paper presented at conference of the International Institute for Self-Management, Ariccia, Italy, 26 October 1992.

Morrison, Roy. *We Build the Road As We Travel.* Philadelphia: New Society Publishers, 1991.

Moynihan, Daniel P. *The Politics of a Guaranteed Income: The Nixon Administration and the Family Assistance Plan.* New York: Random House, 1973.

Nagel, Thomas. "A Defense of Affirmative Action." In *Values and Public Policy,* ed. Claudia Mills. New York: Harcourt Brace Jovanovich, 1992.

National Center for Employee Ownership. "Companies." *Employee Ownership Report* 19, no. 2 (March–April 1999): 14.

_____. "Employee Ownership and Corporate Performance" <http://www.nceo.org/library/corpperf.html> (10 March 1999).

_____. "The Employee Ownership 100." *Employee Ownership Report* 17, no. 4 (July–August 1997): 8–9.

_____. "ESOPs, Stock Options, and 401(k) Plans Now Control 9% of Corporate Equity." <http://www.nceo.org/library/control_eq.html> (20 July 1997).

_____. "Excerpts from *Employee Ownership and Corporate Performance.*" <http://www.nceo.org/nceo/perf.html> (18 July 1997).

_____. "1998 an Eventful Year for Employee Ownership Research." *Employee Ownership Report* 19, no. 2 (March–April 1999): 3.

_____. "An Overview of ESOPs, Stock Options, and Employee Ownership." <http://www.nceo.org/library/overview.html> (20 July 1997).

_____. "A Statistical Profile of Employee Ownership." Updated January 1999. <http://www.nceo.org/library/eo_stat.html> (24 March 1999).

Nielsen, Kai. *Equality and Liberty: A Defense of Radical Egalitarianism.* Totowa, N.J.: Rowman and Allanheld, 1985.

Nove, Alec. *The Economics of Feasible Socialism.* London: Allen and Unwin, 1983.

_____. *The Economics of Feasible Socialism Revisited.* London: HarperCollins, 1991.

_____. "Markets and Socialism." *New Left Review* 161 (January–February 1987): 98–104.

Nozick, Robert. *Anarchy, State, and Utopia.* New York: Basic Books, 1974.

Nussbaum, Martha C. "Aristotelian Social Democracy." In *Liberalism and the Good*, ed. R. Bruce Douglass, Gerald M. Mara, and Henry S. Richardson. New York: Routledge, 1990.

Nussbaum, Martha C., and A. K. Sen, eds. *The Quality of Life*. Oxford: Clarendon Press, 1992.

Nuti, D. M. "Socialism on Earth." *Cambridge Journal of Economics* 5 (1981): 391–403.

Oakeshott, Robert. *Majority Employee Ownership at United Airlines: Evidence of Big Wins for Both Jobs* and *Investors*. London: Partnership Research, 1997.

O'Connor, James. "Is Sustainable Capitalism Possible?" In *Is Capitalism Sustainable? Political Economy and the Politics of Ecology*, ed. Martin O'Connor. New York: Guilford Press, 1994.

Okin, Susan Moller. *Justice, Gender, and the Family*. New York: Basic Books, 1989.

————. "Politics and the Complex Inequalities of Gender." In Miller and Walzer, *Pluralism, Justice, and Equality*.

Ollman, Bertell, ed. *Market Socialism: The Debate among Socialists*. New York: Routledge, 1998.

Pateman, Carole. *The Disorder of Women*. Stanford, Calif.: Stanford University Press, 1989.

————. *Participation and Democratic Theory*. Cambridge: Cambridge University Press, 1970.

Paul, Jeffrey, ed. *Reading Nozick*. Totowa, N.J.: Rowman & Littlefield, 1981.

Peffer, Rodney G. *Marxism, Morality, and Social Justice*. Princeton: Princeton University Press, 1990.

"Permanent Fund Dividend Division's Yearly Dividend Amounts." Updated 12 January 1999. <http://www.revenue.state.ak.us/pfd/YEARAMOU.htm> (9 March 1999).

Picard, Robert G. *The Press and the Decline of Democracy: The Democratic Socialist Response in Public Policy*. Westport, Conn.: Greenwood Press, 1985.

Pilati, Paulo. "Lega di Denari." *L'Espresso*, 20 September 1987, 243–44.

Pitkin, Hannah. "Justice: On Relating Public and Private." *Political Theory* 9 (August 1981): 327–52.

Pontusson, Jonas. "Radicalization and Retreat in Swedish Social Democracy." *New Left Review* 165 (September–October 1987): 5–33.

Pool, Ithiel de Sola. *Technologies of Freedom*. Cambridge: Harvard University Press, Belknap Press, 1983.

Potts, George A. *The Development of the System of Representation in Yugoslavia with Special Reference to the Period since 1974*. New York: University Press of America, 1996.

Przeworski, Adam. *Capitalism and Social Democracy*. Cambridge: Cambridge University Press, 1985.

————. "The Feasibility of Universal Grants under Democratic Capitalism." *Theory and Society* 15, no. 5 (1986): 695–707.

Putnam, Robert D. *Making Democracy Work: Civic Traditions in Modern Italy*. Princeton: Princeton University Press, 1993.

Putterman, Louis. "Incentive Problems Favoring Noncentralized Investment Fund Ownership." In Bardhan and Roemer, *Market Socialism*.

Rawls, John. "The Basic Liberties and Their Priority." *Tanner Lectures on Human Values*, vol. 3. Salt Lake City: University of Utah Press, 1982.

_____. *Political Liberalism*. New York: Columbia University Press, 1993.

_____. "Reply to Habermas." *Journal of Philosophy* 92, no. 3 (March 1995): 132–80.

_____. *A Theory of Justice*. Cambridge: Harvard University Press, 1971.

Raz, Joseph. *The Morality of Freedom*. Oxford: Clarendon Press, 1986.

Redmon, Gene, Chuck Mueller, and Gene Daniels. "A Lost Dream: Worker Control at Rath Packing." *Labor Research Review* 1, no. 6 (Spring 1985): 5–23.

Rifkin, Jeremy. *The End of Work*. New York: G. P. Putnam's Sons, 1995.

Roemer, John E. "Can There Be Socialism after Communism?" In Bardhan and Roemer *Market Socialism*.

_____. *A Future for Socialism*. Cambridge: Harvard University Press, 1994.

_____. *A General Theory of Exploitation and Class*. Cambridge: Harvard University Press, 1982.

_____. "The Possibility of Market Socialism." In Copp, Hampton, and Roemer. *The Idea of Democracy*.

Rosen, Corey. "ESOPs: Hype or Hope?" In Krimerman and Lindenfeld, *When Workers Decide*.

Rousseau, Jean-Jacques. "The Social Contract." In *Social Contract Essays by Locke, Hume, and Rousseau*, ed. Ernest Barker. London: Oxford University Press, 1947.

Sabel, Charles F. *Work and Politics*. Cambridge: Cambridge University Press, 1982.

Sabel, Charles F., and Michael J. Piore. *The Second Industrial Divide: Possibilities for Prosperity*. New York: Basic Books, 1984.

Sacks, Stephen R. "Giant Corporations in Yugoslavia." In *Participatory and Self-Managed Firms*, ed. Derek Jones and Jan Svejnar. Lexington, Mass.: Lexington Books, 1982.

Sandel, Michael. *Liberalism and the Limits of Justice*. Cambridge: Cambridge University Press, 1982.

Schlosser, Eric. "The Prison–Industrial Complex." *Atlantic Monthly*, December 1998, 51–77.

Schmitt, John, Lawrence Mischel, and Jared Bernstein. "Dangers for European Workers in the U.S. Economic Model." *WorkingUSA* (May–June 1998): 73–85.

Schor, Juliet. *The Overworked American: The Unexpected Decline of Leisure*. New York: Basic Books, 1991.

Schutz, Robert. *The $30,000 Solution*. Santa Barbara, Calif.: Fithian Press, 1996.

Schwartz, Justin. "Where Did Mill Go Wrong? or If Market Socialism Is So Wonderful, Why Doesn't It Already Exist?" Paper presented to the American Philosophical Association, Central Division, Kansas City, Missouri, May 1994.

Schweickart, David. *Against Capitalism*. Cambridge: Cambridge University Press, 1994.

Schweke, William, Carl Rist, and Brian Dabson. *Bidding for Business: Are Cities and States Selling Themselves Short?* Washington, D.C.: Corporation for Enterprise Development, 1994.

Schwoebel, Jean. *Newsroom Democracy: The Case for Independence of the Press*. Iowa City: University of Iowa Center for Communication Study, 1976.

Sen, A. K. *Inequality Reexamined*. Cambridge: Harvard University Press, 1992.

Shklar, Judith N. *The Faces of Injustice*. New Haven: Yale University Press, 1990.

Simon, Herbert. Interview by Philippe Van Parijs. In *Basic Income* 29 (Spring 1998). <http://www.econ.ucl.ac.be/etes/bien/previous_newsletters.html> (4 April 1999).

Simon, Thomas W. *Democracy and Social Injustice: Law, Politics, and Philosophy.* Lanham, Md.: Rowman & Littlefield Publishers, 1995.

Slott, Mike. "The Case against Worker Ownership." *Labor Research Review* 1, no. 6 (Spring 1985): 83–98.

Somers, Amy Borgstrom. "Grassroots Economic Networking in Ohio." *Grassroots Economic Organizing Newsletter* 7 (January–February 1993): 3–8.

Somers, Amy Borgstrom, Jim Converse, Cathy Ivanic, and Ray West. "Grassroots Economic Networking in Ohio" *Grassroots Economic Organizing Newsletter* 8 (March–April 1993): 3–8.

Sterba, James P., ed. *Morality and Social Justice: Point/Counterpoint.* Lanham, Md.: Rowman & Littlefield, 1995.

Stojanović, Svetozar. "Social Self-Government and Socialist Community." *Praxis* (International Ed.) 4 (1968): 104–16.

Strom, Stephanie. "Mitsubishi Electric to Cut Global Workforce by 10 Percent." *New York Times*, 1 April 1999.

————. "A Revolution by Degrees." *New York Times*, 6 April 1999.

Tannen, Deborah. *Talking 9 to 5.* New York: William Morrow, 1994.

Taylor, Charles. *Sources of the Self.* Cambridge: Harvard University Press, 1989.

Thomas, Henk, and Chris Logan. *Mondragon: An Economic Analysis.* London: Allen and Unwin, 1982.

Turner, Lowell. "Industrial Relations and the Reorganization of Work in West Germany: Lessons for the U.S." In Mischel and Voos, *Unions and Economic Competitiveness.*

Union of Concerned Scientists."The Hidden Costs of Transportation." <http://www.ucsusa.org/transportation/index.html?hidden.html> (1 April 1999).

United Nations High Commission for Refugees. "UNHCR by numbers." <http://www.unhcr.ch/un&ref/numbers/table1.htm> (12 March 1999).

United Parcel Service. "UPS Extends Stock Ownership to Nonmanagement Employees." <http://www.ups.com/news/950828stock.html> (6 August 1997).

Vail, David. "The Past and Future of Swedish Social Democracy: A Reply to Kenneth Hermele." *Monthly Review* 45, no. 5 (October 1993): 24–31.

Van Anda, Jackie. "Colt Enterprises, Inc.: Union-Based Self-Determination in Texas." In Krimerman and Lindenfeld, *When Workers Decide.*

van der Veen, Robert J., and Philippe Van Parijs. "A Capitalist Road to Communism." *Theory and Society* 15, no. 5 (1986): 635–55.

————. "Universal Grants versus Socialism: Reply to Six Critics." *Theory and Society* 15, no. 5 (1986): 723–57.

Van Parijs, Philippe. "Basic Income: A Green Strategy for the New Europe." In *Green Light on Europe*, ed. Sara Parkin. London: Heretic Books, 1991.

————. "Competing Justifications of Basic Income." In Van Parijs, *Arguing for Basic Income.*

————. "Justice as the Fair Distribution of Freedom: Fetishism or Stoicism?" Unpublished manuscript.

————. *Marxism Recycled.* Cambridge: Cambridge University Press, 1993.

————. *Real Freedom for All: What (If Anything) Can Justify Capitalism?* Oxford: Clarendon Press, 1995.

————. The Second Marriage of Justice and Efficiency." In Van Parijs, *Arguing for Basic Income.*

_____, ed. *Arguing for Basic Income: Ethical Foundations for a Radical Reform.* London: Verso, 1992.

Vanek, Jaroslav. *The General Theory of Labor-Managed Market Economies.* Ithaca: Cornell University Press, 1970.

Wallach, Lori, and Michelle Sforza, "NAFTA at 5." *Nation,* 25 January 1999, 7.

Walzer, Michael. *Spheres of Justice: A Defense of Pluralism and Equality.* New York: Basic Books, 1983.

Warren, Paul. "Should Marxists Be Liberal Egalitarians?" *Journal of Political Philosophy* 5 no. 1 (March 1997): 47–68.

Wartenberg, Thomas. *The Forms of Power.* Philadelphia: Temple University Press, 1990.

Weisskopf, Thomas E. "A Democratic Enterprise–Based Market Socialism." In Bardhan and Roemer, *Market Socialism.*

Whyte, William Foote, and Kathleen King Whyte. *Making Mondragon: The Growth and Dynamics of the Worker Cooperative Complex.* Ithaca: Cornell University Press, 1988.

Will, George. "A New Chapter in Capitalism." *Boston Globe,* 6 December 1996.

Williams, Lynn. "Worker Ownership: A Better Alternative for the United Steel Workers: Interview with Lynn Williams." In Krimerman and Lindenfeld, *When Workers Decide.*

Williams, Raymond. *Keywords.* New York: Oxford University Press, 1983.

Wilson, William Julius. "Race-Specific Policies and the Truly Disadvantaged." In *Justice,* ed. Milton Fisk. Atlantic Highlands, N.J.: Humanities Press, 1993.

Wood, Stephan, ed. *The Degradation of Work?* London: Heinemann, 1982.

Wright, Eric Olin. "Why Something like Socialism Is Necessary for the Transition to Something like Communism." *Theory and Society* 15, no. 5 (1986): 657–72.

Wright, Eric Olin, et al. *The Debate on Classes.* London: Verso, 1989.

Young, Iris. *Justice and the Politics of Difference.* Princeton: Princeton University Press, 1990.

Zimbalist, Andrew, Howard Sherman, and Stuart Brown. *Comparing Economic Systems: A Political Economic Approach.* Fort Worth, Tex.: Harcourt Brace Jovanovich, 1989.

# Author Index

Page references followed by "n" indicate endnotes.

265

# Subject Index

Page references followed by "n" indicate endnotes.

# About the Author

Michael W. Howard is associate professor of philosophy at the University of Maine. He is the author of numerous articles in social and political philosophy in such journals as *Social Theory and Practice*, *The Journal of Social Philosophy*, *Philosophy and Social Criticism*, *Studies in East European Thought*, and *Radical Philosophy Review*.